MATTHEW ARNOLD

From the painting by G. F. Watts in the National Portrait Gallery

(*By permission of Mr. Frederick Hollyer*)

The Poems of
MATTHEW ARNOLD
1840–1867

With an Introduction by
SIR A. T. QUILLER-COUCH

London
OXFORD UNIVERSITY PRESS
HUMPHREY MILFORD
1930

OXFORD UNIVERSITY PRESS
AMEN HOUSE, E.C. 4
LONDON EDINBURGH GLASGOW
LEIPZIG NEW YORK TORONTO
MELBOURNE CAPETOWN BOMBAY
CALCUTTA MADRAS SHANGHAI
HUMPHREY MILFORD
PUBLISHER TO THE
UNIVERSITY

PRINTED IN GREAT BRITAIN AT THE UNIVERSITY PRESS, OXFORD
BY JOHN JOHNSON, PRINTER TO THE UNIVERSITY

O.S.A.

INTRODUCTION

'I do not hold up Joubert as a very astonishing and powerful genius, but rather as a delightful and edifying genius. . . . He is the most prepossessing and convincing of witnesses to the good of loving light. Because he sincerely loved light, and did not prefer to it any little private darkness of his own, he found light. . . . And because he was full of light he was also full of happiness. . . . His life was as charming as his thoughts. For certainly it is natural that the love of light, which is already, in some measure, the possession of light, should irradiate and beatify the whole life of him who has it.'

MANY a reader of *Essays in Criticism* must have paused and in thought transferred to Matthew Arnold these words of his in praise of Joubert, as well as the fine passage in which he goes on to ask What, in literature, we mean by fame? Only two kinds of authors (he tells us) are secure of fame: the first being the Homers, Dantes, Shakespeares, 'the great abiding fountains of truth,' whose praise is for ever and ever. But beside these sacred personages stand certain elect ones, less majestic, yet to be recognized as of the same family and character with the greatest, 'exercising like them an immortal function, and like them inspiring a permanent interest.' The fame of these also is assured. 'They will never, like the Shakespeares, command the homage of the multitude; but they are safe; the multitude will not trample them down.'

To this company Matthew Arnold belongs. We all feel it, and some of us can give reasons for our confidence; but perhaps, if all our reasons were collected, the feeling would be found to reach deeper into certainty than any of them. He was never popular, and never will be. Yet no one can say that, although at one time he seemed to vie with the public in distrusting it, his poetry missed its mark. On the other hand, while his critical writings had swift and almost instantaneous effect for good, the repute they brought him was moderate, and largely made up of misconception. For the mass of his countrymen he came somehow to personify a number of things which their minds vaguely associated with kid gloves, and by his ironical way of playing with the misconception he did more than a little to confirm it. But in truth Arnold was a serious man who saw life as a serious business, and chiefly relied, for making the best of it, upon a serene common sense. He had elegance, to be sure, and was inclined —at any rate, in controversy—to be conscious of it ; but it was elegance of that plain Attic order to which common sense gives the law and almost the inspiration. The man and the style were one. Alike in his life and his writings he observed and preached the golden mean, with a mind which was none the less English and practical if, in expressing it, he deliberately and almost defiantly avoided that emphasis which Englishmen love to a fault.

Matthew Arnold, eldest son of Dr. Thomas Arnold, the famous Head Master of Rugby, was born on Christmas Eve, 1822, at Laleham on the Thames, where his father at that time taught private pupils. The child was barely six years old when the family removed to Rugby, and at seven he returned to Laleham to be taught by his uncle, the Rev. John Buckland. In August, 1836, he proceeded to Winchester, but was removed at the end of a year and entered Rugby, where he remained until he went up to Balliol College,

Oxford, in 1841, with an open scholarship. He had written a prize poem at Rugby—the subject, *Alaric at Rome*; and on this performance he improved by taking the Newdigate in 1843—the subject, *Cromwell*. But we need waste no time on these exercises. It is better worth noting that the boy had been used to spending his holidays, and now spent a great part of his vacations, at Fox How, near Grasmere, a house which Dr. Arnold had taken to refresh his eyes and his spirits after the monotonous ridge and furrow, field and hedgerow, around Rugby; and that, as Mr. Herbert Paul puts it, young Matthew 'thus grew up under the shadow of Wordsworth, whose brilliant and penetrating interpreter he was destined to become'. Genius collects early, and afterwards distils from recollection; and if its spirit, like that of the licentiate Pedro Garcias, is to be disinterred, he who would find Matthew Arnold's must dig in and around Fox How and Oxford.

At Oxford, which he loved passionately, he 'missed his first', but atoned for this, three months later, by winning a fellowship at Oriel. (This was in 1844–5. His father had died in 1842.) He stayed up, however, but a short while after taking his degree; went back to Rugby as an assistant master; relinquished this in 1847 to become private secretary to Lord Lansdowne, then President of the Council; and was by him appointed in 1851 to an Inspectorship of Schools, which he retained for five-and-thirty years. In 1851, too, he married Frances Lucy Wightman, daughter of a Judge of the Queen's Bench; and so settled down at the same time to domestic happiness and to daily work which, if dull sometimes, was not altogether ungrateful, as it was never less than conscientiously performed.

Meanwhile, in 1849, he had put forth a thin volume,

The Strayed Reveller, and other Poems, by A ; which was followed in 1852 by *Empedocles on Etna, and other Poems, by A*. In 1853 he dropped anonymity and under the title of *Poems, by Matthew Arnold* republished the contents of these two volumes, omitting *Empedocles*, with a few minor pieces, and adding some priceless things, such as *Sohrab and Rustum, The Church of Brou, Requiescat*, and *The Scholar Gipsy.*

'It was received, we believe, with general indifference,' wrote Mr. Froude of the first volume, in the *Westminster Review*, 1854. We need not trouble to explain the fact, beyond saying that English criticism was just then at about the lowest ebb it reached in the last century, and that the few capable ears were occupied by the far more confident voice of Tennyson and the far more disconcerting one of Browning : but the fact—surprising when all allowance has been made—must be noted, for it is important to remember that the most and best of Arnold's poetry was written before he gained the world's ear, and that he gained it not as a poet but as a critic. In 1855 appeared *Poems by Matthew Arnold, Second Series*, of which only *Balder Dead* and *Separation* were new ; and in 1858 *Merope* with its Preface : but in the interval between them he had been elected Professor of Poetry at Oxford (May 1857).

The steps by which a reputation grows, the precise moment at which it becomes established, are often difficult to trace and fix. The poems, negligently though they had been received at first, must have helped : and, since men who improve an office are themselves usually improved by it, assuredly the Professorship helped too. The Lectures on Homer which adorned Arnold's first tenure of the Chair strike a new note of criticism, speak with a growing undertone of authority beneath their modest professions, and would suffice to explain—if mere custom did not even more easily explain—why in 1862 he was re-elected for another five years. But before 1865, no doubt, the judicious who knew him had tested him by more than his lectures, and were prepared for *Essays in Criticism*.

Although we are mainly concerned here with the poems, a word must be said on *Essays in Criticism*, which Mr. Paul pronounces to be 'Mr. Arnold's most important work in prose, the central book, so to speak,' of his life'. Mr. Saintsbury calls it 'the first full and varied, and perhaps always the best, expression and illustration of the author's critical attitude, the detailed manifesto and exemplar of the new critical method, and so one of the epoch-making books of the later nineteenth century in English'—and on this subject Mr. Saintsbury has a peculiar right to be heard.

Now for a book to be 'epoch-making' it must bring to its age something which its age conspicuously lacks: and *Essays in Criticism* did this. No one remembering what Dryden did, and Johnson, and Coleridge, and Lamb, and Hazlitt, will pretend that Arnold invented English Criticism, or that he did well what these men had done ill. What he did, and they missed doing, was to treat Criticism as a deliberate disinterested art, with laws and methods of its own, a proper temper, and certain standards or touchstones of right taste by which the quality of any writing, as literature, could be tested. In other words, he introduced authority and, with authority, responsibility, into a business which had hitherto been practised at the best by brilliant nonconformists and at the worst by Quarterly Reviewers—who, taking for their motto *Iudex damnatur cum nocens absolvitur*, either forgot or never surmised that to punish the guilty can be but a corollary of a higher obligation, to discover the truth. Nor can any one now read the literature of that period without a sense that Arnold's teaching was indispensably needed just then. A page of Macaulay or of Carlyle dazzles us with its rhetoric; strikes, arrests, excites us with a number of things tellingly put and in ways we had scarcely guessed to be possible; but it no longer convinces. It does not even dispose us to be convinced, since (to put it vulgarly) we feel that the author 'is not out after' truth; that Macaulay's William III is a figure dressed up and adjusted to prove Macaulay's thesis, and that the France of Carlyle's *French Revolution* not only never existed but, had it ever existed, would not be France. Arnold helping us, we see these failures—for surely that history is a failure which, like Cremorne, will not bear the daylight—to be inevitable in a republic of letters where laws are not and wherein each author writes at the top of his own bent, indulging and exploiting his personal eccentricity to the fullest. It has probably been the salvation of our literature that in the fourteenth century the Latin prevailed over the Anglo-Saxon line of its descent, and that in the forming of our verse as well as of our prose we had, at the critical moments, the literatures of Latin races, Italian or French, for models and correctives; as it was the misfortune of the Victorian period before 1865 that its men of genius wrote with eyes turned inward upon themselves or, if outward, upon that German literature which, for all its great qualities, must ever be dangerous to Englishmen because it flatters and encourages their special faults [1].

Of Arnold from 1865 onward — of the books in which he enforced rather than developed his critical

---

[1] That Matthew Arnold himself over-valued contemporary German literature does not really affect our argument.

method (for all the gist of it may be found in *Essays in Criticism*)—of his incursions into the fields of politics and theology—much might be written, but it would not be germane to our purpose. *New Poems*, including *Bacchanalia, or the New Age, Dover Beach*, and the beautiful *Thyrsis*, appeared in 1867, and thenceforward for the last twenty years of his life he wrote very little in verse, though the fine *Westminster Abbey* [1] proved that the Muse had not died in him. He used his hold upon the public ear to preach some sermons which, as a good citizen, he thought the nation needed. In his hard-working official life he rendered services which those of us who engage in the work of English education are constantly and gratefully recognizing in their effects, as we still toil in the wake of his ideals. He retired in November, 1886. He died on April 15th, 1888, of heart-failure: he had gone to Liverpool to meet his eldest daughter on her return from the United States, and there, in running to catch a tram-car, he fell and died in a moment. He was sixty-five, but in appearance carried his years lightly. He looked, and was, a distinguished and agreeable man. Of good presence and fine manners ; perfect in his domestic relations, genial in company and radiating cheerfulness ; setting a high aim to his official work yet ever conscientious in details ; he stands (apart from his literary achievement) as an example of the Englishman at his best. He cultivated this best deliberately. His daily note-books were filled with quotations, high thoughts characteristically chosen and jotted down to be borne in mind ; and some of these—such as *Semper aliquid certi proponendum est* and *Ecce labora et noli contristari!*—recur again and again. But the result owed its amiability also to that 'timely relaxation' counselled by Milton—

[1] Published in *The Nineteenth Century*, January, 1882.

> To measure life learn thou betimes, and know
>   Toward solid good what leads the nearest way ;
>   For other things mild Heav'n a time ordains,
> And disapproves that care, though wise in show,
>   That with superfluous burden loads the day
>   And, when God sends a cheerful hour, refrains.

To those, then, who tell us that Arnold's poetic period
was brief, and imply that it was therefore dis-
appointing, we might answer that this is but testimony to the perfect development of a life which in
due season used poetry and at the due hour cast it
away, to proceed to things more practical. But this
would be to err almost as deeply as those who tell us
that Arnold, as he himself said of Gray, 'never spoke
out '—whereas Arnold habitually spoke out, and now
and then even too insistently. Again it would be
a mistake for us to apply to him *au pied de la lettre*
the over-sad verses—

> Youth rambles on life's arid mount,
>   And strikes the rock, and finds the vein,
> And brings the water from the fount,
>   The fount which shall not flow again.
>
> The man mature with labour chops
>   For the bright stream a channel grand,
> And sees not that the sacred drops
>   Ran off and vanish'd out of hand.
>
> And then the old man totters nigh
>   And feebly rakes among the stones.
> The mount is mute, the channel dry ;
>   And down he lays his weary bones.

Yet it were stupid not to recognize that here is
contained a certain amount of general truth, and of
truth particularly applicable to Arnold. 'The poet,'
Mr. Saintsbury writes of him (and it sums up the

matter), 'has in him a vein, or, if the metaphor be pre-
ferred, a spring, of the most real and rarest poetry. But
the vein is constantly broken by faults, and never very
thick ; the spring is intermittent, and runs at times
by drops only.' Elsewhere Mr. Saintsbury speaks of
his 'elaborate assumption of the singing-robe', a phrase
very happily critical. Arnold felt—no man more
deeply—the majesty of the poet's function : he
solemnly attired himself to perform it : but the singing-robe was not his daily wear. The ample pall in
which Tennyson swept, his life through, as to the
manner born ; the stiffer skirts in which Wordsworth
walked so complacently ; these would have intolerably
cumbered the man who protested that even the title
of Professor made him uneasy. Wordsworth and
Tennyson were bards, authentic and unashamed ;
whereas in Arnold, as Mr. Watson has noted,

> Something of worldling mingled still
> With bard and sage.

There was never a finer worldling than Matthew Arnold :
but the criticism is just.

The critics, while noting this, have missed something
which to us seems to explain much in Arnold's verse.
We said just now that English literature has been
fortunate in what it owes to the Latin races : we may
add that it has been most fortunate in going to Italy
for instruction in its verse, to France for instruction
in its prose. This will be denied by no one who has
studied Elizabethan poetry or the prose of the 'Augus-
tan' age : and as little will any one who has studied
the structure of poetry deny that Italy is the natural,
France the unnatural, school for an English poet. The
reason is not that we understand Italian better than
French history and with more sympathy—though this,

too, scarcely admits of dispute; nor again that the past of Italy appeals to emotions of which poetry is the consecrated language. It lies in the very structure and play of the language; so that an Englishman who has but learnt how to pronounce the Italian vowels can read Italian poetry passably. The accent comes to him at once; the lack of accent in French remains foreign after many months of study. Now although Arnold was no great admirer of French poetry (and indeed had a particular dislike for the Alexandrine), France was to him, among modern nations, the heir of those classical qualities which differentiate the Greek from the barbarian, and his poetry seems ever to be striving to reproduce the Greek note through verse subdued to a French flatness of tone, as though (to borrow a metaphor from another art) its secret lay in low relief. But an English poet fighting against emphasis is as a man fighting water with a broom: and an English poet, striving to be unemphatic, must yet contrive to be various or he is naught. Successfully as he managed his prose, when he desired it to be emphatic Arnold had, in default of our native methods of emphasis, to fall back upon that simple repetition which irritates so many readers. In his poetry the devices are yet more clumsy. We suppose that no English poet before or since has so overworked the interjection 'Ah!' But far worse than any number of ah!s is Arnold's trick of italic type—

> How *I* bewail you!
> We mortal millions live *alone*.
>
> In the rustling night-air came the answer—
> 'Wouldst thou *be* as these are? *Live* as they.'

—a device almost unpardonable in poetry. So when he would give us variety, as in *Tristram and Iseult,*

Arnold has no better resource than frequent change
of metre: and although every reader must have felt
the effect of that sudden fine outburst—

> What voices are these on the clear night air?
> What lights in the court? what steps on the stair?

yet some must also have reflected that the great
masters, having to tell a story, choose their one metre
and, having chosen, so adapt and handle it that it tells
all. *Sohrab and Rustum* indeed tells itself perfectly,
from its first line to its noble close. But *Sohrab and
Rustum* is, and professes to be, an episode. *Balder* is
little more, and most readers find *Balder*, in spite of
its fine passages and general dignity, long enough.
Arnold—let it be repeated—was not a bard; not
a Muse-intoxicated man. He had not the bardic, the
architectonic, gift. 'Something of worldling' in him
forbade any such fervour as, sustained day after day
for years, gave the world *Paradise Lost*, and incidentally,
no doubt, made Milton's daughters regret at times that
their father was not as ordinary men.

Nor had Arnold an impeccable ear for rhyme (in *The
New Sirens*, for instance, he rhymes 'dawning' with
'morning'): and if we hesitate to follow the many
who have doubted his ear for rhythm, it is not for lack
of apparently good evidence, but because some of his
rhythms which used to give us pause have come, upon
longer acquaintance, to fascinate us: and the explanation may be, as we have hinted, that they follow the
French rather than the Italian use of accent, and are
strange to us rather than in themselves unmusical.
Certainly the critics who would have us believe that
The Strayed Reveller is an unmusical poem will not at
this time of day persuade us by the process of taking
a stanza or two and writing them down in the form of
prose. We could do the same with a dozen lines of

The Tempest or *Antony and Cleopatra*, were it worth doing, and prove just as much, or as little.

Something of Arnold's own theory of poetry may be extracted from the prefaces, here reprinted, of 1853 and 1854. They contain, like the prefaces of Dryden and of Wordsworth, much wisdom ; but the world, perhaps even more wisely, refuses to judge a poet by his theory, which (however admirable) seldom yields up his secret. Yet Arnold had a considered view of what the poet should attempt and what avoid ; and that he followed it would remain certain although much evidence were accumulated to prove that he who denounced 'poetry's eternal enemy, Caprice', could himself be, on occasion, capricious. He leaves the impression that he wrote with difficulty ; his raptures, though he knew rapture, are infrequent. But through all his work there runs a strain of serious elevated thought, and on it all there rests an air of composure equally serious and elevated—a trifle statu-esque, perhaps, but by no means deficient in feeling. No one can read, say, the closing lines of *Mycerinus* and fail to perceive these qualities. No one can read this volume from cover to cover and deny that they are characteristic. Nor, we think, can any one study the poetry of 1850 and thereabouts without being forced to admit that it wanted these qualities of thoughtfulness and composure. Arnold has been criti-cized for discovering in Tennyson a certain 'deficiency in intellectual power'. But is he by this time alone in that discovery? And if no lack of thoughtfulness can be charged against Browning—as it cannot—is not Browning violent, unchastened, far too often energetic for energy's sake? Be it granted that Arnold in poetical strength was no match for these champions : yet he brought to literature, and in a happy hour, that which

they lacked, insisting by the example of his verse as
well as by the precepts of his criticism that before
anything becomes literature it must observe two conditions—it must be worth saying, and it must be
worthily said.

Also he continued, if with a difference, that noble
Wordsworthian tradition which stood in some danger
of perishing—chiefly, we think, beneath the accumula-
tion of rubbish piled upon it by its own author during
his later years. That which Matthew Arnold disinterred
and re-polished may have been but a fragment. His
page has not, says Mr. Watson, 'the deep, authentic
mountain-thrill.' We grant that Arnold's feeling for
Nature has not the Wordsworthian depth ; but so far
as it penetrates it is genuine. Lines such as—

> While the deep-burnish'd foliage overhead
> Splinter'd the silver arrows of the moon—

may owe their felicity to phrase rather than to feeling.
The Mediterranean landscape in *A Southern Night* may
seem almost too exquisitely elaborated. Yet who can
think of Arnold's poetry as a whole without feeling
that Nature is always behind it as a living background ?
—whether it be the storm of wind and rain shaking
Tintagel—

> I forgot, thou comest from thy voyage.
> Yes, the spray is on thy cloak and hair —

or the scent-laden water-meadows along Thames, or
the pine forests on the flank of Etna, or an English
garden in June, or Oxus, its mists and fens and 'the
hush'd Chorasmian waste '. If Arnold's love of natural
beauty have not those moments of piercing *apprehension*
which in his master's poetry seem to break through
dullness into the very heaven : if we have not that
secret which Wordsworth must have learnt upon the

Cumbrian Mountains, from moments when the clouds drift apart and the surprised climber sees all Windermere, all Derwentwater, shining at his feet; if on the other hand his philosophy of life, rounded and complete, seem none too hopeful, but call man back from eager speculations which man will never resign ; if it repress, where Browning encouraged, our quest after

> Thoughts hardly to be packed
> Into a narrow act,
> Fancies that broke through language and escaped . . .

yet his sense of atmosphere, of background, of the great stage on which man plays his part, gives Arnold's teaching a wonderful *comprehension*, within its range. 'This,' we say, 'is poetry we can trust, not to flatter us, but to sustain, console.' If the reader mistake it for the last word on life his trust in it will be illusory. It brings rather that

> lull in the hot race
> Wherein he doth for ever chase
> That flying and elusive shadow, Rest.
> An air of coolness plays upon his face
> And an unwonted calm pervades his breast ;

and then—if after protesting against italics in poetry we may italicize where, for once, Arnold missed the opportunity—

> And then he *thinks* he knows
> The Hills where his life rose,
> And the Sea where it goes.

ARTHUR T. QUILLER-COUCH.

BIBLIOGRAPHICAL NOTE

THIS volume contains all the poems that Matthew Arnold published between 1840 and 1867. They are printed in chronological order, and when more than one version of any poem is available the latest version is printed in the text, and all earlier verbal variations are noted at the bottom of the page.

Pp. xix to xxvii give the contents of the ten published volumes (*Alaric* 1840, *Cromwell* 1843, *The Strayed Reveller* 1849, *Empedocles on Etna* 1852, *Poems* 1853, *Poems, Second Edition* 1854, *Poems, Second Series* 1855, *Poems, Third Edition* 1857, *Merope* 1858, *New Poems* 1867) in order, giving also under their several dates the poems which appeared in various magazines before publication in volume form.

The order of the poems in this edition being chronological, the reader should remember that the text of (for example) the 1849 version of *The Forsaken Merman* must be reconstructed from the footnotes, the text as here printed being that of the latest available edition, viz., for this poem, 1857.

Arnold's own notes are printed at the end of the book, and a few others have been added, some textual, others giving brief explanations of allusions in the text or references for passages quoted.

Mr. T. J. Wise has kindly given permission for his privately printed edition (1893) of *Alaric at Rome* to be used as the basis of the present reprint of the poem, no copy of the original issue (1840) being accessible; and the *Horatian Echo* is included by kind permission of the Rev. Arthur Galton, to whom the poem was given in 1886 for publication in *The Century Guild Hobby Horse*.

H. S. M.

BIBLIOGRAPHICAL NOTE

This volume contains all the poems that Matthew
Arnold published between 1849 and 1867. They are
printed in chronological order, and when more than
one version of any poem is available the latest version
is printed in the text, and all earlier verbal variants
are noted at the bottom of the page.

Pp. xxv to xxvii give the contents of the ten published
volumes: *The Strayed Reveller*, 1849; *Empedocles
on Etna*, 1852; *Poems*, 1853; *Poems, Second
Series*, 1854; *Poems, Second Edition*, 1854; *Poems,
Third Edition*, 1857; *Merope*, 1858; *New Poems*,
1867, in order, giving also under their several dates
the poems which appeared in various magazines before
publication in volume form.

The order of the poems in this edition being chronological, the reader should remember that the text of
(for example) the 1849 version of *The Strayed Reveller*
must be reconstructed from the footnotes, the text, as
here printed, being that of the latest available edition,
i.e. in this case, 1867.

Arnold's own notes are printed at the end of the
book, and a few others have been added; some textual,
others giving brief explanations of allusions in the text,
as references for passages quoted.

Mr T. J. Wise has kindly given permission for his
privately printed edition (1893) of *Alaric at Rome* to be
used as the basis of the present reprint of the poem, no
copy of the original issue (1840) being accessible; and
the *Horatian Echo* is included by kind permission of the
late Arthur Galton, to whom the poem was given in
1886 for publication in *The Century Guild Hobby Horse*.

H. S. M.

CONTENTS

CONTENTS

PREFACE

[First published 1853. Reprinted 1854 and 1857.]

In two small volumes of Poems, published anonymously, one in 1849, the other in 1852, many of the Poems which compose the present volume have already appeared. The rest are now published for the first time.

I have, in the present collection, omitted the Poem from which the volume published in 1852 took its title. I have done so, not because the subject of it was a Sicilian Greek born between two and three thousand years ago, although many persons would think this a sufficient reason. Neither have I done so 10 because I had, in my own opinion, failed in the delineation which I intended to effect. I intended to delineate the feelings of one of the last of the Greek religious philosophers, one of the family of Orpheus and Musaeus, having survived his fellows, living on into a time when the habits of Greek thought and feeling had begun fast to change, character to dwindle, the influence of the Sophists to prevail. Into the feelings of a man so situated there entered much that we are accustomed to consider as exclusively modern ; how much, the frag- 20 ments of Empedocles himself which remain to us are sufficient at least to indicate. What those who are familiar only with the great monuments of early Greek genius suppose to be its exclusive characteristics, have disappeared ; the calm, the cheerfulness, the disinterested objectivity have disappeared : the dialogue of the mind with itself has commenced ; modern problems have presented themselves ; we hear already the doubts, we witness the discouragement, of Hamlet and of Faust.

The representation of such a man's feelings must be 30 interesting, if consistently drawn. We all naturally take pleasure, says Aristotle, in any imitation or representation whatever : this is the basis of our love of

Preface, *Title*] Preface to the First Edition *1854*.

Poetry : and we take pleasure in them, he adds, because all knowledge is naturally agreeable to us; not to the philosopher only, but to mankind at large. Every representation therefore which is consistently drawn may be supposed to be interesting, inasmuch as it gratifies this natural interest in knowledge of all kinds. What is *not* interesting, is that which does not add to our knowledge of any kind ; that which is vaguely conceived and loosely drawn ; a representation
10 which is general, indeterminate, and faint, instead of being particular, precise, and firm.

Any accurate representation may therefore be expected to be interesting ; but, if the representation be a poetical one, more than this is demanded. It is demanded, not only that it shall interest, but also that it shall inspirit and rejoice the reader : that it shall convey a charm, and infuse delight. For the Muses, as Hesiod says, were born that they might be 'a forgetfulness of evils, and a truce from cares': and it is
20 not enough that the Poet should add to the knowledge of men, it is required of him also that he should add to their happiness. 'All Art,' says Schiller, 'is dedicated to Joy, and there is no higher and no more serious problem, than how to make men happy. The right Art is that alone, which creates the highest enjoyment.

A poetical work, therefore, is not yet justified when it has been shown to be an accurate, and therefore interesting representation ; it has to be shown also that it is a representation from which men can derive en-
30 joyment. In presence of the most tragic circumstances, represented in a work of Art, the feeling of enjoyment, as is well known, may still subsist : the representation of the most utter calamity, of the liveliest anguish, is not sufficient to destroy it : the more tragic the situation, the deeper becomes the enjoyment ; and the situation is more tragic in proportion as it becomes more terrible.

What then are the situations, from the representation of which, though accurate, no poetical enjoyment
40 can be derived ? They are those in which the suffering finds no vent in action ; in which a continuous state of mental distress is prolonged, unrelieved by incident,

hope, or resistance ; in which there is everything to
be endured, nothing to be done. In such situations
there is inevitably something morbid, in the descrip-
tion of them something monotonous. When they
occur in actual life, they are painful, not tragic ; the
representation of them in poetry is painful also.

To this class of situations, poetically faulty as it
appears to me, that of Empedocles, as I have endeavoured to represent him, belongs ; and I have therefore excluded the Poem from the present collection. 10

And why, it may be asked, have I entered into this
explanation respecting a matter so unimportant as the
admission or exclusion of the Poem in question ? I
have done so, because I was anxious to avow that the
sole reason for its exclusion was that which has been
stated above ; and that it has not been excluded in
deference to the opinion which many critics of the
present day appear to entertain against subjects chosen
from distant times and countries: against the choice,
in short, of any subjects but modern ones. 20

'The Poet,' it is said,[1] and by an intelligent critic,
'the Poet who would really fix the public attention
must leave the exhausted past, and draw his subjects
from matters of present import, and *therefore* both of
interest and novelty.'

Now this view I believe to be completely false. It
is worth examining, inasmuch as it is a fair sample of
a class of critical dicta everywhere current at the
present day, having a philosophical form and air, but
no real basis in fact ; and which are calculated to 30
vitiate the judgement of readers of poetry, while they
exert, so far as they are adopted, a misleading influence
on the practice of those who write it.

What are the eternal objects of Poetry, among all
nations and at all times ? They are actions ; human
actions ; possessing an inherent interest in themselves,
and which are to be communicated in an interesting
manner by the art of the Poet. Vainly will the latter

[1] In *The Spectator* of April 2nd, 1853. The words quoted were
not used with reference to poems of mine. *1854 first*

---

21 intelligent] apparently intelligent *1853*

imagine that he has everything in his own power ; that
he can make an intrinsically inferior action equally
delightful with a more excellent one by his treatment
of it ; he may indeed compel us to admire his skill,
but his work will possess, within itself, an incurable
defect.

The Poet, then, has in the first place to select an
excellent action ; and what actions are the most excellent ? Those, certainly, which most powerfully appeal
to the great primary human affections : to those elementary feelings which subsist permanently in the
race, and which are independent of time. These feelings
are permanent and the same ; that which interests
them is permanent and the same also. The modern-
ness or antiquity of an action, therefore, has nothing
to do with its fitness for poetical representation ; this
depends upon its inherent qualities. To the elementary part of our nature, to our passions, that which is
great and passionate is eternally interesting ; and
interesting solely in proportion to its greatness and to
its passion. A great human action of a thousand years
ago is more interesting to it than a smaller human
action of to-day, even though upon the representation
of this last the most consummate skill may have been
expended, and though it has the advantage of appeal-
ing by its modern language, familiar manners, and
contemporary allusions, to all our transient feelings and
interests. These, however, have no right to demand
of a poetical work that it shall satisfy them ; their
claims are to be directed elsewhere. Poetical works
belong to the domain of our permanent passions : let
them interest these, and the voice of all subordinate
claims upon them is at once silenced.

Achilles, Prometheus, Clytemnestra, Dido—what
modern poem presents personages as interesting, even
to us moderns, as these personages of an 'exhausted
past'? We have the domestic epic dealing with the
details of modern life which pass daily under our eyes ;
we have poems representing modern personages in
contact with the problems of modern life, moral, intellectual, and social ; these works have been produced
by poets the most distinguished of their nation and

time ; yet I fearlessly assert that Hermann and Dorothea,
Childe Harold, Jocelyn, The Excursion, leave the reader
cold in comparison with the effect produced upon him
by the latter books of the Iliad, by the Orestea, or by
the episode of Dido. And why is this ? Simply
because in the three latter cases the action is greater,
the personages nobler, the situations more intense :
and this is the true basis of the interest in a poetical
work, and this alone.

It may be urged, however, that past actions may be 10
interesting in themselves, but that they are not to be
adopted by the modern Poet, because it is impossible
for him to have them clearly present to his own mind,
and he cannot therefore feel them deeply, nor represent them forcibly. But this is not necessarily the
case. The externals of a past action, indeed, he cannot
know with the precision of a contemporary ; but his
business is with its essentials. The outward man of
Oedipus or of Macbeth, the houses in which they lived,
the ceremonies of their courts, he cannot accurately 20
figure to himself ; but neither do they essentially concern him. His business is with their inward man ;
with their feelings and behaviour in certain tragic
situations, which engage their passions as men ; these
have in them nothing local and casual ; they are as
accessible to the modern Poet as to a contemporary.

The date of an action, then, signifies nothing : the
action itself, its selection and construction, this is what
is all-important. This the Greeks understood far more
clearly than we do. The radical difference between 30
their poetical theory and ours consists, as it appears
to me, in this : that, with them, the poetical character
of the action in itself, and the conduct of it, was the
first consideration ; with us, attention is fixed mainly
on the value of the separate thoughts and images which
occur in the treatment of an action. They regarded
the whole ; we regard the parts. With them, the
action predominated over the expression of it ; with
us, the expression predominates over the action. Not
that they failed in expression, or were inattentive to it ; 40
on the contrary, they are the highest models of expression, the unapproached masters of the *grand style :* but

their expression is so excellent because it is so admirably kept in its right degree of prominence ; because it is so simple and so well subordinated ; because it draws its force directly from the pregnancy of the matter which it conveys. For what reason was the Greek tragic poet confined to so limited a range of subjects ? Because there are so few actions which unite in themselves, in the highest degree, the conditions of excellence : and it was not thought that on any but
10 an excellent subject could an excellent Poem be constructed. A few actions, therefore, eminently adapted for tragedy, maintained almost exclusive possession of the Greek tragic stage ; their significance appeared inexhaustible ; they were as permanent problems, perpetually offered to the genius of every fresh poet. This too is the reason of what appears to us moderns a certain baldness of expression in Greek tragedy ; of the triviality with which we often reproach the remarks of the chorus, where it takes part in the dialogue : that
20 the action itself, the situation of Orestes, or Merope, or Alcmaeon, was to stand the central point of interest, unforgotten, absorbing, principal ; that no accessories were for a moment to distract the spectator's attention from this ; that the tone of the parts was to be perpetually kept down, in order not to impair the grandiose effect of the whole. The terrible old mythic story on which the drama was founded stood, before he entered the theatre, traced in its bare outlines upon the spectator's mind ; it stood in his memory, as a group of statu-
30 ary, faintly seen, at the end of a long and dark vista : then came the Poet, embodying outlines, developing situations, not a word wasted, not a sentiment capriciously thrown in : stroke upon stroke, the drama proceeded : the light deepened upon the group ; more and more it revealed itself to the rivetted gaze of the spectator : until at last, when the final words were spoken, it stood before him in broad sunlight, a model of immortal beauty.

This was what a Greek critic demanded ; this was
40 what a Greek poet endeavoured to effect. It signified nothing to what time an action belonged ; we do not find that the Persae occupied a particularly high rank

among the dramas of Aeschylus, because it represented
a matter of contemporary interest : this was not what
a cultivated Athenian required ; he required that the ×
permanent elements of his nature should be moved ;
and dramas of which the action, though taken from a
long-distant mythic time, yet was calculated to accomplish this in a higher degree than that of the Persae,
stood higher in his estimation accordingly. The Greeks
felt, no doubt, with their exquisite sagacity of taste,
that an action of present times was too near them, too 10 ×
much mixed up with what was accidental and passing,
to form a sufficiently grand, detached, and self-subsis-
tent object for a tragic poem : such objects belonged
to the domain of the comic poet, and of the lighter
kinds of poetry. For the more serious kinds, for *pragmatic* poetry, to use an excellent expression of Polybius,
they were more difficult and severe in the range of
subjects which they permitted. Their theory and
practice alike, the admirable treatise of Aristotle, and
the unrivalled works of their poets, exclaim with a 20
thousand tongues—'All depends upon the subject ;
choose a fitting action, penetrate yourself with the
feeling of its situations ; this done, everything else will
follow.'

But for all kinds of poetry alike there was one point
on which they were rigidly exacting ; the adaptability ×
of the subject to the kind of poetry selected, and the
careful construction of the poem.

How different a way of thinking from this is ours !
We can hardly at the present day understand what 30
Menander meant, when he told a man who inquired
as to the progress of his comedy that he had finished
it, not having yet written a single line, because he had
constructed the action of it in his mind. A modern ×
critic would have assured him that the merit of his
piece depended on the brilliant things which arose
under his pen as he went along. We have poems
which seem to exist merely for the sake of single lines
and passages ; not for the sake of producing any total-
impression. We have critics who seem to direct their 40

18 *1853 inserts after* permitted, *and omits below, the sentence :* 'But
for all kinds of poetry alike . . . careful construction of the poem.'

attention merely to detached expressions, to the language about the action, not to the action itself. I verily think that the majority of them do not in their hearts believe that there is such a thing as a total-impression to be derived from a poem at all, or to be demanded from a poet; they think the term a common-place of metaphysical criticism. They will permit the Poet to select any action he pleases, and to suffer that action to go as it will, provided he gratifies them with

10 occasional bursts of fine writing, and with a shower of isolated thoughts and images. That is, they permit him to leave their poetical sense ungratified, provided that he gratifies their rhetorical sense and their curiosity. Of his neglecting to gratify these, there is little danger; he needs rather to be warned against the danger of attempting to gratify these alone; he needs rather to be perpetually reminded to prefer his action to every-thing else; so to treat this, as to permit its inherent excellences to develop themselves, without interruption

20 from the intrusion of his personal peculiarities: most fortunate, when he most entirely succeeds in effacing himself, and in enabling a noble action to subsist as it did in nature.

But the modern critic not only permits a false practice; he absolutely prescribes false aims.—'A true allegory of the state of one's own mind in a repre-sentative history,' the Poet is told, 'is perhaps the highest thing that one can attempt in the way of poetry.' —And accordingly he attempts it. An allegory of the

30 state of one's own mind, the highest problem of an art which imitates actions! No assuredly, it is not, it never can be so: no great poetical work has ever been produced with such an aim. Faust itself, in which something of the kind is attempted, wonderful passages as it contains, and in spite of the unsurpassed beauty of the scenes which relate to Margaret, Faust itself, judged as a whole, and judged strictly as a poetical work, is defective: its illustrious author, the greatest poet of modern times, the greatest critic of all times,

40 would have been the first to acknowledge it; he only defended his work, indeed, by asserting it to be 'some-thing incommensurable.'

The confusion of the present times is great, the multitude of voices counselling different things bewildering, the number of existing works capable of attracting a young writer's attention and of becoming his models, immense : what he wants is a hand to guide him through the confusion, a voice to prescribe to him the aim which he should keep in view, and to explain to him that the value of the literary works which offer themselves to his attention is relative to their power of helping him forward on his road towards 10 this aim. Such a guide the English writer at the present day will nowhere find. Failing this, all that can be looked for, all indeed that can be desired, is, that his attention should be fixed on excellent models ; that he may reproduce, at any rate, something of their excellence, by penetrating himself with their works and by catching their spirit, if he cannot be taught to produce what is excellent independently.

Foremost among these models for the English writer stands Shakespeare : a name the greatest perhaps of all 20 poetical names ; a name never to be mentioned without reverence. I will venture, however, to express a doubt, whether the influence of his works, excellent and fruitful for the readers of poetry, for the great majority, has been of unmixed advantage to the writers of it. Shakespeare indeed chose excellent subjects ; the world could afford no better than Macbeth, or Romeo and Juliet, or Othello: he had no theory respecting the necessity of choosing subjects of present import, or the paramount interest attaching to allegories 30 of the state of one's own mind ; like all great poets, he knew well what constituted a poetical action; like them, wherever he found such an action, he took it ; like them, too, he found his best in past times. But to these general characteristics of all great poets he added a special one of his own ; a gift, namely, of happy, abundant, and ingenious expression, eminent and unrivalled : so eminent as irresistibly to strike the attention first in him, and even to throw into comparative shade his other excellences as a poet. Here has 40 been the mischief. These other excellences were his fundamental excellences *as a poet ;* what distinguishes

the artist from the mere amateur, says Goethe, is
Architectonicè in the highest sense ; that power of
execution, which creates, forms, and constitutes : not
the profoundness of single thoughts, not the richness
of imagery, not the abundance of illustration. But
these attractive accessories of a poetical work being
more easily seized than the spirit of the whole, and
these accessories being possessed by Shakespeare in an
unequalled degree, a young writer having recourse to
10 Shakespeare as his model runs great risk of being vanquished and absorbed by them, and, in consequence,
of reproducing, according to the measure of his power,
these, and these alone. Of this preponderating quality
of Shakespeare's genius, accordingly, almost the whole
of modern English poetry has, it appears to me, felt
the influence. To the exclusive attention on the part
of his imitators to this it is in a great degree owing,
that of the majority of modern poetical works the
details alone are valuable, the composition worthless.
20 In reading them one is perpetually reminded of that
terrible sentence on a modern French poet—*il dit tout
ce qu'il veut, mais malheureusement il n'a rien à dire.*

Let me give an instance of what I mean. I will
take it from the works of the very chief among those
who seem to have been formed in the school of Shakespeare : of one whose exquisite genius and pathetic
death render him for ever interesting. I will take
the poem of Isabella, or the Pot of Basil, by Keats.
I choose this rather than the Endymion, because the
30 latter work (which a modern critic has classed with
the Fairy Queen !), although undoubtedly there blows
through it the breath of genius, is yet as a whole so
utterly incoherent, as not strictly to merit the name of
a poem at all. The poem of Isabella, then, is a perfect
treasure-house of graceful and felicitous words and
images : almost in every stanza there occurs one of
those vivid and picturesque turns of expression, by
which the object is made to flash upon the eye of the
mind, and which thrill the reader with a sudden delight.
40 This one short poem contains, perhaps, a greater
number of happy single expressions which one could
quote than all the extant tragedies of Sophocles. But

the action, the story? The action in itself is an excellent
one; but so feebly is it conceived by the Poet, so
loosely constructed, that the effect produced by it, in
and for itself, is absolutely null. Let the reader, after
he has finished the poem of Keats, turn to the same
story in the Decameron: he will then feel how pregnant and interesting the same action has become in
the hands of a great artist, who above all things
delineates his object; who subordinates expression to
that which it is designed to express.   10

I have said that the imitators of Shakespeare, fixing
their attention on his wonderful gift of expression,
have directed their imitation to this, neglecting his
other excellences.   These excellences, the fundamental excellences of poetical art, Shakespeare no
doubt possessed them—possessed many of them in a
splendid degree; but it may perhaps be doubted
whether even he himself did not sometimes give scope
to his faculty of expression to the prejudice of a higher
poetical duty.   For we must never forget that Shake- 20
speare is the great poet he is from his skill in discerning
and firmly conceiving an excellent action, from his
power of intensely feeling a situation, of intimately
associating himself with a character; not from his gift
of expression, which rather even leads him astray, de-
generating sometimes into a fondness for curiosity of
expression, into an irritability of fancy, which seems
to make it impossible for him to say a thing plainly,
even when the press of the action demands the very
directest language, or its level character the very sim- 30
plest.   Mr. Hallam, than whom it is impossible to find
a saner and more judicious critic, has had the courage
(for at the present day it needs courage) to remark,
how extremely and faultily difficult Shakespeare's language often is.   It is so: you may find main scenes in
some of his greatest tragedies, King Lear for instance,
where the language is so artificial, so curiously tortured,
and so difficult, that every speech has to be read two
or three times before its meaning can be comprehended.
This over-curiousness of expression is indeed but the 40
excessive employment of a wonderful gift—of the
power of saying a thing in a happier way than any

other man ; nevertheless, it is carried so far that one
understands what M. Guizot meant, when he said that
Shakespeare appears in his language to have tried all
styles except that of simplicity.   He has not the severe
and scrupulous self-restraint of the ancients, partly no
doubt, because he had a far less cultivated and exacting
audience : he has indeed a far wider range than they
had, a far richer fertility of thought ; in this respect
he rises above them : in his strong conception of his
10 subject, in the genuine way in which he is penetrated
with it, he resembles them, and is unlike the moderns :
but in the accurate limitation of it, the conscientious
rejection of superfluities, the simple and rigorous
development of it from the first line of his work to the
last, he falls below them, and comes nearer to the
moderns.   In his chief works, besides what he has
of his own, he has the elementary soundness of the
ancients ; he has their important action and their
large and broad manner : but he has not their purity
20 of method.   He is therefore a less safe model ; for what
he has of his own is personal, and inseparable from his
own rich nature ; it may be imitated and exaggerated,
it cannot be learned or applied as an art ; he is above all
suggestive ; more valuable, therefore, to young writers
as men than as artists.   But clearness of arrangement, rigour of development, simplicity of style—these
may to a certain extent be learned : and these may, I am
convinced, be learned best from the ancients, who although infinitely less suggestive than Shakespeare, are
30 thus, to the artist, more instructive.

What, then, it will be asked, are the ancients to be
our sole models ? the ancients with their comparatively
narrow range of experience, and their widely different
circumstances ?   Not, certainly, that which is narrow
in the ancients, nor that in which we can no longer
sympathize.   An action like the action of the Antigone
of Sophocles, which turns upon the conflict between
the heroine's duty to her brother's corpse and that to
the laws of her country, is no longer one in which
40 it is possible that we should feel a deep interest.   I
am speaking too, it will be remembered, not of the
best sources of intellectual stimulus for the general

reader, but of the best models of instruction for the individual writer. This last may certainly learn of the ancients, better than anywhere else, three things which it is vitally important for him to know:—the all-im- portance of the choice of a subject; the necessity of accurate construction; and the subordinate character of expression. He will learn from them how unspeak- ably superior is the effect of the one moral impression left by a great action treated as a whole, to the effect produced by the most striking single thought or by the 10 happiest image. As he penetrates into the spirit of the great classical works, as he becomes gradually aware of their intense significance, their noble simplicity, and their calm pathos, he will be convinced that it is this effect, unity and profoundness of moral impression, at which the ancient Poets aimed; that it is this which constitutes the grandeur of their works, and which makes them immortal. He will desire to direct his own efforts towards producing the same effect. Above all, he will deliver himself from the jargon of modern 20 criticism, and escape the danger of producing poetical works conceived in the spirit of the passing time, and which partake of its transitoriness.

The present age makes great claims upon us: we owe it service, it will not be satisfied without our admiration. I know not how it is, but their commerce with the ancients appears to me to produce, in those who constantly practise it, a steadying and composing effect upon their judgement, not of literary works only, but of men and events in general. They are like 30 persons who have had a very weighty and impressive experience: they are more truly than others under the empire of facts, and more independent of the language current among those with whom they live. They wish neither to applaud nor to revile their age: they wish to know what it is, what it can give them, and whether this is what they want. What they want, they know very well; they want to educe and cultivate what is best and noblest in themselves: they know, too, that this is no easy task—χαλεπὸν, as Pittacus said, χαλεπὸν 40 ἐσθλὸν ἔμμεναι—and they ask themselves sincerely whether their age and its literature can assist them in

the attempt. If they are endeavouring to practise any art, they remember the plain and simple proceedings of the old artists, who attained their grand results by penetrating themselves with some noble and significant action, not by inflating themselves with a belief in the pre-eminent importance and greatness of their own times. They do not talk of their mission, nor of interpreting their age, nor of the coming Poet ; all this, they know, is the mere delirium of vanity ; their business is not to
10 praise their age, but to afford to the men who live in it the highest pleasure which they are capable of feeling. If asked to afford this by means of subjects drawn from the age itself, they ask what special fitness the present age has for supplying them : they are told that it is an era of progress, an age commissioned to carry out the great ideas of industrial development and social amelioration. They reply that with all this they can do nothing ; that the elements they need for the exercise of their art are great actions, calculated power-
20 fully and delightfully to affect what is permanent in the human soul ; that so far as the present age can supply such actions, they will gladly make use of them ; but that an age wanting in moral grandeur can with difficulty supply such, and an age of spiritual discom- fort with difficulty be powerfully and delightfully affected by them.

A host of voices will indignantly rejoin that the pre- sent age is inferior to the past neither in moral gran- deur nor in spiritual health. He who possesses the
30 discipline I speak of will content himself with remem- bering the judgements passed upon the present age, in this respect, by the two men, the one of strongest head, the other of widest culture, whom it has produced ; by Goethe and by Niebuhr. It will be sufficient for him that he knows the opinions held by these two great men respecting the present age and its literature ; and that he feels assured in his own mind that their aims and demands upon life were such as he would wish, at any rate, his own to be ; and their judgement as to
40 what is impeding and disabling such as he may safely

32–33 the two men . . . culture] the men of strongest head and widest culture 1853, 1854.

follow. He will not, however, maintain a hostile attitude towards the false pretensions of his age ; he will
content himself with not being overwhelmed by them.
He will esteem himself fortunate if he can succeed in
banishing from his mind all feelings of contradiction,
and irritation, and impatience ; in order to delight
himself with the contemplation of some noble action
of a heroic time, and to enable others, through his representation of it, to delight in it also.

I am far indeed from making any claim, for myself, 10
that I possess this discipline ; or for the following
Poems, that they breathe its spirit. But I say, that
in the sincere endeavour to learn and practise, amid
the bewildering confusion of our times, what is sound
and true in poetical art, I seemed to myself to find the
only sure guidance, the only solid footing, among the
ancients. They, at any rate, knew what they wanted in x
Art, and we do not. It is this uncertainty which is
disheartening, and not hostile criticism. How often
have I felt this when reading words of disparagement 20
or of cavil : that it is the uncertainty as to what is
really to be aimed at which makes our difficulty, not
the dissatisfaction of the critic, who himself suffers
from the same uncertainty. *Non me tua fervida
terrent Dicta : Dii me terrent, et Jupiter hostis.*

Two kinds of *dilettanti*, says Goethe, there are in
poetry : he who neglects the indispensable mechanical
part, and thinks he has done enough if he shows
spirituality and feeling ; and he who seeks to arrive at
poetry merely by mechanism, in which he can acquire 30
an artisan's readiness, and is without soul and matter.
And he adds, that the first does most harm to Art, and
the last to himself. If we must be *dilettanti :* if it
is impossible for us, under the circumstances amidst
which we live, to think clearly, to feel nobly, and to
delineate firmly : if we cannot attain to the mastery of
the great artists—let us, at least, have so much respect
for our Art as to prefer it to ourselves : let us not bewilder our successors : let us transmit to them the
practice of Poetry, with its boundaries and wholesome 40
regulative laws, under which excellent works may
again, perhaps, at some future time, be produced, not

yet fallen into oblivion through our neglect, not yet condemned and cancelled by the influence of their eternal enemy, Caprice.

Fox How, Ambleside,
October 1, 1853.

ADVERTISEMENT TO THE SECOND EDITION

[First published 1854. Reprinted 1857.]

I HAVE allowed the Preface to the former edition of these Poems to stand almost without change, because I still believe it to be, in the main, true. I must not, however, be supposed insensible to the force of much 10 that has been alleged against portions of it, or unaware that it contains many things incompletely stated, many things which need limitation. It leaves, too, untouched the question, how far, and in what manner, the opinions there expressed respecting the choice of subjects apply to lyric poetry ; that region of the poetical field which is chiefly cultivated at present. But neither have I time now to supply these deficiencies, nor is this the proper place for attempting it : on one or two points alone I wish to offer, in the briefest 20 possible way, some explanation.

An objection has been ably urged to the classing together, as subjects equally belonging to a past time, Oedipus and Macbeth. And it is no doubt true that to Shakespeare, standing on the verge of the middle ages, the epoch of Macbeth was more familiar than that of Oedipus. But I was speaking of actions as they presented themselves to us moderns : and it will hardly be said that the European mind, since Voltaire, has much more affinity with the times of Macbeth than 30 with those of Oedipus. As moderns, it seems to me, we have no longer any direct affinity with the circumstances and feelings of either ; as individuals, we are attracted towards this or that personage, we have a capacity for imagining him, irrespective of his times, solely according to a law of personal sympathy ; and

Advertisement, &c. *Title*] Preface *1854*.

those subjects for which we feel this personal attraction most strongly, we may hope to treat successfully. Alcestis or Joan of Arc, Charlemagne or Agamemnon —one of these is not really nearer to us now than another ; each can be made present only by an act of poetic imagination : but this man's imagination has an affinity for one of them, and that man's for another.

It has been said that I wish to limit the Poet in his choice of subjects to the period of Greek and Roman antiquity : but it is not so : I only counsel him to 10 choose for his subjects great actions, without regarding to what time they belong. Nor do I deny that the poetic faculty can and does manifest itself in treating the most trifling action, the most hopeless subject. But it is a pity that power should be wasted ; and that the Poet should be compelled to impart interest and force to his subject, instead of receiving them from it, and thereby doubling his impressiveness. There is, it has been excellently said, an immortal strength in the stories of great actions : the most gifted poet, then, 20 may well be glad to supplement with it that mortal weakness, which, in presence of the vast spectacle of life and the world, he must for ever feel to be his individual portion.

Again, with respect to the study of the classical writers of antiquity : it has been said that we should emulate rather than imitate them. I make no objection : all I say is, let us study them. They can help to cure us of what is, it seems to me, the great vice of our intellect, manifesting itself in our incredible vagaries 30 in literature, in art, in religion, in morals ; namely, that it is *fantastic*, and wants *sanity*. Sanity—that is the great virtue of the ancient literature : the want of that is the great defect of the modern, in spite of all its variety and power. It is impossible to read carefully the great ancients, without losing something of our caprice and eccentricity · and to emulate them we must at least read them.

London,
    June 1, 1854.

3 Alcestis] Prometheus *1854.*

ALARIC AT ROME

[A prize poem recited in Rugby School, June 12, 1840. Published at Rugby the same year.]

> Admire, exult, despise, laugh, weep, for here
> There is such matter for all feeling.
> *Childe Harold.*

I

UNWELCOME shroud of the forgotten dead,
Oblivion's dreary fountain, where art thou:
Why speed'st thou not thy deathlike wave to shed
O'er humbled pride, and self-reproaching woe:
Or time's stern hand, why blots it not away
The saddening tale that tells of sorrow and decay?

II

There are, whose glory passeth not away—
Even in the grave their fragrance cannot fade:
Others there are as deathless full as they,
Who for themselves a monument have made   10
By their own crimes—a lesson to all eyes—
Of wonder to the fool—of warning to the wise.

III

Yes, there are stories registered on high,
Yes, there are stains time's fingers cannot blot,
Deeds that shall live when they who did them, die;
Things that may cease, but never be forgot:
Yet some there are, their very lives would give
To be remembered thus, and yet they cannot live.

IV

But thou, imperial City! that hast stood
In greatness once, in sackcloth now and tears,   20
A mighty name, for evil or for good,
Even in the loneness of thy widowed years:
Thou that hast gazed, as the world hurried by,
Upon its headlong course with sad prophetic eye.

V

Is thine the laurel-crown that greatness wreathes
Round the wan temples of the hallowed dead—
Is it the blighting taint dishonour breathes
In fires undying o'er the guilty head,
  Or the brief splendour of that meteor light
That for a moment gleams, and all again is night?   30

VI

Fain would we deem that thou hast risen so high
Thy dazzling light an eagle's gaze should tire;
No meteor brightness to be seen and die,
No passing pageant, born but to expire,
  But full and deathless as the deep dark hue
Of ocean's sleeping face, or heaven's unbroken blue.

VII

Yet stains there are to blot thy brightest page,
And wither half the laurels on thy tomb;
A glorious manhood, yet a dim old age,
And years of crime, and nothingness, and gloom:
  And then that mightiest crash, that giant fall,   41
Ambition's boldest dream might sober and appal.

VIII

Thou wondrous chaos, where together dwell
Present and past, the living and the dead,
Thou shattered mass, whose glorious ruins tell
The vanisht might of that discrownèd head:
  Where all we see, or do, or hear, or say,
Seems strangely echoed back by tones of yesterday:

IX

Thou solemn grave, where every step we tread
Treads on the slumbering dust of other years;   50
The while there sleeps within thy precincts dread
What once had human passions, hopes, and fears;
  And memory's gushing tide swells deep and full
And makes thy very ruin fresh and beautiful.

X

Alas, no common sepulchre art thou,
No habitation for the nameless dead,
Green turf above, and crumbling dust below,
Perchance some mute memorial at their head,
But one vast fane where all unconscious sleep
Earth's old heroic forms in peaceful slumbers deep. 60

XI

Thy dead are kings, thy dust are palaces,
Relics of nations thy memorial-stones :
And the dim glories of departed days
Fold like a shroud around thy withered bones :
And o'er thy towers the wind's half-uttered sigh
Whispers, in mournful tones, thy silent elegy.

XII

Yes, in such eloquent silence didst thou lie
When the Goth stooped upon his stricken prey,
And the deep hues of an Italian sky
Flasht on the rude barbarian's wild array : 70
While full and ceaseless as the ocean roll,
Horde after horde streamed up thy frowning Capitol.

XIII

Twice, ere that day of shame, the embattled foe
Had gazed in wonder on that glorious sight ;
Twice had the eternal city bowed her low
In sullen homage to the invader's might :
Twice had the pageant of that vast array
Swept, from thy walls, O Rome, on its triumphant way.

XIV

Twice, from without thy bulwarks, hath the din
Of Gothic clarion smote thy startled ear ; 80
Anger, and strife, and sickness are within,
Famine and sorrow are no strangers here :
Twice hath the cloud hung o'er thee, twice been
    stayed
Even in the act to burst, twice threatened, twice delayed.

XV

Yet once again, stern Chief, yet once again,
Pour forth the foaming vials of thy wrath:
There lies thy goal, to miss or to attain,
Gird thee, and on upon thy fateful path.
The world hath bowed to Rome, oh! cold were he
Who would not burst his bonds, and in his turn be free.

XVI

Therefore arise and arm thee! lo, the world   91
Looks on in fear! and when the seal is set,
The doom pronounced, the battle-flag unfurled,
Scourge of the nations, wouldst thou linger yet?
Arise and arm thee! spread thy banners forth,
Pour from a thousand hills thy warriors of the north!

XVII

Hast thou not marked on a wild autumn day
When the wind slumbereth in a sudden lull,
What deathlike stillness o'er the landscape lay,
How calmly sad, how sadly beautiful;   100
How each bright tint of tree, and flower, and heath
Were mingling with the sere and withered hues of death?

XVIII

And thus, beneath the clear, calm vault of heaven
In mournful loveliness that city lay,
And thus, amid the glorious hues of even
That city told of languor and decay:
Till what at morning's hour lookt warm and bright
Was cold and sad beneath that breathless, voiceless
          night.

XIX

Soon was that stillness broken: like the cry
Of the hoarse onset of the surging wave,   110
Or louder rush of whirlwinds sweeping by
Was the wild shout those Gothic myriads gave,
As towered on high, above their moonlit road,
Scenes where a Caesar triumpht, or a Scipio trod.

XX

Think ye it strikes too slow, the sword of fate,
Think ye the avenger loiters on his way,
That your own hands must open wide the gate,
And your own voice⟨s⟩ guide him to his prey ;
Alas, it needs not ; is it hard to know
Fate's threat'nings are not vain, the spoiler comes not
      slow ?   120

XXI

And were there none, to stand and weep alone,
And as the pageant swept before their eyes
To hear a dim and long forgotten tone
Tell of old times, and holiest memories,
Till fanciful regret and dreamy woe
Peopled night's voiceless shades with forms of long Ago?

XXII

Oh yes ! if fancy feels, beyond to-day,
Thoughts of the past and of the future time,
How should that mightiest city pass away
And not bethink her of her glorious prime,   130
Whilst every chord that thrills at thoughts of home
Jarr'd with the bursting shout, ' they come, the Goth,
      they come ! '

XXIII

The trumpet swells yet louder : they are here !
Yea, on your fathers' bones the avengers tread,
Not this the time to weep upon the bier
That holds the ashes of your hero-dead,
If wreaths may twine for you, or laurels wave,
They shall not deck your life, but sanctify your grave.

XXIV

Alas ! no wreaths are here.   Despair may teach
Cowards to conquer and the weak to die ;   140
Nor tongue of man, nor fear, nor shame can preach
So stern a lesson as necessity,
Yet here it speaks not.   Yea, though all around
Unhallowed feet are trampling on this haunted ground,

XXV

Though every holiest feeling, every tie
That binds the heart of man with mightiest power,
All natural love, all human sympathy
Be crusht, and outraged in this bitter hour,
Here is no echo to the sound of home,
No shame that suns should rise to light a conquer'd
　　　　Rome.　　　　　　　　　　　　　　　150

XXVI

That troublous night is over : on the brow
Of thy stern hill, thou mighty Capitol,
One form stands gazing : silently below
The morning mists from tower and temple roll,
And lo ! the eternal city, as they rise,
Bursts, in majestic beauty, on her conqueror's eyes.

XXVII

Yes, there he stood, upon that silent hill,
And there beneath his feet his conquest lay :
Unlike that ocean-city, gazing still
Smilingly forth upon her sunny bay,　　　　　160
But o'er her vanisht might and humbled pride
Mourning, as widowed Venice o'er her Adrian tide.

XXVIII

Breathe there not spirits on the peopled air ?
Float there not voices on the murmuring wind ?
Oh ! sound there not some strains of sadness there,
To touch with sorrow even a victor's mind,
And wrest one tear from joy !　Oh ! who shall pen
The thoughts that toucht thy breast, thou lonely
　　　　conqueror, then ?

XXIX

Perchance his wandering heart was far away,
Lost in dim memories of his early home,　　　　170
And his young dreams of conquest ; how to-day
Beheld him master of Imperial Rome,
Crowning his wildest hopes : perchance his eyes
As they looked sternly on, beheld new victories,

XXX

New dreams of wide dominion, mightier, higher,
Come floating up from the abyss of years ;
Perchance that solemn sight might quench the fire
Even of that ardent spirit ; hopes and fears
Might well be mingling at that murmured sigh,
Whispering from all around, 'All earthly things must
    die.'   180

XXXI

Perchance that wondrous city was to him
But as one voiceless blank ; a place of graves,
And recollections indistinct and dim,
Whose sons were conquerors once, and now were
    slaves :
It may be in that desolate sight his eye
Saw but another step to climb to victory !

XXXII

Alas ! that fiery spirit little knew
The change of life, the nothingness of power,
How both were hastening, as they flowered and grew,
Nearer and nearer to their closing hour :   190
How every birth of time's miraculous womb
Swept off the withered leaves that hide the naked
    tomb.

XXXIII

One little year ; that restless soul shall rest,
That frame of vigour shall be crumbling clay,
And tranquilly, above that troubled breast,
The sunny waters hold their joyous way :
And gently shall the murmuring ripples flow,
Nor wake the weary soul that slumbers on below.

XXXIV

Alas ! far other thoughts might well be ours
And dash our holiest raptures while we gaze :   200
Energies wasted, unimproved hours,
The saddening visions of departed days :
And while they rise here might we stand alone,
And mingle with thy ruins somewhat of our own.

XXXV

Beautiful city !   If departed things
Ever again put earthly likeness on,
Here should a thousand forms on fancy's wings
Float up to tell of ages that are gone :
Yea, though hand touch thee not, nor eye should see,
Still should the spirit hold communion, Rome, with
 thee !   210

XXXVI

O ! it is bitter, that each fairest dream
Should fleet before us but to melt away ;
That wildest visions still should loveliest seem
And soonest fade in the broad glare of day :
That while we feel the world is dull and low,
Gazing on thee, we wake to find it is not so.

XXXVII

A little while, alas ! a little while,
And the same world has tongue, and ear, and eye,
The careless glance, the cold unmeaning smile,
The thoughtless word, the lack of sympathy ! 220
Who would not turn him from the barren sea
And rest his weary eyes on the green land and thee !

XXXVIII

So pass we on.   But oh ! to harp aright
The vanisht glories of thine early day,
There needs a minstrel of diviner might,
A holier incense than this feeble lay ;
To chant thy requiem with more passionate breath,
And twine with bolder hand thy last memorial wreath !

CROMWELL

[A prize poem recited in the Sheldonian Theatre, Oxford, June 28, 1843. First published by J. Vincent, Oxford, 1843. Reprinted in *Oxford Prize Poems*, 1846, and separately in 1863.]

SYNOPSIS

Introduction—The mountains and the sea the cradles of Freedom —contrasted with the birth-place of Cromwell—His childhood and youth—The germs of his future character probably formed during his life of inaction—Cromwell at the moment of his intended embarkation—Retrospect of his past life and profligate youth—Temptations held out by the prospect of a life of rest in America—How far such rest was allowable—Vision of his future life—Different persons represented in it—Charles the First—Cromwell himself—His victories and maritime glory—Pym—Strafford—Laud—Hampden—Falkland—Milton —Charles the First—Cromwell on his death-bed—His character—Dispersion of the vision—Conclusion.

> Schrecklich ist es, deiner Wahrheit
> Sterbliches Gefäss zu seyn.
>
> Schiller.

High fate is theirs, ye sleepless waves, whose ear
Learns Freedom's lesson from your voice of fear ;
Whose spell-bound sense from childhood's hour hath
    known
Familiar meanings in your mystic tone :
Sounds of deep import—voices that beguile
Age of its tears and childhood of its smile,
To yearn with speechless impulse to the free
And gladsome greetings of the buoyant sea !
High fate is theirs, who where the silent sky
Stoops to the soaring mountains, live and die;   10
Who scale the cloud-capt height, or sink to rest
In the deep stillness of its shelt'ring breast ;—
Around whose feet the exulting waves have sung,
The eternal hills their giant shadows flung.

No wonders nurs'd thy childhood ; not for thee
Did the waves chant their song of liberty !

Thine was no mountain home, where Freedom's form
Abides enthron'd amid the mist and storm,
And whispers to the listening winds, that swell
With solemn cadence round her citadel !   20
These had no sound for thee : that cold calm eye
Lit with no rapture as the storm swept by,
To mark with shiver'd crest the reeling wave
Hide his torn head beneath his sunless cave ;
Or hear, 'mid circling crags, the impatient cry
Of the pent winds, that scream in agony !
Yet all high sounds that mountain children hear
Flash'd from thy soul upon thine inward ear ;
All Freedom's mystic language—storms that roar
By hill or wave, the mountain or the shore,—   30
All these had stirr'd thy spirit, and thine eye
In common sights read secret sympathy ;
Till all bright thoughts that hills or waves can yield,
Deck'd the dull waste, and the familiar field ;
Or wondrous sounds from tranquil skies were borne
Far o'er the glistening sheets of windy corn :
Skies—that unbound by clasp of mountain chain,
Slope stately down, and melt into the plain ;
Sounds—such as erst the lone wayfaring man
Caught, as he journeyed, from the lips of Pan ;   40
Or that mysterious cry, that smote with fear,
Like sounds from other worlds, the Spartan's ear,
While o'er the dusty plain, the murmurous throng
Of Heaven's embattled myriads swept along.

Say not such dreams are idle : for the man
Still toils to perfect what the child began ;
And thoughts, that were but outlines, time engraves
Deep on his life ; and childhood's baby waves,
Made rough with care, become the changeful sea,
Stemm'd by the strength of manhood fearlessly ;   50
And fleeting thoughts, that on the lonely wild
Swept o'er the fancy of that heedless child,
Perchance had quicken'd with a living truth
The cold dull soil of his unfruitful youth ;
Till, with his daily life, a life, that threw
Its shadows o'er the future, flower'd and grew,
With common cares unmingling, and apart,

Haunting the shrouded chambers of his heart ;
Till life, unstirr'd by action, life became
Threaded and lighten'd by a track of flame ;   60
An inward light, that, with its streaming ray,
On the dark current of his changeless day
Bound all his being with a silver chain—
Like a swift river through a silent plain !

High thoughts were his, when by the gleaming flood,
With heart new strung, and stern resolve, he stood ;
Where rode the tall dark ships, whose loosen'd sail
All idly flutter'd in the eastern gale ;
High thoughts were his ;—but Memory's glance the
    while
Fell on the cherish'd past with tearful smile ;   70
And peaceful joys and gentler thoughts swept by,
Like summer lightnings o'er a darken'd sky.
The peace of childhood, and the thoughts that roam,
Like loving shadows, round that childhood's home ;
Joys that had come and vanish'd, half unknown,
Then slowly brighten'd, as the days had flown ;
Years that were sweet or sad, becalm'd or toss'd
On life's wild waves—the living and the lost.
Youth stain'd with follies : and the thoughts of ill
Crush'd, as they rose, by manhood's sterner will.   80
Repentant prayers, that had been strong to save ;
And the first sorrow, which is childhood's grave !
All shapes that haunt remembrance—soft and fair,
Like a green land at sunset, all were there !
Eyes that he knew, old faces, unforgot,
Gaz'd sadly down on his unrestful lot,
And Memory's calm clear voice, and mournful eye,
Chill'd every buoyant hope that floated by ;
Like frozen winds on southern vales that blow
From a far land—the children of the snow—   90
O'er flowering plain and blossom'd meadow fling
The cold dull shadow of their icy wing.

Then Fancy's roving visions, bold and free,
A moment dispossess'd reality.
All airy hopes that idle hearts can frame,
Like dreams between two sorrows, went and came :

Fond hearts that fain would clothe the unwelcome truth
Of toilsome manhood in the dreams of youth,
To bend in rapture at some idle throne,
Some lifeless soulless phantom of their own ;　　　100
Some shadowy vision of a tranquil life,
Of joys unclouded, years unstirr'd by strife ;
Of sleep unshadow'd by a dream of woe ;
Of many a lawny hill, and streams with silver flow ;
Of giant mountains by the western main,
The sunless forest, and the sea-like plain ;
Those lingering hopes of coward hearts, that still
Would play the traitor to the steadfast will,
One moment's space, perchance, might charm his eye
From the stern future, and the years gone by.　　　110
One moment's space might waft him far away
To western shores—the death-place of the day !
Might paint the calm, sweet peace—the rest of home,
Far o'er the pathless waste of labouring foam—
Peace, that recall'd his childish hours anew,
More calm, more deep, than childhood ever knew !
Green happy places—like a flowery lea
Between the barren mountains and the stormy sea.

　　O pleasant rest, if once the race were run !
O happy slumber, if the day were done !　　　120
Dreams that were sweet at eve, at morn were sin ;
With cares to conquer, and a goal to win !
His were no tranquil years—no languid sleep—
No life of dreams—no home beyond the deep—
No softening ray—no visions false and wild—
No glittering hopes on life's grey distance smiled—
Like isles of sunlight on a mountain's brow,
Lit by a wandering gleam, we know not how,
Far on the dim horizon, when the sky
With glooming clouds broods dark and heavily.　　　130

　　Then his eye slumber'd, and the chain was broke
That bound his spirit, and his heart awoke ;
Then—like a kingly river—swift and strong,
The future roll'd its gathering tides along !
The shout of onset and the shriek of fear
Smote, like the rush of waters, on his ear ;

And his eye kindled with the kindling fray,
The surging battle and the mail'd array !
All wondrous deeds the coming days should see,
And the long Vision of the years to be.   140
Pale phantom hosts, like shadows, faint and far,
Councils, and armies, and the pomp of war !
And one sway'd all, who wore a kingly crown,
Until another rose and smote him down :
A form that tower'd above his brother men ;
A form he knew—but it was shrouded then !
With stern, slow steps—unseen—yet still the same,
By leaguer'd tower and tented field it came ;
By Naseby's hill, o'er Marston's heathy waste,
By Worcester's field the warrior-vision pass'd !   150
From their deep base, thy beetling cliffs, Dunbar,
Rang, as he trode them, with the voice of war !
The soldier kindled at his words of fire ;
The statesman quail'd before his glance of ire !
Worn was his brow with cares no thought could scan,
His step was loftier than the steps of man ;
And the winds told his glory, and the wave
Sonorous witness to his empire gave !

What forms are these, that with complaining sound,
And slow, reluctant steps are gathering round ?   160
Forms that with him shall tread life's changing stage,
Cross his lone path, or share his pilgrimage.
There, as he gazed, a wondrous band—they came,
Pym's look of hate, and Strafford's glance of flame.
There Laud, with noiseless steps and glittering eye,
In priestly garb, a frail old man, went by ;
His drooping head bowed meekly on his breast ;
His hands were folded, like a saint at rest !
There Hampden bent him o'er his saddle bow,
And death's cold dews bedimm'd his earnest brow ; 170
Still turn'd to watch the battle—still forgot
Himself, his sufferings, in his country's lot !
There Falkland eyed the strife that would not cease,
Shook back his tangled locks, and murmur'd—'Peace!'
With feet that spurn'd the ground, lo ! Milton there
Stood like a statue ; and his face was fair—

Fair beyond human beauty ; and his eye,
That knew not earth, soar'd upwards to the sky !

He, too, was there—it was the princely boy,
The child-companion of his childish joy !   180
But oh ! how chang'd—those deathlike features wore
Childhood's bright glance, and sunny smile no more !
That brow so sad, so pale, so full of care—
What trace of careless childhood linger'd there ?
What spring of youth in that majestic mien,
So sadly calm, so kingly, so serene ?
No—all was chang'd—the monarch wept alone,
Between a ruin'd church and shatter'd throne !
Friendless and hopeless—like a lonely tree,
On some bare headland, straining mournfully,   190
That all night long its weary moan doth make
To the vex'd waters of a mountain lake !
Still, as he gaz'd, the phantom's mournful glance
Shook the deep slumber of his deathlike trance ;
Like some forgotten strain that haunts us still,
That calm eye follow'd, turn him where he will ;
Till the pale monarch, and the long array,
Pass'd, like a morning mist, in tears away !

Then all his dream was troubled, and his soul
Thrill'd with a dread no slumber could control ;   200
On that dark form his eyes had gaz'd before,
Nor known it then ;—but it was veil'd no more !
In broad clear light the ghastly vision shone,—
That form was his,—those features were his own !
The night of terrors, and the day of care,
The years of toil, all, all were written there !
Sad faces watch'd around him, and his breath
Came faint and feeble in the embrace of death.
The gathering tempest, with its voice of fear,
His latest loftiest music, smote his ear !   210
That day of boundless hope and promise high,
That day that hail'd his triumphs, saw him die !
Then from those whitening lips, as death drew near,
The imprisoning chains fell off, and all was clear !
Like lowering clouds, that at the close of day,
Bath'd in a blaze of sunset, melt away ;

And with its clear calm tones, that dying prayer
Cheer'd all the failing hearts that sorrow'd there !

A life—whose ways no human thought could scan ;
A life—that was not as the life of man ;   220
A life—that wrote its purpose with a sword,
Moulding itself in action, not in word !
Rent with tumultuous thoughts, whose conflict rung
Deep thro' his soul, and chok'd his faltering tongue ;
A heart that reck'd not of the countless dead
That strew'd the blood-stain'd path where Empire led ;
A daring hand, that shrunk not to fulfil
The thought that spurr'd it ; and a dauntless will,
Bold action's parent ; and a piercing ken
Through the dark chambers of the hearts of men,   230
To read each thought, and teach that master-mind
The fears and hopes and passions of mankind ;
All these were thine—Oh thought of fear !—and thou
Stretch'd on that bed of death, art nothing now.

Then all his vision faded, and his soul
Sprang from its sleep ! and lo, the waters roll
Once more beneath him ; and the fluttering sail,
Where the dark ships rode proudly, woo'd the gale ;
And the wind murmur'd round him, and he stood
Once more alone beside the gleaming flood.   240

HORATIAN ECHO

(TO AN AMBITIOUS FRIEND)

[Written in 1847. First published in *The Century Guild Hobby Horse*, 1887.]

OMIT, omit, my simple friend,
Still to inquire how parties tend,
Or what we fix with foreign powers.
If France and we are really friends,
And what the Russian Czar intends,
  Is no concern of ours.

Us not the daily quickening race
Of the invading populace
Shall draw to swell that shouldering herd.
Mourn will we not your closing hour, 10
Ye imbeciles in present power,
  Doom'd, pompous, and absurd!

And let us bear, that they debate
Of all the engine-work of state,
Of commerce, laws, and policy,
The secrets of the world's machine,
And what the rights of man may mean,
  With readier tongue than we.

Only, that with no finer art
They cloak the troubles of the heart 20
With pleasant smile, let us take care ;
Nor with a lighter hand dispose
Fresh garlands of this dewy rose,
  To crown Eugenia's hair.

Of little threads our life is spun,
And he spins ill, who misses one.
But is thy fair Eugenia cold ?
Yet Helen had an equal grace,
And Juliet's was as fair a face,
  And now their years are told. 30

The day approaches, when we must
Be crumbling bones and windy dust ;
And scorn us as our mistress may,
Her beauty will no better be
Than the poor face she slights in thee,
    When dawns that day, that day.

SONNET TO THE HUNGARIAN NATION

[First published in *The Examiner*, July 21, 1849; not reprinted by the author.]

NOT in sunk Spain's prolong'd death agony ;
Not in rich England, bent but to make pour
The flood of the world's commerce on her shore ;
Not in that madhouse, France, from whence the cry
Afflicts grave Heaven with its long senseless roar ;
Not in American vulgarity,
Nor wordy German imbecility—
Lies any hope of heroism more.
Hungarians !   Save the world !   Renew the stories
Of men who against hope repell'd the chain,   10
And make the world's dead spirit leap again !
On land renew that Greek exploit, whose glories
Hallow the Salaminian promontories,
And the Armada flung to the fierce main.

THE STRAYED REVELLER

AND OTHER POEMS, 1849

Ἀ μάκαρ, ὅστις ἔην κεῖνον χρόνον ἴδρις ἀοιδῆς
Μουσάων θεράπων, ὅτ᾽ ἀκείρατος ἦν ἔτι λειμών·
νῦν δ᾽, ὅτε πάντα δέδασται, ἔχουσι δὲ πείρατα τέχναι,
ὕστατοι ὥστε δρόμου καταλειπόμεθ᾽—

SONNET

[First published 1849.   Reprinted 1853, '54, '57.]

ONE lesson, Nature, let me learn of thee,
One lesson that in every wind is blown,
One lesson of two duties serv'd in one,
Though the loud world proclaim their enmity—
    Of Toil unsever'd from Tranquillity :
Of Labour, that in still advance outgrows
Far noisier schemes, accomplish'd in Repose,
Too great for haste, too high for rivalry.
Yes, while on earth a thousand discords ring,
Man's senseless uproar mingling with his toil,   10
Still do thy sleepless ministers move on,
Their glorious tasks in silence perfecting :
Still working, blaming still our vain turmoil ;
Labourers that shall not fail, when man is gone.

MYCERINUS

[First published 1849.   Reprinted 1853, '54, '57.]

' NOT by the justice that my father spurn'd,
Not for the thousands whom my father slew,
Altars unfed and temples overturn'd,
Cold hearts and thankless tongues, where thanks were
    due ;
Fell this late voice from lips that cannot lie,
Stern sentence of the Powers of Destiny.

1, 2 One lesson] Two lessons *1849*.   2 is] are *1849*.
3 Two blending duties, harmonis'd in one, *1849*.
6 still advance] one short hour *1849*.   7 Far noisier] Man's
noisy *1849*.   10 senseless uproar] weak complainings *1849*.
    12 tasks] course *1849*.   13 blaming] chiding *1849*.

I will unfold my sentence and my crime.
My crime, that, rapt in reverential awe,
I sate obedient, in the fiery prime
Of youth, self-govern'd, at the feet of Law ;　　10
Ennobling this dull pomp, the life of kings,
By contemplation of diviner things.

My father lov'd injustice, and liv'd long ;
Crown'd with grey hairs he died, and full of sway.
I lov'd the good he scorn'd, and hated wrong :
The Gods declare my recompense to-day.
I look'd for life more lasting, rule more high ;
And when six years are measur'd, lo, I die !

Yet surely, O my people, did I deem
Man's justice from the all-just Gods was given :　　20
A light that from some upper fount did beam,
Some better archetype, whose seat was heaven ;
A light that, shining from the blest abodes,
Did shadow somewhat of the life of Gods.

Mere phantoms of man's self-tormenting heart,
Which on the sweets that woo it dares not feed :
Vain dreams, that quench our pleasures, then depart,
When the dup'd soul, self-master'd, claims its meed :
When, on the strenuous just man, Heaven bestows,
Crown of his struggling life, an unjust close.　　30

Seems it so light a thing then, austere Powers,
To spurn man's common lure, life's pleasant things ?
Seems there no joy in dances crown'd with flowers,
Love, free to range, and regal banquetings ?
Bend ye on these, indeed, an unmov'd eye,
Not Gods but ghosts, in frozen apathy ?

Or is it that some Power, too wise, too strong,
Even for yourselves to conquer or beguile,
Whirls earth, and heaven, and men, and gods along,
Like the broad rushing of the insurged Nile ?　　40
And the great powers we serve, themselves may be
Slaves of a tyrannous Necessity ?

40 insurged] column'd *1849.*

Or in mid-heaven, perhaps, your golden cars,
Where earthly voice climbs never, wing their flight,
And in wild hunt, through mazy tracts of stars,
Sweep in the sounding stillness of the night ?
Or in deaf ease, on thrones of dazzling sheen,
Drinking deep draughts of joy, ye dwell serene ?

Oh, wherefore cheat our youth, if thus it be,
Of one short joy, one lust, one pleasant dream ?   50
Stringing vain words of powers we cannot see,
Blind divinations of a will supreme ;
Lost labour : when the circumambient gloom
But hides, if Gods, Gods careless of our doom ?

The rest I give to joy.   Even while I speak
My sand runs short ; and as yon star-shot ray,
Hemm'd by two banks of cloud, peers pale and weak,
Now, as the barrier closes, dies away ;
Even so do past and future intertwine,
Blotting this six years' space, which yet is mine.   60

Six years—six little years—six drops of time—
Yet suns shall rise, and many moons shall wane,
And old men die, and young men pass their prime,
And languid Pleasure fade and flower again ;
And the dull Gods behold, ere these are flown,
Revels more deep, joy keener than their own.

Into the silence of the groves and woods
I will go forth ; but something would I say—
Something—yet what I know not : for the Gods
The doom they pass revoke not, nor delay ;   70
And prayers, and gifts, and tears, are fruitless all,
And the night waxes, and the shadows fall.

Ye men of Egypt, ye have heard your king.
I go, and I return not.   But the will
Of the great Gods is plain ; and ye must bring
Ill deeds, ill passions, zealous to fulfil
Their pleasure, to their feet ; and reap their praise,
The praise of Gods, rich boon ! and length of days.'

—So spake he, half in anger, half in scorn ;
And one loud cry of grief and of amaze   80
Broke from his sorrowing people : so he spake ;
And turning, left them there ; and with brief pause,
Girt with a throng of revellers, bent his way
To the cool region of the groves he lov'd.
There by the river banks he wander'd on,
From palm-grove on to palm-grove, happy trees,
Their smooth tops shining sunwards, and beneath
Burying their unsunn'd stems in grass and flowers :
Where in one dream the feverish time of Youth
Might fade in slumber, and the feet of Joy   90
Might wander all day long and never tire :
Here came the king, holding high feast, at morn,
Rose-crown'd ; and ever, when the sun went down,
A hundred lamps beam'd in the tranquil gloom,
From tree to tree, all through the twinkling grove,
Revealing all the tumult of the feast,
Flush'd guests, and golden goblets, foam'd with wine ;
While the deep-burnish'd foliage overhead
Splinter'd the silver arrows of the moon.

  It may be that sometimes his wondering soul   100
From the loud joyful laughter of his lips
Might shrink half startled, like a guilty man
Who wrestles with his dream ; as some pale Shape,
Gliding half hidden through the dusky stems,
Would thrust a hand before the lifted bowl,
Whispering, 'A little space, and thou art mine.'
It may be on that joyless feast his eye
Dwelt with mere outward seeming ; he, within,
Took measure of his soul, and knew its strength,
And by that silent knowledge, day by day,   110
Was calm'd, ennobled, comforted, sustain'd.
It may be ; but not less his brow was smooth,
And his clear laugh fled ringing through the gloom,
And his mirth quail'd not at the mild reproof
Sigh'd out by Winter's sad tranquillity ;
Nor, pall'd with its own fullness, ebb'd and died
In the rich languor of long summer days ;
Nor wither'd, when the palm-tree plumes that roof'd
With their mild dark his grassy banquet-hall,
Bent to the cold winds of the showerless Spring ;   120

No, nor grew dark when Autumn brought the clouds.
  So six long years he revell'd, night and day ;
And when the mirth wax'd loudest, with dull sound
Sometimes from the grove's centre echoes came,
To tell his wondering people of their king ;
In the still night, across the steaming flats,
Mix'd with the murmur of the moving Nile.

TO A FRIEND

[First published 1849.   Reprinted 1853, '54, '57.]

WHO prop, thou ask'st, in these bad days, my mind ?
He much, the old man, who, clearest-soul'd of men,
Saw The Wide Prospect,[1] and the Asian Fen,
And Tmolus' hill, and Smyrna's bay, though blind.
Much he, whose friendship I not long since won,
That halting slave, who in Nicopolis
Taught Arrian, when Vespasian's brutal son
Clear'd Rome of what most sham'd him.   But be his
My special thanks, whose even-balanc'd soul,
From first youth tested up to extreme old age,   10
Business could not make dull, nor Passion wild :
Who saw life steadily, and saw it whole :
The mellow glory of the Attic stage ;
Singer of sweet Colonus, and its child.

[1] Εὐρώπη.

THE STRAYED REVELLER

[First published 1849.   Reprinted 1853, '54, '57.]

The portico of Circe's Palace.   Evening

A YOUTH.   CIRCE

THE YOUTH

FASTER, faster,
O Circe, Goddess,
Let the wild, thronging train,
The bright procession
Of eddying forms,
Sweep through my soul !

The portico of Circe's Palace.   Evening]   *First inserted in 1853.*

Thou standest, smiling
Down on me; thy right arm,
Lean'd up against the column there,
Props thy soft cheek;   10
Thy left holds, hanging loosely,
The deep cup, ivy-cinctur'd,
I held but now.

Is it then evening
So soon?   I see, the night dews,
Cluster'd in thick beads, dim
The agate brooch-stones
On thy white shoulder.
The cool night-wind, too,
Blows through the portico,   20
Stirs thy hair, Goddess,
Waves thy white robe.

CIRCE

Whence art thou, sleeper?

THE YOUTH

When the white dawn first
Through the rough fir-planks
Of my hut, by the chestnuts,
Up at the valley-head,
Came breaking, Goddess,
I sprang up, I threw round me
My dappled fawn-skin: ·   30
Passing out, from the wet turf,
Where they lay, by the hut door,
I snatch'd up my vine-crown, my fir-staff,
All drench'd in dew:
Came swift down to join
The rout early gather'd
In the town, round the temple,
Iacchus' white fane
On yonder hill.

Quick I pass'd, following   40
The wood-cutters' cart-track
Down the dark valley;—I saw

On my left, through the beeches,
Thy palace, Goddess,
Smokeless, empty:
Trembling, I enter'd; beheld
The court all silent,
The lions sleeping;
On the altar, this bowl.
I drank, Goddess—   50
And sunk down here, sleeping,
On the steps of thy portico.

CIRCE

Foolish boy! Why tremblest thou?
Thou lovest it, then, my wine?
Wouldst more of it? See, how glows,
Through the delicate flush'd marble,
The red creaming liquor,
Strown with dark seeds!
Drink, then! I chide thee not,
Deny thee not my bowl.   60
Come, stretch forth thy hand, then—so,—
Drink, drink again!

THE YOUTH

Thanks, gracious One!
Ah, the sweet fumes again!
More soft, ah me!
More subtle-winding
Than Pan's flute-music.
Faint—faint! Ah me!
Again the sweet sleep.

CIRCE

Hist! Thou—within there!   70
Come forth, Ulysses!
Art tired with hunting?
While we range the woodland,
See what the day brings.

ULYSSES

Ever new magic!
Hast thou then lur'd hither,

Wonderful Goddess, by thy art,
The young, languid-ey'd Ampelus,
Iacchus' darling—
Or some youth belov'd of Pan,   80
Of Pan and the Nymphs?
That he sits, bending downward
His white, delicate neck
To the ivy-wreath'd marge
Of thy cup :—the bright, glancing vine-leaves
That crown his hair,
Falling forwards, mingling
With the dark ivy-plants,
His fawn-skin, half untied,
Smear'd with red wine-stains?   Who is he,   90
That he sits, overweigh'd
By fumes of wine and sleep,
So late, in thy portico?
What youth, Goddess,—what guest
Of Gods or mortals?

Circe

Hist! he wakes!
I lur'd him not hither, Ulysses.
Nay, ask him!

The Youth

Who speaks?   Ah!   Who comes forth
To thy side, Goddess, from within?   100
How shall I name him?
This spare, dark-featur'd,
Quick-ey'd stranger?
Ah! and I see too
His sailor's bonnet,
His short coat, travel-tarnish'd,
With one arm bare.—
Art thou not he, whom fame
This long time rumours
The favour'd guest of Circe, brought by the waves?   110
Art thou he, stranger?
The wise Ulysses,
Laertes' son?

Ulysses

I am Ulysses.
And thou, too, sleeper?
Thy voice is sweet.
It may be thou hast follow'd
Through the islands some divine bard,
By age taught many things,
Age and the Muses;
And heard him delighting
The chiefs and people
In the banquet, and learn'd his songs,
Of Gods and Heroes,
Of war and arts,
And peopled cities
Inland, or built
By the grey sea.—If so, then hail!
I honour and welcome thee.

120

The Youth

The Gods are happy.
They turn on all sides
Their shining eyes:
And see, below them,
The Earth, and men.

130

They see Tiresias
Sitting, staff in hand,
On the warm, grassy
Asopus' bank:
His robe drawn over
His old, sightless head:
Revolving inly
The doom of Thebes.

140

They see the Centaurs
In the upper glens
Of Pelion, in the streams,
Where red-berried ashes fringe
The clear-brown shallow pools;
With streaming flanks, and heads
Rear'd proudly, snuffing
The mountain wind.

150

They see the Indian
Drifting, knife in hand,
His frail boat moor'd to
A floating isle thick matted
With large-leav'd, low-creeping melon-plants,
And the dark cucumber.
He reaps, and stows them,
Drifting—drifting :—round him,
Round his green harvest-plot,
Flow the cool lake-waves :   160
The mountains ring them.

They see the Scythian
On the wide Stepp, unharnessing
His wheel'd house at noon.
He tethers his beast down, and makes his meal,
Mares' milk, and bread
Bak'd on the embers :—all around
The boundless waving grass-plains stretch, thick-starr'd
With saffron and the yellow hollyhock
And flag-leav'd iris flowers.   170
Sitting in his cart
He makes his meal : before him, for long miles,
Alive with bright green lizards,
And the springing bustard fowl,
The track, a straight black line,
Furrows the rich soil : here and there
Clusters of lonely mounds
Topp'd with rough-hewn,
Grey, rain-blear'd statues, overpeer
The sunny Waste.   180

They see the Ferry
On the broad, clay-laden
Lone Chorasmian stream : thereon
With snort and strain,
Two horses, strongly swimming, tow
The ferry-boat, with woven ropes
To either bow
Firm-harness'd by the mane :—a Chief,
With shout and shaken spear
Stands at the prow, and guides them : but astern,   190
The cowering Merchants, in long robes,

Sit pale beside their wealth
Of silk-bales and of balsam-drops,
Of gold and ivory,
Of turquoise-earth and amethyst,
Jasper and chalcedony,
And milk-barr'd onyx stones.
The loaded boat swings groaning
In the yellow eddies.
The Gods behold them.   200

They see the Heroes
Sitting in the dark ship
On the foamless, long-heaving,
Violet sea:
At sunset nearing
The Happy Islands.

These things, Ulysses,
The wise Bards also
Behold and sing.
But oh, what labour!   210
O Prince, what pain!

They too can see
Tiresias:—but the Gods,
Who give them vision,
Added this law:
That they should bear too
His groping blindness,
His dark foreboding,
His scorn'd white hairs;
Bear Hera's anger   220
Through a life lengthen'd
To seven ages.

They see the Centaurs
On Pelion:—then they feel,
They too, the maddening wine
Swell their large veins to bursting: in wild pain
They feel the biting spears
Of the grim Lapithae, and Theseus, drive,
Drive crashing through their bones: they feel
High on a jutting rock in the red stream   230

Alcmena's dreadful son
Ply his bow :—such a price
The Gods exact for song ;
To become what we sing.

They see the Indian
On his mountain lake :—but squalls
Make their skiff reel, and worms
In the unkind spring have gnaw'd
Their melon-harvest to the heart: They see
The Scythian :—but long frosts   240
Parch them in winter-time on the bare Stepp,
Till they too fade like grass : they crawl
Like shadows forth in spring.

They see the Merchants
On the Oxus' stream :—but care
Must visit first them too, and make them pale.
Whether, through whirling sand,
A cloud of desert robber-horse has burst
Upon their caravan : or greedy kings,
In the wall'd cities the way passes through,   250
Crush'd them with tolls : or fever-airs,
On some great river's marge,
Mown them down, far from home.

They see the Heroes
Near harbour :—but they share
Their lives, and former violent toil, in Thebes,
Seven-gated Thebes, or Troy :
Or where the echoing oars
Of Argo, first,
Startled the unknown Sea.   260

The old Silenus
Came, lolling in the sunshine,
From the dewy forest coverts,
This way, at noon.
Sitting by me, while his Fauns
Down at the water side
Sprinkled and smooth'd
His drooping garland,
He told me these things.

238 In] I' *1849*.

But I, Ulysses,   270
Sitting on the warm steps,
Looking over the valley,
All day long, have seen,
Without pain, without labour,
Sometimes a wild-hair'd Maenad ;
Sometimes a Faun with torches ;
And sometimes, for a moment,
Passing through the dark stems
Flowing-rob'd—the belov'd,
The desir'd, the divine,   280
Belov'd Iacchus.

Ah cool night-wind, tremulous stars !
Ah glimmering water—
Fitful earth-murmur—
Dreaming woods !
Ah golden-hair'd, strangely-smiling Goddess,
And thou, prov'd, much enduring,
Wave-toss'd Wanderer !
Who can stand still ?
Ye fade, ye swim, ye waver before me.   290
The cup again !

Faster, faster,
O Circe, Goddess,
Let the wild thronging train,
The bright procession
Of eddying forms,
Sweep through my soul !

FRAGMENT OF AN 'ANTIGONE'

[First published 1849.   Reprinted 1855.]

THE CHORUS

WELL hath he done who hath seiz'd happiness.
For little do the all-containing Hours,
        Though opulent, freely give.
        Who, weighing that life well
        Fortune presents unpray'd,
Declines her ministry, and carves his own :
        And, justice not infring'd,
Makes his own welfare his unswerv'd-from law.

He does well too, who keeps that clue the mild
Birth-Goddess and the austere Fates first gave.   10
  For from the day when these
 Bring him, a weeping child,
 First to the light, and mark
A country for him, kinsfolk, and a home,
  Unguided he remains,
Till the Fates come again, alone, with death.

  In little companies,
 And, our own place once left,
 Ignorant where to stand, or whom to avoid,
By city and household group'd, we live : and many
    shocks   20
  Our order heaven-ordain'd
  Must every day endure.
Voyages, exiles, hates, dissensions, wars.
  Besides what waste He makes,
  The all-hated, order-breaking,
  Without friend, city, or home,
   Death, who dissevers all.

  Him then I praise, who dares
  To self-selected good
 Prefer obedience to the primal law,   30
Which consecrates the ties of blood : for these, indeed,
   Are to the Gods a care :
   That touches but himself.
For every day man may be link'd and loos'd
  With strangers : but the bond
   Original, deep-inwound,
  Of blood, can he not bind :
  Nor, if Fate binds, not bear.

  But hush !   Haemon, whom Antigone,
  Robbing herself of life in burying,   40
  Against Creon's law, Polynices,
  Robs of a lov'd bride ; pale, imploring,
   Waiting her passage,
  Forth from the palace hitherward comes.

HAEMON

No, no, old men, Creon I curse not.
            I weep, Thebans,
            One than Creon crueller far.
For he, he, at least, by slaying her,
August laws doth mightily vindicate:
But thou, too-bold, headstrong, pitiless,   50
Ah me!—honourest more than thy lover,
            O Antigone,
A dead, ignorant, thankless corpse.

THE CHORUS

            Nor was the love untrue
            Which the Dawn-Goddess bore
            To that fair youth she erst
            Leaving the salt sea-beds
And coming flush'd over the stormy frith
            Of loud Euripus, saw:
            Saw and snatch'd, wild with love,   60
            From the pine-dotted spurs
            Of Parnes, where thy waves,
            Asopus, gleam rock-hemm'd;
The Hunter of the Tanagraean Field.
            But him, in his sweet prime,
            By severance immature,
            By Artemis' soft shafts,
            She, though a Goddess born,
Saw in the rocky isle of Delos die.
            Such end o'ertook that love.   70
            For she desir'd to make
            Immortal mortal man,
            And blend his happy life,
            Far from the Gods, with hers:
To him postponing an eternal law.

HAEMON

But, like me, she, wroth, complaining,
Succumb'd to the envy of unkind Gods:
And, her beautiful arms unclasping,
Her fair Youth unwillingly gave.

The Chorus

Nor, though enthron'd too high   80
To fear assault of envious Gods,
His belov'd Argive Seer would Zeus retain
    From his appointed end
    In this our Thebes : but when

His flying steeds came near
To cross the steep Ismenian glen,
The broad Earth open'd and whelm'd them and him ;
    And through the void air sang
    At large his enemy's spear.

And fain would Zeus have sav'd his tired son   90
Beholding him where the Two Pillars stand
    O'er the sun-redden'd Western Straits :
Or at his work in that dim lower world.
    Fain would he have recall'd
    The fraudulent oath which bound
To a much feebler wight the heroic man :

But he preferr'd Fate to his strong desire.
Nor did there need less than the burning pile
    Under the towering Trachis crags,
And the Spercheius' vale, shaken with groans,   100
    And the rous'd Maliac gulph,
    And scar'd Oetaean snows,
To achieve his son's deliverance, O my child.

THE SICK KING IN BOKHARA

[First published 1849. Reprinted 1855.]

Hussein

O most just Vizier, send away
The cloth-merchants, and let them be,
Them and their dues, this day : the King
Is ill at ease, and calls for thee.

The Vizier

O merchants, tarry yet a day
Here in Bokhara : but at noon
To-morrow, come, and ye shall pay
Each fortieth web of cloth to me,
As the law is, and go your way.

O Hussein, lead me to the King.   10
Thou teller of sweet tales, thine own,
Ferdousi's, and the others', lead.
How is it with my lord ?

HUSSEIN
                              Alone,
Ever since prayer-time, he doth wait,
O Vizier, without lying down,
In the great window of the gate,
Looking into the Registàn ;
Where through the sellers' booths the slaves
Are this way bringing the dead man.
O Vizier, here is the King's door.   20

THE KING
O Vizier, I may bury him ?

THE VIZIER
O King, thou know'st, I have been sick
These many days, and heard no thing
(For Allah shut my ears and mind),
Not even what thou dost, O King.
Wherefore, that I may counsel thee,
Let Hussein, if thou wilt, make haste
To speak in order what hath chanc'd.

THE KING
O Vizier, be it as thou say'st.

HUSSEIN
Three days since, at the time of prayer,   30
A certain Moollah, with his robe
All rent, and dust upon his hair,
Watch'd my lord's coming forth, and push'd
The golden mace-bearers aside,
And fell at the King's feet, and cried ;

'Justice, O King, and on myself !
On this great sinner, who hath broke
The law, and by the law must die !
Vengeance, O King !'
                        But the King spoke :

12 Ferdousi's] Ferdusi's *1849*.

'What fool is this, that hurts our ears   40
With folly? or what drunken slave?
My guards, what, prick him with your spears!
Prick me the fellow from the path!'
As the King said, so was it done,
And to the mosque my lord pass'd on.

But on the morrow, when the King
Went forth again, the holy book
Carried before him, as is right,
And through the square his path he took;

My man comes running, fleck'd with blood   50
From yesterday, and falling down
Cries out most earnestly; 'O King,
My lord, O King, do right, I pray!

'How canst thou, ere thou hear, discern
If I speak folly? but a king,
Whether a thing be great or small,
Like Allah, hears and judges all.

'Wherefore hear thou! Thou know'st, how fierce
In these last days the sun hath burn'd:
That the green water in the tanks   60
Is to a putrid puddle turn'd:
And the canal, that from the stream
Of Samarcand is brought this way,
Wastes, and runs thinner every day.

'Now I at nightfall had gone forth
Alone, and in a darksome place
Under some mulberry trees I found
A little pool; and in brief space
With all the water that was there
I fill'd my pitcher, and stole home   70
Unseen: and having drink to spare,
I hid the can behind the door,
And went up on the roof to sleep.

'But in the night, which was with wind
And burning dust, again I creep
Down, having fever, for a drink.

'Now meanwhile had my brethren found
The water-pitcher, where it stood
Behind the door upon the ground,
And call'd my mother : and they all,   80
As they were thirsty, and the night
Most sultry, drain'd the pitcher there ;
That they sate with it, in my sight,
Their lips still wet, when I came down.

'Now mark ! I, being fever'd, sick,
(Most unblest also) at that sight
Brake forth, and curs'd them—dost thou hear ?~
One was my mother—Now, do right ! '

But my lord mus'd a space, and said :
' Send him away, Sirs, and make on.   90
It is some madman,' the King said :
As the King said, so was it done.

The morrow at the self-same hour
In the King's path, behold, the man,
Not kneeling, sternly fix'd : he stood
Right opposite, and thus began,
Frowning grim down :—' Thou wicked King,
Most deaf where thou shouldst most give ear !
What, must I howl in the next world,
Because thou wilt not listen here ?   100

'What, wilt thou pray, and get thee grace,
And all grace shall to me be grudg'd ?
Nay but, I swear, from this thy path
I will not stir till I be judg'd.'

Then they who stood about the King
Drew close together and conferr'd :
Till that the King stood forth and said,
'Before the priests thou shalt be heard.'

But when the Ulemas were met
And the thing heard, they doubted not ;   110
But sentenc'd him, as the law is,
To die by stoning on the spot.

109 Ulemas] Ulema *1849.*

Now the King charg'd us secretly :
' Ston'd must he be, the law stands so :
Yet, if he seek to fly, give way :
Forbid him not, but let him go.'

So saying, the King took a stone,
And cast it softly : but the man,
With a great joy upon his face,
Kneel'd down, and cried not, neither ran.   120

So they, whose lot it was, cast stones ;
That they flew thick and bruis'd him sore :
But he prais'd Allah with loud voice,
And remain'd kneeling as before.

My lord had cover'd up his face :
But when one told him, ' He is dead,'
Turning him quickly to go in,
' Bring thou to me his corpse,' he said.

And truly, while I speak, O King,
I hear the bearers on the stair.   130
Wilt thou they straightway bring him in ?
—Ho ! enter ye who tarry there !

The Vizier

O King, in this I praise thee not.
Now must I call thy grief not wise.
Is he thy friend, or of thy blood,
To find such favour in thine eyes ?

Nay, were he thine own mother's son,
Still, thou art king, and the Law stands.
It were not meet the balance swerv'd,
The sword were broken in thy hands.   140

But being nothing, as he is,
Why for no cause make sad thy face ?
Lo, I am old : three kings, ere thee,
Have I seen reigning in this place.

But who, through all this length of time,
Could bear the burden of his years,
If he for strangers pain'd his heart
Not less than those who merit tears ?

Fathers we *must* have, wife and child ;
And grievous is the grief for these :   150
This pain alone, which *must* be borne,
Makes the head white, and bows the knees.

But other loads than this his own
One man is not well made to bear.
Besides, to each are his own friends,
To mourn with him, and show him care.

Look, this is but one single place,
Though it be great : all the earth round,
If a man bear to have it so,
Things which might vex him shall be found.   160

Upon the Russian frontier, where
The watchers of two armies stand
Near one another, many a man,
Seeking a prey unto his hand,

Hath snatch'd a little fair-hair'd slave :
They snatch also, towards Mervè,
The Shiah dogs, who pasture sheep,
And up from thence to Orgunjè.

And these all, labouring for a lord,
Eat not the fruit of their own hands :   170
Which is the heaviest of all plagues,
To that man's mind, who understands.

The kaffirs also (whom God curse !)
Vex one another, night and day :
There are the lepers, and all sick :
There are the poor, who faint alway.

All these have sorrow, and keep still,
Whilst other men make cheer, and sing.
Wilt thou have pity on all these ?
No, nor on this dead dog, O King !   180

The King

O Vizier, thou art old, I young.
Clear in these things I cannot see.
My head is burning ; and a heat
Is in my skin which angers me.

161 Russian] northern *1849*.   168 Orgunjè] Urghendjè *1849*.

But hear ye this, ye sons of men !
They that bear rule, and are obey'd,
Unto a rule more strong than theirs
Are in their turn obedient made.

In vain therefore, with wistful eyes
Gazing up hither, the poor man,   190
Who loiters by the high-heap'd booths,
Below there, in the Registàn,

Says, ' Happy he, who lodges there !
With silken raiment, store of rice,
And for this drought, all kinds of fruits,
Grape syrup, squares of colour'd ice,

' With cherries serv'd in drifts of snow.'
In vain hath a king power to build
Houses, arcades, enamell'd mosques ;
And to make orchard closes, fill'd   200

With curious fruit trees, bought from far ;
With cisterns for the winter rain ;
And in the desert, spacious inns
In divers places ;—if that pain

Is not more lighten'd, which he feels,
If his will be not satisfied :
And that it be not, from all time
The Law is planted, to abide.

Thou wert a sinner, thou poor man !
Thou wert athirst ; and didst not see,   210
That, though we snatch what we desire,
We must not snatch it eagerly.

And I have meat and drink at will,
And rooms of treasures, not a few.
But I am sick, nor heed I these :
And what I would, I cannot do.

Even the great honour which I have,
When I am dead, will soon grow still.
So have I neither joy, nor fame.
But what I can do, that I will.   220

I have a fretted brick-work tomb
Upon a hill on the right hand,
Hard by a close of apricots,
Upon the road of Samarcand :

Thither, O Vizier, will I bear
This man my pity could not save ;
And, plucking up the marble flags,
There lay his body in my grave.

Bring water, nard, and linen rolls.
Wash off all blood, set smooth each limb.   230
Then say ; ' He was not wholly vile,
Because a king shall bury him.'

SHAKESPEARE

[First published 1849.   Reprinted 1853, '54, '57.]

OTHERS abide our question.   Thou art free.
We ask and ask : Thou smilest and art still,
Out-topping knowledge.   For the loftiest hill
That to the stars uncrowns his majesty,
Planting his steadfast footsteps in the sea,
Making the Heaven of Heavens his dwelling-place,
Spares but the cloudy border of his base
To the foil'd searching of mortality :
And thou, who didst the stars and sunbeams know,
Self-school'd, self-scann'd, self-honour'd, self-secure,   10
Didst walk on Earth unguess'd at.   Better so !
All pains the immortal spirit must endure,
   All weakness that impairs, all griefs that bow,
   Find their sole voice in that victorious brow.

227 plucking] tearing *1849.*

TO THE DUKE OF WELLINGTON

ON HEARING HIM MISPRAISED

[First published 1849.]

BECAUSE thou hast believ'd, the wheels of life
Stand never idle, but go always round :
Not by their hands, who vex the patient ground,
Mov'd only ; but by genius, in the strife
Of all its chafing torrents after thaw,
Urg'd ; and to feed whose movement, spinning sand,
The feeble sons of pleasure set their hand :
And, in this vision of the general law,
Hast labour'd with the foremost, hast become
Laborious, persevering, serious, firm ;   10
For this, thy track, across the fretful foam
Of vehement actions without scope or term,
 Call'd History, keeps a splendour : due to wit,
 Which saw *one* clue to life, and follow'd it

WRITTEN IN BUTLER'S SERMONS

[First published 1849.]

AFFECTIONS, Instincts, Principles, and Powers,
Impulse and Reason, Freedom and Control—
So men, unravelling God's harmonious whole,
Rend in a thousand shreds this life of ours.
Vain labour ! Deep and broad, where none may see,
Spring the foundations of the shadowy throne
Where man's one Nature, queen-like, sits alone,
Centred in a majestic unity ;
And rays her powers, like sister islands, seen
Linking their coral arms under the sea :   10
Or cluster'd peaks, with plunging gulfs between
Spann'd by aërial arches, all of gold ;
Whereo'er the chariot wheels of Life are roll'd
In cloudy circles, to eternity.

WRITTEN IN EMERSON'S ESSAYS

[First published 1849. Reprinted 1853.]

'O MONSTROUS, dead, unprofitable world,
That thou canst hear, and hearing, hold thy way.
A voice oracular hath peal'd to-day,
To-day a hero's banner is unfurl'd.
Hast thou no lip for welcome?' So I said.
Man after man, the world smil'd and pass'd by:
A smile of wistful incredulity
As though one spake of noise unto the dead:
Scornful, and strange, and sorrowful; and full
Of bitter knowledge. Yet the Will is free: 10
Strong is the Soul, and wise, and beautiful:
The seeds of godlike power are in us still:
Gods are we, Bards, Saints, Heroes, if we will.—
   Dumb judges, answer, truth or mockery?

TO AN INDEPENDENT PREACHER

WHO PREACHED THAT WE SHOULD BE 'IN HARMONY
WITH NATURE'

[First published 1849.]

'IN harmony with Nature'? Restless fool,
Who with such heat dost preach what were to thee,
When true, the last impossibility;
To be like Nature strong, like Nature cool:—
Know, man hath all which Nature hath, but more,
And in that *more* lie all his hopes of good.
Nature is cruel; man is sick of blood:
Nature is stubborn; man would fain adore:
Nature is fickle; man hath need of rest:
Nature forgives no debt, and fears no grave;   10
Man would be mild, and with safe conscience blest.
Man must begin, know this, where Nature ends;
Nature and man can never be fast friends.
Fool, if thou canst not pass her, rest her slave!

TO GEORGE CRUIKSHANK, ESQ.

ON SEEING FOR THE FIRST TIME HIS PICTURE OF 'THE
BOTTLE', IN THE COUNTRY

[First published 1849.   Reprinted 1853, '54, '57.]

ARTIST, whose hand, with horror wing'd, hath torn
From the rank life of towns this leaf : and flung
The prodigy of full-blown crime among
Valleys and men to middle fortune born,
Not innocent, indeed, yet not forlorn :
Say, what shall calm us, when such guests intrude,
Like comets on the heavenly solitude ?
Shall breathless glades, cheer'd by shy Dian's horn,
Cold-bubbling springs, or caves ?   Not so !   The Soul
Breasts her own griefs : and, urg'd too fiercely, says :
'Why tremble ?   True, the nobleness of man   11
May be by man effac'd : man can control
To pain, to death, the bent of his own days.
Know thou the worst.   So much, not more, he *can*.'

TO A REPUBLICAN FRIEND, 1848

[First published 1849.   Reprinted 1853, '54, '57.]

GOD knows it, I am with you.   If to prize
Those virtues, priz'd and practis'd by too few,
But priz'd, but lov'd, but eminent in you,
Man's fundamental life : if to despise
The barren optimistic sophistries
Of comfortable moles, whom what they do
Teaches the limit of the just and true—
And for such doing have no need of eyes :
If sadness at the long heart-wasting show
Wherein earth's great ones are disquieted :   10
If thoughts, not idle, while before me flow
The armies of the homeless and unfed :—
    If these are yours, if this is what you are,
    Then am I yours, and what you feel, I share.

To a Republican Friend, 1848.   *Title*] *date first inserted in 1853.*

TO A REPUBLICAN FRIEND, 1848

Continued

[First published 1849.   Reprinted 1853, '54, '57.]

YET, when I muse on what life is, I seem
Rather to patience prompted, than that proud
Prospect of hope which France proclaims so loud,
France, fam'd in all great arts, in none supreme.
Seeing this Vale, this Earth, whereon we dream,
Is on all sides o'ershadow'd by the high
Uno'erleap'd Mountains of Necessity,
Sparing us narrower margin than we deem.
Nor will that day dawn at a human nod,
When, bursting through the network superpos'd   10
By selfish occupation—plot and plan,
Lust, avarice, envy—liberated man,
All difference with his fellow man compos'd,
Shall be left standing face to face with God.

RELIGIOUS ISOLATION

TO THE SAME

[First published 1849.   Reprinted 1853, '54, '57.]

CHILDREN (as such forgive them) have I known,
Ever in their own eager pastime bent
To make the incurious bystander, intent
On his own swarming thoughts, an interest own ;
Too fearful or too fond to play alone.
Do thou, whom light in thine own inmost soul
(Not less thy boast) illuminates, control
Wishes unworthy of a man full-grown.
What though the holy secret which moulds thee
Moulds not the solid Earth ? though never Winds   10
Have whisper'd it to the complaining Sea,
Nature's great law, and law of all men's minds ?
　　To its own impulse every creature stirs :
　　Live by thy light, and Earth will live by hers.

TO MY FRIENDS

WHO RIDICULED A TENDER LEAVE-TAKING

[First published 1849.   Reprinted 1853, '54, '57.]

LAUGH, my Friends, and without blame
Lightly quit what lightly came:
Rich to-morrow as to-day
Spend as madly as you may.
I, with little land to stir,
Am the exacter labourer.
  Ere the parting hour go by,
  Quick, thy tablets, Memory!

But my Youth reminds me—'Thou
Hast liv'd light as these live now: 10
As these are, thou too wert such:
Much hast had, hast squander'd much.'
Fortune's now less frequent heir,
Ah! I husband what's grown rare.
  Ere the parting hour go by,
  Quick, thy tablets, Memory!

Young, I said: 'A face is gone
If too hotly mus'd upon:
And our best impressions are
Those that do themselves repair.'   20
Many a face I then let by,
Ah! is faded utterly.
  Ere the parting hour go by,
  Quick, thy tablets, Memory!

Marguerite says: 'As last year went,
So the coming year'll be spent:
Some day next year, I shall be,
Entering heedless, kiss'd by thee.'
Ah! I hope—yet, once away,
What may chain us, who can say?   30
  Ere the parting hour go by,
  Quick, thy tablets, Memory!

To my Friends, &c.   *Title*] Switzerland. I. To my friends who
ridiculed a tender leave-taking *1853, 1854, 1857.*
  7, 15, 23, 31, 39, 47, 55, 71 hour go by] kiss be dry *1849, 1853, 1854.*

Paint that lilac kerchief, bound
Her soft face, her hair around:
Tied under the archest chin
Mockery ever ambush'd in.
Let the fluttering fringes streak
All her pale, sweet-rounded cheek.
   Ere the parting hour go by,
   Quick, thy tablets, Memory!   40

Paint that figure's pliant grace
As she towards me lean'd her face,
Half refus'd and half resign'd,
Murmuring, 'Art thou still unkind?'
Many a broken promise then
Was new made—to break again.
   Ere the parting hour go by,
   Quick, thy tablets, Memory!

Paint those eyes, so blue, so kind,
Eager tell-tales of her mind: 50
Paint, with their impetuous stress
Of inquiring tenderness,
Those frank eyes, where deep doth lie
An angelic gravity.
   Ere the parting hour go by,
   Quick, thy tablets, Memory!

What, my Friends, these feeble lines
Show, you say, my love declines?
To paint ill as I have done,
Proves forgetfulness begun?   60
Time's gay minions, pleas'd you see,
Time, your master, governs me.
   Pleas'd, you mock the fruitless cry
   'Quick, thy tablets, Memory!'

Ah! too true. Time's current strong
Leaves us true to nothing long.
Yet, if little stays with man,
Ah! retain we all we can!
If the clear impression dies,
Ah! the dim remembrance prize!   70
   Ere the parting hour go by,
   Quick, thy tablets, Memory!

A MODERN SAPPHO

[First published 1849. Reprinted 1853.]

THEY are gone : all is still : Foolish heart, dost thou
      quiver ?
Nothing moves on the lawn but the quick lilac shade.
Far up gleams the house, and beneath flows the river.
Here lean, my head, on this cool balustrade.

Ere he come : ere the boat, by the shining-branch'd
      border
Of dark elms come round, dropping down the proud
      stream ;
Let me pause, let me strive, in myself find some order,
Ere their boat-music sound, ere their broider'd flags
      gleam.

Is it hope makes me linger ? the dim thought, that
      sorrow
Means parting ? that only in absence lies pain ?   10
It was well with me once if I saw him : to-morrow
May bring one of the old happy moments again.

Last night we stood earnestly talking together—
She enter'd—that moment his eyes turn'd from me.
Fasten'd on her dark hair and her wreath of white
      heather—
As yesterday was, so to-morrow will be.

Their love, let me know, must grow strong and yet
      stronger,
Their passion burn more, ere it ceases to burn :
They must love—while they must : But the hearts
      that love longer
Are rare : ah ! most loves but flow once, and return. 20

I shall suffer ; but they will outlive their affection :
I shall weep ; but their love will be cooling : and he,
As he drifts to fatigue, discontent, and dejection,
Will be brought, thou poor heart ! how much nearer
      to thee !

For cold is his eye to mere beauty, who, breaking
The strong band which beauty around him hath furl'd,
Disenchanted by habit, and newly awaking,
Looks languidly round on a gloom-buried world.

Through that gloom he will see but a shadow appearing,
Perceive but a voice as I come to his side:　　30
But deeper their voice grows, and nobler their bearing,
Whose youth in the fires of anguish hath died.

Then—to wait.　But what notes down the wind, hark!
　　are driving?
'Tis he! 'tis the boat, shooting round by the trees!
Let my turn, if it will come, be swift in arriving!
Ah! hope cannot long lighten torments like these.

Hast thou yet dealt him, O Life, thy full measure?
World, have thy children yet bow'd at his knee?
Hast thou with myrtle-leaf crown'd him, O Pleasure?
Crown, crown him quickly, and leave him for me.　　40

THE NEW SIRENS

A PALINODE

[First published 1849.]

In the cedar shadow sleeping,
　Where cool grass and fragrant glooms
Oft at noon have lur'd me, creeping
　From your darken'd palace rooms:
I, who in your train at morning
　Stroll'd and sang with joyful mind,
Heard, at evening, sounds of warning;
Heard the hoarse boughs labour in the wind.

Who are they, O pensive Graces,
　— For I dream'd they wore your forms—　　10
Who on shores and sea-wash'd places
　Scoop the shelves and fret the storms?
Who, when ships are that way tending,
　Troop across the flushing sands,
To all reefs and narrows wending,
With blown tresses, and with beckoning hands?

Yet I see, the howling levels
Of the deep are not your lair ;
And your tragic-vaunted revels
Are less lonely than they were.   20
In a Tyrian galley steering
From the golden springs of dawn,
Troops, like Eastern kings, appearing,
Stream all day through your enchanted lawn.

And we too, from upland valleys,
Where some Muse, with half-curv'd frown,
Leans her ear to your mad sallies
Which the charm'd winds never drown ;
By faint music guided, ranging
The scar'd glens, we wander'd on :   30
Left our awful laurels hanging,
And came heap'd with myrtles to your throne.

From the dragon-warder'd fountains
Where the springs of knowledge are :
From the watchers on the mountains,
And the bright and morning star :
We are exiles, we are falling,
We have lost them at your call.
O ye false ones, at your calling
Seeking ceilèd chambers and a palace hall.   40

Are the accents of your luring
More melodious than of yore ?
Are those frail forms more enduring
Than the charms Ulysses bore ?
That we sought you with rejoicings
Till at evening we descry
At a pause of Siren voicings
These vext branches and this howling sky ?

Oh ! your pardon. The uncouthness
Of that primal age is gone :   50
And the skin of dazzling smoothness
Screens not now a heart of stone.
Love has flush'd those cruel faces ;
And your slacken'd arms forego
The delight of fierce embraces :
And those whitening bone-mounds do not grow.

F 2

'Come,' you say ; 'the large appearance
Of man's labour is but vain :
And we plead as firm adherence
Due to pleasure as to pain.'   60
Pointing to some world-worn creatures,
'Come,' you murmur with a sigh :
'Ah ! we own diviner features,
Loftier bearing, and a prouder eye.

'Come,' you say, 'the hours are dreary :
Life is long, and will not fade :
Time is lame, and we grow weary
In this slumbrous cedarn shade.
Round our hearts, with long caresses,
With low sighs hath Silence stole ;   70
And her load of steaming tresses
Weighs, like Ossa, on the aery soul.

'Come,' you say, 'the Soul is fainting
Till she search, and learn her own :
And the wisdom of man's painting
Leaves her riddle half unknown.
Come,' you say, 'the brain is seeking,
When the princely heart is dead :
Yet this glean'd, when Gods were speaking,
Rarer secrets than the toiling head.   80

'Come,' you say, 'opinion trembles,
Judgement shifts, convictions go :
Life dries up, the heart dissembles :
Only, what we feel, we know.
Hath your wisdom known emotions ?
Will it weep our burning tears ?
Hath it drunk of our love-potions
Crowning moments with the weight of years ? '

I am dumb.   Alas ! too soon, all
Man's grave reasons disappear :   90
Yet, I think, at God's tribunal
Some large answer you shall hear.
But for me, my thoughts are straying
Where at sunrise, through the vines,
On these lawns I saw you playing,
Hanging garlands on the odorous pines.

When your showering locks enwound you,
And your heavenly eyes shone through:
When the pine-boughs yielded round you,
And your brows were starr'd with dew: 100
And immortal forms to meet you
Down the statued alleys came:
And through golden horns, to greet you,
Blew such music as a God may frame.

Yes—I muse:—And, if the dawning
Into daylight never grew—
If the glistering wings of morning
On the dry noon shook their dew—
If the fits of joy were longer—
Or the day were sooner done—   110
Or, perhaps, if Hope were stronger—
No weak nursling of an earthly sun . . .
        Pluck, pluck cypress, O pale maidens,
        Dusk the hall with yew!

But a bound was set to meetings,
And the sombre day dragg'd on:
And the burst of joyful greetings,
And the joyful dawn, were gone:
For the eye was fill'd with gazing,
And on raptures follow calms:—   120
And those warm locks men were praising
Droop'd, unbraided, on your listless arms.

Storms unsmooth'd your folded valleys,
And made all your cedars frown;
Leaves are whirling in the alleys
Which your lovers wander'd down.
—Sitting cheerless in your bowers,
The hands propping the sunk head,
Do they gall you, the long hours?
And the hungry thought, that must be fed?   130

Is the pleasure that is tasted
Patient of a long review?
Will the fire joy hath wasted,
Mus'd on, warm the heart anew?

—Or, are those old thoughts returning,
Guests the dull sense never knew,
Stars, set deep, yet inly burning,
Germs, your untrimm'd Passion overgrew?

Once, like me, you took your station
Watchers for a purer fire: 140
But you droop'd in expectation,
And you wearied in desire.
When the first rose flush was steeping
All the frore peak's awful crown,
Shepherds say, they found you sleeping
In a windless valley, further down.

Then you wept, and slowly raising
Your doz'd eyelids, sought again,
Half in doubt, they say, and gazing
Sadly back, the seats of men.   150
Snatch'd an earthly inspiration
From some transient human Sun,
And proclaim'd your vain ovation
For the mimic raptures you had won.
     Pluck, pluck cypress, O pale maidens,
      Dusk the hall with yew!

With a sad, majestic motion—
With a stately, slow surprise—
From their earthward-bound devotion
Lifting up your languid eyes: 160
Would you freeze my louder boldness
Dumbly smiling as you go?
One faint frown of distant coldness
Flitting fast across each marble brow?

Do I brighten at your sorrow
O sweet Pleaders? doth my lot
Find assurance in to-morrow
Of one joy, which you have not?
O speak once! and let my sadness,
And this sobbing Phrygian strain,   170
Sham'd and baffled by your gladness,
Blame the music of your feasts in vain.

Scent, and song, and light, and flowers—
Gust on gust, the hoarse winds blow.
Come, bind up those ringlet showers !
Roses for that dreaming brow !
Come, once more that ancient lightness,
Glancing feet, and eager eyes !
Let your broad lamps flash the brightness
Which the sorrow-stricken day denies !　　　180

Through black depths of serried shadows,
Up cold aisles of buried glade ;
In the mist of river meadows
Where the looming kine are laid ;
From your dazzled windows streaming,
From the humming festal room,
Deep and far, a broken gleaming
Reels and shivers on the ruffled gloom.

Where I stand, the grass is glowing :
Doubtless, you are passing fair :　　　190
But I hear the north wind blowing ;
And I feel the cold night-air.
Can I look on your sweet faces,
And your proud heads backward thrown,
From this dusk of leaf-strewn places
With the dumb woods and the night alone ?

But, indeed, this flux of guesses—
Mad delight, and frozen calms—
Mirth to-day and vine-bound tresses,
And to-morrow—folded palms—　　　200
Is this all ? this balanc'd measure ?
Could life run no easier way ?
Happy at the noon of pleasure,
Passive, at the midnight of dismay ?

But, indeed, this proud possession—
This far-reaching magic chain,
Linking in a mad succession
Fits of joy and fits of pain :
Have you seen it at the closing ?
Have you track'd its clouded ways ?　　　210
Can your eyes, while fools are dozing,
Drop, with mine, adown life's latter days ?

When a dreary light is wading
Through this waste of sunless greens—
When the flashing lights are fading
On the peerless cheek of queens—
When the mean shall no more sorrow
And the proudest no more smile—
While the dawning of the morrow
Widens slowly westward all that while?   220

Then, when change itself is over,
When the slow tide sets one way,
Shall you find the radiant lover,
Even by moments, of to-day?
The eye wanders, faith is failing:
O, loose hands, and let it be!
Proudly, like a king bewailing,
O, let fall one tear, and set us free!

All true speech and large avowal
Which the jealous soul concedes: 230
All man's heart—which brooks bestowal:
All frank faith—which passion breeds:
These we had, and we gave truly:
Doubt not, what we had, we gave:
False we were not, nor unruly:
Lodgers in the forest and the cave.

Long we wander'd with you, feeding
Our sad souls on your replies:
In a wistful silence reading
All the meaning of your eyes: 240
By moss-border'd statues sitting,
By well-heads, in summer days.
But we turn, our eyes are flitting.
See, the white east, and the morning rays!

And you too, O weeping Graces,
Sylvan Gods of this fair shade!
Is there doubt on divine faces?
Are the happy Gods dismay'd?
Can men worship the wan features,
The sunk eyes, the wailing tone,   250
Of unspher'd discrownèd creatures,
Souls as little godlike as their own?

Come, loose hands! The wingèd fleetness
Of immortal feet is gone.
And your scents have shed their sweetness,
And your flowers are overblown.
And your jewell'd gauds surrender
Half their glories to the day:
Freely did they flash their splendour,
Freely gave it—but it dies away.   260

In the pines the thrush is waking—
Lo, yon orient hill in flames:
Scores of true love knots are breaking
At divorce which it proclaims.
When the lamps are pal'd at morning,
Heart quits heart, and hand quits hand.
—Cold in that unlovely dawning,
Loveless, rayless, joyless you shall stand.

Strew no more red roses, maidens,
Leave the lilies in their dew: 270
Pluck, pluck cypress, O pale maidens!
Dusk, O dusk the hall with yew!
—Shall I seek, that I may scorn her,
Her I lov'd at eventide?
Shall I ask, what faded mourner
Stands, at daybreak, weeping by my side?
　　Pluck, pluck cypress, O pale maidens!
　　Dusk the hall with yew!

THE VOICE

[First published 1849.]

As the kindling glances,
Queen-like and clear,
Which the bright moon lances
From her tranquil sphere
At the sleepless waters
Of a lonely mere,
On the wild whirling waves, mournfully, mournfully,
　　Shiver and die.

As the tears of sorrow
    Mothers have shed—   10
Prayers that to-morrow
    Shall in vain be sped
When the flower they flow for
    Lies frozen and dead—
Fall on the throbbing brow, fall on the burning breast,
        Bringing no rest.

    Like bright waves that fall
    With a lifelike motion
On the lifeless margin of the sparkling Ocean:—
A wild rose climbing up a mould'ring wall—   20
A gush of sunbeams through a ruin'd hall—
Strains of glad music at a funeral : —
      So sad, and with so wild a start
      To this long sober'd heart,
      So anxiously and painfully,
      So drearily and doubtfully
And, oh, with such intolerable change
    Of thought, such contrast strange,
O unforgotten Voice, thy whispers come,
Like wanderers from the world's extremity,   30
    Unto their ancient home.

In vain, all, all in vain,
They beat upon mine ear again,
Those melancholy tones so sweet and still;
Those lute-like tones which in long distant years
    Did steal into mine ears:
Blew such a thrilling summons to my will
    Yet could not shake it:
Drain'd all the life my full heart had to spill ;
    Yet could not break it.   40

TO FAUSTA
[First published 1849.]

Joy comes and goes: hope ebbs and flows,
    Like the wave.
Change doth unknit the tranquil strength of men.
    Love lends life a little grace,
    A few sad smiles: and then,
      Both are laid in one cold place,
      In the grave.

Dreams dawn and fly : friends smile and die,
    Like spring flowers.
Our vaunted life is one long funeral.   10
    Men dig graves, with bitter tears,
    For their dead hopes ; and all,
    Maz'd with doubts, and sick with fears,
        Count the hours.

We count the hours : these dreams of ours,
      False and hollow,
Shall we go hence and find they are not dead ?
    Joys we dimly apprehend,
    Faces that smil'd and fled,
    Hopes born here, and born to end,   20
        Shall we follow ?

DESIRE

[First published 1849.   Reprinted 1855.]

    THOU, who dost dwell alone—
    Thou, who dost know thine own—
    Thou, to whom all are known
    From the cradle to the grave—
        Save, oh, save.
    From the world's temptations,
      From tribulations ;
    From that fierce anguish
    Wherein we languish ;
    From that torpor deep   10
    Wherein we lie asleep,
Heavy as death, cold as the grave ;
        Save, oh, save.

    When the Soul, growing clearer,
      Sees God no nearer :
    When the Soul, mounting higher,
      To God comes no nigher :
    But the arch-fiend Pride
    Mounts at her side,
    Foiling her high emprize,   20
    Sealing her eagle eyes,

Desire *Title*] Stagyrus *1849*.

And, when she fain would soar,
Makes idols to adore ;
Changing the pure emotion
Of her high devotion,
To a skin-deep sense
Of her own eloquence :
Strong to deceive, strong to enslave—
        Save, oh, save.

From the ingrain'd fashion   30
Of this earthly nature
That mars thy creature.
From grief, that is but passion ;
From mirth, that is but feigning ;
From tears, that bring no healing ;
From wild and weak complaining ;
    Thine old strength revealing,
        Save, oh, save.
From doubt, where all is double :
Where wise men are not strong :   40
Where comfort turns to trouble :
Where just men suffer wrong :
Where sorrow treads on joy :
Where sweet things soonest cloy :
Where faiths are built on dust :
Where Love is half mistrust,
Hungry, and barren, and sharp as the sea ;
        Oh, set us free.
O let the false dream fly
Where our sick souls do lie   50
    Tossing continually.
O where thy voice doth come
    Let all doubts be dumb :
    Let all words be mild :
    All strifes be reconcil'd :
    All pains beguil'd.
Light bring no blindness ;
Love no unkindness ;
Knowledge no ruin ;
Fear no undoing.   60
From the cradle to the grave,
        Save, oh, save.

TO A GIPSY CHILD BY THE SEA-SHORE

DOUGLAS, ISLE OF MAN

[First published 1849.   Reprinted 1855.]

Who taught this pleading to unpractis'd eyes ?
Who hid such import in an infant's gloom ?
Who lent thee, child, this meditative guise ?
What clouds thy forehead, and fore-dates thy doom ?

Lo ! sails that gleam a moment and are gone ;
The swinging waters, and the cluster'd pier.
Not idly Earth and Ocean labour on,
Nor idly do these sea-birds hover near.

But thou, whom superfluity of joy
Wafts not from thine own thoughts, nor longings vain,
Nor weariness, the full-fed soul's annoy ;   11
Remaining in thy hunger and thy pain :

Thou, drugging pain by patience ; half averse
From thine own mother's breast, that knows not thee ;
With eyes that sought thine eyes thou didst converse,
And that soul-searching vision fell on me.

Glooms that go deep as thine I have not known :
Moods of fantastic sadness, nothing worth.
Thy sorrow and thy calmness are thine own :
Glooms that enhance and glorify this earth.   20

What mood wears like complexion to thy woe?—
His, who in mountain glens, at noon of day,
Sits rapt, and hears the battle break below ?—
Ah ! thine was not the shelter, but the fray.

What exile's, changing bitter thoughts with glad ?
What seraph's, in some alien planet born ?—
No exile's dream was ever half so sad,
Nor any angel's sorrow so forlorn.

4 Who mass'd, round that slight brow, these clouds of doom ?
1849.

Is the calm thine of stoic souls, who weigh
Life well, and find it wanting, nor deplore: 30
But in disdainful silence turn away,
Stand mute, self-centred, stern, and dream no more?

Or do I wait, to hear some grey-hair'd king
Unravel all his many-colour'd lore:
Whose mind hath known all arts of governing,
Mus'd much, lov'd life a little, loath'd it more?

Down the pale cheek long lines of shadow slope,
Which years, and curious thought, and suffering give—
Thou hast foreknown the vanity of hope,
Foreseen thy harvest—yet proceed'st to live.   40

O meek anticipant of that sure pain
Whose sureness grey-hair'd scholars hardly learn!
What wonder shall time breed, to swell thy strain?
What heavens, what earth, what suns shalt thou discern?

Ere the long night, whose stillness brooks no star,
Match that funereal aspect with her pall,
I think, thou wilt have fathom'd life too far,
Have known too much—or else forgotten all.

The Guide of our dark steps a triple veil
Betwixt our senses and our sorrow keeps: 50
Hath sown with cloudless passages the tale
Of grief, and eas'd us with a thousand sleeps.

Ah! not the nectarous poppy lovers use,
Not daily labour's dull, Lethaean spring,
Oblivion in lost angels can infuse
Of the soil'd glory, and the trailing wing;

And though thou glean, what strenuous gleaners may,
In the throng'd fields where winning comes by strife;
And though the just sun gild, as all men pray,
Some reaches of thy storm-vext stream of life;   60

Though that blank sunshine blind thee: though the
    cloud
That sever'd the world's march and thine, is gone:
Though ease dulls grace, and Wisdom be too proud
To halve a lodging that was all her own:

Once, ere the day decline, thou shalt discern,
Oh once, ere night, in thy success, thy chain.
Ere the long evening close, thou shalt return,
And wear this majesty of grief again.

THE HAYSWATER BOAT

[First published 1849. Not reprinted by the author.]

A REGION desolate and wild,
Black, chafing water : and afloat,
And lonely as a truant child
In a waste wood, a single boat :
No mast, no sails are set thereon ;
It moves, but never moveth on :
And welters like a human thing
Amid the wild waves weltering.

Behind, a buried vale doth sleep,
Far down the torrent cleaves its way :   10
In front the dumb rock rises steep,
A fretted wall of blue and grey ;
Of shooting cliff and crumbled stone
With many a wild weed overgrown :
All else, black water : and afloat,
One rood from shore, that single boat.

Last night the wind was up and strong ;
The grey-streak'd waters labour still :
The strong blast brought a pigmy throng
From that mild hollow in the hill ;   20
From those twin brooks, that beachèd strand
So featly strewn with drifted sand ;
From those weird domes of mounded green
That spot the solitary scene.

This boat they found against the shore :
The glossy rushes nodded by.
One rood from land they push'd, no more ;
Then rested, listening silently.
The loud rains lash'd the mountain's crown,
The grating shingle straggled down :   30
All night they sate ; then stole away,
And left it rocking in the bay.

Last night ?—I look'd, the sky was clear.
The boat was old, a batter'd boat.
In sooth, it seems a hundred year
Since that strange crew did ride afloat.
The boat hath drifted in the bay—
The oars have moulder'd as they lay—
The rudder swings—yet none doth steer.
   What living hand hath brought it here ?   40

THE FORSAKEN MERMAN

[First published 1849.   Reprinted 1853, '54, '57.]

COME, dear children, let us away ;
Down and away below.
Now my brothers call from the bay ;
Now the great winds shorewards blow ;
Now the salt tides seawards flow ;
Now the wild white horses play,
Champ and chafe and toss in the spray.
Children dear, let us away.
This way, this way.

Call her once before you go.   10
Call once yet.
In a voice that she will know :
' Margaret ! Margaret !'
Children's voices should be dear
(Call once more) to a mother's ear :
Children's voices, wild with pain.
Surely she will come again.
Call her once and come away.
This way, this way.
' Mother dear, we cannot stay.'   20
The wild white horses foam and fret.
Margaret ! Margaret !

Come, dear children, come away down.
Call no more.
One last look at the white-wall'd town,
And the little grey church on the windy shore.
Then come down.

She will not come though you call all day.
Come away, come away.

Children dear, was it yesterday   30
We heard the sweet bells over the bay?
In the caverns where we lay,
Through the surf and through the swell,
The far-off sound of a silver bell?
Sand-strewn caverns, cool and deep,
Where the winds are all asleep;
Where the spent lights quiver and gleam;
Where the salt weed sways in the stream;
Where the sea-beasts rang'd all round
Feed in the ooze of their pasture-ground;   40
Where the sea-snakes coil and twine,
Dry their mail and bask in the brine;
Where great whales come sailing by,
Sail and sail, with unshut eye,
Round the world for ever and aye?
When did music come this way?
Children dear, was it yesterday?

Children dear, was it yesterday
(Call yet once) that she went away?
Once she sate with you and me,   50
On a red gold throne in the heart of the sea,
And the youngest sate on her knee.
She comb'd its bright hair, and she tended it well,
When down swung the sound of the far-off bell.
She sigh'd, she look'd up through the clear green sea.
She said; 'I must go, for my kinsfolk pray
In the little grey church on the shore to-day.
'Twill be Easter-time in the world—ah me!
And I lose my poor soul, Merman, here with thee.
I said; 'Go up, dear heart, through the waves;   60
Say thy prayer, and come back to the kind sea-caves.'
She smil'd, she went up through the surf in the bay.
Children dear, was it yesterday?

   Children dear, were we long alone?
'The sea grows stormy, the little ones moan.
Long prayers,' I said, 'in the world they say.
Come,' I said, and we rose through the surf in the bay.

We went up the beach, by the sandy down
Where the sea-stocks bloom, to the white-wall'd town.
Through the narrow pav'd streets, where all was still,
To the little grey church on the windy hill.   71
From the church came a murmur of folk at their prayers,
But we stood without in the cold blowing airs.
We climb'd on the graves, on the stones, worn with
           rains,
And we gaz'd up the aisle through the small leaded panes.
She sate by the pillar ; we saw her clear :
' Margaret, hist ! come quick, we are here.
Dear heart,' I said, ' we are long alone.
The sea grows stormy, the little ones moan.'
But, ah, she gave me never a look,   80
For her eyes were seal'd to the holy book.
' Loud prays the priest ; shut stands the door.'
Come away, children, call no more.
Come away, come down, call no more.

   Down, down, down.
Down to the depths of the sea.
She sits at her wheel in the humming town,
Singing most joyfully.
Hark, what she sings ; ' O joy, O joy,
For the humming street, and the child with its toy. 90
For the priest, and the bell, and the holy well.
For the wheel where I spun,
And the blessed light of the sun.'
And so she sings her fill,
Singing most joyfully,
Till the shuttle falls from her hand,
And the whizzing wheel stands still.
She steals to the window, and looks at the sand ;
And over the sand at the sea ;
And her eyes are set in a stare ;   100
And anon there breaks a sigh,
And anon there drops a tear,
From a sorrow-clouded eye,
And a heart sorrow-laden,
A long, long sigh,
For the cold strange eyes of a little Mermaiden,
And the gleam of her golden hair.

Come away, away children.
Come children, come down.
The hoarse wind blows colder ;   110
Lights shine in the town.
She will start from her slumber
When gusts shake the door ;
She will hear the winds howling,
Will hear the waves roar.
We shall see, while above us
The waves roar and whirl,
A ceiling of amber,
A pavement of pearl.
Singing, 'Here came a mortal,   120
But faithless was she.
And alone dwell for ever
The kings of the sea.'

But, children, at midnight,
When soft the winds blow ;
When clear falls the moonlight ;
When spring-tides are low :
When sweet airs come seaward
From heaths starr'd with broom ;
And high rocks throw mildly   130
On the blanch'd sands a gloom :
Up the still, glistening beaches,
Up the creeks we will hie ;
Over banks of bright seaweed
The ebb-tide leaves dry.
We will gaze, from the sand-hills,
At the white, sleeping town ;
At the church on the hill-side—
    And then come back down.
Singing, 'There dwells a lov'd one,   140
But cruel is she.
She left lonely for ever
The kings of the sea.'

110 The salt tide rolls seaward *1849*.

THE WORLD AND THE QUIETIST

TO CRITIAS

[First published 1849. Reprinted 1855.]

WHY, when the World's great mind
Hath finally inclin'd,
Why, you say, Critias, *be debating still?*
Why, with these mournful rhymes
Learn'd in more languid climes,
Blame our activity,
Who, with such passionate will,
Are, what we mean to be?

Critias, long since, I know,
(For Fate decreed it so,)   10
Long since the World hath set its heart to live.
Long since with credulous zeal
It turns Life's mighty wheel;
Still doth for labourers send,
Who still their labour give;
And still expects an end.

Yet, as the wheel flies round,
With no ungrateful sound
Do adverse voices fall on the World's ear.
Deafen'd by his own stir   20
The rugged Labourer
Caught not till then a sense
So glowing and so near
Of his omnipotence.

So, when the feast grew loud
In Susa's palace proud,
A white-rob'd slave stole to the Monarch's side.
He spoke: the Monarch heard:
Felt the slow-rolling word
Swell his attentive soul.   30
Breath'd deeply as it died,
And drain'd his mighty bowl.

IN UTRUMQUE PARATUS

[First published 1849.]

IF, in the silent mind of One all-pure,
    At first imagin'd lay
The sacred world ; and by procession sure
From those still deeps, in form and colour drest,
Seasons alternating, and night and day,
The long-mus'd thought to north south east and west
    Took then its all-seen way :

O waking on a world which thus-wise springs !
    Whether it needs thee count
Betwixt thy waking and the birth of things   10
Ages or hours : O waking on Life's stream !
By lonely pureness to the all-pure Fount
(Only by this thou canst) the colour'd dream
    Of Life remount.

Thin, thin the pleasant human noises grow ;
    And faint the city gleams ;
Rare the lone pastoral huts : marvel not thou !
The solemn peaks but to the stars are known,
But to the stars, and the cold lunar beams :
Alone the sun arises, and alone   20
    Spring the great streams.

But, if the wild unfather'd mass no birth
    In divine seats hath known :
In the blank, echoing solitude, if Earth,
Rocking her obscure body to and fro,
Ceases not from all time to heave and groan,
Unfruitful oft, and, at her happiest throe,
    Forms, what she forms, alone :

O seeming sole to awake, thy sun-bath'd head
    Piercing the solemn cloud   30
Round thy still dreaming brother-world outspread !
O man, whom Earth, thy long-vext mother, bare
Not without joy ; so radiant, so endow'd—
(Such happy issue crown'd her painful care)
    Be not too proud !

O when most self-exalted most alone,
    Chief dreamer, own thy dream !
Thy brother-world stirs at thy feet unknown ;
Who hath a monarch's hath no brother's part ;
Yet doth thine inmost soul with yearning teem.   40
O what a spasm shakes the dreamer's heart——
    'I too but seem !'

RESIGNATION

TO FAUSTA

[First published 1849.   Reprinted 1855.]

To die be given us, or attain !
Fierce work it were, to do again.
So pilgrims, bound for Mecca, pray'd
At burning noon : so warriors said,
Scarf'd with the cross, who watch'd the miles
Of dust that wreath'd their struggling files
Down Lydian mountains : so, when snows
Round Alpine summits eddying rose,
The Goth, bound Rome-wards : so the Hun,
Crouch'd on his saddle, when the sun   10
Went lurid down o'er flooded plains
Through which the groaning Danube strains
To the drear Euxine : so pray all,
Whom labours, self-ordain'd, enthrall ;
Because they to themselves propose
On this side the all-common close
A goal which, gain'd, may give repose.
So pray they : and to stand again
Where they stood once, to them were pain ;
Pain to thread back and to renew   20
Past straits, and currents long steer'd through.

   But milder natures, and more free ;
Whom an unblam'd serenity
Hath freed from passions, and the state
Of struggle these necessitate ;

Whom schooling of the stubborn mind
Hath made, or birth hath found, resign'd ;
These mourn not, that their goings pay
Obedience to the passing day :
These claim not every laughing Hour   30
For handmaid to their striding power ;
Each in her turn, with torch uprear'd,
To await their march ; and when appear'd,
Through the cold gloom, with measur'd race,
To usher for a destin'd space,
(Her own sweet errands all foregone)
The too imperious Traveller on.
These, Fausta, ask not this : nor thou,
Time's chafing prisoner, ask it now.

We left, just ten years since, you say,   40
That wayside inn we left to-day :
Our jovial host, as forth we fare,
Shouts greeting from his easy chair ;
High on a bank our leader stands,
Reviews and ranks his motley bands ;
Makes clear our goal to every eye,
The valley's western boundary.
A gate swings to : our tide hath flow'd
Already from the silent road.
The valley pastures, one by one,   50
Are threaded, quiet in the sun :
And now beyond the rude stone bridge
Slopes gracious up the western ridge.
Its woody border, and the last
Of its dark upland farms is past ;
Cool farms, with open-lying stores,
Under their burnish'd sycamores :
All past : and through the trees we glide
Emerging on the green hill-side.
There climbing hangs, a far-seen sign,   60
Our wavering, many-colour'd line ;
There winds, upstreaming slowly still
Over the summit of the hill.
And now, in front, behold outspread
Those upper regions we must tread ;

56 Cool] Lone *1849.*

Mild hollows, and clear heathy swells,
The cheerful silence of the fells.
Some two hours' march, with serious air,
Through the deep noontide heats we fare:
The red-grouse, springing at our sound,   70
Skims, now and then, the shining ground;
No life, save his and ours, intrudes
Upon these breathless solitudes.
O joy! again the farms appear;
Cool shade is there, and rustic cheer:
There springs the brook will guide us down,
Bright comrade, to the noisy town.
Lingering, we follow down: we gain
The town, the highway, and the plain.
And many a mile of dusty way,   80
Parch'd and road-worn, we made that day;
But, Fausta, I remember well
That, as the balmy darkness fell,
We bath'd our hands, with speechless glee,
That night, in the wide-glimmering Sea.

Once more we tread this self-same road
Fausta, which ten years since we trod:
Alone we tread it, you and I;
Ghosts of that boisterous company.
Here, where the brook shines, near its head,   90
In its clear, shallow, turf-fring'd bed;
Here, whence the eye first sees, far down,
Capp'd with faint smoke, the noisy town;
Here sit we, and again unroll,
Though slowly, the familiar whole.
The solemn wastes of heathy hill
Sleep in the July sunshine still:
The self-same shadows now, as then,
Play through this grassy upland glen:
The loose dark stones on the green way   100
Lie strewn, it seems, where then they lay:
On this mild bank above the stream,
(You crush them) the blue gentians gleam.
Still this wild brook, the rushes cool,
The sailing foam, the shining pool.—

These are not chang'd : and we, you say,
Are scarce more chang'd, in truth, than they.

The Gipsies, whom we met below,
They too have long roam'd to and fro.
They ramble, leaving, where they pass,   110
Their fragments on the cumber'd grass.
And often to some kindly place,
Chance guides the migratory race
Where, though long wanderings intervene,
They recognize a former scene.
The dingy tents are pitch'd : the fires
Give to the wind their wavering spires ;
In dark knots crouch round the wild flame
Their children, as when first they came ;
They see their shackled beasts again   120
Move, browsing, up the grey-wall'd lane.
Signs are not wanting, which might raise
The ghosts in them of former days :
Signs are not wanting, if they would ;
Suggestions to disquietude.
For them, for all, Time's busy touch,
While it mends little, troubles much :
Their joints grow stiffer ; but the year
Runs his old round of dubious cheer :
Chilly they grow ; yet winds in March,   130
Still, sharp as ever, freeze and parch :
They must live still ; and yet, God knows,
Crowded and keen the country grows :
It seems as if, in their decay,
The Law grew stronger every day.
So might they reason ; so compare,
Fausta, times past with times that are.
But no :—they rubb'd through yesterday
In their hereditary way ;
And they will rub through, if they can,   140
To-morrow on the self-same plan ;
Till death arrives to supersede,
For them, vicissitude and need.

The Poet, to whose mighty heart
Heaven doth a quicker pulse impart,

Subdues that energy to scan
Not his own course, but that of Man.
Though he move mountains ; though his day
Be pass'd on the proud heights of sway ;
Though he hath loos'd a thousand chains ;   150
Though he hath borne immortal pains ;
Action and suffering though he know ;
—He hath not liv'd, if he lives so.
He sees, in some great-historied land,
A ruler of the people stand ;
Sees his strong thought in fiery flood
Roll through the heaving multitude ;
Exults : yet for no moment's space
Envies the all-regarded place.
Beautiful eyes meet his ; and he   160
Bears to admire uncravingly :
They pass ; he, mingled with the crowd,
Is in their far-off triumphs proud.
From some high station he looks down,
At sunset, on a populous town ;
Surveys each happy group that fleets,
Toil ended, through the shining streets,
Each with some errand of its own ;—
And does not say, *I am alone.*
He sees the gentle stir of birth   170
When Morning purifies the earth ;
He leans upon a gate, and sees
The pastures, and the quiet trees.
Low woody hill, with gracious bound,
Folds the still valley almost round ;
The cuckoo, loud on some high lawn,
Is answer'd from the depth of dawn ;
In the hedge straggling to the stream,
Pale, dew-drench'd, half-shut roses gleam :
But where the further side slopes down   180
He sees the drowsy new-wak'd clown
In his white quaint-embroider'd frock
Make, whistling, towards his mist-wreath'd flock ;
Slowly, behind the heavy tread,
The wet flower'd grass heaves up its head.—
Lean'd on his gate, he gazes : tears
Are in his eyes, and in his ears

The murmur of a thousand years:
Before him he sees Life unroll,
A placid and continuous whole ;   190
That general Life, which does not cease,
Whose secret is not joy, but peace ;
That Life, whose dumb wish is not miss'd
If birth proceeds, if things subsist :
The Life of plants, and stones, and rain :
The Life he craves ; if not in vain
Fate gave, what Chance shall not control,
His sad lucidity of soul.

You listen :—but that wandering smile,
Fausta, betrays you cold the while.   200
Your eyes pursue the bells of foam
Wash'd, eddying, from this bank, their home.
Those Gipsies, so your thoughts I scan,
Are less, the Poet more, than man.
They feel not, though they move and see :
Deeply the Poet feels ; but he
Breathes, when he will, immortal air,
Where Orpheus and where Homer are.
In the day's life, whose iron round
Hems us all in, he is not bound.   210
He escapes thence, but we abide.
Not deep the Poet sees, but wide.

The World in which we live and move
Outlasts aversion, outlasts love :
Outlasts each effort, interest, hope,
Remorse, grief, joy :—and were the scope
Of these affections wider made,
Man still would see, and see dismay'd,
Beyond his passion's widest range
Far regions of eternal change.   220
Nay, and since death, which wipes out man,
Finds him with many an unsolv'd plan,
With much unknown, and much untried,
Wonder not dead, and thirst not dried,
Still gazing on the ever full
Eternal mundane spectacle ;
This World in which we draw our breath,
In some sense, Fausta, outlasts death.

Blame thou not therefore him, who dares
Judge vain beforehand human cares.   230
Whose natural insight can discern
What through experience others learn.
Who needs not love and power, to know
Love transient, power an unreal show.
Who treads at ease life's uncheer'd ways:—
Him blame not, Fausta, rather praise.
Rather thyself for some aim pray
Nobler than this—to fill the day.
Rather, that heart, which burns in thee,
Ask, not to amuse, but to set free.   240
Be passionate hopes not ill resign'd
For quiet, and a fearless mind.
And though Fate grudge to thee and me
The Poet's rapt security,
Yet they, believe me, who await
No gifts from Chance, have conquer'd Fate.
They, winning room to see and hear,
And to men's business not too near,
Through clouds of individual strife
Draw homewards to the general Life.   250
Like leaves by suns not yet uncurl'd:
To the wise, foolish; to the world,
Weak: yet not weak, I might reply,
Not foolish, Fausta, in His eye,
To whom each moment in its race,
Crowd as we will its neutral space,
Is but a quiet watershed
Whence, equally, the Seas of Life and Death are fed.

Enough, we live:—and if a life,
With large results so little rife,   260
Though bearable, seem hardly worth
This pomp of worlds, this pain of birth;
Yet, Fausta, the mute turf we tread,
The solemn hills around us spread,
This stream that falls incessantly,
The strange-scrawl'd rocks, the lonely sky,

255 Each moment as it flies, to whom *1849*.
256 space] room *1849*.

If I might lend their life a voice,
Seem to bear rather than rejoice.
And even could the intemperate prayer
Man iterates, while these forbear, 270
For movement, for an ampler sphere,
Pierce Fate's impenetrable ear ;
Not milder is the general lot
Because our spirits have forgot,
In action's dizzying eddy whirl'd,
The something that infects the world.

EMPEDOCLES ON ETNA

AND OTHER POEMS, 1852

Σοφώτατον χρόνος· ἀνευρίσκει γὰρ πάντα.

EMPEDOCLES ON ETNA

A DRAMATIC POEM

[First published 1852. Fragments reprinted 1853, '54, '55, '57.
Reprinted in complete form as below 1867.]

PERSONS

EMPEDOCLES.
PAUSANIAS, *a Physician.*
CALLICLES, *a young Harp-player.*

The Scene of the Poem is on Mount Etna ; at first in the forest region,
afterwards on the summit of the mountain.

ACT I : SCENE I

A Pass in the forest region of Etna.   Morning

CALLICLES

(Alone, resting on a rock by the path)

THE mules, I think, will not be here this hour.
They feel the cool wet turf under their feet
By the stream-side, after the dusty lanes
In which they have toil'd all night from Catana,
And scarcely will they budge a yard.   O Pan !
How gracious is the mountain at this hour !
A thousand times have I been here alone
Or with the revellers from the mountain towns,
But never on so fair a morn ;—the sun
Is shining on the brilliant mountain crests,   10
And on the highest pines : but further down
Here in the valley is in shade ; the sward
Is dark, and on the stream the mist still hangs ;
One sees one's foot-prints crush'd in the wet grass,
One's breath curls in the air ; and on these pines

That climb from the stream's edge, the long grey tufts,
Which the goats love, are jewell'd thick with dew.
Here will I stay till the slow litter comes.
I have my harp too—that is well.—Apollo!
What mortal could be sick or sorry here?   20
I know not in what mind Empedocles,
Whose mules I follow'd, may be coming up,
But if, as most men say, he is half mad
With exile, and with brooding on his wrongs,
Pausanias, his sage friend, who mounts with him,
Could scarce have lighted on a lovelier cure.
The mules must be below, far down.   I hear
Their tinkling bells, mix'd with the song of birds,
Rise faintly to me—now it stops!—Who's here?
Pausanias! and on foot? alone?   30

PAUSANIAS

                And thou, then?
I left thee supping with Peisianax,
With thy head full of wine, and thy hair crown'd,
Touching thy harp as the whim came on thee,
And prais'd and spoil'd by master and by guests
Almost as much as the new dancing girl.
Why hast thou follow'd us?

CALLICLES

            The night was hot,
And the feast past its prime; so we slipp'd out,
Some of us, to the portico to breathe;—
Peisianax, thou know'st, drinks late;—and then,
As I was lifting my soil'd garland off,   40
I saw the mules and litter in the court,
And in the litter sate Empedocles;
Thou, too, wert with him. Straightway I sped home;
I saddled my white mule, and all night long
Through the cool lovely country follow'd you,
Pass'd you a little since as morning dawn'd,
And have this hour sate by the torrent here,
Till the slow mules should climb in sight again.
And now?

     31 *and throughout* Peisianax] Pisianax *1852.*

Pausanias

And now, back to the town with speed !
Crouch in the wood first, till the mules have pass'd; 50
They do but halt, they will be here anon.
Thou must be viewless to Empedocles ;
Save mine, he must not meet a human eye.
One of his moods is on him that thou know'st.
I think, thou would'st not vex him.

Callicles

No—and yet
I would fain stay and help thee tend him ; once
He knew me well, and would oft notice me.
And still, I know not how, he draws me to him,
And I could watch him with his proud sad face,
His flowing locks and gold-encircled brow   60
And kingly gait, for ever ; such a spell
In his severe looks, such a majesty
As drew of old the people after him,
In Agrigentum and Olympia,
When his star reign'd, before his banishment,
Is potent still on me in his decline.
But oh, Pausanias, he is changed of late !
There is a settled trouble in his air
Admits no momentary brightening now ;
And when he comes among his friends at feasts,   70
'Tis as an orphan among prosperous boys.
Thou know'st of old he loved this harp of mine,
When first he sojourn'd with Peisianax ;
He is now always moody, and I fear him.
But I would serve him, soothe him, if I could,
Dared one but try.

Pausanias

Thou wert a kind child ever.
He loves thee, but he must not see thee now.
Thou hast indeed a rare touch on thy harp,
He loves that in thee, too ; there was a time
(But that is pass'd) he would have paid thy strain 80
With music to have drawn the stars from heaven.
He has his harp and laurel with him still,
But he has laid the use of music by,

And all which might relax his settled gloom.
Yet thou may'st try thy playing if thou wilt,
But thou must keep unseen ; follow us on,
But at a distance ; in these solitudes,
In this clear mountain air, a voice will rise,
Though from afar, distinctly ; it may soothe him.
Play when we halt, and, when the evening comes   90
And I must leave him (for his pleasure is
To be left musing these soft nights alone
In the high unfrequented mountain spots),
Then watch him, for he ranges swift and far,
Sometimes to Etna's top, and to the cone ;
But hide thee in the rocks a great way down,
And try thy noblest strains, my Callicles,
With the sweet night to help thy harmony.
Thou wilt earn my thanks sure, and perhaps his.

CALLICLES

More than a day and night, Pausanias,   100
Of this fair summer weather, on these hills,
Would I bestow to help Empedocles.
That needs no thanks ; one is far better here
Than in the broiling city in these heats.
But tell me, how hast thou persuaded him
In this his present fierce, man-hating mood,
To bring thee out with him alone on Etna ?

PAUSANIAS

Thou hast heard all men speaking of Pantheia,
The woman who at Agrigentum lay
Thirty long days in a cold trance of death,   110
And whom Empedocles call'd back to life.
Thou art too young to note it, but his power
Swells with the swelling evil of this time,
And holds men mute to see where it will rise.
He could stay swift diseases in old days,
Chain madmen by the music of his lyre,
Cleanse to sweet airs the breath of poisonous streams,
And in the mountain chinks inter the winds.
This he could do of old ; but now, since all
Clouds and grows daily worse in Sicily,   120
Since broils tear us in twain, since this new swarm
        108 Pantheia]. Panthea *1852, and so throughout.*

Of sophists has got empire in our schools
Where he was paramount, since he is banish'd,
And lives a lonely man in triple gloom,
He grasps the very reins of life and death.
I ask'd him of Pantheia yesterday,
When we were gather'd with Peisianax,
And he made answer, I should come at night
On Etna here, and be alone with him,
And he would tell me, as his old, tried friend,   130
Who still was faithful, what might profit me ;
That is, the secret of this miracle.

Callicles

Bah !   Thou a doctor ?   Thou art superstitious.
Simple Pausanias, 'twas no miracle !
Pantheia, for I know her kinsmen well,
Was subject to these trances from a girl.
Empedocles would say so, did he deign ;
But he still lets the people, whom he scorns,
Gape and cry wizard at him, if they list.
But thou, thou art no company for him ;   140
Thou art as cross, as soured as himself.
Thou hast some wrong from thine own citizens,
And then thy friend is banish'd, and on that,
Straightway thou fallest to arraign the times,
As if the sky was impious not to fall.
The sophists are no enemies of his ;
I hear, Gorgias, their chief, speaks nobly of him,
As of his gifted master and once friend.
He is too scornful, too high-wrought, too bitter.
'Tis not the times, 'tis not the sophists vex him ;   150
There is some root of suffering in himself,
Some secret and unfollow'd vein of woe,
Which makes the time look black and sad to him.
Pester him not in this his sombre mood
With questionings about an idle tale,
But lead him through the lovely mountain paths,
And keep his mind from preying on itself,
And talk to him of things at hand and common,
Not miracles ; thou art a learned man,
But credulous of fables as a girl.   160

153 time] times *1852.*

PAUSANIAS

And thou, a boy whose tongue outruns his knowledge,
And on whose lightness blame is thrown away.
Enough of this! I see the litter wind
Up by the torrent-side, under the pines.
I must rejoin Empedocles. Do thou
Crouch in the brush-wood till the mules have pass'd;
Then play thy kind part well. Farewell till night!

SCENE II

*Noon. A Glen on the highest skirts of the woody
region of Etna*

EMPEDOCLES. PAUSANIAS

PAUSANIAS

The noon is hot; when we have cross'd the stream
We shall have left the woody tract, and come
Upon the open shoulder of the hill.
See how the giant spires of yellow bloom
Of the sun-loving gentian, in the heat,
Are shining on those naked slopes like flame!
Let us rest here; and now, Empedocles,
Pantheia's history.   [*A harp-note below is heard.*

EMPEDOCLES

   Hark! what sound was that
Rose from below? If it were possible,
And we were not so far from human haunt,   10
I should have said that some one touch'd a harp.
Hark! there again!

PAUSANIAS

   'Tis the boy Callicles,
The sweetest harp-player in Catana,
He is for ever coming on these hills,
In summer, to all country festivals,
With a gay revelling band; he breaks from them
Sometimes, and wanders far among the glens.
But heed him not, he will not mount to us;
I spoke with him this morning. Once more, therefore,
Instruct me of Pantheia's story, Master,   20
As I have pray'd thee.

H 2

EMPEDOCLES

That? and to what end?

PAUSANIAS

It is enough that all men speak of it.
But I will also say, that when the Gods
Visit us as they do with sign and plague,
To know those spells of time that stay their hand
Were to live free from terror.

EMPEDOCLES

Spells? Mistrust them.
Mind is the spell which governs earth and heaven.
Man has a mind with which to plan his safety;
Know that, and help thyself.

PAUSANIAS

But thy own words?
' The wit and counsel of man was never clear,   30
Troubles confuse the little wit he has.'
Mind is a light which the Gods mock us with,
To lead those false who trust it.

[*The harp sounds again*

EMPEDOCLES

Hist! once more!
Listen, Pausanias!—Aye, 'tis Callicles!
I know those notes among a thousand.   Hark!

CALLICLES

[*Sings unseen, from below.*

The track winds down to the clear stream,
To cross the sparkling shallows; there
The cattle love to gather, on their way
To the high mountain pastures, and to stay,
Till the rough cow-herds drive them past,   40
Knee-deep in the cool ford; for 'tis the last
Of all the woody, high, well-water'd dells
On Etna; and the beam
Of noon is broken there by chestnut boughs

26 free] free'd *1852*.
36–76 *in 1855 as* The harp-player on Etna. I. The Last Glen.

Down its steep verdant sides ; the air
Is freshen'd by the leaping stream, which throws
Eternal showers of spray on the moss'd roots
Of trees, and veins of turf, and long dark shoots
Of ivy-plants, and fragrant hanging bells
Of hyacinths, and on late anemonies,   50
That muffle its wet banks ; but glade,
And stream, and sward, and chestnut trees,
End here ; Etna beyond, in the broad glare
Of the hot noon, without a shade,
Slope behind slope, up to the peak, lies bare ;
The peak, round which the white clouds play.

    In such a glen, on such a day,
    On Pelion, on the grassy ground,
    Chiron, the aged Centaur, lay,
    The young Achilles standing by.   60
    The Centaur taught him to explore
    The mountains ; where the glens are dry,
    And the tired Centaurs come to rest,
    And where the soaking springs abound,
    And the straight ashes grow for spears,
    And where the hill-goats come to feed,
    And the sea-eagles build their nest.
    He show'd him Phthia far away,
    And said : O boy, I taught this lore
    To Peleus, in long distant years !   70
    He told him of the Gods, the stars,
    The tides ;—and then of mortal wars,
    And of the life which heroes lead
    Before they reach the Elysian place
    And rest in the immortal mead ;
    And all the wisdom of his race.

     [*The music below ceases, and* EMPEDOCLES *speaks,*
        accompanying himself in a solemn manner
        on his harp.

The out-spread world to span
A cord the Gods first slung,
And then the soul of man
There, like a mirror, hung,   80
And bade the winds through space impel the gusty toy.

    73 which] that *1852, 1855.*
    77 out-spread world] howling void *1852.*

Hither and thither spins
The wind-borne mirroring soul,
A thousand glimpses wins,
And never sees a whole ;
Looks once, and drives elsewhere, and leaves its last
      employ.

The Gods laugh in their sleeve
To watch man doubt and fear,
Who knows not what to believe
Since he sees nothing clear,   90
And dares stamp nothing false where he finds nothing
      sure.

Is this, Pausanias, so ?
And can our souls not strive,
But with the winds must go,
And hurry where they drive ?
Is Fate indeed so strong, man's strength indeed so poor ?

I will not judge ! that man,
Howbeit, I judge as lost,
Whose mind allows a plan
Which would degrade it most ;   100
And he treats doubt the best who tries to see least ill.

Be not, then, fear's blind slave !
Thou art my friend ; to thee,
All knowledge that I have,
All skill I wield, are free ;
Ask not the latest news of the last miracle,

Ask not what days and nights
In trance Pantheia lay,
But ask how thou such sights
May'st see without dismay ;   110
Ask what most helps when known, thou son of Anchitus !

What ? hate, and awe, and shame
Fill thee to see our world ;
Thou feelest thy soul's frame
Shaken and rudely hurl'd.
What ? life and time go hard with thee too, as with us ;

90 Since] Where *1852*.   113 world] day *1852*.
115 rudely hurl'd.] in dismay : *1852*.

Thy citizens, 'tis said,
Envy thee and oppress,
Thy goodness no men aid,
All strive to make it less ;   120
Tyranny, pride, and lust fill Sicily's abodes ;

Heaven is with earth at strife,
Signs make thy soul afraid,
The dead return to life,
Rivers are dried, winds stay'd ;
Scarce can one think in calm, so threatening are the
     Gods ;

And we feel, day and night,
The burden of ourselves—
Well, then, the wiser wight
In his own bosom delves,   130
And asks what ails him so, and gets what cure he can.

The sophist sneers : Fool, take
Thy pleasure, right or wrong !
The pious wail : Forsake
A world these sophists throng !
Be neither saint nor sophist-led, but be a man.

These hundred doctors try
To preach thee to their school.
We have the truth ! they cry.
And yet their oracle,   140
Trumpet it as they will, is but the same as thine.

Once read thy own breast right,
And thou has⁺ done with fears !
Man gets no other light,
Search he a thousand years.
Sink in thyself ! there ask what ails thee, at that shrine !

What makes thee struggle and rave ?
Why are men ill at ease ?—
'Tis that the lot they have
Fails their own will to please ;   150
For man would make no murmuring, were his will
     obey'd.

And why is it, that still
Man with his lot thus fights ?—
'Tis that he makes this *will*
The measure of his *rights*,
And believes Nature outraged if his will's gainsaid.

Couldst thou, Pausanias, learn
How deep a fault is this !
Couldst thou but once discern
Thou hast no *right* to bliss,   160
No title from the Gods to welfare and repose ;

Then thou wouldst look less mazed
Whene'er from bliss debarr'd,
Nor think the Gods were crazed
When thy own lot went hard.
But we are all the same—the fools of our own woes !

For, from the first faint morn
Of life, the thirst for bliss
Deep in man's heart is born ;
And, sceptic as he is,   170
He fails not to judge clear if this be quench'd or no.

Nor is that thirst to blame !
Man errs not that he deems
His welfare his true aim,
He errs because he dreams
The world does but exist that welfare to bestow.

We mortals are no kings
For each of whom to sway
A new-made world up-springs
Meant merely for his play ;   180
No, we are strangers here ; the world is from of old.

In vain our pent wills fret,
And would the world subdue.
Limits we did not set
Condition all we do ;
Born into life we are, and life must be our mould.

Born into life—man grows
Forth from his parents' stem,
And blends their bloods, as those
Of theirs are blent in them ;   190
So each new man strikes root into a far fore-time.

Born into life—we bring
A bias with us here,
And, when here, each new thing
Affects us we come near ;
To tunes we did not call our being must keep chime.

Born into life—in vain,
Opinions, those or these,
Unalter'd to retain
The obstinate mind decrees ;   200
Experience, like a sea, soaks all-effacing in.

Born into life—who lists
May what is false hold dear,
And for himself make mists
Through which to see less clear ;
The world is what it is, for all our dust and din.

Born into life—'tis we,
And not the world, are new.
Our cry for bliss, our plea,
Others have urged it too ;   210
Our wants have all been felt, our errors made before.

No eye could be too sound
To observe a world so vast,
No patience too profound
To sort what 's here amass'd ;
How man may here best live no care too great to explore.

But we—as some rude guest
Would change, where'er he roam,
The manners there profess'd
To those he brings from home—   220
We mark not the world's course, but would have *it* take
   ours.

187–196 *first inserted in 1867.*   197–201 *follow* 202–206 *in 1852.*
203 hold dear] maintain *1852.*   205 clear] plain *1852.*
221 course . . . take] ways . . . learn *1852.*

The world's course proves the terms
On which man wins content ;
Reason the proof confirms ;
We spurn it, and invent
A false course for the world, and for ourselves, false
    powers.

Riches we wish to get,
Yet remain spendthrifts still ;
We would have health, and yet
Still use our bodies ill ;   230
Bafflers of our own prayers, from youth to life's last
    scenes.

We would have inward peace,
Yet will not look within ;
We would have misery cease,
Yet will not cease from sin ;
We want all pleasant ends, but will use no harsh means ;

We do not what we ought,
What we ought not, we do,
And lean upon the thought
That chance will bring us through ;   240
But our own acts, for good or ill, are mightier powers.

Yet, even when man forsakes
All sin,—is just, is pure,
Abandons all which makes
His welfare insecure—
Other existences there are, that clash with ours.

Like us, the lightning fires
Love to have scope and play ;
The stream, like us, desires
An unimpeded way ;   250
Like us, the Libyan wind delights to roam at large.

222 world's course proves] world proclaims *1852.*   224 the
proof] its voice *1852.*   225 it] them *1852.*   226 A false
course for . . . for] False weakness in . . . in *1852.*   244 which]
that *1852.*   246 that] which *1852.*

Streams will not curb their pride
The just man not to entomb,
Nor lightnings go aside
To leave his virtues room ;
Nor is that wind less rough which blows a good man's
    barge.

Nature, with equal mind,
Sees all her sons at play ;
Sees man control the wind,
The wind sweep man away ;   260
Allows the proudly-riding and the founder'd bark.

And, lastly, though of ours
No weakness spoil our lot,
Though the non-human powers
Of Nature harm us not,
The ill-deeds of other men make often *our* life dark.

What were the wise man's plan ?—
Through this sharp, toil-set life,
To fight as best he can,
And win what 's won by strife.   270
But we an easier way to cheat our pains have found.

Scratch'd by a fall, with moans
As children of weak age
Lend life to the dumb stones
Whereon to vent their rage,
And bend their little fists, and rate the senseless ground;

So, loath to suffer mute,
We, peopling the void air,
Make Gods to whom to impute
The ills we ought to bear ;   280
With God and Fate to rail at, suffering easily.

Yet grant—as sense long miss'd
Things that are now perceiv'd,
And much may still exist
Which is not yet believ'd—
Grant that the world were full of Gods we cannot see ;

256 that . . . which] the . . . that *1852*

All things the world which fill
Of but one stuff are spun,
That we who rail are still,
With what we rail at, one ;   290
One with the o'er-labour'd Power that through the
      breadth and length

Of earth, and air, and sea,
In men, and plants, and stones,
Hath toil perpetually,
And struggles, pants, and moans ;
Fain would do all things well, but sometimes fails in
      strength.

And patiently exact
This universal God
Alike to any act
Proceeds at any nod,   300
And quietly declaims the cursings of himself.

This is not what man hates,
Yet he can curse but this.
Harsh Gods and hostile Fates
Are dreams ! this only *is ;*
Is everywhere ; sustains the wise, the foolish elf.

Nor only, in the intent
To attach blame elsewhere,
Do we at will invent
Stern Powers who make their care   310
To embitter human life, malignant Deities ;

But, next, we would reverse
The scheme ourselves have spun,
And what we made to curse
We now would lean upon,
And feign kind Gods who perfect what man vainly tries.

Look, the world tempts our eye,
And we would know it all !
We map the starry sky,
We mine this earthen ball,   320
We measure the sea-tides, we number the sea-sands ;

---

287 which] that *1852*.   294 hath] has *1852*.
297 patiently] punctually *1852*.   301 quietly] patiently *1852*.

We scrutinize the dates
Of long-past human things,
The bounds of effac'd states,
The lines of deceas'd kings ;
We search out dead men's words, and works of dead
    men's hands ;

We shut our eyes, and muse
How our own minds are made,
What springs of thought they use,
How righten'd, how betray'd ;   330
And spend our wit to name what most employ unnam'd ;

But still, as we proceed,
The mass swells more and more
Of volumes yet to read,
Of secrets yet to explore.
Our hair grows grey, our eyes are dimm'd, our heat is
    tamed.

We rest our faculties,
And thus address the Gods :
'True science if there is,
It stays in your abodes ;   340
Man's measures cannot mete the immeasurable All ;

'You only can take in
The world's immense design,
Our desperate search was sin,
Which henceforth we resign,
Sure only that *your* mind sees all things which befall !'

Fools ! that in man's brief term
He cannot all things view,
Affords no ground to affirm
That there are Gods who do !   350
Nor does being weary prove that he has where to rest !

Again : our youthful blood
Claims rapture as its right ;
The world, a rolling flood
Of newness and delight,
Draws in the enamour'd gazer to its shining breast ;

341 mete . . . immeasurable] span . . . illimitable *1852.*

Pleasure to our hot grasp
Gives flowers after flowers,
With passionate warmth we clasp
Hand after hand in ours ;   360
Nor do we soon perceive how fast our youth is spent.

At once our eyes grow clear ;
We see in blank dismay
Year posting after year,
Sense after sense decay ;
Our shivering heart is mined by secret discontent ;

Yet still, in spite of truth,
In spite of hopes entomb'd,
That longing of our youth
Burns ever unconsum'd,   370
Still hungrier for delight as delights grow more rare.

We pause ; we hush our heart,
And then address the Gods :
' The world hath fail'd to impart
The joy our youth forbodes,
Fail'd to fill up the void which in our breasts we bear.

' Changeful till now, we still
Look'd on to something new ;
Let us, with changeless will,
Henceforth look on to you,   380
To find with you the joy we in vain *here* require ! '

Fools ! that so often here
Happiness mock'd our prayer,
I think, might make us fear
A like event elsewhere !
Make us, not fly to dreams, but moderate desire !

And yet, for those who know
Themselves, who wisely take
Their way through life, and bow
To what they cannot break,   390
Why should I say that life need yield but *moderate* bliss?

Shall we, with temper spoil'd,
Health sapp'd by living ill,
And judgement all embroil'd
By sadness and self-will,
Shall *we* judge what for man is not true bliss or is?

Is it so small a thing
To have enjoy'd the sun,
To have lived light in the spring,
To have loved, to have thought, to have done;   400
To have advanc'd true friends, and beat down baffling
    foes;

That we must feign a bliss
Of doubtful future date,
And, while we dream on this,
Lose all our present state,
And relegate to worlds yet distant our repose?

Not much, I know, you prize
What pleasures may be had,
Who look on life with eyes
Estrang'd, like mine, and sad;   410
And yet the village churl feels the truth more than you,

Who's loath to leave this life
Which to him little yields;
His hard-task'd sunburnt wife,
His often-labour'd fields,
The boors with whom he talk'd, the country spots he
    knew.

But thou, because thou hear'st
Men scoff at Heaven and Fate,
Because the Gods thou fear'st
Fail to make blest thy state,   420
Tremblest, and wilt not dare to trust the joys there are.

I say: Fear not! Life still
Leaves human effort scope.
But, since life teems with ill,
Nurse no extravagant hope;
Because thou must not dream, thou need'st not then
    despair!

392 temper] tempers *1852.*   396 true] high *1852.*

[*A long pause.   At the end of it the notes of a
     harp below are again heard, and* CALLICLES
     sings :—

Far, far from here,
The Adriatic breaks in a warm bay
Among the green Illyrian hills ; and there
The sunshine in the happy glens is fair,   430
And by the sea, and in the brakes.
The grass is cool, the sea-side air
Buoyant and fresh, the mountain flowers
As virginal and sweet as ours.
And there, they say, two bright and agèd snakes,
Who once were Cadmus and Harmonia,
Bask in the glens or on the warm sea-shore,
In breathless quiet, after all their ills.
Nor do they see their country, nor the place
Where the Sphinx lived among the frowning hills, 440
Nor the unhappy palace of their race,
Nor Thebes, nor the Ismenus, any more.

There those two live, far in the Illyrian brakes.
They had stay'd long enough to see,
In Thebes, the billow of calamity
Over their own dear children roll'd,
Curse upon curse, pang upon pang,
For years, they sitting helpless in their home,
A grey old man and woman ; yet of old
The Gods had to their marriage come,   450
And at the banquet all the Muses sang.

Therefore they did not end their days
In sight of blood ; but were rapt, far away,
To where the west wind plays,
And murmurs of the Adriatic come
To those untrodden mountain lawns ; and there
Placed safely in changed forms, the Pair
Wholly forget their first sad life, and home,
And all that Theban woe, and stray
For ever through the glens, placid and dumb.   460

427–460 *in 1853, 1854, 1857 as* Cadmus and Harmonia.
434 As . . . as] more . . than *1853, 1854, 1857.*

EMPEDOCLES

That was my harp-player again!—where is he?
Down by the stream?

PAUSANIAS

Yes, Master, in the wood.

EMPEDOCLES

He ever loved the Theban story well!
But the day wears. Go now, Pausanias,
For I must be alone. Leave me one mule;
Take down with thee the rest to Catana.
And for young Callicles, thank him from me;
Tell him I never fail'd to love his lyre:
But he must follow me no more to-night.

PAUSANIAS

Thou wilt return to-morrow to the city?   470

EMPEDOCLES

Either to-morrow or some other day,
In the sure revolutions of the world,
Good friend, I shall revisit Catana.
I have seen many cities in my time
Till my eyes ache with the long spectacle,
And I shall doubtless see them all again;
Thou know'st me for a wanderer from of old.
Meanwhile, stay me not now. Farewell, Pausanias!
          [*He departs on his way up the mountain.*

PAUSANIAS (*alone*)

I dare not urge him further; he must go.
But he is strangely wrought!—I will speed back   480
And bring Peisianax to him from the city;
His counsel could once soothe him. But, Apollo!
How his brow lighten'd as the music rose!
Callicles must wait here, and play to him;
I saw him through the chestnuts far below,
Just since, down at the stream.—Ho! Callicles!
          [*He descends, calling.*

ARNOLD   I

ACT II

Evening.   The Summit of Etna

EMPEDOCLES

Alone !—
On this charr'd, blacken'd, melancholy waste,
Crown'd by the awful peak, Etna's great mouth,
Round which the sullen vapour rolls—alone !
Pausanias is far hence, and that is well,
For I must henceforth speak no more with man.
He has his lesson too, and that debt 's paid ;
And the good, learned, friendly, quiet man,
May bravelier front his life, and in himself
Find henceforth energy and heart ; but I,   10
The weary man, the banish'd citizen—
Whose banishment is not his greatest ill,
Whose weariness no energy can reach,
And for whose hurt courage is not the cure—
What should I do with life and living more ?

No, thou art come too late, Empedocles !
And the world hath the day, and must break thee,
Not thou the world.   With men thou canst not live,
Their thoughts, their ways, their wishes, are not thine ;
And being lonely thou art miserable,   20
For something has impair'd thy spirit's strength,
And dried its self-sufficing fount of joy.
Thou canst not live with men nor with thyself—
Oh sage ! oh sage !—Take then the one way left ;
And turn thee to the elements, thy friends,
Thy well-tried friends, thy willing ministers,
And say :—Ye servants, hear Empedocles,
Who asks this final service at your hands !
Before the sophist brood hath overlaid
The last spark of man's consciousness with words—   30
Ere quite the being of man, ere quite the world
Be disarray'd of their divinity—
Before the soul lose all her solemn joys,
And awe be dead, and hope impossible,
And the soul's deep eternal night come on,
Receive me, hide me, quench me, take me home !

*[He advances to the edge of the crater. Smoke
and fire break forth with a loud noise, and
CALLICLES is heard below singing :—*

The lyre's voice is lovely everywhere !
In the court of Gods, in the city of men,
And in the lonely rock-strewn mountain glen,
In the still mountain air.   40

Only to Typho it sounds hatefully !
To Typho only, the rebel o'erthrown,
Through whose heart Etna drives her roots of stone,
To imbed them in the sea.

Wherefore dost thou groan so loud ?
Wherefore do thy nostrils flash,
Through the dark night, suddenly,
Typho, such red jets of flame ?—
Is thy tortur'd heart still proud ?
Is thy fire-scath'd arm still rash ?   50
Still alert thy stone-crush'd frame ?
Doth thy fierce soul still deplore
The ancient rout by the Cilician hills,
And that curst treachery on the Mount of Gore ?
Do thy bloodshot eyes still see
The fight that crown'd thy ills,
Thy last defeat in this Sicilian sea ?
Hast thou sworn, in thy sad lair,
Where erst the strong sea-currents suck'd thee down,
Never to cease to writhe, and try to sleep,   60
Letting the sea-stream wander through thy hair ?
That thy groans, like thunder deep,
Begin to roll, and almost drown
The sweet notes, whose lulling spell
Gods and the race of mortals love so well,
When through thy caves thou hearest music swell ?

But an awful pleasure bland
Spreading o'er the Thunderer's face,
When the sound climbs near his seat,
The Olympian council sees ;   70

37–88 *in 1855 as* The harp-player on Etna. II. Typho.
42 To Typho only] Only to Typho, *1852, 1855.* 52 Doth] Does
1852, 1855. 53 The] Thy *1852, 1855.* by] *in 1855.*

I 2

As he lets his lax right hand,
Which the lightnings doth embrace,
Sink upon his mighty knees.
And the eagle, at the beck
Of the appeasing gracious harmony,
Droops all his sheeny, brown, deep-feather'd neck,
Nestling nearer to Jove's feet;
While o'er his sovereign eye
The curtains of the blue films slowly meet,
And the white Olympus peaks   80
Rosily brighten, and the sooth'd Gods smile
At one another from their golden chairs,
And no one round the charmèd circle speaks.
Only the loved Hebe bears
The cup about, whose draughts beguile
Pain and care, with a dark store
Of fresh-pull'd violets wreath'd and nodding o'er;
And her flush'd feet glow on the marble floor.

EMPEDOCLES

He fables, yet speaks truth.
The brave impetuous heart yields everywhere   90
To the subtle, contriving head;
Great qualities are trodden down,
And littleness united
Is become invincible.

These rumblings are not Typho's groans, I know!
These angry smoke-bursts
Are not the passionate breath
Of the mountain-crush'd, tortur'd, intractable Titan
    king!
But over all the world
What suffering is there not seen   100
Of plainness oppress'd by cunning,
As the well-counsell'd Zeus oppress'd
The self-helping son of earth!
What anguish of greatness
Rail'd and hunted from the world,
Because its simplicity rebukes

90 heart] hand 1852.

This envious, miserable age !
I am weary of it !—
Lie there, ye ensigns
Of my unloved pre-eminence   110
In an age like this !
Among a people of children,
Who throng'd me in their cities,
Who worshipp'd me in their houses,
And ask'd, not wisdom,
But drugs to charm with,
But spells to mutter—
All the fool's-armoury of magic !—Lie there,
My golden circlet !
My purple robe !   120

CALLICLES (*from below*)

As the sky-brightening south-wind clears the day,
And makes the mass'd clouds roll,
The music of the lyre blows away
The clouds that wrap the soul.

Oh, that Fate had let me see
That triumph of the sweet persuasive lyre !
That famous, final victory
When jealous Pan with Marsyas did conspire !

When, from far Parnassus' side,
Young Apollo, all the pride   130
Of the Phrygian flutes to tame,
To the Phrygian highlands came !
Where the long green reed-beds sway
In the rippled waters grey
Of that solitary lake
Where Maeander's springs are born ;
Where the ridg'd pine-wooded roots
Of Messogis westward break,
Mounting westward, high and higher.
There was held the famous strife ;   140
There the Phrygian brought his flutes,
And Apollo brought his lyre ;

121–190 *in 1855 as* The harp-player on Etna. III. Marsyas.
137 pine-wooded] pine-darken'd *1852*, pine-muffled *1855*.

And, when now the westering sun
Touch'd the hills, the strife was done,
And the attentive Muses said :
' Marsyas ! thou art vanquishèd.'
Then Apollo's minister
Hang'd upon a branching fir
Marsyas, that unhappy Faun,
And began to whet his knife.   150
But the Maenads, who were there,
Left their friend, and with robes flowing
In the wind, and loose dark hair
O'er their polish'd bosoms blowing,
Each her ribbon'd tambourine
Flinging on the mountain sod,
With a lovely frighten'd mien
Came about the youthful God.
But he turn'd his beauteous face
Haughtily another way,   160
From the grassy sun-warm'd place,
Where in proud repose he lay,
With one arm over his head,
Watching how the whetting sped.

But aloof, on the lake strand,
Did the young Olympus stand,
Weeping at his master's end ;
For the Faun had been his friend.
For he taught him how to sing,
And he taught him flute-playing.   170
Many a morning had they gone
To the glimmering mountain lakes,
And had torn up by the roots
The tall crested water-reeds
With long plumes, and soft brown seeds,
And had carved them into flutes,
Sitting on a tabled stone
Where the shoreward ripple breaks.
And he taught him how to please
The red-snooded Phrygian girls,   180
Whom the summer evening sees
Flashing in the dance's whirls
Underneath the starlit trees

In the mountain villages.
Therefore now Olympus stands,
At his master's piteous cries
Pressing fast with both his hands
His white garment to his eyes,
Not to see Apollo's scorn ;
Ah, poor Faun, poor Faun ! ah, poor Faun !   190

EMPEDOCLES

And lie thou there,
My laurel bough !
Scornful Apollo's ensign, lie thou there !
Though thou hast been my shade in the world's heat—
Though I have loved thee, lived in honouring thee—
Yet lie thou there,
My laurel bough !

I am weary of thee !
I am weary of the solitude
Where he who bears thee must abide !   200
Of the rocks of Parnassus,
Of the gorge of Delphi,
Of the moonlit peaks, and the caves.
Thou guardest them, Apollo !
Over the grave of the slain Pytho,
Though young, intolerably severe ;
Thou keepest aloof the profane,
But the solitude oppresses thy votary !
The jars of men reach him not in thy valley—
But can life reach him ?   210
Thou fencest him from the multitude—
Who will fence him from himself ?
He hears nothing but the cry of the torrents
And the beating of his own heart.
The air is thin, the veins swell—
The temples tighten and throb there—
Air ! air !

Take thy bough ; set me free from my solitude !
I have been enough alone !

Where shall thy votary fly then ? back to men ?—   220

193 first inserted in 1867.

But they will gladly welcome him once more,
And help him to unbend his too tense thought,
And rid him of the presence of himself,
And keep their friendly chatter at his ear,
And haunt him, till the absence from himself,
That other torment, grow unbearable ;
And he will fly to solitude again,
And he will find its air too keen for him,
And so change back ; and many thousand times
Be miserably bandied to and fro   230
Like a sea-wave, betwixt the world and thee,
Thou young, implacable God ! and only death
Shall cut his oscillations short, and so
Bring him to poise.   There is no other way.

And yet what days were those, Parmenides !
When we were young, when we could number friends
In all the Italian cities like ourselves,
When with elated hearts we join'd your train,
Ye Sun-born Virgins ! on the road of truth.
Then we could still enjoy, then neither thought   240
Nor outward things were clos'd and dead to us,
But we receiv'd the shock of mighty thoughts
On simple minds with a pure natural joy ;
And if the sacred load oppress'd our brain,
We had the power to feel the pressure eased,
The brow unbound, the thoughts flow free again,
In the delightful commerce of the world.
We had not lost our balance then, nor grown
Thought's slaves, and dead to every natural joy !
The smallest thing could give us pleasure then !   250
The sports of the country people,
A flute-note from the woods
Sunset over the sea ;
Seed-time and harvest,
The reapers in the corn,
The vinedresser in his vineyard,
The village-girl at her wheel !

Fullness of life and power of feeling, ye
Are for the happy, for the souls at ease,
Who dwell on a firm basis of content !—   260

But he, who has outliv'd his prosperous days,
But he, whose youth fell on a different world
From that on which his exiled age is thrown,
Whose mind was fed on other food, was train'd
By other rules than are in vogue to-day,
Whose habit of thought is fix'd, who will not change,
But in a world he loves not must subsist
In ceaseless opposition, be the guard
Of his own breast, fetter'd to what he guards,
That the world win no mastery over him ;   270
Who has no friend, no fellow left, not one ;
Who has no minute's breathing space allow'd
To nurse his dwindling faculty of joy—
Joy and the outward world must die to him,
As they are dead to me !

    [A long pause, during which EMPEDOCLES *remains
    motionless, plunged in thought. The night deepens.
    He moves forward and gazes round him, and pro-
    ceeds :—*

And you, ye stars,
Who slowly begin to marshal,
As of old, in the fields of heaven,
Your distant, melancholy lines !
Have *you*, too, survived yourselves ?   280
Are *you*, too, what I fear to become ?
You, too, once lived !
You too moved joyfully
Among august companions
In an older world, peopled by Gods,
In a mightier order,
The radiant, rejoicing, intelligent Sons òf Heaven !
But now, you kindle
Your lonely, cold-shining lights,
Unwilling lingerers   290
In the heavenly wilderness,
For a younger, ignoble world ;
And renew, by necessity,
Night after night your courses,
In echoing unnear'd silence,
Above a race you know not.

276-300 *in 1855 as* The Philosopher and the Stars.

Uncaring and undelighted,
Without friend and without home ;
Weary like us, though not
Weary with our weariness.   300

No, no, ye stars ! there is no death with you,
No languor, no decay !   Languor and death,
They are with me, not you ! ye are alive !
Ye and the pure dark ether where ye ride
Brilliant above me !   And thou, fiery world,
That sapp'st the vitals of this terrible mount
Upon whose charr'd and quaking crust I stand,
Thou, too, brimmest with life !—the sea of cloud
That heaves its white and billowy vapours up
To moat this isle of ashes from the world,   310
Lives !—and that other fainter sea, far down,
O'er whose lit floor a road of moonbeams leads
To Etna's Liparëan sister-fires
And the long dusky line of Italy—
That mild and luminous floor of waters lives,
With held-in joy swelling its heart !—I only,
Whose spring of hope is dried, whose spirit has fail'd—
I, who have not, like these, in solitude
Maintain'd courage and force, and in myself
Nursed an immortal vigour—I alone   320
Am dead to life and joy ; therefore I read
In all things my own deadness.
                    [*A long silence. He continues :—*

Oh that I could glow like this mountain !
Oh that my heart bounded with the swell of the sea !
Oh that my soul were full of light as the stars !
Oh that it brooded over the world like the air !

But no, this heart will glow no more ! thou art
A living man no more, Empedocles !
Nothing but a devouring flame of thought—
But a naked, eternally restless mind !   330
                    [*After a pause :—*

To the elements it came from
Everything will return.

Our bodies to earth,
Our blood to water,
Heat to fire,
Breath to air.
They were well born, they will be well entomb'd!
But mind?...

And we might gladly share the fruitful stir
Down in our mother earth's miraculous womb! 340
Well might it be
With what roll'd of us in the stormy main!
We might have joy, blent with the all-bathing air,
Or with the nimble radiant life of fire!

But mind—but thought—
If these have been the master part of us—
Where will *they* find their parent element?
What will receive *them*, who will call *them* home?
But we shall still be in them, and they in us,
And we shall be the strangers of the world, 350
And they will be our lords, as they are now;
And keep us prisoners of our consciousness,
And never let us clasp and feel the All
But through their forms, and modes, and stifling veils.
And we shall be unsatisfied as now,
And we shall feel the agony of thirst,
The ineffable longing for the life of life
Baffled for ever: and still thought and mind
Will hurry us with them on their homeless march,
Over the unallied unopening earth, 360
Over the unrecognizing sea; while air
Will blow us fiercely back to sea and earth,
And fire repel us from its living waves.
And then we shall unwillingly return
Back to this meadow of calamity,
This uncongenial place, this human life;
And in our individual human state
Go through the sad probation all again,
To see if we will poise our life at last,
To see if we will now at last be true 370

341 might] would *1852*.　　342 main] deep *1852*.
343 might] should *1852*.　344 nimble] active *1852*.

To our own only true, deep-buried selves,
Being one with which we are one with the whole world ;
Or whether we will once more fall away
Into some bondage of the flesh or mind,
Some slough of sense, or some fantastic maze
Forg'd by the imperious lonely thinking-power.
And each succeeding age in which we are born
Will have more peril for us than the last ;
Will goad our senses with a sharper spur,
Will fret our minds to an intenser play,   380
Will make ourselves harder to be discern'd.
And we shall struggle awhile, gasp and rebel ;
And we shall fly for refuge to past times,
Their soul of unworn youth, their breath of greatness ;
And the reality will pluck us back,
Knead us in its hot hand, and change our nature.
And we shall feel our powers of effort flag,
And rally them for one last fight, and fail ;
And we shall sink in the impossible strife,
And be astray for ever.

      Slave of sense   390
I have in no wise been ; but slave of thought ?—
 And who can say :—I have been always free,
Lived ever in the light of my own soul ?—
I cannot ! I have lived in wrath and gloom,
Fierce, disputatious, ever at war with man,
Far from my own soul, far from warmth and light.
But I have not grown easy in these bonds—
But I have not denied what bonds these were !
Yea, I take myself to witness,
That I have loved no darkness,   400
Sophisticated no truth,
Nursed no delusion,
Allow'd no fear !

And therefore, O ye elements, I know—
Ye know it too—it hath been granted me
Not to die wholly, not to be all enslav'd.
I feel it in this hour ! The numbing cloud
Mounts off my soul ; I feel it, I breathe free !

Is it but for a moment ?
Ah ! boil up, ye vapours !   410

Leap and roar, thou sea of fire !
My soul glows to meet you.
Ere it flag, ere the mists
Of despondency and gloom
Rush over it again,
Receive me ! Save me ! [*He plunges into the crater.*

CALLICLES (*from below*)

Through the black, rushing smoke-bursts,
Thick breaks the red flame ;
All Etna heaves fiercely
Her forest-cloth'd frame.   420

Not here, O Apollo !
Are haunts meet for thee.
But, where Helicon breaks down
In cliff to the sea,

Where the moon-silver'd inlets
Send far their light voice
Up the still vale of Thisbe,
O speed, and rejoice !

On the sward at the cliff-top
Lie strewn the white flocks ;   430
On the cliff-side the pigeons
Roost deep in the rocks.

In the moonlight the shepherds,
Soft lull'd by the rills,
Lie wrapt in their blankets,
Asleep on the hills.

—What forms are these coming
So white through the gloom ?
What garments out-glistening
The gold-flower'd broom ?   440

What sweet-breathing presence
Out-perfumes the thyme ?
What voices enrapture
The night's balmy prime ?—

417 *to* 468 *in 1855 as* The harp-player on Etna. IV. Apollo.

'Tis Apollo comes leading
His choir, the Nine.
—The leader is fairest,
But all are divine.

They are lost in the hollows !
They stream up again !　　　　　　450
What seeks on this mountain
The glorified train ?—

They bathe on this mountain,
In the spring by their road ;
Then on to Olympus,
Their endless abode !

—Whose praise do they mention ?
Of what is it told ?—
What will be for ever ;
What was from of old.　　　　　　460

First hymn they the Father
Of all things ; and then
The rest of immortals,
The action of men.

The day in his hotness,
The strife with the palm ;
The night in her silence,
The stars in their calm.

THE RIVER

[First published 1852.　Reprinted 1855.]

STILL glides the stream, slow drops the boat
Under the rustling poplars' shade ;
Silent the swans beside us float :
None speaks, none heeds—ah, turn thy head.

Let those arch eyes now softly shine,
That mocking mouth grow sweetly bland :
Ah, let them rest, those eyes, on mine ;
On mine let rest that lovely hand.

465 his] its *1852, 1855*.　　　467 her] its *1852, 1855*.
The River *Title*] Faded Leaves.　I.　The River *1855*.

My pent-up tears oppress my brain,
My heart is swoln with love unsaid :   10
Ah, let me weep, and tell my pain,
And on thy shoulder rest my head.

Before I die, before the soul,
Which now is mine, must re-attain
Immunity from my control,
And wander round the world again :

Before this teas'd o'erlabour'd heart
For ever leaves its vain employ,
Dead to its deep habitual smart,
And dead to hopes of future joy.   20

EXCUSE

[First published 1852.   Reprinted 1855.]

I TOO have suffer'd : yet I know
She is not cold, though she seems so :
She is not cold, she is not light ;
But our ignoble souls lack might.

She smiles and smiles, and will not sigh,
While we for hopeless passion die ;
Yet she could love, those eyes declare,
Were but men nobler than they are.

Eagerly once her gracious ken
Was turn'd upon the sons of men.   10
But light the serious visage grew—
She look'd, and smiled, and saw them through.

Our petty souls, our strutting wits,
Our labour'd puny passion-fits—
Ah, may she scorn them still, till we
Scorn them as bitterly as she !

Yet oh, that Fate would let her see
One of some worthier race than we ;
One for whose sake she once might prove
How deeply she who scorns can love.   20

Excuse] 18 worthier] better *1852*.

His eyes be like the starry lights—
His voice like sounds of summer nights—
In all his lovely mien let pierce
The magic of the universe.

And she to him will reach her hand,
And gazing in his eyes will stand,
And know her friend, and weep for glee,
And cry—*Long, long I've look'd for thee.*—

Then will she weep—with smiles, till then,
Coldly she mocks the sons of men.   30
Till then her lovely eyes maintain
Their gay, unwavering, deep disdain.

INDIFFERENCE

[First published 1852.   Reprinted 1855.]

I MUST not say that thou wert true,
Yet let me say that thou wert fair.
And they that lovely face who view,
They will not ask if truth be there.

Truth—what is truth?   Two bleeding hearts
Wounded by men, by Fortune tried,
Outwearied with their lonely parts,
Vow to beat henceforth side by side.

The world to them was stern and drear;
Their lot was but to weep and moan.   10
Ah, let them keep their faith sincere,
For neither could subsist alone!

But souls whom some benignant breath
Has charm'd at birth from gloom and care,
These ask no love—these plight no faith,
For they are happy as they are.

The world to them may homage make,
And garlands for their forehead weave.
And what the world can give, they take:
But they bring more than they receive.   20

They smile upon the world : their ears
To one demand alone are coy.
They will not give us love and tears—
They bring us light, and warmth, and joy.

It was not love that heav'd thy breast,
Fair child ! it was the bliss within.
Adieu ! and say that one, at least,
Was just to what he did not win.

TOO LATE

[First published 1852. Reprinted 1855.]

EACH on his own strict line we move,
And some find death ere they find love.
So far apart their lives are thrown
From the twin soul that halves their own.

And sometimes, by still harder fate,
The lovers meet, but meet too late.
—Thy heart is mine !—*True, true ! ah true !*
—Then, love, thy hand !—*Ah no ! adieu !*

ON THE RHINE

[First published 1852. Reprinted 1855.]

VAIN is the effort to forget.
Some day I shall be cold, I know,
As is the eternal moon-lit snow
Of the high Alps, to which I go :
But ah, not yet ! not yet !

Vain is the agony of grief.
'Tis true, indeed, an iron knot
Ties straitly up from mine thy lot,
And were it snapt—thou lov'st me not !
But is despair relief ?   10

Too late *Title*] Faded Leaves. II. Too late *1855*.
On the Rhine *Title*] Faded Leaves. IV. On the Rhine *1855*.

Awhile let me with thought have done ;
And as this brimm'd unwrinkled Rhine
And that far purple mountain line
Lie sweetly in the look divine
Of the slow-sinking sun ;

So let me lie, and calm as they
Let beam upon my inward view
Those eyes of deep, soft, lucent hue—
Eyes too expressive to be blue,
Too lovely to be grey.   20

Ah Quiet, all things feel thy balm !
Those blue hills too, this river's flow,
Were restless once, but long ago.
Tam'd is their turbulent youthful glow :
Their joy is in their calm.

LONGING

[First published 1852.   Reprinted 1855.]

COME to me in my dreams, and then
By day I shall be well again.
For then the night will more than pay
The hopeless longing of the day.

Come, as thou cam'st a thousand times,
A messenger from radiant climes,
And smile on thy new world, and be
As kind to others as to me.

Or, as thou never cam'st in sooth,
Come now, and let me dream it truth.   10
And part my hair, and kiss my brow,
And say—*My love ! why sufferest thou ?*

Come to me in my dreams, and then
By day I shall be well again.
For then the night will more than pay
The hopeless longing of the day.

Longing *Title*] Faded Leaves. V. Longing *1855*.
8 to others as to me] to all the rest as me *1852*.

THE LAKE

[First published 1852. Reprinted 1853, '54, '57.]

AGAIN I see my bliss at hand ;
The town, the lake are here.
My Marguerite smiles upon the strand
Unalter'd with the year.

I know that graceful figure fair,
That cheek of languid hue ;
I know that soft enkerchief'd hair,
And those sweet eyes of blue.

Again I spring to make my choice ;
Again in tones of ire   10
I hear a God's tremendous voice—
'Be counsell'd, and retire !'

Ye guiding Powers, who join and part,
What would ye have with me ?
Ah, warn some more ambitious heart,
And let the peaceful be !

PARTING

[First published 1852. Reprinted 1853, '54, '57.]

YE storm-winds of Autumn
Who rush by, who shake
The window, and ruffle
The gleam-lighted lake ;
Who cross to the hill-side
Thin-sprinkled with farms,
Where the high woods strip sadly
Their yellowing arms ;—
Ye are bound for the mountains—
Ah, with you let me go   10
Where your cold distant barrier,
The vast range of snow,

The Lake *Title*] Switzerland. II. The Lake *1853, 1854, 1857.*
Parting *Title*] Switzerland. IV. Parting *1853, 1854, 1857.*

Through the loose clouds lifts dimly
Its white peaks in air—
How deep is their stillness!
Ah! would I were there!

But on the stairs what voice is this I hear,
Buoyant as morning, and as morning clear?
Say, has some wet bird-haunted English lawn
Lent it the music of its trees at dawn?   20
Or was it from some sun-fleck'd mountain-brook
That the sweet voice its upland clearness took?
    Ah! it comes nearer—
    Sweet notes, this way!

Hark! fast by the window
The rushing winds go,
To the ice-cumber'd gorges,
The vast seas of snow.
There the torrents drive upward
Their rock-strangled hum,   30
There the avalanche thunders
The hoarse torrent dumb.
—I come, O ye mountains!
Ye torrents, I come!

But who is this, by the half-open'd door,
Whose figure casts a shadow on the floor?
The sweet blue eyes—the soft, ash-colour'd hair—
The cheeks that still their gentle paleness wear—
The lovely lips, with their arch smile, that tells
The unconquer'd joy in which her spirit dwells—   40
    Ah! they bend nearer—
    Sweet lips, this way!

Hark! the wind rushes past us—
Ah! with that let me go
To the clear waning hill-side
Unspotted by snow,
There to watch, o'er the sunk vale,
The frore mountain wall,
Where the nich'd snow-bed sprays down
Its powdery fall.   50
There its dusky blue clusters
The aconite spreads;

There the pines slope, the cloud-strips
Hung soft in their heads.
No life but, at moments,
The mountain-bee's hum.
—I come, O ye mountains !
Ye pine-woods, I come !

Forgive me ! forgive me !
  Ah, Marguerite, fain   60
Would these arms reach to clasp thee :—
  But see ! 'tis in vain.

In the void air towards thee
  My strain'd arms are cast.
But a sea rolls between us—
  Our different past.

To the lips, ah ! of others,
  Those lips have been prest,
And others, ere I was,
  Were clasp'd to that breast ;   70

Far, far from each other
  Our spirits have grown.
And what heart knows another ?
  Ah ! who knows his own ?

Blow, ye winds ! lift me with you !
  I come to the wild.
Fold closely, O Nature !
  Thine arms round thy child.

To thee only God granted
  A heart ever new :   80
To all always open ;
  To all always true.

Ah, calm me ! restore me !
  And dry up my tears
On thy high mountain platforms,
  Where Morn first appears,

Where the white mists, for ever,
  Are spread and upfurl'd ;
In the stir of the forces
  Whence issued the world.   90

ABSENCE

[First published 1852.   Reprinted 1853, '54, '57.]

In this fair stranger's eyes of grey
Thine eyes, my love, I see.
I shudder : for the passing day
Had borne me far from thee.

This is the curse of life : that not
A nobler calmer train
Of wiser thoughts and feelings blot
Our passions from our brain ;

But each day brings its petty dust
Our soon-chok'd souls to fill,   10
And we forget because we must,
And not because we will.

I struggle towards the light ; and ye,
Once-long'd-for storms of love !
If with the light ye cannot be,
I bear that ye remove.

I struggle towards the light ; but oh,
While yet the night is chill,
Upon Time's barren, stormy flow,
Stay with me, Marguerite, still !   20

DESTINY

[First published 1852.   Not reprinted by the author.]

Why each is striving, from of old,
To love more deeply than he can ?
Still would be true, yet still grows cold ?
—Ask of the Powers that sport with man !

They yok'd in him, for endless strife,
A heart of ice, a soul of fire ;
And hurl'd him on the Field of Life,
An aimless unallay'd Desire.

Absence *Title*] Switzerland. VI. Absence *1853*.. Switzerland.
VII. Absence *1854*. Switzerland. VIII. Absence *1857*.

TO MARGUERITE, IN RETURNING A VOLUME OF THE LETTERS OF ORTIS

[First published 1852. Reprinted 1853, '54, '57.]

YES: in the sea of life enisl'd,
With echoing straits between us thrown,
Dotting the shoreless watery wild,
We mortal millions live *alone*.
    The islands feel the enclasping flow,
And then their endless bounds they know.

But when the moon their hollows lights
And they are swept by balms of spring,
And in their glens, on starry nights,
The nightingales divinely sing ;   10
And lovely notes, from shore to shore,
Across the sounds and channels pour ;

Oh then a longing like despair
Is to their farthest caverns sent ;
For surely once, they feel, we were
Parts of a single continent.
Now round us spreads the watery plain—
Oh might our marges meet again !

Who order'd, that their longing's fire
Should be, as soon as kindled, cool'd ?   20
Who renders vain their deep desire ?—
    A God, a God their severance rul'd ;
And bade betwixt their shores to be
The unplumb'd, salt, estranging sea.

HUMAN LIFE

[First published 1852. Reprinted 1867.]

WHAT mortal, when he saw,
Life's voyage done, his heavenly Friend,
Could ever yet dare tell him fearlessly :
' I have kept uninfring'd my nature's law ;
The inly-written chart thou gavest me
To guide me, I have steer'd by to the end ' ?

To Marguerite *Title*] Switzerland. V. To Marguerite *1853*.
Switzerland. VI. To Marguerite *1854*. Switzerland. VII. Isolation *1857*

Ah ! let us make no claim
On life's incognizable sea
To too exact a steering of our way !
Let us not fret and fear to miss our aim　　　　10
If some fair coast has lured us to make stay,
Or some friend hail'd us to keep company !

Aye, we would each fain drive
At random, and not steer by rule !
Weakness ! and worse, weakness bestow'd in vain !
Winds from our side the unsuiting consort rive,
We rush by coasts where we had lief remain ;
Man cannot, though he would, live chance's fool.

No ! as the foaming swathe
Of torn-up water, on the main,　　　　20
Falls heavily away with long-drawn roar
On either side the black deep-furrow'd path
Cut by an onward-labouring vessel's prore,
And never touches the ship-side again ;

Even so we leave behind,
As, charter'd by some unknown Powers,
We stem across the sea of life by night,
The joys which were not for our use design'd,
The friends to whom we had no natural right,
The homes that were not destined to be ours.　　　　30

DESPONDENCY

[First published 1852.　Reprinted 1855.]

THE thoughts that rain their steady glow
Like stars on life's cold sea,
Which others know, or say they know—
They never shone for me.

Thoughts light, like gleams, my spirit's sky,
But they will not remain.
They light me once, they hurry by,
And never come again.

YOUTH'S AGITATIONS

[First published 1852. Reprinted 1867.]

When I shall be divorced, some ten years hence,
From this poor present self which I am now ;
When youth has done its tedious vain expense
Of passions that for ever ebb and flow ;
Shall I not joy youth's heats are left behind,
And breathe more happy in an even clime ?
Ah no ! for then I shall begin to find
A thousand virtues in this hated time.
Then I shall wish its agitations back,
And all its thwarting currents of desire ;   10
Then I shall praise the heat which then I lack,
And call this hurrying fever, generous fire,
And sigh that one thing only has been lent
To youth and age in common—discontent.

SELF-DECEPTION

[First published 1852. Reprinted 1855.]

Say, what blinds us, that we claim the glory
Of possessing powers not our share ?—
Since man woke on earth, he knows his story,
But, before we woke on earth, we were.

Long, long since, undower'd yet, our spirit
Roam'd, ere birth, the treasuries of God :
Saw the gifts, the powers it might inherit ;
Ask'd an outfit for its earthly road.

Then, as now, this tremulous, eager Being
Strain'd, and long'd, and grasp'd each gift it saw. 10
Then, as now, a Power beyond our seeing
Stav'd us back, and gave our choice the law.

Ah, whose hand that day through heaven guided
Man's blank spirit, since it was not we ?
Ah, who sway'd our choice, and who decided
What our gifts, and what our wants should be ?

Youth's Agitations *Title*] Sonnet *1852*.
Self-Deception] 14 blank] new *1852*.   16 our gifts] the
parts *1852*. our wants] the whole *1852*.

For, alas! he left us each retaining
Shreds of gifts which he refus'd in full.
Still these waste us with their hopeless straining—
Still the attempt to use them proves them null.   20

And on earth we wander, groping, reeling;
Powers stir in us, stir and disappear.
Ah, and he, who placed our master-feeling,
Fail'd to place our master-feeling clear.

We but dream we have our wish'd-for powers.
Ends we seek we never shall attain.
Ah, *some* power exists there, which is ours?
Some end is there, we indeed may gain?

LINES WRITTEN BY A DEATH-BED

[First published 1852.]

YES, now the longing is o'erpast,
Which, dogg'd by fear and fought by shame,
Shook her weak bosom day and night,
Consum'd her beauty like a flame,
And dimm'd it like the desert blast.
And though the curtains hide her face,
Yet were it lifted to the light
The sweet expression of her brow
Would charm the gazer, till his thought
Eras'd the ravages of time,   10
Fill'd up the hollow cheek, and brought
A freshness back as of her prime—
So healing is her quiet now.
So perfectly the lines express
A placid, settled loveliness;
Her youngest rival's freshest grace.

But ah, though peace indeed is here,
And ease from shame, and rest from fear;
Though nothing can dismarble now
The smoothness of that limpid brow;   20

24 our] that *1852.*
Lines written by a death-bed] 17–41 *were printed as a separate poem in 1867 under the title* Youth and Calm.   17 'Tis death! and peace, indeed, is here, *1867.*   19 Though] There's *1867.*

Yet is a calm like this, in truth,
The crowning end of life and youth?
And when this boon rewards the dead,
Are all debts paid, has all been said?
And is the heart of youth so light,
Its step so firm, its eye so bright,
Because on its hot brow there blows
A wind of promise and repose
From the far grave, to which it goes?
Because it has the hope to come,   30
One day, to harbour in the tomb?
Ah no, the bliss youth dreams is one
For daylight, for the cheerful sun,
For feeling nerves and living breath—
Youth dreams a bliss on this side death.
It dreams a rest, if not more deep,
More grateful than this marble sleep.
It hears a voice within it tell—
'Calm's not life's crown, though calm is well.'
'Tis all perhaps which man acquires: 40
But 'tis not what our youth desires.

TRISTRAM AND ISEULT

[First published 1852. Reprinted 1853, '54, '57.]

I

TRISTRAM

TRISTRAM

Is she not come? The messenger was sure.
Prop me upon the pillows once again—
Raise me, my Page: this cannot long endure.
Christ! what a night! how the sleet whips the pane!
  What lights will those out to the northward be?

THE PAGE

The lanterns of the fishing-boats at sea.

21 Yet] But *1867.*
Tristram and Iseult *Title*] Tristan and Iseult *1857. See notes at end.*

TRISTRAM

Soft—who is that stands by the dying fire?

THE PAGE

Iseult.

TRISTRAM

Ah! not the Iseult I desire.

.   .   .   .   .

What Knight is this so weak and pale,
Though the locks are yet brown on his noble head, 10
Propt on pillows in his bed,
Gazing seawards for the light
Of some ship that fights the gale
On this wild December night?
Over the sick man's feet is spread
A dark green forest dress.
A gold harp leans against the bed,
Ruddy in the fire's light.
   I know him by his harp of gold,
Famous in Arthur's court of old: 20
I know him by his forest dress.
   The peerless hunter, harper, knight—
Tristram of Lyoness.

What Lady is this, whose silk attire
Gleams so rich in the light of the fire?
The ringlets on her shoulders lying
In their flitting lustre vying
With the clasp of burnish'd gold
Which her heavy robe doth hold.
Her looks are mild, her fingers slight   30
As the driven snow are white;
And her cheeks are sunk and pale.
   Is it that the bleak sea-gale
Beating from the Atlantic sea

<hr>

Between 25 *and* 26 *1852 reads*

    Never surely has been seen
    So slight a form in so rich a dress.

30, 31 *first inserted in 1853.*   32 And] But *1852.*
33 bleak] black *1854.*

On this coast of Brittany,
Nips too keenly the sweet Flower?—
  Is it that a deep fatigue
Hath come on her, a chilly fear,
Passing all her youthful hour
Spinning with her maidens here,   40
Listlessly through the window bars
Gazing seawards many a league
From her lonely shore-built tower,
While the knights are at the wars?
  Or, perhaps, has her young heart
Felt already some deeper smart,
Of those that in secret the heart-strings rive,
Leaving her sunk and pale, though fair?—
  Who is this snowdrop by the sea?
I know her by her mildness rare,   50
Her snow-white hands, her golden hair;
I know her by her rich silk dress,
And her fragile loveliness.
The sweetest Christian soul alive,
Iseult of Brittany.

Iseult of Brittany?—but where
Is that other Iseult fair,
That proud, first Iseult, Cornwall's queen?
She, whom Tristram's ship of yore
From Ireland to Cornwall bore,   60
To Tyntagel, to the side
Of King Marc, to be his bride?
She who, as they voyag'd, quaff'd
With Tristram that spic'd magic draught,
Which since then for ever rolls
Through their blood, and binds their souls,
  Working love, but working teen?—
There were two Iseults, who did sway
Each her hour of Tristram's day;
But one possess'd his waning time,   70
The other his resplendent prime.

50 mildness rare] golden hair *1852.*   51 *first inserted in 1853.*
56-82 *first inserted in 1853.*
60, 61   To Tyntagil from Ireland bore,
          To Cornwall's palace, to the side *1853, 1854.*

Behold her here, the patient Flower,
Who possess'd his darker hour.
Iseult of the Snow-White Hand
   Watches pale by Tristram's bed.—
She is here who had his gloom,
Where art thou who hadst his bloom?
One such kiss as those of yore
Might thy dying knight restore—
   Does the love-draught work no more?   80
Art thou cold, or false, or dead,
   Iseult of Ireland?

Loud howls the wind, sharp patters the rain,
And the knight sinks back on his pillows again:
He is weak with fever and pain,
And his spirit is not clear.
Hark! he mutters in his sleep,
As he wanders far from here,
Changes place and time of year,
And his closèd eye doth sweep   90
O'er some fair unwintry sea,
Not this fierce Atlantic deep,
   As he mutters brokenly—

TRISTRAM

The calm sea shines, loose hang the vessel's sails—
Before us are the sweet green fields of Wales,
And overhead the cloudless sky of May.—
' *Ah, would I were in those green fields at play,*
Not pent on ship-board this delicious day.
Tristram, I pray thee, of thy courtesy,
Reach me my golden cup that stands by thee,   100
And pledge me in it first for courtesy.—'
Ha! dost thou start? are thy lips blanch'd like mine?
Child, 'tis no water this, 'tis poison'd wine!
Iseult! . . .

   .   .   .   .   .

   Ah, sweet angels, let him dream!
Keep his eyelids! let him seem
Not this fever-wasted wight
Thinn'd and pal'd before his time,

But the brilliant youthful knight
In the glory of his prime,   110
Sitting in the gilded barge,
At thy side, thou lovely charge !
Bending gaily o'er thy hand,
Iseult of Ireland !
And she too, that princess fair,
If her bloom be now less rare,
Let her have her youth again—
   Let her be as she was then !
Let her have her proud dark eyes,
And her petulant quick replies,   120
Let her sweep her dazzling hand
With its gesture of command,
And shake back her raven hair
With the old imperious air.
   As of old, so let her be,
That first Iseult, princess bright,
Chatting with her youthful knight
As he steers her o'er the sea,
Quitting at her father's will
The green isle where she was bred,   130
   And her bower in Ireland,
For the surge-beat Cornish strand,
Where the prince whom she must wed
Dwells on proud Tyntagel's hill,
Fast beside the sounding sea.
And that golden cup her mother
Gave her, that her future lord,
Gave her, that King Marc and she,
Might drink it on their marriage day,
And for ever love each other,   140
   Let her, as she sits on board,
Ah, sweet saints, unwittingly,
See it shine, and take it up,
And to Tristram laughing say—
' Sir Tristram, of thy courtesy,
Pledge me in my golden cup ! '
Let them drink it—let their hands

134 Keeps his court in Tyntagil, *1852, 1853, 1854.*   137 future
lord] lord and she *1852.*   138 *first inserted in 1853.*

Tremble, and their cheeks be flame,
As they feel the fatal bands
Of a love they dare not name,   150
With a wild delicious pain,
   Twine about their hearts again.
Let the early summer be
Once more round them, and the sea
Blue, and o'er its mirror kind
Let the breath of the May wind,
Wandering through their drooping sails,
   Die on the green fields of Wales.
Let a dream like this restore
What his eye must see no more.   160

Tristram

Chill blows the wind, the pleasaunce walks are drear.
Madcap, what jest was this, to meet me here?
Were feet like those made for so wild a way?
The southern winter-parlour, by my fay,
Had been the likeliest trysting-place to-day.—
' Tristram!—nay, nay—thou must not take my hand—
Tristram—sweet love—we are betray'd—out-plann'd.
Fly—save thyself—save me.   I dare not stay.'—
One last kiss first!—''Tis vain—to horse—away!'

.   .   .   .   .

Ah, sweet saints, his dream doth move   170
Faster surely than it should,
From the fever in his blood.
All the spring-time of his love
Is already gone and past,
And instead thereof is seen
Its winter, which endureth still—
Tyntagel on its surge-beat hill,
The pleasaunce walks, the weeping queen,
The flying leaves, the straining blast,
And that long, wild kiss—their last.   180
And this rough December night
And his burning fever pain

177 The palace towers of Tyntagil, *1852, 1853, 1854*.

Mingle with his hurrying dream
Till they rule it, till he seem
The press'd fugitive again,
The love-desperate banish'd knight
With a fire in his brain
Flying o'er the stormy main.
    Whither does he wander now?
Haply in his dreams the wind   190
Wafts him here, and lets him find
The lovely Orphan Child again
In her castle by the coast,
The youngest, fairest chatelaine,
That this realm of France can boast,
    Our Snowdrop by the Atlantic sea,
Iseult of Brittany.
And—for through the haggard air,
The stain'd arms, the matted hair
Of that stranger-knight ill-starr'd,   200
There gleam'd something that recall'd
The Tristram who in better days
Was Launcelot's guest at Joyous Gard—
Welcom'd here, and here install'd,
Tended of his fever here,
Haply he seems again to move
His young guardian's heart with love;
    In his exil'd loneliness,
In his stately deep distress,
Without a word, without a tear.—   210
    Ah, 'tis well he should retrace
His tranquil life in this lone place;
His gentle bearing at the side
Of his timid youthful bride;
His long rambles by the shore
On winter evenings, when the roar
Of the near waves came, sadly grand,
Through the dark, up the drown'd sand:
    Or his endless reveries
In the woods, where the gleams play   220
On the grass under the trees,
Passing the long summer's day
Idle as a mossy stone
In the forest depths alone;

The chase neglected, and his hound
Couch'd beside him on the ground.—
    Ah, what trouble's on his brow?
Hither let him wander now,
Hither, to the quiet hours
Pass'd among these heaths of ours   230
By the grey Atlantic sea.
    Hours, if not of ecstasy,
From violent anguish surely free.

TRISTRAM

All red with blood the whirling river flows,
The wide plain rings, the daz'd air throbs with blows.
Upon us are the chivalry of Rome—
Their spears are down, their steeds are bath'd in foam.
' Up, Tristram, up,' men cry, 'thou moonstruck knight!
What foul fiend rides thee? On into the fight! '—
Above the din her voice is in my ears—   240
I see her form glide through the crossing spears.—
Iseult! . . .

    .   .   .   .   .

    Ah, he wanders forth again;
We cannot keep him; now as then
There's a secret in his breast
    That will never let him rest.
These musing fits in the green wood
They cloud the brain, they dull the blood.
    His sword is sharp—his horse is good—
Beyond the mountains will he see   250
The famous towns of Italy,
And label with the blessed sign
The heathen Saxons on the Rhine.
At Arthur's side he fights once more
With the Roman Emperor.
There's many a gay knight where he goes
Will help him to forget his care.
The march—the leaguer—Heaven's blithe air—
The neighing steeds—the ringing blows;
    Sick pining comes not where these are.   260
Ah, what boots it, that the jest
Lightens every other brow.

What, that every other breast
Dances as the trumpets blow,
If one's own heart beats not light
On the waves of the toss'd fight,
If oneself cannot get free
From the clog of misery?
　　Thy lovely youthful Wife grows pale
Watching by the salt sea tide   270
With her children at her side
For the gleam of thy white sail.
Home, Tristram, to thy halls again!
To our lonely sea complain,
　　To our forests tell thy pain.

TRISTRAM

All round the forest sweeps off, black in shade,
But it is moonlight in the open glade:
And in the bottom of the glade shine clear
The forest chapel and the fountain near.

　　I think, I have a fever in my blood: 280
Come, let me leave the shadow of this wood,
Ride down, and bathe my hot brow in the flood.

　　Mild shines the cold spring in the moon's clear light.
God! 'tis *her* face plays in the waters bright.—
' Fair love,' she says, ' canst thou forget so soon,
At this soft hour, under this sweet moon?'—
Iseult! . . .
　　　　　　　.　　.　　.　　.　　.

　　　　Ah poor soul, if this be so,
　　　　Only death can balm thy woe.
　　　　The solitudes of the green wood   290
　　　　Had no medicine for thy mood.
　　　　　　The rushing battle clear'd thy blood
　　　　As little as did solitude.
　　　　　　Ah, his eyelids slowly break
　　　　Their hot seals, and let him wake.
　　　　What new change shall we now see?
　　　　　　A happier? Worse it cannot be.

TRISTRAM

Is my Page here? Come, turn me to the fire.
Upon the window panes the moon shines bright;

266 On] In *1852.*

L 2

The wind is down : but she'll not come to-night.   300
Ah no—she is asleep in Cornwall now,
Far hence—her dreams are fair—smooth is her brow.
Of me she recks not, nor my vain desire.
    I have had dreams, I have had dreams, my Page,
Would take a score years from a strong man's age;
And with a blood like mine, will leave, I fear,
Scant leisure for a second messenger.
    My Princess, art thou there ? Sweet, 'tis too late.
To bed, and sleep: my fever is gone by:
To-night my Page shall keep me company.   310
Where do the children sleep ? kiss them for me.
Poor child, thou art almost as pale as I :
This comes of nursing long and watching late.
To bed—good night !

       .   .   .   .   .

    She left the gleam-lit fire-place,
      She came to the bed-side.
    She took his hands in hers : her tears
    Down on her slender fingers rain'd.
    She rais'd her eyes upon his face—
    Not with a look of wounded pride,   320
    A look as if the heart complain'd :—
      Her look was like a sad embrace ;
    The gaze of one who can divine
    A grief, and sympathize.
    Sweet Flower, thy children's eyes
      Are not more innocent than thine.
      But they sleep in shelter'd rest,
    Like helpless birds in the warm nest,
    On the Castle's southern side ;
    Where feebly comes the mournful roar   330
    Of buffeting wind and surging tide
    Through many a room and corridor.
    Full on their window the Moon's ray
    Makes their chamber as bright as day ;
    It shines upon the blank white walls,
    And on the snowy pillow falls,

   301 Cornwall now] Tyntagil *1852, 1853, 1854.*   302 smooth is
her brow.] her sleep is still. *1852, 1853, 1854*   303 my vain]
of my *1852, 1853*

And on two angel-heads doth play
Turn'd to each other :—the eyes clos'd—
  The lashes on the cheeks repos'd.
Round each sweet brow the cap close-set   340
Hardly lets peep the golden hair ;
Through the soft-open'd lips the air
Scarcely moves the coverlet.
One little wandering arm is thrown
At random on the counterpane,
And often the fingers close in haste
As if their baby owner chas'd
  The butterflies again.
This stir they have and this alone ;
But else they are so still.   350
  Ah, tired madcaps, you lie still
But were you at the window now
To look forth on the fairy sight
Of your illumin'd haunts by night ;
To see the park-glades where you play
Far lovelier than they are by day ;
To see the sparkle on the eaves,
And upon every giant bough
Of those old oaks, whose wet red leaves
Are jewell'd with bright drops of rain—   360
  How would your voices run again !
And far beyond the sparkling trees
Of the castle park one sees
The bare heaths spreading, clear as day,
Moor behind moor, far, far away,
Into the heart of Brittany.
And here and there, lock'd by the land,
Long inlets of smooth glittering sea,
And many a stretch of watery sand
All shining in the white moon-beams.   370
But you see fairer in your dreams.

What voices are these on the clear night air ?
What lights in the court? what steps on the stair ?

II

ISEULT OF IRELAND

TRISTRAM

RAISE the light, my Page, that I may see her.—
  Thou art come at last then, haughty Queen !
Long I've waited, long I've fought my fever :
  Late thou comest, cruel thou hast been.

ISEULT

Blame me not, poor sufferer, that I tarried :
  I was bound, I could not break the band.
Chide not with the past, but feel the present :
  I am here—we meet—I hold thy hand.

TRISTRAM

Thou art come, indeed—thou hast rejoin'd me ;
  Thou hast dar'd it : but too late to save.   10
Fear not now that men should tax thy honour.
  I am dying : build—(thou may'st)—my grave !

ISEULT

Tristram, for the love of Heaven, speak kindly !
  What, I hear these bitter words from thee ?
Sick with grief I am, and faint with travel—
  Take my hand—dear Tristram, look on me !

TRISTRAM

I forgot, thou comest from thy voyage.
  Yes, the spray is on thy cloak and hair.
But thy dark eyes are not dimm'd, proud Iseult !
  And thy beauty never was more fair.   20

ISEULT

Ah, harsh flatterer ! let alone my beauty.
  I, like thee, have left my youth afar.
Take my hand, and touch these wasted fingers—
  See my cheek and lips, how white they are.

TRISTRAM

Thou art paler :—but thy sweet charm, Iseult !
  Would not fade with the dull years away.
Ah, how fair thou standest in the moonlight !
  I forgive thee, Iseult !—thou wilt stay ?

ISEULT

Fear me not, I will be always with thee ;
  I will watch thee, tend thee, soothe thy pain ;   30
Sing thee tales of true long-parted lovers
  Join'd at evening of their days again.

TRISTRAM

No, thou shalt not speak ; I should be finding
  Something alter'd in thy courtly tone.
Sit—sit by me : I will think, we've liv'd so
  In the greenwood, all our lives, alone.

ISEULT

Alter'd, Tristram ?   Not in courts, believe me,
  Love like mine is alter'd in the breast.
Courtly life is light and cannot reach it.
  Ah, it lives, because so deep suppress'd.   40

Royal state with Marc, my deep-wrong'd husband—
  That was bliss to make my sorrows flee !
Silken courtiers whispering honied nothings—
  Those were friends to make me false to thee !

What, thou think'st, men speak in courtly chambers
  Words by which the wretched are consol'd ?
What, thou think'st, this aching brow was cooler,
  Circled, Tristram, by a band of gold ?

Ah, on which, if both our lots were balanc'd,
  Was indeed the heaviest burden thrown,   50
Thee, a weeping exile in thy forest—
  Me, a smiling queen upon my throne ?

Vain and strange debate, where both have suffer'd :
  Both have pass'd a youth constrain'd and sad ;
Both have brought their anxious day to evening,
  And have now short space for being glad.

41-44 *first inserted in 1853.*

Join'd we are henceforth : nor will thy people,
　　Nor thy younger Iseult take it ill,
That a former rival shares her office,
　　When she sees her humbled, pale, and still.　　60

I, a faded watcher by thy pillow,
　　I, a statue on thy chapel floor,
Pour'd in grief before the Virgin Mother,
　　Rouse no anger, make no rivals more.

She will cry—'Is this the foe I dreaded ?
　　This his idol ? this that royal bride ?
Ah, an hour of health would purge his eyesight :
　　Stay, pale queen ! for ever by my side.'

Hush, no words ! that smile, I see, forgives me.
　　I am now thy nurse, I bid thee sleep.　　70
Close thine eyes—this flooding moonlight blinds
　　　them—
　　Nay, all 's well again : thou must not weep.

TRISTRAM

I am happy : yet I feel, there 's something
　　Swells my heart, and takes my breath away :
Through a mist I see thee : near !—come nearer !
　　Bend—bend down—I yet have much to say

ISEULT

Heaven ! his head sinks back upon the pillow !—
　　Tristram ! Tristram ! let thy heart not fail.
Call on God and on the holy angels !
　　What, love, courage !—Christ ! he is so pale.　　80

TRISTRAM

Hush, 'tis vain, I feel my end approaching.
　　This is what my mother said should be,
When the fierce pains took her in the forest,
　　The deep draughts of death, in bearing me.

'Son,' she said, ' thy name shall be of sorrow !
　　Tristram art thou call'd for my death's sake ! '
So she said, and died in the drear forest.
　　Grief since then his home with me doth make.

59 a former] an ancient *1852, 1853.*
65 cry . . . foe] say . . . form *1852.*

I am dying.—Start not, nor look wildly !
  Me, thy living friend, thou canst not save.   90
But, since living we were ununited,
  Go not far, O Iseult ! from my grave.

Rise, go hence, and seek the princess Iseult :
  Speak her fair, she is of royal blood.
Say, I charg'd her, that ye live together :—
  She will grant it—she is kind and good.

Now to sail the seas of Death I leave thee ;
  One last kiss upon the living shore !

ISEULT

Tristram !—Tristram !—stay—receive me with thee !
  Iseult leaves thee, Tristram, never more.   100

   .   .   .   .   .

You see them clear : the moon shines bright.
Slow—slow and softly, where she stood,
She sinks upon the ground : her hood
Had fallen back : her arms outspread
Still hold her lover's hands : her head
Is bow'd, half-buried, on the bed.
O'er the blanch'd sheet her raven hair
Lies in disorder'd streams ; and there,
Strung like white stars, the pearls still are,
And the golden bracelets heavy and rare   110
Flash on her white arms still.
The very same which yesternight
Flash'd in the silver sconces' light,
When the feast was gay and the laughter loud
In Tyntagel's palace proud.
But then they deck'd a restless ghost

97–100   Now stand clear before me in the moonlight.
    Fare, farewell, thou long, thou deeply lov'd !
ISEULT
    Tristram !—Tristram—stay—I come ! Ah Sorrow—
    Fool ! thou missest—we are both unmov'd ! *1852.*
114 gay . . . loud] loud . . . shrill *1852, 1853, 1854.*   115 In
the banquet-hall of Tyntagil. *1852, 1853, 1854.*

With hot-flush'd cheeks and brilliant eyes,
And quivering lips on which the tide
Of courtly speech abruptly died,
And a glance that over the crowded floor,   120
The dancers, and the festive host,
   Flew ever to the door.
That the knights eyed her in surprise,
And the dames whisper'd scoffingly—
'Her moods, good lack, they pass like showers!
But yesternight and she would be
As pale and still as wither'd flowers,
And now to-night she laughs and speaks
And has a colour in her cheeks.
   Christ keep us from such fantasy!'—   130
   The air of the December night
Steals coldly around the chamber bright,
Where those lifeless lovers be.
Swinging with it, in the light
Flaps the ghostlike tapestry.
And on the arras wrought you see
A stately Huntsman, clad in green,
And round him a fresh forest scene.
On that clear forest knoll he stays
With his pack round him, and delays.   140
He stares and stares, with troubled face,
At this huge gleam-lit fireplace,
At the bright iron-figur'd door,
And those blown rushes on the floor.

130 Christ] Heaven *1852, 1853.*   133 *first inserted in 1853.*
135 Flaps] Shines *1852.*   136 on the arras wrought] there
upon the wall *1852.*   139 On that clear forest knoll] 'Tis noon
with him, and yet *1852.*   *After* 140 *1852 has these seven lines
peculiar to itself:—*

      As rooted to the earth, nor sounds
      His lifted horn, nor cheers his hounds
      Into the tangled glen below.
      Yet in the sedgy bottom there
      Where the deep forest stream creeps slow
      Fring'd with dead leaves and mosses rare,
      The wild boar harbours close, and feeds.

and continues with lines 145, 146, 149–158, 141–144, 159–166 *in
roman type with differences as noted on next page, and* 167 *to end as in
later editions.*   142 this] the *1852.*   144 those] the *1852.*

He gazes down into the room
With heated cheeks and flurried air,
And to himself he seems to say—
' *What place is this, and who are they?*
Who is that kneeling Lady fair?
And on his pillows that pale Knight   150
Who seems of marble on a tomb?
How comes it here, this chamber bright
Through whose mullion'd windows clear
The castle court all wet with rain,
The drawbridge and the moat appear,
And then the beach, and, mark'd with spray,
The sunken reefs, and far away
The unquiet bright Atlantic plain?—
   What, has some glamour made me sleep,
And sent me with my dogs to sweep,   160
By night, with boisterous bugle peal,
Through some old, sea-side, knightly hall,
Not in the free greenwood at all?
That Knight's asleep, and at her prayer
That Lady by the bed doth kneel:
Then hush, thou boisterous bugle peal!'—
   The wild boar rustles in his lair—
The fierce hounds snuff the tainted air—
But lord and hounds keep rooted there.

   Cheer, cheer thy dogs into the brake,   170
O Hunter! and without a fear
Thy golden-tassell'd bugle blow,
And through the glades thy pastime take!
   For thou wilt rouse no sleepers here.
For these thou seest are unmov'd;
Cold, cold as those who liv'd and lov'd
   A thousand years ago.

147–148 *first inserted in 1853.*   159 *What, has . . . me*] **Has** then
. . . **him** *1852.*   160 *me . . . my*] **him . . . his** *1852.*

III

ISEULT OF BRITTANY

A YEAR had flown, and o'er the sea away,
In Cornwall, Tristram and queen Iseult lay ;
In King Marc's chapel, in Tyntagel old :
There in a ship they bore those lovers cold.
The young surviving Iseult, one bright day,
Had wander'd forth : her children were at play
In a green circular hollow in the heath
Which borders the sea-shore ; a country path
Creeps over it from the till'd fields behind.
The hollow's grassy banks are soft inclin'd,   10
And to one standing on them, far and near
The lone unbroken view spreads bright and clear
Over the waste :—This cirque of open ground
Is light and green ; the heather, which all round
Creeps thickly, grows not here ; but the pale grass
Is strewn with rocks, and many a shiver'd mass
Of vein'd white-gleaming quartz, and here and there
Dotted with holly trees and juniper.
In the smooth centre of the opening stood
Three hollies side by side, and made a screen   20
Warm with the winter sun, of burnish'd green,
With scarlet berries gemm'd, the fell-fare's food.
Under the glittering hollies Iseult stands
Watching her children play : their little hands
Are busy gathering spars of quartz, and streams
Of stagshorn for their hats : anon, with screams
Of mad delight they drop their spoils, and bound
Among the holly clumps and broken ground,
Racing full speed, and startling in their rush
The fell-fares and the speckled missel-thrush   30
Out of their glossy coverts : but when now
Their cheeks were flush'd, and over each hot brow
Under the feather'd hats of the sweet pair
In blinding masses shower'd the golden hair—

1 o'er the sea away] in the chapel old *1852*.   2 Lay Tristram
and queen Iseult dead and cold. *1852*.   3, 4 *not in 1852*.
3 At Tyntagil in King Marc's chapel old : *1853, 1854*.   13
cirque] ring *1852*.

Then Iseult called them to her, and the three
Cluster'd under the holly screen, and she
Told them an old-world Breton history.

    Warm in their mantles wrapt, the three stood there,
Under the hollies, in the clear still air—
Mantles with those rich furs deep glistering   40
Which Venice ships do from swart Egypt bring.
Long they stayed still—then, pacing at their ease,
Mov'd up and down under the glossy trees ;
But still as they pursued their warm dry road
From Iseult's lips the unbroken story flow'd,
And still the children listen'd, their blue eyes
Fix'd on their mother's face in wide surprise ;
Nor did their looks stray once to the sea-side,
Nor to the brown heaths round them, bright and wide,
Nor to the snow which, though 'twas all away   50
From the open heath, still by the hedgerows lay,
Nor to the shining sea-fowl that with screams
Bore up from where the bright Atlantic gleams,
Swooping to landward ; nor to where, quite clear,
The fell-fares settled on the thickets near.
And they would still have listen'd, till dark night
Came keen and chill down on the heather bright ;
But, when the red glow on the sea grew cold,
And the grey turrets of the castle old
Look'd sternly through the frosty evening air,—   60
Then Iseult took by the hand those children fair,
And brought her tale to an end, and found the path,
And led them home over the darkening heath.

    And is she happy ? Does she see unmov'd
The days in which she might have liv'd and lov'd
Slip without bringing bliss slowly away,
One after one, to-morrow like to-day ?
Joy has not found her yet, nor ever will :—
Is it this thought that makes her mien so still,
Her features so fatigued, her eyes, though sweet,   70
So sunk, so rarely lifted save to meet
Her children's ? She moves slow : her voice alone
Has yet an infantine and silver tone,
But even that comes languidly : in truth,
She seems one dying in a mask of youth.

And now she will go home, and softly lay
Her laughing children in their beds, and play
Awhile with them before they sleep ; and then
She'll light her silver lamp, which fishermen
Dragging their nets through the rough waves, afar,   80
Along this iron coast, know like a star,
And take her broidery frame, and there she'll sit
Hour after hour, her gold curls sweeping it,
Lifting her soft-bent head only to mind
Her children, or to listen to the wind.
And when the clock peals midnight, she will move
Her work away, and let her fingers rove
Across the shaggy brows of Tristram's hound
Who lies, guarding her feet, along the ground :
Or else she will fall musing, her blue eyes   90
Fix'd, her slight hands clasp'd on her lap ; then rise,
And at her prie-dieu kneel, until she have told
Her rosary beads of ebony tipp'd with gold,
Then to her soft sleep: and to-morrow'll be
To-day's exact repeated effigy.

Yes, it is lonely for her in her hall.
The children, and the grey-hair'd seneschal,
Her women, and Sir Tristram's agèd hound,
Are there the sole companions to be found.
But these she loves ; and noisier life than this   100
She would find ill to bear, weak as she is :
She has her children too, and night and day
Is with them ; and the wide heaths where they play,
The hollies, and the cliff, and the sea-shore,
The sand, the sea-birds, and the distant sails,
These are to her dear as to them: the tales
With which this day the children she beguil'd
She glean'd from Breton grandames when a child
In every hut along this sea-coast wild.
She herself loves them still, and, when they are told,
Can forget all to hear them, as of old.   111

Dear saints, it is not sorrow, as I hear,
Not suffering, that shuts up eye and ear

112–150 *omitted in 1853, 1854, reinserted in 1857.*

To all which has delighted them before,
And lets us be what we were once no more.
No : we may suffer deeply, yet retain
Power to be mov'd and sooth'd, for all our pain,
By what of old pleas'd us, and will again.
No : 'tis the gradual furnace of the world,
In whose hot air our spirits are upcurl'd   120
Until they crumble, or else grow like steel—
Which kills in us the bloom, the youth, the spring—
Which leaves the fierce necessity to feel,
But takes away the power—this can avail,
By drying up our joy in everything,
To make our former pleasures all seem stale.
This, or some tyrannous single thought, some fit
Of passion, which subdues our souls to it,
Till for its sake alone we live and move—
Call it ambition, or remorse, or love—   130
This too can change us wholly, and make seem
All that we did before, shadow and dream.

And yet, I swear, it angers me to see
How this fool passion gulls men potently ;
Being, in truth, but a diseas'd unrest,
And an unnatural overheat at best.
How they are full of languor and distress
Not having it ; which, when they do possess,
They straightway are burnt up with fume and care,
And spend their lives in posting here and there   140
Where this plague drives them ; and have little ease,
Are fretful with themselves, and hard to please.
Like that bold Caesar, the fam'd Roman wight,
Who wept at reading of a Grecian knight
Who made a name at younger years than he :
Or that renown'd mirror of chivalry,
Prince Alexander, Philip's peerless son,
Who carried the great war from Macedon
Into the Soudan's realm, and thundered on
To die at thirty-five in Babylon.   150

What tale did Iseult to the children say,
Under the hollies, that bright winter's day ?

142 Can never end their tasks, are hard to please. *1852*.
143 bold] bald *1852*.

She told them of the fairy-haunted land
Away the other side of Brittany,
Beyond the heaths, edg'd by the lonely sea ;
Of the deep forest-glades of Broce-liande,
Through whose green boughs the golden sunshine
creeps,
Where Merlin by the enchanted thorn-tree sleeps.
For here he came with the fay Vivian,
One April, when the warm days first began ;   160
He was on foot, and that false fay, his friend,
On her white palfrey ; here he met his end,
In these lone sylvan glades, that April day.
This tale of Merlin and the lovely fay
Was the one Iseult chose, and she brought clear
Before the children's fancy him and her.

Blowing between the stems the forest air
Had loosen'd the brown curls of Vivian's hair,
Which play'd on her flush'd cheek, and her blue eyes
Sparkled with mocking glee and exercise.   170
Her palfrey's flanks were mired and bath'd in sweat,
For they had travell'd far and not stopp'd yet.
A brier in that tangled wilderness
Had scor'd her white right hand, which she allows
To rest unglov'd on her green riding-dress ;
The other warded off the drooping boughs.
But still she chatted on, with her blue eyes
Fix'd full on Merlin's face, her stately prize :
Her 'haviour had the morning's fresh clear grace,
The spirit of the woods was in her face ;   180
She look'd so witching fair, that learnèd wight
Forgot his craft, and his best wits took flight,
And he grew fond, and eager to obey
His mistress, use her empire as she may.

They came to where the brushwood ceas'd, and day
Peer'd 'twixt the stems ; and the ground broke away
In a slop'd sward down to a brawling brook,
And up as high as where they stood to look
On the brook's further side was clear ; but then
The underwood and trees began again.   190

This open glen was studded thick with thorns
Then white with blossom ; and you saw the horns,
Through the green fern, of the shy fallow-deer
Which come at noon down to the water here.
You saw the bright-eyed squirrels dart along
Under the thorns on the green sward ; and strong
The blackbird whistled from the dingles near,
And the light chipping of the woodpecker
Rang lonelily and sharp : the sky was fair,
And a fresh breath of spring stirr'd everywhere.   200
Merlin and Vivian stopp'd on the slope's brow
To gaze on the green sea of leaf and bough
Which glistering lay all round them, lone and mild,
As if to itself the quiet forest smil'd.
Upon the brow-top grew a thorn ; and here
The grass was dry and moss'd, and you saw clear
Across the hollow : white anemonies
Starr'd the cool turf, and clumps of primroses
Ran out from the dark underwood behind.
No fairer resting-place a man could find.   210
' Here let us halt,' said Merlin then ; and she
Nodded, and tied her palfrey to a tree.

They sate them down together, and a sleep
Fell upon Merlin, more like death, so deep.
Her finger on her lips, then Vivian rose,
And from her brown-lock'd head the wimple throws,
And takes it in her hand, and waves it over
The blossom'd thorn-tree and her sleeping lover.
Nine times she wav'd the fluttering wimple round,
And made a little plot of magic ground.   220
And in that daisied circle, as men say,
Is Merlin prisoner till the judgement-day,
But she herself whither she will can rove,
For she was passing weary of his love.

MEMORIAL VERSES

APRIL, 1850

[First published in *Fraser's Magazine*, June, 1850.
Reprinted 1852, '55.]

GOETHE in Weimar sleeps, and Greece,
Long since, saw Byron's struggle cease.
But one such death remain'd to come.
The last poetic voice is dumb.
What shall be said o'er Wordsworth's tomb?

When Byron's eyes were shut in death,
We bow'd our head and held our breath.
He taught us little: but our soul
Had *felt* him like the thunder's roll.
With shivering heart the strife we saw   10
Of Passion with Eternal Law;
And yet with reverential awe
We watch'd the fount of fiery life
Which serv'd for that Titanic strife.

When Goethe's death was told, we said—
Sunk, then, is Europe's sagest head.
Physician of the Iron Age,
Goethe has done his pilgrimage.
He took the suffering human race,
He read each wound, each weakness clear—   20
And struck his finger on the place
And said—*Thou ailest here, and here.*—
He look'd on Europe's dying hour
Of fitful dream and feverish power;
His eye plung'd down the weltering strife,
The turmoil of expiring life;
He said—*The end is everywhere:*
Art still has truth, take refuge there.

April *in Title*] April 27 *Fraser*.   5 We stand to-day at
Wordsworth's tomb *Fraser*.   7 head] heads *Fraser*.   14
serv'd] flow'd *Fraser*.   15 Goethe's death was told] Goethe
pass'd away *Fraser*.   20 read . . . weakness clear—] scann'd
. . . weakness, near, *Fraser*.   25 weltering] seething *Fraser*.

And he was happy, if to know
Causes of things, and far below 30
His feet to see the lurid flow
Of terror, and insane distress,
And headlong fate, be happiness.

And Wordsworth !—Ah, pale Ghosts, rejoice !
For never has such soothing voice
Been to your shadowy world convey'd,
Since erst, at morn, some wandering shade
Heard the clear song of Orpheus come
Through Hades, and the mournful gloom.
Wordsworth has gone from us—and ye, 40
Ah, may ye feel his voice as we.
He too upon a wintry clime
Had fallen—on this iron time
Of doubts, disputes, distractions, fears.
He found us when the age had bound
Our souls in its benumbing round ;
He spoke, and loos'd our heart in tears.
He laid us as we lay at birth
On the cool flowery lap of earth ;
Smiles broke from us and we had ease. 50
The hills were round us, and the breeze
Went o'er the sun-lit fields again :
Our foreheads felt the wind and rain.
Our youth return'd : for there was shed
On spirits that had long been dead,
Spirits dried up and closely-furl'd,
The freshness of the early world.

Ah, since dark days still bring to light
Man's prudence and man's fiery might,
Time may restore us in his course 60
Goethe's sage mind and Byron's force :

40 has] is *Fraser, 1852.* 43 Had . . . this] Was . . . the
Fraser. 44 *first inserted in 1852.* 46 Our spirits in a
brazen round *Fraser.* *Between 47 and 48 Fraser reads :—*
He tore us from the prison-cell
Of festering thoughts and personal fears,
Where we had long been doom'd to dwell.
54 return'd] came back *Fraser.* 56 dried up] deep-crush'd,
Fraser. 60 his] its *Fraser.*

But where will Europe's latter hour
Again find Wordsworth's healing power?
Others will teach us how to dare,
And against fear our breast to steel:
Others will strengthen us to bear—
But who, ah who, will make us feel?
The cloud of mortal destiny,
Others will front it fearlessly—
But who, like him, will put it by?　　　　70

Keep fresh the grass upon his grave,
O Rotha! with thy living wave.
Sing him thy best! for few or none
Hears thy voice right, now he is gone.

COURAGE

[First published 1852.　Not reprinted by the author.]

TRUE, we must tame our rebel will:
True, we must bow to Nature's law:
Must bear in silence many an ill;
Must learn to wait, renounce, withdraw.

Yet now, when boldest wills give place,
When Fate and Circumstance are strong,
And in their rush the human race
Are swept, like huddling sheep, along;

Those sterner spirits let me prize,
Who, though the tendence of the whole　　　10
They less than us might recognize,
Kept, more than us, their strength of soul.

Yes, be the second Cato prais'd!
Not that he took the course to die—
But that, when 'gainst himself he rais'd
His arm, he rais'd it dauntlessly.

And, Byron! let us dare admire,
If not thy fierce and turbid song,
Yet that, in anguish, doubt, desire,
Thy fiery courage still was strong.　　　　20

62 will] shall *Fraser.*

The sun that on thy tossing pain
Did with such cold derision shine,
He crush'd thee not with his disdain—
   He had his glow, and thou hadst thine.

Our bane. disguise it as we may,
Is weakness, is a faltering course.
Oh that past times could give our day,
Join'd to its clearness, of their force !

SELF-DEPENDENCE

[First published 1852.   Reprinted 1853, '54, '57.]

WEARY of myself, and sick of asking
What I am, and what I ought to be,
At the vessel's prow I stand, which bears me
Forwards, forwards, o'er the starlit sea.

And a look of passionate desire
O'er the sea and to the stars I send:
' Ye who from my childhood up have calm'd me,
Calm me, ah, compose me to the end.

' Ah, once more,' I cried, ' ye Stars, ye Waters,
On my heart your mighty charm renew :   10
Still, still let me, as I gaze upon you,
Feel my soul becoming vast like you.'

From the intense, clear, star-sown vault of heaven,
Over the lit sea's unquiet way,
In the rustling night-air came the answer—
' Wouldst thou *be* as these are ?   *Live* as they.

' Unaffrighted by the silence round them,
Undistracted by the sights they see,
These demand not that the things without them
Yield them love, amusement, sympathy.   20

' And with joy the stars perform their shining,
And the sea its long moon-silver'd roll.
For alone they live, nor pine with noting
All the fever of some differing soul.

'Bounded by themselves, and unobservant
In what state God's other works may be,
In their own tasks all their powers pouring,
These attain the mighty life you see.'

O air-born Voice! long since, severely clear,
A cry like thine in my own heart I hear. 30
'Resolve to be thyself: and know, that he
Who finds himself, loses his misery.'

A SUMMER NIGHT

[First published 1852. Reprinted 1855.]

In the deserted moon-blanch'd street
How lonely rings the echo of my feet!
Those windows, which I gaze at, frown,
Silent and white, unopening down,
Repellent as the world:—but see!
A break between the housetops shows
The moon, and, lost behind her, fading dim
Into the dewy dark obscurity
Down at the far horizon's rim,
    Doth a whole tract of heaven disclose. 10

And to my mind the thought
Is on a sudden brought
Of a past night, and a far different scene.
Headlands stood out into the moon-lit deep
As clearly as at noon;
The spring-tide's brimming flow
Heav'd dazzlingly between;
Houses with long white sweep
Girdled the glistening bay:
Behind, through the soft air, 20
The blue haze-cradled mountains spread away.
    That night was far more fair;
But the same restless pacings to and fro,
And the same vainly-throbbing heart was there,
And the same bright calm moon.

24 vainly-throbbing] agitated *1852*.

And the calm moonlight seems to say—
Hast thou then still the old unquiet breast
That neither deadens into rest
Nor ever feels the fiery glow
That whirls the spirit from itself away,   30
But fluctuates to and fro
Never by passion quite possess'd
And never quite benumb'd by the world's sway?—
And I, I know not if to pray
Still to be what I am, or yield, and be
Like all the other men I see.

For most men in a brazen prison live,
Where in the sun's hot eye,
With heads bent o'er their toil, they languidly
Their lives to some unmeaning taskwork give,   40
Dreaming of naught beyond their prison wall.
And as, year after year,
Fresh products of their barren labour fall
From their tired hands, and rest
Never yet comes more near,
Gloom settles slowly down over their breast.
And while they try to stem
The waves of mournful thought by which they are prest,
Death in their prison reaches them
Unfreed, having seen nothing, still unblest.   50

And the rest, a few,
Escape their prison, and depart
On the wide Ocean of Life anew.
There the freed prisoner, where'er his heart
Listeth, will sail;
Nor does he know how there prevail,
Despotic on life's sea,
Trade-winds that cross it from eternity.
Awhile he holds some false way, undebarr'd
By thwarting signs, and braves   60
The freshening wind and blackening waves.
And then the tempest strikes him, and between
The lightning bursts is seen
Only a driving wreck,
And the pale Master on his spar-strewn deck

With anguish'd face and flying hair
Grasping the rudder hard,
Still bent to make some port he knows not where,
Still standing for some false impossible shore.
 And sterner comes the roar   70
Of sea and wind, and through the deepening gloom
Fainter and fainter wreck and helmsman loom,
And he too disappears, and comes no more.

 Is there no life, but these alone?
Madman or slave, must man be one?

 Plainness and clearness without shadow of stain!
Clearness divine!
Ye Heavens, whose pure dark regions have no sign
Of languor, though so calm, and though so great
Are yet untroubled and unpassionate: 80
Who though so noble share in the world's toil,
And though so task'd keep free from dust and soil:
I will not say that your mild deeps retain
A tinge, it may be, of their silent pain
Who have long'd deeply once, and long'd in vain;
But I will rather say that you remain
A world above man's head, to let him see
How boundless might his soul's horizons be,
How vast, yet of what clear transparency.
How it were good to sink there, and breathe free. 90
How fair a lot to fill
Is left to each man still.

THE BURIED LIFE

[First published 1852.   Reprinted 1855.]

LIGHT flows our war of mocking words, and yet,
Behold, with tears my eyes are wet.
I feel a nameless sadness o'er me roll.
 Yes, yes, we know that we can jest,
We know, we know that we can smile;
But there 's a something in this breast
To which thy light words bring no rest,

91 fair] high 1852.

And thy gay smiles no anodyne.
  Give me thy hand, and hush awhile,
And turn those limpid eyes on mine,   10
And let me read there, love, thy inmost soul.

  Alas, is even Love too weak
To unlock the heart, and let it speak ?
Are even lovers powerless to reveal
To one another what indeed they feel ?
I knew the mass of men conceal'd
Their thoughts, for fear that if reveal'd
They would by other men be met
With blank indifference, or with blame reprov'd :
I knew they liv'd and mov'd   20
Trick'd in disguises, alien to the rest
Of men, and alien to themselves—and yet
The same heart beats in every human breast.

  But we, my love—does a like spell benumb
Our hearts—our voices ?—must we too be dumb ?

  Ah, well for us, if even we,
Even for a moment, can get free
Our heart, and have our lips unchain'd :
For that which seals them hath been deep ordain'd.

  Fate, which foresaw   30
How frivolous a baby man would be,
By what distractions he would be possess'd,
How he would pour himself in every strife,
And well-nigh change his own identity ;
That it might keep from his capricious play
His genuine self, and force him to obey,
Even in his own despite, his being's law,
Bade through the deep recesses of our breast
The unregarded River of our Life
Pursue with indiscernible flow its way ;   40
And that we should not see
The buried stream, and seem to be
Eddying about in blind uncertainty,
Though driving on with it eternally.

    23 The same heart beats] There beats one heart *1852*.

But often, in the world's most crowded streets,
But often, in the din of strife,
There rises an unspeakable desire
After the knowledge of our buried life,
A thirst to spend our fire and restless force
In tracking out our true, original course ;   50
A longing to inquire
Into the mystery of this heart that beats
So wild, so deep in us, to know
Whence our thoughts come and where they go.
And many a man in his own breast then delves,
But deep enough, alas, none ever mines :
And we have been on many thousand lines,
And we have shown on each talent and power,
But hardly have we, for one little hour,
Been on our own line, have we been ourselves ;   60
Hardly had skill to utter one of all
The nameless feelings that course through our breast,
But they course on for ever unexpress'd.
And long we try in vain to speak and act
Our hidden self, and what we say and do
Is eloquent, is well—but 'tis not true :
    And then we will no more be rack'd
With inward striving, and demand
Of all the thousand nothings of the hour
Their stupefying power ;   70
Ah yes, and they benumb us at our call :
Yet still, from time to time, vague and forlorn,
From the soul's subterranean depth upborne
As from an infinitely distant land,
Come airs, and floating echoes, and convey
A melancholy into all our day.

    Only—but this is rare—
When a belovèd hand is laid in ours,
When, jaded with the rush and glare
Of the interminable hours,   80
Our eyes can in another's eyes read clear,
When our world-deafen'd ear
Is by the tones of a lov'd voice caress'd,—
    A bolt is shot back somewhere in our breast

And a lost pulse of feeling stirs again :
The eye sinks inward, and the heart lies plain,
And what we mean, we say, and what we would, we
    know.
A man becomes aware of his life's flow,
And hears its winding murmur, and he sees
The meadows where it glides, the sun, the breeze.   90

And there arrives a lull in the hot race
Wherein he doth for ever chase
That flying and elusive shadow, Rest.
An air of coolness plays upon his face,
And an unwonted calm pervades his breast.
    And then he thinks he knows
The Hills where his life rose,
And the Sea where it goes.

A FAREWELL

[First published 1852.   Reprinted 1854, '57.]

My horse's feet beside the lake,
Where sweet the unbroken moonbeams lay,
Sent echoes through the night to wake
Each glistening strand, each heath-fring'd bay.

The poplar avenue was pass'd,
And the roof'd bridge that spans the stream.
Up the steep street I hurried fast,
Led by thy taper's starlike beam.

I came ; I saw thee rise :—the blood
Came flushing to thy languid cheek.   10
Lock'd in each other's arms we stood,
In tears, with hearts too full to speak.

Days flew : ah, soon I could discern
A trouble in thine alter'd air.
Thy hand lay languidly in mine—
Thy cheek was grave, thy speech grew rare.

A Farewell *Title*] Switzerland. V. A Farewell *1854, 1857*.
8 Led] Lit *1852*.   10 flushing] flooding *1852*.

I blame thee not:—this heart, I know,
To be long lov'd was never fram'd ;
For something in its depths doth glow
Too strange, too restless, too untam'd.   20

And women—things that live and move
Min'd by the fever of the soul—
They seek to find in those they love
Stern strength, and promise of control.

They ask not kindness, gentle ways ;
These they themselves have tried and known :
They ask a soul that never sways
With the blind gusts which shake their own.

I too have felt the load I bore
In a too strong emotion's sway ;   30
I too have wish'd, no woman more,
This starting, feverish heart, away :

I too have long'd for trenchant force
And will like a dividing spear ;
Have prais'd the keen, unscrupulous course,
Which knows no doubt, which feels no fear.

But in the world I learnt, what there
Thou too wilt surely one day prove,
That will, that energy, though rare,
Are yet far, far less rare than love.   40

Go then ! till Time and Fate impress
This truth on thee, be mine no more !
They will : for thou, I feel, no less
Than I, wert destin'd to this lore.

We school our manners, act our parts :
But He, who sees us through and through,
Knows that the bent of both our hearts
Was to be gentle, tranquil, true.

And though we wear out life, alas,
Distracted as a homeless wind,   50
In beating where we must not pass,
In seeking what we shall not find ;

Yet we shall one day gain, life past,
Clear prospect o'er our being's whole ;
Shall see ourselves, and learn at last
Our true affinities of soul.

We shall not then deny a course
To every thought the mass ignore ;
We shall not then call hardness force,
Nor lightness wisdom any more.   60

Then, in the eternal Father's smile,
Our sooth'd, encourag'd souls will dare
To *seem* as free from pride and guile,
As good, as generous, as they *are*.

Then we shall know our friends : though much
Will have been lost—the help in strife ;
The thousand sweet still joys of such
As hand in hand face earthly life ;—

Though these be lost, there will be yet
A sympathy august and pure ;   70
Ennobled by a vast regret,
And by contrition seal'd thrice sure.

And we, whose ways were unlike here,
May then more neighbouring courses ply ;
May to each other be brought near,
And greet across infinity.

How sweet, unreach'd by earthly jars,
My sister ! to behold with thee
The hush among the shining stars,
The calm upon the moonlit sea.   80

How sweet to feel, on the boon air,
All our unquiet pulses cease ;
To feel that nothing can impair
The gentleness, the thirst for peace—

The gentleness too rudely hurl'd
On this wild earth of hate and fear :
The thirst for peace a raving world
Would never let us satiate here.

OBERMANN

[First published 1852.   Reprinted 1855.]

In front the awful Alpine track
Crawls up its rocky stair ;
The autumn storm-winds drive the rack
Close o'er it, in the air.

Behind are the abandon'd baths
Mute in their meadows lone ;
The leaves are on the valley paths ;
The mists are on the Rhone—

The white mists rolling like a sea.
I hear the torrents roar.   10
—Yes, Obermann, all speaks of thee !
I feel thee near once more.

I turn thy leaves : I feel their breath
Once more upon me roll ;
That air of languor, cold, and death,
Which brooded o'er thy soul.

Fly hence, poor Wretch, whoe'er thou art,
Condemn'd to cast about,
All shipwreck in thy own weak heart,
For comfort from without :   20

A fever in these pages burns
Beneath the calm they feign ;
A wounded human spirit turns
Here, on its bed of pain.

Yes, though the virgin mountain air
Fresh through these pages blows,
Though to these leaves the glaciers spare
The soul of their white snows,

Obermann *Title*] Stanzas in memory of the author of ' Obermann' *1852*.   28 white] mute *1852*.

Though here a mountain murmur swells
Of many a dark-bough'd pine,   30
Though, as you read, you hear the bells
Of the high-pasturing kine—

Yet, through the hum of torrent lone,
And brooding mountain bee,
There sobs I know not what ground tone
Of human agony.

Is it for this, because the sound
Is fraught too deep with pain,
That, Obermann! the world around
So little loves thy strain?   40

Some secrets may the poet tell,
For the world loves new ways.
To tell too deep ones is not well;
It knows not what he says.

Yet of the spirits who have reign'd
In this our troubled day,
I know but two, who have attain'd,
Save thee, to see their way.

By England's lakes, in grey old age,
His quiet home one keeps;[1]   50
And one, the strong much-toiling Sage,
In German Weimar sleeps.

But Wordsworth's eyes avert their ken
From half of human fate;
And Goethe's course few sons of men
May think to emulate.

For he pursued a lonely road,
His eyes on Nature's plan;
Neither made man too much a God,
Nor God too much a man.   60

[1] Written in November, 1849.

Strong was he, with a spirit free
From mists, and sane, and clear;
Clearer, how much! than ours: yet we
Have a worse course to steer.

For though his manhood bore the blast
Of Europe's stormiest time,
Yet in a tranquil world was pass'd
His tenderer youthful prime.

But we, brought forth and rear'd in hours
Of change, alarm, surprise—   70
What shelter to grow ripe is ours?
What leisure to grow wise?

Like children bathing on the shore,
Buried a wave beneath,
The second wave succeeds, before
We have had time to breathe.

Too fast we live, too much are tried,
Too harass'd, to attain
Wordsworth's sweet calm, or Goethe's wide
And luminous view to gain.   80

And then we turn, thou sadder Sage!
To thee: we feel thy spell.
The hopeless tangle of our age—
Thou too hast scann'd it well.

Immovable thou sittest; still
As death; compos'd to bear.
Thy head is clear, thy feeling chill—
And icy thy despair.

Yes, as the Son of Thetis said,
One hears thee saying now—   90
Greater by far than thou are dead:
Strive not: die also thou.—

66 Europe's stormiest] a tremendous *1852.*

Ah ! Two desires toss about
The poet's feverish blood.
One drives him to the world without,
And one to solitude.

The glow, he cries, *the thrill of life—*
Where, where do these abound ?—
Not in the world, not in the strife
Of men, shall they be found.   100

He who hath watch'd, not shar'd, the strife,
Knows how the day hath gone ;
He only lives with the world's life
Who hath renounc'd his own.

To thee we come, then.   Clouds are roll'd
Where thou, O Seer, art set ;
Thy realm of thought is drear and cold—
The world is colder yet !

And thou hast pleasures too to share
With those who come to thee :   110
Balms floating on thy mountain air,
And healing sights to see.

How often, where the slopes are green
On Jaman, hast thou sate
By some high chalet door, and seen
The summer day grow late,

And darkness steal o'er the wet grass
With the pale crocus starr'd,
And reach that glimmering sheet of glass
Beneath the piny sward,   120

Lake Leman's waters, far below :
And watch'd the rosy light
Fade from the distant peaks of snow :
And on the air of night

97 The glow of thought, the thrill of life— *1852.*

Heard accents of the eternal tongue
Through the pine branches play:
Listen'd, and felt thyself grow young;
Listen'd, and wept——Away!

Away the dreams that but deceive!
And thou, sad Guide, adieu!   130
I go; Fate drives me: but I leave
Half of my life with you.

We, in some unknown Power's employ,
Move on a rigorous line:
Can neither, when we will, enjoy;
Nor, when we will, resign.

I in the world must live:—but thou,
Thou melancholy Shade!
Wilt not, if thou canst see me now,
Condemn me, nor upbraid.   140

For thou art gone away from earth,
And place with those dost claim,
The Children of the Second Birth
Whom the world could not tame;

And with that small transfigur'd Band,
Whom many a different way
Conducted to their common land,
Thou learn'st to think as they.

Christian and pagan, king and slave,
Soldier and anchorite,   150
Distinctions we esteem so grave,
Are nothing in their sight.

They do not ask, who pin'd unseen,
Who was on action hurl'd,
Whose one bond is that all have been
Unspotted by the world.

There without anger thou wilt see
Him who obeys thy spell
No more, so he but rest, like thee,
Unsoil'd :—and so, Farewell !   160

Farewell !—Whether thou now liest near
That much-lov'd inland sea,
The ripples of whose blue waves cheer
Vevey and Meillerie,

And in that gracious region bland,
Where with clear-rustling wave
The scented pines of Switzerland
Stand dark round thy green grave,

Between the dusty vineyard walls
Issuing on that green place   170
The early peasant still recalls
The pensive stranger's face,

And stoops to clear thy moss-grown date
Ere he plods on again ;—
Or whether, by maligner Fate,
Among the swarms of men,

Where between granite terraces
The blue Seine rolls her wave,
The Capital of Pleasure sees
Thy hardly-heard-of grave—   180

Farewell !   Under the sky we part,
In this stern Alpine dell.
O unstrung will !   O broken heart !
A last, a last farewell !

178 blue Seine rolls] Seine conducts *1852*.

CONSOLATION

[First published 1852. Reprinted 1853, '54, '57.]

MIST clogs the sunshine,
Smoky dwarf houses
Hem me round everywhere.
 A vague dejection
Weighs down my soul.

Yet, while I languish,
Everywhere, countless
Prospects unroll themselves,
 And countless beings
Pass countless moods.   10

Far hence, in Asia,
On the smooth convent-roofs,
On the gold terraces
 Of holy Lassa,
Bright shines the sun.

Grey time-worn marbles
Hold the pure Muses.
In their cool gallery,
 By yellow Tiber,
They still look fair.   20

Strange unlov'd uproar [1]
Shrills round their portal.
Yet not on Helicon
 Kept they more cloudless
Their noble calm.

Written during the siege of Rome by the French [1849].

Consolation] *In 1853 and 1854 the following lines are printed as
a motto to the poem :—*

        The wide earth is still
Wider than one man's passion : there's no mood,
No meditation, no delight, no sorrow,
Cas'd in one man's dimensions, can distil
Such pregnant and infectious quality,
Six yards round shall not ring it.—

Through sun-proof alleys
In a lone, sand-hemm'd
City of Africa,
  A blind, led beggar,
Age-bow'd, asks alms.   30

No bolder Robber
Erst abode ambush'd
Deep in the sandy waste :
  No clearer eyesight
Spied prey afar.

Saharan sand-winds
Sear'd his keen eyeballs.
Spent is the spoil he won.
  For him the present
Holds only pain.   40

Two young, fair lovers,
Where the warm June wind,
Fresh from the summer fields,
  Plays fondly round them,
Stand, tranc'd in joy.

With sweet, join'd voices,
And with eyes brimming —
'Ah,' they cry, 'Destiny !
  Prolong the present !
Time ! stand still here ! '   50

The prompt stern Goddess
Shakes her head, frowning.
Time gives his hour-glass
  Its due reversal.
Their hour is gone.

With weak indulgence
Did the just Goddess
Lengthen their happiness,
  She lengthen'd also
Distress elsewhere.   60

The hour, whose happy
Unalloy'd moments
I would eternalize,
    Ten thousand mourners
Well pleas'd see end.

The bleak stern hour,
Whose severe moments
I would annihilate,
    Is pass'd by others
In warmth, light, joy.   70

Time, so complain'd of,
Who to no one man
Shows partiality,
    Brings round to all men
Some undimm'd hours.

LINES WRITTEN
IN KENSINGTON GARDENS

[First published 1852.   Reprinted 1867.]

IN this lone open glade I lie,
Screen'd by deep boughs on either hand;
And at its head, to stay the eye,
Those black-crown'd, red-boled pine-trees stand.

Birds here make song, each bird has his,
Across the girdling city's hum.
How green under the boughs it is!
How thick the tremulous sheep-cries come!

Sometimes a child will cross the glade
To take his nurse his broken toy;   10
Sometimes a thrush flit overhead
Deep in her unknown day's employ.

2 deep boughs] dark trees *1852.*   4 black-crown'd] black-
topp'd *1852.*   *Between 4 and 5 1852 reads :—*
            The clouded sky is still and grey,
            Through silken rifts soft peers the sun.
            Light the green-foliag'd chestnuts play,
            The darker elms stand grave and dun.
5 The birds sing sweetly in these trees *1852.*

Here at my feet what wonders pass,
What endless, active life is here !
What blowing daisies, fragrant grass !
An air-stirr'd forest, fresh and clear.

Scarce fresher is the mountain sod
Where the tired angler lies, stretch'd out,
And, eased of basket and of rod,
Counts his day's spoil, the spotted trout.   20

In the huge world which roars hard by
Be others happy, if they can !
But in my helpless cradle I
Was breathed on by the rural Pan.

I, on men's impious uproar hurl'd,
Think often, as I hear them rave,
That peace has left the upper world,
And now keeps only in the grave.

Yet here is peace for ever new !
When I, who watch them, am away,   30
Still all things in this glade go through
The changes of their quiet day.

Then to their happy rest they pass ;
The flowers close, the birds are fed,
The night comes down upon the grass,
The child sleeps warmly in his bed.

Calm soul of all things ! make it mine
To feel, amid the city's jar,
That there abides a peace of thine,
Man did not make, and cannot mar !   40

The will to neither strive nor cry,
The power to feel with others give !
Calm, calm me more ! nor let me die
Before I have begun to live.

21-24 *first inserted in 1867.*   26 often] sometimes *1852.*

THE WORLD'S TRIUMPHS

[First published 1852.   Reprinted in 1853, '54, '57.]

So far as I conceive the World's rebuke
To him address'd who would recast her new,
Not from herself her fame of strength she took,
But from their weakness, who would work her rue.
  'Behold,' she cries, ' so many rages lull'd,
So many fiery spirits quite cool'd down :
Look how so many valours, long undull'd,
After short commerce with me, fear my frown.
Thou too, when thou against my crimes wouldst cry,
Let thy foreboded homage check thy tongue.'—   10
The World speaks well : yet might her foe reply—
  'Are wills so weak ? then let not mine wait long.
Hast thou so rare a poison ? let me be
Keener to slay thee, lest thou poison me.'

THE SECOND BEST

[First published 1852.   Reprinted 1867.]

MODERATE tasks and moderate leisure,
Quiet living, strict-kept measure
Both in suffering and in pleasure—
  'Tis for this thy nature yearns.

But so many books thou readest,
But so many schemes thou breedest,
But so many wishes feedest,
  That thy poor head almost turns.

And (the world's so madly jangled,
Human things so fast entangled)
Nature's wish must now be strangled   10
  For that best which she discerns.

The World's Triumphs *Title*] Sonnet *1852*. Sonnets. VIII. The
World's Triumphs *1853*. Sonnets. VII. The World's Triumphs
1854, 1857.

So it *must* be ! yet, while leading
A strain'd life, while overfeeding,
Like the rest, his wit with reading,
   No small profit that man earns,

Who through all he meets can steer him,
Can reject what cannot clear him,
Cling to what can truly cheer him !
   Who each day more surely learns   20

That an impulse, from the distance
Of his deepest, best existence,
To the words 'Hope, Light, Persistence,'
   Strongly stirs and truly burns !

REVOLUTIONS

[First published 1852. Reprinted 1855.]

BEFORE Man parted for this earthly strand,
While yet upon the verge of heaven he stood,
God put a heap of letters in his hand,
And bade him make with them what word he could.

And Man has turn'd them many times : made Greece,
Rome, England, France :—yes, nor in vain essay'd
Way after way, changes that never cease.
The letters have combin'd : something was made.

But ah, an inextinguishable sense
Haunts him that he has not made what he should.   10
That he has still, though old, to recommence,
Since he has not yet found the word God would.

And Empire after Empire, at their height
Of sway, have felt this boding sense come on.
Have felt their huge frames not constructed right,
And droop'd, and slowly died upon their throne.

One day, thou say'st, there will at last appear
The word, the order, which God meant should be.—
Ah, we shall know *that* well when it comes near :   19
The band will quit Man's heart :—he will breathe free.

THE YOUTH OF NATURE

[First published 1852.   Reprinted 1855.]

RAIS'D are the dripping oars—
Silent the boat : the lake,
Lovely and soft as a dream,
Swims in the sheen of the moon.
The mountains stand at its head
Clear in the pure June night,
But the valleys are flooded with haze.
Rydal and Fairfield are there ;
In the shadow Wordsworth lies dead.
So it is, so it will be for aye.   10
    Nature is fresh as of old,
Is lovely : a mortal is dead.

The spots which recall him survive,
For he lent a new life to these hills.
The Pillar still broods o'er the fields
Which border Ennerdale Lake,
And Egremont sleeps by the sea.
The gleam of The Evening Star
Twinkles on Grasmere no more,
But ruin'd and solemn and grey   20
The sheepfold of Michael survives,
And far to the south, the heath
Still blows in the Quantock coombs,
    By the favourite waters of Ruth.
These survive : yet not without pain,
Pain and dejection to-night,
Can I feel that their Poet is gone.

He grew old in an age he condemn'd.
He look'd on the rushing decay
Of the times which had shelter'd his youth.   30
Felt the dissolving throes
Of a social order he lov'd.
Outliv'd his brethren, his peers.
And, like the Theban seer,
    Died in his enemies' day.

16 Which] That *1852*.

Cold bubbled the spring of Tilphusa,
Copais lay bright in the moon ;
Helicon glass'd in the lake
Its firs, and afar, rose the peaks
Of Parnassus, snowily clear :   40
Thebes was behind him in flames,
And the clang of arms in his ear,
When his awe-struck captors led
The Theban seer to the spring.
    Tiresias drank and died.
Nor did reviving Thebes
See such a prophet again.

Well may we mourn, when the head
Of a sacred poet lies low
In an age which can rear them no more.   50
The complaining millions of men
Darken in labour and pain ;
But he was a priest to us all
Of the wonder and bloom of the world,
Which we saw with his eyes, and were glad.
    He is dead, and the fruit-bearing day
Of his race is past on the earth ;
And darkness returns to our eyes.

For oh, is it you, is it you,
Moonlight, and shadow, and lake,   60
And mountains, that fill us with joy,
Or the Poet who sings you so well ?
Is it you, O Beauty, O Grace,
O Charm, O Romance, that we feel,
Or the voice which reveals what you are ?
Are ye, like daylight and sun,
Shar'd and rejoic'd in by all ?
Or are ye immers'd in the mass
Of matter, and hard to extract,
Or sunk at the core of the world   70
Too deep for the most to discern ?
    Like stars in the deep of the sky,
Which arise on the glass of the sage,
But are lost when their watcher is gone.

They are here '—I heard, as men heard
In Mysian Ida the voice
Of the Mighty Mother, or Crete,
The murmur of Nature reply—
' Loveliness, Magic, and Grace,
They are here—they are set in the world—   80
They abide—and the finest of souls
Has not been thrill'd by them all,
Nor the dullest been dead to them quite.
The poet who sings them may die,
But they are immortal, and live,
For they are the life of the world.
    Will ye not learn it, and know,
When ye mourn that a poet is dead,
That the singer was less than his themes,
    Life, and Emotion, and I ?   90

' More than the singer are these.
Weak is the tremor of pain
That thrills in his mournfullest chord
To that which once ran through his soul.
Cold the elation of joy
In his gladdest, airiest song,
To that which of old in his youth
Fill'd him and made him divine.
Hardly his voice at its best
Gives us a sense of the awe,   100
The vastness, the grandeur, the gloom
Of the unlit gulph of himself.

' Ye know not yourselves—and your bards,
The clearest, the best, who have read
Most in themselves, have beheld
Less than they left unreveal'd.
Ye express not yourselves—can ye make
With marble, with colour, with word,
What charm'd you in others re-live ?
Can thy pencil, O Artist, restore   110
The figure, the bloom of thy love,
As she was in her morning of spring ?
Canst thou paint the ineffable smile
Of her eyes as they rested on thine ?

Can the image of life have the glow,
The motion of life itself?

'Yourselves and your fellows ye know not—and me
The Mateless, the One, will ye know?
Will ye scan me, and read me, and tell
Of the thoughts that ferment in my breast,   120
My longing, my sadness, my joy?
Will ye claim for your great ones the gift
To have render'd the gleam of my skies,
To have echoed the moan of my seas,
Utter'd the voice of my hills?
When your great ones depart, will ye say—
All things have suffer'd a loss—
Nature is hid in their grave?

'Race after race, man after man,
Have dream'd that my secret was theirs,   130
Have thought that I liv'd but for them,
That they were my glory and joy.—
They are dust, they are chang'd, they are gone.—
    I remain.'

THE YOUTH OF MAN

[First published 1852. Two fragments 1853. Reprinted in its
complete form, as below, 1855.]

    WE, O Nature, depart:
    Thou survivest us: this,
    This, I know, is the law.
    Yes, but more than this,
    Thou who seest us die
    Seest us change while we live;
    Seest our dreams one by one,
    Seest our errors depart:
        Watchest us, Nature, throughout,
    Mild and inscrutably calm.   10

        Well for us that we change!
    Well for us that the Power
    Which in our morning prime
    Saw the mistakes of our youth,
    Sweet, and forgiving, and good,
    Sees the contrition of age!

Behold, O Nature, this pair!
See them to-night where they stand,
Not with the halo of youth
Crowning their brows with its light,   20
Not with the sunshine of hope,
Not with the rapture of spring,
Which they had of old, when they stood
Years ago at my side
In this self-same garden, and said ;—
'We are young, and the world is ours,
For man is the king of the world.
Fools that these mystics are
Who prate of Nature! but she
Has neither beauty, nor warmth,   30
Nor life, nor emotion, nor power.
But Man has a thousand gifts,
And the generous dreamer invests
The senseless world with them all.
    Nature is nothing! her charm
Lives in our eyes which can paint,
Lives in our hearts which can feel!'

    Thou, O Nature, wert mute,
Mute as of old: days flew,
Days and years; and Time   40
With the ceaseless stroke of his wings
Brush'd off the bloom from their soul.
Clouded and dim grew their eye ;
Languid their heart; for Youth
Quicken'd its pulses no more.
Slowly within the walls
Of an ever-narrowing world
They droop'd, they grew blind, they grew old.
Thee and their Youth in thee,
Nature, they saw no more.   50

    Murmur of living!
Stir of existence!
Soul of the world!
Make, oh make yourselves felt
To the dying spirit of Youth.

51–60 *were printed as a separate poem in 1853 under the title*
Richmond Hill.

Come, like the breath of the spring.
Leave not a human soul
To grow old in darkness and pain.
  Only the living can feel you:
But leave us not while we live.   60

  Here they stand to-night—
Here, where this grey balustrade
Crowns the still valley: behind
Is the castled house with its woods
Which shelter'd their childhood, the sun
On its ivied windows: a scent
From the grey-wall'd gardens, a breath
Of the fragrant stock and the pink,
Perfumes the evening air.
Their children play on the lawns.   70
They stand and listen: they hear
The children's shouts, and, at times,
Faintly, the bark of a dog
From a distant farm in the hills:—
Nothing besides: in front
The wide, wide valley outspreads
To the dim horizon, repos'd
In the twilight, and bath'd in dew,
  Corn-field and hamlet and copse
Darkening fast; but a light,   80
Far off, a glory of day,
Still plays on the city spires:
And there in the dusk by the walls,
With the grey mist marking its course
Through the silent flowery land,
  On, to the plains, to the sea,
Floats the Imperial Stream.

  Well I know what they feel.
They gaze, and the evening wind
Plays on their faces: they gaze;   90
Airs from the Eden of Youth
Awake and stir in their soul:
The Past returns; they feel
What they are, alas! what they were.
They, not Nature, are chang'd.
Well I know what they feel.

Hush! for tears
Begin to steal to their eyes.
Hush! for fruit
Grows from such sorrow as theirs.   100

And they remember
With piercing untold anguish
The proud boasting of their youth.
And they feel how Nature was fair.
And the mists of delusion,
And the scales of habit,
Fall away from their eyes.
And they see, for a moment,
Stretching out, like the Desert
In its weary, unprofitable length,   110
Their faded, ignoble lives.

While the locks are yet brown on thy head,
While the soul still looks through thine eyes,
While the heart still pours
The mantling blood to thy cheek,
    Sink, O Youth, in thy soul!
Yearn to the greatness of Nature!
Rally the good in the depths of thyself!

MORALITY

[First published 1852. Reprinted 1853, '54, '57.]

WE cannot kindle when we will
The fire that in the heart resides,
The spirit bloweth and is still,
In mystery our soul abides:
    But tasks in hours of insight will'd
Can be through hours of gloom fulfill'd.

With aching hands and bleeding feet
We dig and heap, lay stone on stone;
We bear the burden and the heat
Of the long day, and wish 'twere done.   10
    Not till the hours of light return
All we have built do we discern.

112-118 *were printed as a separate poem in 1853 under the title*
Power of Youth.

Then, when the clouds are off the soul,
When thou dost bask in Nature's eye,
Ask, how *she* view'd thy self-control,
Thy struggling task'd morality.
    Nature, whose free, light, cheerful air,
Oft made thee, in thy gloom, despair.

And she, whose censure thou dost dread,
Whose eye thou wert afraid to seek,   20
See, on her face a glow is spread,
A strong emotion on her cheek.
    ' Ah child,' she cries, ' that strife divine—
Whence was it, for it is not mine ?

' There is no effort on *my* brow—
I do not strive, I do not weep.
I rush with the swift spheres, and glow
In joy, and, when I will, I sleep.—
    Yet that severe, that earnest air,
I saw, I felt it once—but where ?   30

' I knew not yet the gauge of Time,
Nor wore the manacles of Space.
I felt it in some other clime—
I saw it in some other place.
    —'Twas when the heavenly house I trod,
And lay upon the breast of God.'

PROGRESS

[First published 1852.   Reprinted 1867.]

THE Master stood upon the mount, and taught.
He saw a fire in his disciples' eyes ;
' The old law,' they said, ' is wholly come to naught !
    Behold the new world rise !'

' Was it,' the Lord then said, ' with scorn ye saw
The old law observed by Scribes and Pharisees ?
I say unto you, see *ye* keep that law
    More faithfully than these !

' Too hasty heads for ordering worlds, alas !
Think not that I to annul the law have will'd ;   10
No jot, no tittle from the law shall pass,
    Till all hath been fulfill'd.'

              12 hath been] shall be *1852.*

So Christ said eighteen hundred years ago.
And what then shall be said to those to-day
Who cry aloud to lay the old world low
　　To clear the new world's way?

'Religious fervours! ardour misapplied!
Hence, hence,' they cry, 'ye do but keep man blind!
But keep him self-immersed, preoccupied,
　　And lame the active mind.'　　　　　　　　　　20

Ah! from the old world let some one answer give:
'Scorn ye this world, their tears, their inward cares?
I say unto you, see that *your* souls live
　　A deeper life than theirs.

'Say ye: The spirit of man has found new roads,
And we must leave the old faiths, and walk therein?—
Leave then the Cross as ye have left carved gods,
　　But guard the fire within!

'Bright, else, and fast the stream of life may roll,
And no man may the other's hurt behold;　　　　　30
Yet each will have one anguish—his own soul
　　Which perishes of cold.'

Here let that voice make end! then let a strain
From a far lonelier distance, like the wind
Be heard, floating through heaven, and fill again
　　These men's profoundest mind:

'Children of men! the unseen Power, whose eye
For ever doth accompany mankind,
Hath look'd on no religion scornfully
　　That man did ever find.　　　　　　　　　　　40

27, 28　Quench then the altar fires of your old Gods!
　　　　　　Quench not the fire within!　*1852.*

38-40　Ever accompanies the march of man,
　　　　　　Hath without pain seen *no* religion die,
　　　　　　Since first the world began.　*1852.*

Between 40 and 41 1852 reads:—

That man must still to some new worship press
Hath in his eye ever but serv'd to show
The depth of that consuming restlessness
　　Which makes man's greatest woe.

'Which has not taught weak wills how much they can,
Which has not fall'n on the dry heart like rain,
Which has not cried to sunk, self-weary man:
   Thou must be born again!

'Children of men! not that your age excel   45
In pride of life the ages of your sires,
But that *you* think clear, feel deep, bear fruit well,
   The Friend of man desires '

THE FUTURE

[First published 1852.   Reprinted 1853, '54, '57.]

A WANDERER is man from his birth.
   He was born in a ship
On the breast of the River of Time.
Brimming with wonder and joy
He spreads out his arms to the light,
Rivets his gaze on the banks of the stream.

   As what he sees is, so have his thoughts been.
Whether he wakes
Where the snowy mountainous pass
Echoing the screams of the eagles   10
Hems in its gorges the bed
   Of the new-born clear-flowing stream:
Whether he first sees light
Where the river in gleaming rings
   Sluggishly winds through the plain:
Whether in sound of the swallowing sea:—
   As is the world on the banks
So is the mind of the man.

47 *you* think clear, feel deep] you too feel deeply *1852.*

   The Future] *In 1853 and 1854 the following lines were printed as a
motto to the poem :—*
         For Nature hath long kept this inn, the Earth,
         And many a guest hath she therein received—

Vainly does each as he glides
Fable and dream   20
Of the lands which the River of Time
Had left ere he woke on its breast,
Or shall reach when his eyes have been clos'd.
Only the tract where he sails
He wots of : only the thoughts,
Rais'd by the objects he passes, are his.

Who can see the green Earth any more
As she was by the sources of Time?
Who imagines her fields as they lay
In the sunshine, unworn by the plough?   30
Who thinks as they thought,
The tribes who then roam'd on her breast,
  Her vigorous primitive sons?

What girl
Now reads in her bosom as clear
As Rebekah read, when she sate
At eve by the palm-shaded well?
Who guards in her breast
As deep, as pellucid a spring
Of feeling, as tranquil, as sure?   40

What Bard,
At the height of his vision, can deem
Of God, of the world, of the soul,
With a plainness as near,
As flashing as Moses felt,
When he lay in the night by his flock
On the starlit Arabian waste?
Can rise and obey
The beck of the Spirit like him?

This tract which the River of Time   50
Now flows through with us, is the Plain.
Gone is the calm of its earlier shore.
Border'd by cities and hoarse
With a thousand cries is its stream.
And we on its breast, our minds
Are confus'd as the cries which we hear,
  Changing and shot as the sights which we see.

32 roam'd] liv'd *1852, 1853, 1854.*

And we say that repose has fled
For ever the course of the River of Time.
That cities will crowd to its edge 60
In a blacker incessanter line;
That the din will be more on its banks,
Denser the trade on its stream,
Flatter the plain where it flows,
   Fiercer the sun overhead.
That never will those on its breast
See an ennobling sight,
Drink of the feeling of quiet again.

But what was before us we know not,
And we know not what shall succeed. 70

Haply, the River of Time,
As it grows, as the towns on its marge
Fling their wavering lights
On a wider statelier stream—
May acquire, if not the calm
Of its early mountainous shore,
   Yet a solemn peace of its own.

And the width of the waters, the hush
Of the grey expanse where he floats,
Freshening its current and spotted with foam 80
As it draws to the Ocean, may strike
Peace to the soul of the man on its breast:
   As the pale Waste widens around him—
As the banks fade dimmer away—
As the stars come out, and the night-wind
Brings up the stream
Murmurs and scents of the infinite Sea.

POEMS; A NEW EDITION, 1853

SOHRAB AND RUSTUM

AN EPISODE

[First published 1853.   Reprinted 1854, '57.]

AND the first grey of morning fill'd the east,
And the fog rose out of the Oxus stream.
But all the Tartar camp along the stream
Was hush'd, and still the men were plunged in sleep:
Sohrab alone, he slept not: all night long
He had lain wakeful, tossing on his bed;
But when the grey dawn stole into his tent,
He rose, and clad himself, and girt his sword,
And took his horseman's cloak, and left his tent,
And went abroad into the cold wet fog,   10
Through the dim camp to Peran-Wisa's tent.

    Through the black Tartar tents he pass'd, which stood
Clustering like bee-hives on the low flat strand
Of Oxus, where the summer floods o'erflow
When the sun melts the snows in high Pamere:
Through the black tents he pass'd, o'er that low strand,
And to a hillock came, a little back
From the stream's brink, the spot where first a boat,
Crossing the stream in summer, scrapes the land.
The men of former times had crown'd the top   20
With a clay fort: but that was fall'n; and now
The Tartars built there Peran-Wisa's tent,
A dome of laths, and o'er it felts were spread.
And Sohrab came there, and went in, and stood
Upon the thick-pil'd carpets in the tent,
And found the old man sleeping on his bed
Of rugs and felts, and near him lay his arms.
And Peran-Wisa heard him, though the step
Was dull'd; for he slept light, an old man's sleep;
And he rose quickly on one arm, and said:—   30
    'Who art thou? for it is not yet clear dawn.
Speak! is there news, or any night alarm?'

But Sohrab came to the bedside, and said :—
'Thou know'st me, Peran-Wisa : it is I.
The sun is not yet risen, and the foe
Sleep ; but I sleep not ; all night long I lie
Tossing and wakeful, and I come to thee.
For so did King Afrasiab bid me seek
Thy counsel, and to heed thee as thy son,
In Samarcand, before the army march'd ;   40
And I will tell thee what my heart desires.
Thou know'st if, since from Ader-baijan first
I came among the Tartars, and bore arms,
I have still serv'd Afrasiab well, and shown,
At my boy's years, the courage of a man.
This too thou know'st, that, while I still bear on
The conquering Tartar ensigns through the world,
And beat the Persians back on every field,
I seek one man, one man, and one alone—
Rustum, my father ; who, I hop'd, should greet,   50
Should one day greet, upon some well-fought field,
His not unworthy, not inglorious son.
So I long hop'd, but him I never find.
Come then, hear now, and grant me what I ask.
Let the two armies rest to-day : but I
Will challenge forth the bravest Persian lords
To meet me, man to man : if I prevail,
Rustum will surely hear it ; if I fall—
Old man, the dead need no one, claim no kin.
Dim is the rumour of a common fight,   60
Where host meets host, and many names are sunk :
But of a single combat Fame speaks clear.'
He spoke : and Peran-Wisa took the hand
Of the young man in his, and sigh'd, and said :—
'O Sohrab, an unquiet heart is thine !
Canst thou not rest among the Tartar chiefs,
And share the battle's common chance with us
Who love thee, but must press for ever first,
In single fight incurring single risk,
To find a father thou hast never seen ?   70
That were far best, my son, to stay with us
Unmurmuring ; in our tents, while it is war,

And when 'tis truce, then in Afrasiab's towns.
But, if this one desire indeed rules all,
To seek out Rustum—seek him not through fight:
Seek him in peace, and carry to his arms,
O Sohrab, carry an unwounded son!
But far hence seek him, for he is not here.
For now it is not as when I was young,
When Rustum was in front of every fray: 80
But now he keeps apart, and sits at home,
In Seistan, with Zal, his father old.
Whether that his own mighty strength at last
Feels the abhorr'd approaches of old age;
Or in some quarrel with the Persian King.
There go:—Thou wilt not?   Yet my heart forebodes
Danger or death awaits thee on this field.
Fain would I know thee safe and well, though lost
To us: fain therefore send thee hence, in peace
To seek thy father, not seek single fights   90
In vain:—but who can keep the lion's cub
From ravening? and who govern Rustum's son?
Go: I will grant thee what thy heart desires.'

So said he, and dropp'd Sohrab's hand, and left
His bed, and the warm rugs whereon he lay,
And o'er his chilly limbs his woollen coat
He pass'd, and tied his sandals on his feet,
And threw a white cloak round him, and he took
In his right hand a ruler's staff, no sword;
And on his head he plac'd his sheep-skin cap,   100
Black, glossy, curl'd, the fleece of Kara-Kul;
And rais'd the curtain of his tent, and call'd
His herald to his side, and went abroad.

The sun, by this, had risen, and clear'd the fog
From the broad Oxus and the glittering sands:
And from their tents the Tartar horsemen fil'd
Into the open plain; so Haman bade;
Haman, who next to Peran-Wisa rul'd
The host, and still was in his lusty prime.
From their black tents, long files of horse, they stream'd:
As when, some grey November morn, the files,   111
In marching order spread, of long-neck'd cranes

74 But, if this one desire indeed] Or, if indeed this one desire *1853*.

Stream over Casbin, and the southern slopes
Of Elburz, from the Aralian estuaries,
Or some frore Caspian reed-bed, southward bound
For the warm Persian sea-board : so they stream'd
The Tartars of the Oxus, the King's guard,
First, with black sheep-skin caps and with long spears ;
Large men, large steeds ; who from Bokhara come
And Khiva, and ferment the milk of mares.   120
Next the more temperate Toorkmuns of the south,
The Tukas, and the lances of Salore,
And those from Attruck and the Caspian sands ;
Light men, and on light steeds, who only drink
The acrid milk of camels, and their wells.
And then a swarm of wandering horse, who came
From far, and a more doubtful service own'd ;
The Tartars of Ferghana, from the banks
Of the Jaxartes, men with scanty beards
And close-set skull-caps ; and those wilder hordes   130
Who roam o'er Kipchak and the northern waste,
Kalmuks and unkemp'd Kuzzaks, tribes who stray
Nearest the Pole, and wandering Kirghizzes,
Who come on shaggy ponies from Pamere.
These all fil'd out from camp into the plain.
And on the other side the Persians form'd :
First a light cloud of horse, Tartars they seem'd,
The Ilyats of Khorassan : and behind,
The royal troops of Persia, horse and foot,
Marshall'd battalions bright in burnish'd steel.   140
But Peran-Wisa with his herald came
Threading the Tartar squadrons to the front,
And with his staff kept back the foremost ranks.
And when Ferood, who led the Persians, saw
That Peran-Wisa kept the Tartars back,
He took his spear, and to the front he came,
And check'd his ranks, and fix'd them where they stood.
And the old Tartar came upon the sand
Betwixt the silent hosts, and spake, and said :—
     ' Ferood, and ye, Persians and Tartars, hear !   150
Let there be truce between the hosts to-day.
But choose a champion from the Persian lords
To fight our champion Sohrab, man to man.'
     As, in the country, on a morn in June,

When the dew glistens on the pearled ears,
A shiver runs through the deep corn for joy—
So, when they heard what Peran-Wisa said,
A thrill through all the Tartar squadrons ran
Of pride and hope for Sohrab, whom they lov'd.

But as a troop of pedlars, from Cabool,   160
Cross underneath the Indian Caucasus,
That vast sky-neighbouring mountain of milk snow ;
Winding so high, that, as they mount, they pass
Long flocks of travelling birds dead on the snow,
Chok'd by the air, and scarce can they themselves
Slake their parch'd throats with sugar'd mulberries—
In single file they move, and stop their breath,
For fear they should dislodge the o'erhanging snows—
So the pale Persians held their breath with fear.

And to Ferood his brother Chiefs came up   170
To counsel : Gudurz and Zoarrah came,
And Feraburz, who rul'd the Persian host
Second, and was the uncle of the King :
These came and counsell'd ; and then Gudurz said :—
' Ferood, shame bids us take their challenge up,
Yet champion have we none to match this youth.
He has the wild stag's foot, the lion's heart.
But Rustum came last night ; aloof he sits
And sullen, and has pitch'd his tents apart :
Him will I seek, and carry to his ear   180
The Tartar challenge, and this young man's name.
Haply he will forget his wrath, and fight.
Stand forth the while, and take their challenge up.'

So spake he ; and Ferood stood forth and said :—
' Old man, be it agreed as thou hast said.
Let Sohrab arm, and we will find a man.'

He spoke ; and Peran-Wisa turn'd, and strode
Back through the opening squadrons to his tent.
But through the anxious Persians Gudurz ran,
And cross'd the camp which lay behind, and reach'd,
Out on the sands beyond it, Rustum's tents.   191
Of scarlet cloth they were, and glittering gay,
Just pitch'd : the high pavilion in the midst
Was Rustum's, and his men lay camp'd around.
And Gudurz enter'd Rustum's tent, and found
Rustum : his morning meal was done, but still

The table stood beside him, charg'd with food ;
A side of roasted sheep, and cakes of bread,
And dark green melons ; and there Rustum sate
Listless, and held a falcon on his wrist,   200
And play'd with it ; but Gudurz came and stood
Before him ; and he look'd, and saw him stand ;
And with a cry sprang up, and dropp'd the bird,
And greeted Gudurz with both hands, and said :—
    'Welcome ! these eyes could see no better sight.
What news ? but sit down first, and eat and drink.'
    But Gudurz stood in the tent door, and said :—
' Not now : a time will come to eat and drink,
But not to-day : to-day has other needs.
The armies are drawn out, and stand at gaze :   210
For from the Tartars is a challenge brought
To pick a champion from the Persian lords
To fight their champion—and thou know'st his name—
Sohrab men call him, but his birth is hid.
O Rustum, like thy might is this young man's !
He has the wild stag's foot, the lion's heart.
And he is young, and Iran's Chiefs are old,
Or else too weak ; and all eyes turn to thee.
Come down and help us, Rustum, or we lose.'
    He spoke : but Rustum answer'd with a smile : —
' Go to ! if Iran's Chiefs are old, then I   221
Am older : if the young are weak, the King
Errs strangely : for the King, for Kai-Khosroo,
Himself is young, and honours younger men,
And lets the agèd moulder to their graves.
Rustum he loves no more, but loves the young—
The young may rise at Sohrab's vaunts, not I.
For what care I, though all speak Sohrab's fame ?
For would that I myself had such a son,
And not that one slight helpless girl I have,   230
A son so fam'd, so brave, to send to war,
And I to tarry with the snow-hair'd Zal,
My father, whom the robber Afghans vex,
And clip his borders short, and drive his herds,
And he has none to guard his weak old age.
There would I go, and hang my armour up,
And with my great name fence that weak old man,
And spend the goodly treasures I have got,

And rest my age, and hear of Sohrab's fame,
And leave to death the hosts of thankless kings,   240
And with these slaughterous hands draw sword no
    more.'
    He spoke, and smil'd ; and Gudurz made reply :—
' What then, O Rustum, will men say to this,
When Sohrab dares our bravest forth, and seeks
Thee most of all, and thou, whom most he seeks,
Hidest thy face ?   Take heed, lest men should say,
Like some old miser, Rustum hoards his fame,
And shuns to peril it with younger men.'
    And, greatly mov'd, then Rustum made reply :—
' O Gudurz, wherefore dost thou say such words ?
Thou knowest better words than this to say.   251
What is one more, one less, obscure or fam'd,
Valiant or craven, young or old, to me?
Are not they mortal, am not I myself ?
But who for men of naught would do great deeds ?
Come, thou shalt see how Rustum hoards his fame.
But I will fight unknown, and in plain arms ;
Let not men say of Rustum, he was match'd
In single fight with any mortal man.'
    He spoke, and frown'd ; and Gudurz turn'd, and ran
Back quickly through the camp in fear and joy,   261
Fear at his wrath, but joy that Rustum came.
But Rustum strode to his tent door, and call'd
His followers in, and bade them bring his arms,
And clad himself in steel : the arms he chose
Were plain, and on his shield was no device,
Only his helm was rich, inlaid with gold,
And from the fluted spine atop a plume
Of horsehair wav'd, a scarlet horsehair plume.
So arm'd he issued forth ; and Ruksh, his horse,   270
Follow'd him, like a faithful hound, at heel,
Ruksh, whose renown was nois'd through all the earth,
The horse, whom Rustum on a foray once
Did in Bokhara by the river find
A colt beneath its dam, and drove him home,
And rear'd him ; a bright bay, with lofty crest ;
Dight with a saddle-cloth of broider'd green
Crusted with gold, and on the ground were work'd
All beasts of chase, all beasts which hunters know :

So follow'd, Rustum left his tents, and cross'd   280
The camp, and to the Persian host appear'd.
And all the Persians knew him, and with shouts
Hail'd ; but the Tartars knew not who he was.
And dear as the wet diver to the eyes
Of his pale wife who waits and weeps on shore,
By sandy Bahrein, in the Persian Gulf,
Plunging all day in the blue waves, at night,
Having made up his tale of precious pearls,
Rejoins her in their hut upon the sands—
So dear to the pale Persians Rustum came.   290
    And Rustum to the Persian front advanc'd,
And Sohrab arm'd in Haman's tent, and came.
And as afield the reapers cut a swathe
Down through the middle of a rich man's corn,
And on each side are squares of standing corn,
And in the midst a stubble, short and bare ;
So on each side were squares of men, with spears
Bristling, and in the midst, the open sand.
And Rustum came upon the sand, and cast
His eyes towards the Tartar tents, and saw   300
Sohrab come forth, and ey'd him as he came.
    As some rich woman, on a winter's morn,
Eyes through her silken curtains the poor drudge
Who with numb blacken'd fingers makes her fire—
At cock-crow, on a starlit winter's morn,
When the frost flowers the whiten'd window panes—
And wonders how she lives, and what the thoughts
Of that poor drudge may be ; so Rustum ey'd
The unknown adventurous Youth, who from afar
Came seeking Rustum, and defying forth   310
All the most valiant chiefs : long he perus'd
His spirited air, and wonder'd who he was.
For very young he seem'd, tenderly rear'd ;
Like some young cypress, tall, and dark, and straight,
Which in a queen's secluded garden throws
Its slight dark shadow on the moonlit turf,
By midnight, to a bubbling fountain's sound—
So slender Sohrab seem'd, so softly rear'd.
And a deep pity enter'd Rustum's soul
As he beheld him coming ; and he stood,   320
And beckon'd to him with his hand, and said :—

'O thou young man, the air of Heaven is soft,
And warm, and pleasant ; but the grave is cold.
Heaven's air is better than the cold dead grave.
Behold me : I am vast, and clad in iron,
And tried ; and I have stood on many a field
Of blood, and I have fought with many a foe :
Never was that field lost, or that foe sav'd.
O Sohrab, wherefore wilt thou rush on death ?
Be govern'd : quit the Tartar host, and come   330
To Iran, and be as my son to me,
And fight beneath my banner till I die.
There are no youths in Iran brave as thou.'
    So he spake, mildly : Sohrab heard his voice,
The mighty voice of Rustum ; and he saw
His giant figure planted on the sand,
Sole, like some single tower, which a chief
Has builded on the waste in former years
Against the robbers ; and he saw that head,
Streak'd with its first grey hairs : hope fill'd his soul ;
And he ran forwards and embrac'd his knees,   341
And clasp'd his hand within his own and said :—
    ' Oh, by thy father's head ! by thine own soul !
Art thou not Rustum ?   Speak ! art thou not he ? '
    But Rustum ey'd askance the kneeling youth,
And turn'd away, and spoke to his own soul :—
    ' Ah me, I muse what this young fox may mean.
False, wily, boastful, are these Tartar boys.
For if I now confess this thing he asks,
And hide it not, but say—*Rustum is here*—   350
He will not yield indeed, nor quit our foes,
But he will find some pretext not to fight,
And praise my fame, and proffer courteous gifts,
A belt or sword perhaps, and go his way.
And on a feast-tide, in Afrasiab's hall,
In Samarcand, he will arise and cry—
"I challeng'd once, when the two armies camp'd
Beside the Oxus, all the Persian lords
To cope with me in single fight ; but they
Shrank ; only Rustum dar'd : then he and I   360
Chang'd gifts, and went on equal terms away."

355 feast-tide] feast day *1853, 1854.*

So will he speak, perhaps, while men applaud.
Then were the chiefs of Iran sham'd through me.'
  And then he turn'd, and sternly spake aloud :—
'Rise! wherefore dost thou vainly question thus
Of Rustum? I am here, whom thou hast call'd
By challenge forth : make good thy vaunt, or yield.
Is it with Rustum only thou wouldst fight?
Rash boy, men look on Rustum's face and flee.
For well I know, that did great Rustum stand   370
Before thy face this day, and were reveal'd,
There would be then no talk of fighting more.
But being what I am, I tell thee this ;
Do thou record it in thine inmost soul :
Either thou shalt renounce thy vaunt, and yield ;
Or else thy bones shall strew this sand, till winds
Bleach them, or Oxus with his summer floods,
Oxus in summer wash them all away.'
  He spoke : and Sohrab answer'd, on his feet :—
'Art thou so fierce? Thou wilt not fright me so.
I am no girl, to be made pale by words.   381
Yet this thou hast said well, did Rustum stand
Here on this field, there were no fighting then.
But Rustum is far hence, and we stand here.
Begin : thou art more vast, more dread than I,
And thou art prov'd, I know, and I am young—
But yet Success sways with the breath of Heaven.
And though thou thinkest that thou knowest sure
Thy victory, yet thou canst not surely know.
For we are all, like swimmers in the sea,   390
Pois'd on the top of a huge wave of Fate,
Which hangs uncertain to which side to fall.
And whether it will heave us up to land,
Or whether it will roll us out to sea,
Back out to sea, to the deep waves of death,
We know not, and no search will make us know :
Only the event will teach us in its hour.'
  He spoke ; and Rustum answer'd not, but hurl'd
His spear : down from the shoulder, down it came,
As on some partridge in the corn a hawk   400
That long has tower'd in the airy clouds
Drops like a plummet : Sohrab saw it come,
And sprang aside, quick as a flash : the spear

Hiss'd, and went quivering down into the sand,
Which it sent flying wide:—then Sohrab threw
In turn, and full struck Rustum's shield : sharp rang,
The iron plates rang sharp, but turn'd the spear.
And Rustum seiz'd his club, which none but he
Could wield : an unlopp'd trunk it was, and huge,
Still rough ; like those which men in treeless plains
To build them boats fish from the flooded rivers,   411
Hyphasis or Hydaspes, when, high up
By their dark springs, the wind in winter-time
Has made in Himalayan forests wrack,
And strewn the channels with torn boughs ; so huge
The club which Rustum lifted now, and struck
One stroke ; but again Sohrab sprang aside
Lithe as the glancing snake, and the club came
Thundering to earth, and leapt from Rustum's hand.
And Rustum follow'd his own blow, and fell   420
To his knees, and with his fingers clutch'd the sand :
And now might Sohrab have unsheath'd his sword,
And pierc'd the mighty Rustum while he lay
Dizzy, and on his knees, and chok'd with sand :
But he look'd on, and smil'd, nor bar'd his sword,
But courteously drew back, and spoke, and said :—
　'Thou strik'st too hard: that club of thine will float
Upon the summer floods, and not my bones.
But rise, and be not wroth ; not wroth am I :
No, when I see thee, wrath forsakes my soul.   430
Thou say'st, thou art not Rustum : be it so.
Who art thou then, that canst so touch my soul ?
Boy as I am, I have seen battles too ;
Have waded foremost in their bloody waves,
And heard their hollow roar of dying men ;
But never was my heart thus touch'd before.
Are they from Heaven, these softenings of the heart ?
O thou old warrior, let us yield to Heaven !
Come, plant we here in earth our angry spears,
And make a truce, and sit upon this sand,   440
And pledge each other in red wine, like friends,
And thou shalt talk to me of Rustum's deeds.
There are enough foes in the Persian host
Whom I may meet, and strike, and feel no pang ;
Champions enough Afrasiab has, whom thou

Mayst fight ; fight them, when they confront thy spear.
But oh, let there be peace 'twixt thee and me !'
　　He ceas'd : but while he spake, Rustum had risen,
And stood erect, trembling with rage : his club
He left to lie, but had regain'd his spear,　　　450
Whose fiery point now in his mail'd right-hand
Blaz'd bright and baleful, like that autumn Star,
The baleful sign of fevers : dust had soil'd
His stately crest, and dimm'd his glittering arms.
His breast heav'd ; his lips foam'd ; and twice his voice
Was chok'd with rage: at last these words broke way :—
　　'Girl ! nimble with thy feet, not with thy hands !
Curl'd minion, dancer, coiner of sweet words !
Fight ; let me hear thy hateful voice no more !
Thou art not in Afrasiab's gardens now　　　460
With Tartar girls, with whom thou art wont to dance ;
But on the Oxus sands, and in the dance
Of battle, and with me, who make no play
Of war : I fight it out, and hand to hand.
Speak not to me of truce, and pledge, and wine !
Remember all thy valour : try thy feints
And cunning : all the pity I had is gone :
Because thou hast sham'd me before both the hosts
With thy light skipping tricks, and thy girl's wiles.'
　　He spoke ; and Sohrab kindled at his taunts,　　470
And he too drew his sword : at once they rush'd
Together, as two eagles on one prey
Come rushing down together from the clouds,
One from the east, one from the west : their shields
Dash'd with a clang together, and a din
Rose, such as that the sinewy woodcutters
Make often in the forest's heart at morn,
Of hewing axes, crashing trees : such blows
Rustum and Sohrab on each other hail'd.
And you would say that sun and stars took part　　480
In that unnatural conflict ; for a cloud
Grew suddenly in Heaven, and dark'd the sun
Over the fighters' heads ; and a wind rose
Under their feet, and moaning swept the plain,
And in a sandy whirlwind wrapp'd the pair.
In gloom they twain were wrapp'd, and they alone ;
For both the on-looking hosts on either hand

Stood in broad daylight, and the sky was pure,
And the sun sparkled on the Oxus stream.   489
But in the gloom they fought, with bloodshot eyes
And labouring breath ; first Rustum struck the shield
Which Sohrab held stiff out : the steel-spik'd spear
Rent the tough plates, but fail'd to reach the skin,
And Rustum pluck'd it back with angry groan.
Then Sohrab with his sword smote Rustum's helm,
Nor clove its steel quite through ; but all the crest
He shore away, and that proud horsehair plume
Never till now defil'd, sunk to the dust ;
And Rustum bow'd his head ; but then the gloom
Grew blacker : thunder rumbled in the air,   500
And lightnings rent the cloud ; and Ruksh, the horse,
Who stood at hand, utter'd a dreadful cry :
No horse's cry was that, most like the roar
Of some pain'd desert lion, who all day
Has trail'd the hunter's javelin in his side,
And comes at night to die upon the sand :—
The two hosts heard that cry, and quak'd for fear,
And Oxus curdled as it cross'd his stream.
But Sohrab heard, and quail'd not, but rush'd on,
And struck again ; and again Rustum bow'd   510
His head ; but this time all the blade, like glass,
Sprang in a thousand shivers on the helm,
And in his hand the hilt remain'd alone.
Then Rustum rais'd his head : his dreadful eyes
Glar'd, and he shook on high his menacing spear,
And shouted, *Rustum !* Sohrab heard that shout,
And shrank amaz'd : back he recoil'd one step,
And scann'd with blinking eyes the advancing Form :
And then he stood bewilder'd ; and he dropp'd
His covering shield, and the spear pierc'd his side. 520
He reel'd, and staggering back, sunk to the ground.
And then the gloom dispers'd, and the wind fell,
And the bright sun broke forth, and melted all
The cloud ; and the two armies saw the pair ;
Saw Rustum standing, safe upon his feet,
And Sohrab, wounded, on the bloody sand.
    Then, with a bitter smile, Rustum began :—
'Sohrab, thou thoughtest in thy mind to kill
A Persian lord this day, and strip his corpse,

And bear thy trophies to Afrasiab's tent.   530
Or else that the great Rustum would come down
Himself to fight, and that thy wiles would move
His heart to take a gift, and let thee go.
And then that all the Tartar host would praise
Thy courage or thy craft, and spread thy fame,
To glad thy father in his weak old age.
Fool! thou art slain, and by an unknown man!
Dearer to the red jackals shalt thou be,
Than to thy friends, and to thy father old.'
    And, with a fearless mien, Sohrab replied :—   540
'Unknown thou art; yet thy fierce vaunt is vain.
Thou dost not slay me, proud and boastful man!
No! Rustum slays me, and this filial heart.
For were I match'd with ten such men as thou,
And I were he who till to-day I was,
They should be lying here, I standing there.
But that belovèd name unnerv'd my arm—
That name, and something, I confess, in thee,
Which troubles all my heart, and made my shield
Fall; and thy spear transfix'd an unarm'd foe.   550
And now thou boastest, and insult'st my fate.
But hear thou this, fierce Man, tremble to hear!
The mighty Rustum shall avenge my death!
My father, whom I seek through all the world,
He shall avenge my death, and punish thee!'
    As when some hunter in the spring hath found
A breeding eagle sitting on her nest,
Upon the craggy isle of a hill lake,
And pierc'd her with an arrow as she rose,
And follow'd her to find her where she fell   560
Far off;—anon her mate comes winging back
From hunting, and a great way off descries
His huddling young left sole; at that, he checks
His pinion, and with short uneasy sweeps
Circles above his eyry, with loud screams
Chiding his mate back to her nest; but she
Lies dying, with the arrow in her side,
In some far stony gorge out of his ken,
A heap of fluttering feathers: never more
Shall the lake glass her, flying over it;   570
Never the black and dripping precipices

Echo her stormy scream as she sails by:—
As that poor bird flies home, nor knows his loss—
So Rustum knew not his own loss, but stood
Over his dying son, and knew him not.
    But with a cold, incredulous voice, he said:—
'What prate is this of fathers and revenge?
The mighty Rustum never had a son.'
    And, with a failing voice, Sohrab replied:—
'Ah yes, he had! and that lost son am I.   580
Surely the news will one day reach his ear,
Reach Rustum, where he sits, and tarries long,
Somewhere, I know not where, but far from here;
And pierce him like a stab, and make him leap
To arms, and cry for vengeance upon thee.
Fierce Man, bethink thee, for an only son!
What will that grief, what will that vengeance be!
Oh, could I live, till I that grief had seen!
Yet him I pity not so much, but her,
My mother, who in Ader-baijan dwells   590
With that old King, her father, who grows grey
With age, and rules over the valiant Koords.
Her most I pity, who no more will see
Sohrab returning from the Tartar camp,
With spoils and honour, when the war is done.
But a dark rumour will be bruited up,
From tribe to tribe, until it reach her ear;
And then will that defenceless woman learn
That Sohrab will rejoice her sight no more;
But that in battle with a nameless foe,   600
By the far-distant Oxus, he is slain.'
    He spoke; and as he ceas'd he wept aloud,
Thinking of her he left, and his own death.
He spoke; but Rustum listen'd, plung'd in thought.
Nor did he yet believe it was his son
Who spoke, although he call'd back names he knew;
For he had had sure tidings that the babe,
Which was in Ader-baijan born to him,
Had been a puny girl, no boy at all:
So that sad mother sent him word, for fear   610
Rustum should take the boy, to train in arms;
And so he deem'd that either Sohrab took,
By a false boast, the style of Rustum's son;

Or that men gave it him, to swell his fame.
So deem'd he ; yet he listen'd, plung'd in thought ;
And his soul set to grief, as the vast tide
Of the bright rocking Ocean sets to shore
At the full moon : tears gather'd in his eyes ;
For he remember'd his own early youth,
And all its bounding rapture ; as, at dawn,   620
The Shepherd from his mountain lodge descries
A far bright City, smitten by the sun,
Through many rolling clouds ;—so Rustum saw
His youth ; saw Sohrab's mother, in her bloom ;
And that old King, her father, who lov'd well
His wandering guest, and gave him his fair child
With joy ; and all the pleasant life they led,
They three, in that long-distant summer-time—
The castle, and the dewy woods, and hunt
And hound, and morn on those delightful hills   630
In Ader-baijan.   And he saw that Youth,
Of age and looks to be his own dear son,
Piteous and lovely, lying on the sand,
Like some rich hyacinth, which by the scythe
Of an unskilful gardener has been cut,
Mowing the garden grass-plots near its bed,
And lies, a fragrant tower of purple bloom,
On the mown, dying grass ;—so Sohrab lay,
Lovely in death, upon the common sand.
And Rustum gaz'd on him with grief, and said :—   640
    'O Sohrab, thou indeed art such a son
Whom Rustum, wert thou his, might well have lov'd !
Yet here thou errest, Sohrab, or else men
Have told thee false ;—thou art not Rustum's son.
For Rustum had no son : one child he had—
But one—a girl : who with her mother now
Plies some light female task, nor dreams of us—
Of us she dreams not, nor of wounds, nor war.'
    But Sohrab answer'd him in wrath ; for now
The anguish of the deep-fix'd spear grew fierce,   650
And he desired to draw forth the steel,
And let the blood flow free, and so to die ;
But first he would convince his stubborn foe—
And, rising sternly on one arm, he said :—
    'Man, who art thou who dost deny my words ?

Truth sits upon the lips of dying men,
And Falsehood, while I liv'd, was far from mine.
I tell thee, prick'd upon this arm I bear
That seal which Rustum to my mother gave,
That she might prick it on the babe she bore.'   660
　　He spoke: and all the blood left Rustum's cheeks;
And his knees totter'd, and he smote his hand
Against his breast, his heavy mailed hand,
That the hard iron corslet clank'd aloud:
And to his heart he press'd the other hand,
And in a hollow voice he spake, and said:—
　　'Sohrab, that were a proof which could not lie.
If thou shew this, then art thou Rustum's son.'
　　Then, with weak hasty fingers, Sohrab loos'd
His belt, and near the shoulder bar'd his arm,   670
And shew'd a sign in faint vermilion points
Prick'd: as a cunning workman, in Pekin,
Pricks with vermilion some clear porcelain vase,
An emperor's gift—at early morn he paints,
And all day long, and, when night comes, the lamp
Lights up his studious forehead and thin hands:—
So delicately prick'd the sign appear'd
On Sohrab's arm, the sign of Rustum's seal.
It was that Griffin, which of old rear'd Zal,
Rustum's great father, whom they left to die,   680
A helpless babe, among the mountain rocks.
Him that kind Creature found, and rear'd, and lov'd—
Then Rustum took it for his glorious sign.
And Sohrab bar'd that figure on his arm,
And himself scann'd it long with mournful eyes,
And then he touch'd it with his hand and said:—
　　'How say'st thou? Is that sign the proper sign
Of Rustum's son, or of some other man's?'
　　He spoke: but Rustum gaz'd, and gaz'd, and stood
Speechless; and then he utter'd one sharp cry—   690
O Boy—thy Father!—and his voice chok'd there.
And then a dark cloud pass'd before his eyes,
And his head swam, and he sunk down to earth.
But Sohrab crawl'd to where he lay, and cast
His arms about his neck, and kiss'd his lips,
And with fond faltering fingers strok'd his cheeks,
Trying to call him back to life: and life

Came back to Rustum, and he op'd his eyes,
And they stood wide with horror; and he seiz'd
In both his hands the dust which lay around,   700
And threw it on his head, and smirch'd his hair,
His hair, and face, and beard, and glittering arms:
And strong convulsive groanings shook his breast,
And his sobs chok'd him; and he clutch'd his sword,
To draw it, and for ever let life out.
But Sohrab saw his thought, and held his hands,
And with a soothing voice he spoke, and said:—
    'Father, forbear: for I but meet to-day
The doom that at my birth was written down
In Heaven, and thou art Heaven's unconscious hand.
Surely my heart cried out that it was thou,   711
When first I saw thee; and thy heart spoke too,
I know it: but Fate trod those promptings down
Under its iron heel; Fate, Fate engag'd
The strife, and hurl'd me on my father's spear.
But let us speak no more of this: I find
My father; let me feel that I have found.
Come, sit beside me on this sand, and take
My head betwixt thy hands, and kiss my cheeks,
And wash them with thy tears, and say, *My Son!*   720
Quick! quick! for number'd are my sands of life,
And swift; for like the lightning to this field
I came, and like the wind I go away—
Sudden, and swift, and like a passing wind.
But it was writ in Heaven that this should be.'
    So said he: and his voice releas'd the heart
Of Rustum, and his tears broke forth; he cast
His arms round his son's neck, and wept aloud,
And kiss'd him. And awe fell on both the hosts
When they saw Rustum's grief: and Ruksh, the horse,
With his head bowing to the ground, and mane   731
Sweeping the dust, came near, and in mute woe
First to the one then to the other mov'd
His head, as if inquiring what their grief
Might mean; and from his dark, compassionate eyes,
The big warm tears roll'd down, and cak'd the sand.
But Rustum chid him with stern voice, and said:—
    'Ruksh, now thou grievest; but, O Ruksh, thy feet
Should then have rotted on thy nimble joints,

When first they bore thy Master to this field.'   740
　　But Sohrab look'd upon the horse and said:—
'Is this then Ruksh?　How often, in past days,
My mother told me of thee, thou brave Steed!
My terrible father's terrible horse; and said,
That I should one day find thy lord and thee.
Come, let me lay my hand upon thy mane.
O Ruksh, thou art more fortunate than I;
For thou hast gone where I shall never go,
And snuff'd the breezes of my father's home.
And thou hast trod the sands of Seistan,   750
And seen the River of Helmund, and the Lake
Of Zirrah; and the aged Zal himself
Has often strok'd thy neck, and given thee food,
Corn in a golden platter soak'd with wine,
And said—"O Ruksh! bear Rustum well!"—but I
Have never known my grandsire's furrow'd face,
Nor seen his lofty house in Seistan,
Nor slak'd my thirst at the clear Helmund stream:
But lodg'd among my father's foes, and seen
Afrasiab's cities only, Samarcand,   760
Bokhara, and lone Khiva in the waste,
And the black Toorkmun tents; and only drunk
The desert rivers, Moorghab and Tejend,
Kohik, and where the Kalmuks feed their sheep,
The northern Sir; and this great Oxus stream—
The yellow Oxus, by whose brink I die.'
　　And, with a heavy groan, Rustum replied:—
'Oh that its waves were flowing over me!
Oh that I saw its grains of yellow silt
Roll tumbling in the current o'er my head!'   770
　　And, with a grave mild voice, Sohrab replied:—
'Desire not that, my father; thou must live.
For some are born to do great deeds, and live,
As some are born to be obscur'd, and die.
Do thou the deeds I die too young to do,
And reap a second glory in thine age.
Thou art my father, and thy gain is mine.
But come: thou seest this great host of men
Which follow me; I pray thee, slay not these:
Let me entreat for them: what have they done?   780
They follow'd me, my hope, my fame, my star.

Let them all cross the Oxus back in peace.
But me thou must bear hence, not send with them,
But carry me with thee to Seistan,
And place me on a bed, and mourn for me,
Thou, and the snow-hair'd Zal, and all thy friends.
And thou must lay me in that lovely earth,
And heap a stately mound above my bones,
And plant a far-seen pillar over all :
That so the passing horseman on the waste   790
May see my tomb a great way off, and say—
Sohrab, the mighty Rustum's son, lies there,
Whom his great father did in ignorance kill—
And I be not forgotten in my grave.'
    And, with a mournful voice, Rustum replied :—
' Fear not ; as thou hast said, Sohrab, my son,
So shall it be : for I will burn my tents,
And quit the host, and bear thee hence with me,
And carry thee away to Seistan,
And place thee on a bed, and mourn for thee,   800
With the snow-headed Zal, and all my friends.
And I will lay thee in that lovely earth,
And heap a stately mound above thy bones,
And plant a far-seen pillar over all :
And men shall not forget thee in thy grave.
And I will spare thy host : yea, let them go :
Let them all cross the Oxus back in peace.
What should I do with slaying any more ?
For would that all whom I have ever slain
Might be once more alive ; my bitterest foes,   810
And they who were call'd champions in their time,
And through whose death I won that fame I have ;
And I were nothing but a common man,
A poor, mean soldier, and without renown,
So thou mightest live too, my Son, my Son !
Or rather would that I, even I myself,
Might now be lying on this bloody sand,
Near death, and by an ignorant stroke of thine,
Not thou of mine ; and I might die, not thou ;
And I, not thou, be borne to Seistan ;   820
And Zal might weep above my grave, not thine ;
And say—*O son, I weep thee not too sore,*
For willingly, I know, thou met'st thine end.—

But now in blood and battles was my youth,
And full of blood and battles is my age ;
And I shall never end this life of blood.'
　　Then, at the point of death, Sohrab replied :—
' A life of blood indeed, thou dreadful Man !
But thou shalt yet have peace ; only not now :
Not yet : but thou shalt have it on that day,　　　　830
When thou shalt sail in a high-masted Ship,
Thou and the other peers of Kai-Khosroo,
Returning home over the salt blue sea,
From laying thy dear Master in his grave.'
　　And Rustum gaz'd on Sohrab's face, and said :—
' Soon be that day, my Son, and deep that sea !
Till then, if Fate so wills, let me endure.'
　　He spoke ; and Sohrab smil'd on him, and took
The spear, and drew it from his side, and eas'd
His wound's imperious anguish : but the blood　　840
Came welling from the open gash, and life
Flow'd with the stream : all down his cold white side
The crimson torrent ran, dim now, and soil'd,
Like the soil'd tissue of white violets
Left, freshly gather'd, on their native bank,
By romping children, whom their nurses call
From the hot fields at noon : his head droop'd low,
His limbs grew slack ; motionless, white, he lay—
White, with eyes closed ; only when heavy gasps,
Deep, heavy gasps, quivering through all his frame,
Convuls'd him back to life, he open'd them,　　　　851
And fix'd them feebly on his father's face :
Till now all strength was ebb'd, and from his limbs
Unwillingly the spirit fled away,
Regretting the warm mansion which it left,
And youth and bloom, and this delightful world.
　　So, on the bloody sand, Sohrab lay dead.
And the great Rustum drew his horseman's cloak
Down o'er his face, and sate by his dead son.
As those black granite pillars, once high-rear'd　　860
By Jemshid in Persepolis, to bear
His house, now, mid their broken flights of steps,
Lie prone, enormous, down the mountain side—

　　　　　　843 ran] pour'd *1853*.

So in the sand lay Rustum by his son.
 And night came down over the solemn waste,
And the two gazing hosts, and that sole pair,
And darken'd all ; and a cold fog, with night,
Crept from the Oxus.   Soon a hum arose,
As of a great assembly loos'd, and fires
Began to twinkle through the fog : for now   870
Both armies mov'd to camp, and took their meal :
The Persians took it on the open sands
Southward ; the Tartars by the river marge :
And Rustum and his son were left alone.
 But the majestic River floated on,
Out of the mist and hum of that low land,
Into the frosty starlight, and there mov'd,
Rejoicing, through the hush'd Chorasmian waste,
Under the solitary moon : he flow'd
Right for the Polar Star, past Orgunjè,   880
Brimming, and bright, and large : then sands begin
To hem his watery march, and dam his streams,
And split his currents ; that for many a league
The shorn and parcell'd Oxus strains along
Through beds of sand and matted rushy isles—
Oxus, forgetting the bright speed he had
In his high mountain cradle in Pamere,
A foil'd circuitous wanderer :—till at last
The long'd-for dash of waves is heard, and wide
His luminous home of waters opens, bright   890
And tranquil, from whose floor the new-bath'd stars
Emerge, and shine upon the Aral Sea.

PHILOMELA

[First published 1853.   Reprinted 1854, '57.]

HARK ! ah, the Nightingale !
The tawny-throated !
Hark ! from that moonlit cedar what a burst !
What triumph ! hark—what pain !

O Wanderer from a Grecian shore,
Still, after many years, in distant lands,

Still nourishing in thy bewilder'd brain
That wild, unquench'd, deep-sunken, old-world pain—
   Say, will it never heal?
And can this fragrant lawn   10
With its cool trees, and night,
And the sweet, tranquil Thames,
And moonshine, and the dew,
To thy rack'd heart and brain
   Afford no balm?

   Dost thou to-night behold
Here, through the moonlight on this English grass,
The unfriendly palace in the Thracian wild?
   Dost thou again peruse
With hot cheeks and sear'd eyes   20
The too clear web, and thy dumb Sister's shame?
   Dost thou once more assay
Thy flight, and feel come over thee,
Poor Fugitive, the feathery change
Once more, and once more seem to make resound
With love and hate, triumph and agony,
Lone Daulis, and the high Cephissian vale?
   Listen, Eugenia—
How thick the bursts come crowding through the
   leaves!
Again—thou hearest!   30
Eternal Passion!
Eternal Pain!

THEKLA'S ANSWER

(From Schiller.)

[First published 1853. Not reprinted by the author.]

WHERE I am, thou ask'st, and where I wended
   When my fleeting shadow pass'd from thee?—
Am I not concluded now, and ended?
   Have not life and love been granted me?

Ask, where now those nightingales are singing,
   Who, of late, on the soft nights of May,
Set thine ears with soul-fraught music ringing—
   Only, while their love liv'd, lasted they.

Find I him, from whom I had to sever?—
   Doubt it not, we met, and we are one.   10
There, where what is join'd, is join'd for ever,
   There, where tears are never more to run.

There thou too shalt live with us together,
   When thou too hast borne the love we bore:
There, from sin deliver'd, dwells my Father,
   Track'd by Murder's bloody sword no more.

There he feels, it was no dream deceiving
   Lur'd him starwards to uplift his eye:
God doth match his gifts to man's believing;
   Believe, and thou shalt find the Holy nigh.   20

All thou augurest here of lovely seeming
   There shall find fulfilment in its day:
Dare, O Friend, be wandering, dare be dreaming;
   Lofty thought lies oft in childish play.

THE CHURCH OF BROU

[First published 1853.   Reprinted 1854, '57.]

I

THE CASTLE

Down the Savoy valleys sounding,
   Echoing round this castle old,
'Mid the distant mountain chalets
   Hark! what bell for church is toll'd?

In the bright October morning
   Savoy's Duke had left his bride.
From the Castle, past the drawbridge,
   Flow'd the hunters' merry tide.

Steeds are neighing, gallants glittering.
   Gay, her smiling lord to greet,   10
From her mullion'd chamber casement
   Smiles the Duchess Marguerite.

From Vienna by the Danube
   Here she came, a bride, in spring.
Now the autumn crisps the forest;
   Hunters gather, bugles ring.

Hounds are pulling, prickers swearing,
   Horses fret, and boar-spears glance :
Off !—They sweep the marshy forests,
   Westward, on the side of France.   20

Hark ! the game's on foot ; they scatter :—
   Down the forest ridings lone,
Furious, single horsemen gallop.
   Hark ! a shout—a crash—a groan !

Pale and breathless, came the hunters.
   On the turf dead lies the boar.
God ! the Duke lies stretch'd beside him—
   Senseless, weltering in his gore.

In the dull October evening,
   Down the leaf-strewn forest road,   30
To the Castle, past the drawbridge,
   Came the hunters with their load.

In the hall, with sconces blazing,
   Ladies waiting round her seat,
Cloth'd in smiles, beneath the daïs,
   Sate the Duchess Marguerite.

Hark ! below the gates unbarring !
   Tramp of men and quick commands !
'—'Tis my lord come back from hunting.'—
   And the Duchess claps her hands.   40

Slow and tired, came the hunters ;
   Stopp'd in darkness in the court.
'—Ho, this way, ye laggard hunters !
   To the hall ! What sport, what sport ?'—

Slow they enter'd with their Master ;
   In the hall they laid him down.
On his coat were leaves and blood-stains :
   On his brow an angry frown.

Dead her princely youthful husband
   Lay before his youthful wife ;   50
Bloody 'neath the flaring sconces :
   And the sight froze all her life.

In Vienna by the Danube
    Kings hold revel, gallants meet.
Gay of old amid the gayest
    Was the Duchess Marguerite.

In Vienna by the Danube
    Feast and dance her youth beguil'd.
Till that hour she never sorrow'd ;
    But from then she never smil'd.   60

'Mid the Savoy mountain valleys
    Far from town or haunt of man,
Stands a lonely Church, unfinish'd,
    Which the Duchess Maud began :

Old, that Duchess stern began it ;
    In grey age, with palsied hands.
But she died while it was building,
    And the Church unfinish'd stands ;

Stands as erst the builders left it,
    When she sunk into her grave.   70
Mountain greensward paves the chancel ;
    Harebells flower in the nave.

' In my Castle all is sorrow,'—
    Said the Duchess Marguerite then.
' Guide me, vassals, to the mountains !
    We will build the Church again.'—

Sandall'd palmers, faring homeward,
    Austrian knights from Syria came.
' Austrian wanderers bring, O warders,
    Homage to your Austrian dame.'—   80

From the gate the warders answer'd ;
    ' Gone, O knights, is she you knew.
Dead our Duke, and gone his Duchess.
    Seek her at the Church of Brou.'—

Austrian knights and march-worn palmers
    Climb the winding mountain way.
Reach the valley, where the Fabric
    Rises higher day by day.

67 while] as *1853, 1854.*

Stones are sawing, hammers ringing;
  On the work the bright sun shines :   90
In the Savoy mountain meadows,
  By the stream, below the pines.

On her palfrey white the Duchess
  Sate and watch'd her working train ;
Flemish carvers, Lombard gilders,
  German masons, smiths from Spain.

Clad in black, on her white palfrey ;
  Her old architect beside—
There they found her in the mountains,
  Morn and noon and eventide.   100

There she sate, and watch'd the builders,
  Till the Church was roof'd and done.
Last of all, the builders rear'd her
  In the nave a tomb of stone.

On the tomb two Forms they sculptur'd,
  Lifelike in the marble pale.
One, the Duke in helm and armour ;
  One, the Duchess in her veil.

Round the tomb the carv'd stone fretwork
  Was at Easter tide put on.   110
Then the Duchess clos'd her labours ;
  And she died at the St. John.

II

THE CHURCH

Upon the glistening leaden roof
Of the new Pile, the sunlight shines.
  The stream goes leaping by.
The hills are cloth'd with pines sun-proof.
Mid bright green fields, below the pines,
  Stands the Church on high.
What Church is this, from men aloof?
'Tis the Church of Brou.

At sunrise, from their dewy lair
Crossing the stream, the kine are seen   10
    Round the wall to stray ;
The churchyard wall that clips the square
Of shaven hill-sward trim and green
    Where last year they lay.
But all things now are order'd fair
Round the Church of Brou.

On Sundays, at the matin chime,
The Alpine peasants, two and three,
    Climb up here to pray.
Burghers and dames, at summer's prime,   20
Ride out to church from Chambery,
    Dight with mantles gay.
But else it is a lonely time
Round the Church of Brou.

On Sundays, too, a priest doth come
From the wall'd town beyond the pass,
    Down the mountain way.
And then you hear the organ's hum,
You hear the white-rob'd priest say mass,
    And the people pray.   30
But else the woods and fields are dumb
Round the Church of Brou.

And after church, when mass is done,
The people to the nave repair
    Round the Tomb to stray.
And marvel at the Forms of stone,
And praise the chisell'd broideries rare.
    Then they drop away.
The Princely Pair are left alone
In the Church of Brou.   40

III

THE TOMB

So rest, for ever rest, O Princely Pair !
In your high Church, 'mid the still mountain air,
Where horn, and hound, and vassals, never come.
Only the blessed Saints are smiling dumb
From the rich painted windows of the nave
On aisle, and transept, and your marble grave :

Where thou, young Prince, shalt never more arise
From the fring'd mattress where thy Duchess lies,
On autumn mornings, when the bugle sounds,
And ride across the drawbridge with thy hounds   10
To hunt the boar in the crisp woods till eve.
And thou, O Princess, shalt no more receive,
Thou and thy ladies, in the hall of state,
The jaded hunters with their bloody freight,
Coming benighted to the castle gate.

So sleep, for ever sleep, O Marble Pair!
Or, if ye wake, let it be then, when fair
On the carv'd Western Front a flood of light
Streams from the setting sun, and colours bright
Prophets, transfigur'd Saints, and Martyrs brave,   20
In the vast western window of the nave;
And on the pavement round the Tomb there glints
A chequer-work of glowing sapphire tints,
And amethyst, and ruby;—then unclose
Your eyelids on the stone where ye repose,
And from your broider'd pillows lift your heads,
And rise upon your cold white marble beds;
And looking down on the warm rosy tints
That chequer, at your feet, the illumin'd flints,
Say—'*What is this? we are in bliss—forgiven—*   30
Behold the pavement of the courts of Heaven!'—
Or let it be on autumn nights, when rain
Doth rustlingly above your heads complain
On the smooth leaden roof, and on the walls
Shedding her pensive light at intervals
The Moon through the clere-story windows shines,
And the wind wails among the mountain pines.
Then, gazing up through the dim pillars high,
The foliag'd marble forest where ye lie,
'*Hush*'—ye will say—'*it is eternity.*   40
This is the glimmering verge of Heaven, and these
The columns of the Heavenly Palaces.'—
And in the sweeping of the wind your ear
The passage of the Angels' wings will hear,
And on the lichen-crusted leads above
The rustle of the eternal rain of Love.

37 wails among] washes in *1853*.

THE NECKAN

[First published 1853.   Reprinted 1854, '57.]

In summer, on the headlands,
  The Baltic Sea along,
Sits Neckan with his harp of gold,
  And sings his plaintive song.

Green rolls beneath the headlands,
  Green rolls the Baltic Sea.
And there, below the Neckan's feet,
  His wife and children be.

He sings not of the ocean,
  Its shells and roses pale.   10
Of earth, of earth the Neckan sings ;
  He hath no other tale.

He sits upon the headlands,
  And sings a mournful stave
Of all he saw and felt on earth,
  Far from the green sea wave.

Sings how, a knight, he wander'd
  By castle, field, and town.—
But earthly knights have harder hearts
  Than the Sea Children own.   20

Sings of his earthly bridal—
  Priest, knights, and ladies gay.
'And who art thou,' the priest began,
  'Sir Knight, who wedd'st to-day ?'—

'I am no knight,' he answer'd ;
  'From the sea waves I come.'—
The knights drew sword, the ladies scream'd,
  The surplic'd priest stood dumb.

He sings how from the chapel
  He vanish'd with his bride,   30
And bore her down to the sea halls,
  Beneath the cold sea tide.

32 cold] salt *1853, 1854.*

He sings how she sits weeping
   'Mid shells that round her lie.
'False Neckan shares my bed,' she weeps ;
   'No Christian mate have I.'—

He sings how through the billows
   He rose to earth again,
And sought a priest to sign the cross,
   That Neckan Heaven might gain.   40

He sings how, on an evening,
   Beneath the birch trees cool,
He sate and play'd his harp of gold,
   Beside the river pool.

Beside the pool sate Neckan—
   Tears fill'd his cold blue eye.
On his white mule, across the bridge,
   A cassock'd priest rode by.

'Why sitt'st thou there, O Neckan,
   And play'st thy harp of gold ?   50
Sooner shall this my staff bear leaves,
   Than thou shalt Heaven behold.'—

The cassock'd priest rode onwards,
   And vanish'd with his mule.
And Neckan in the twilight grey
   Wept by the river pool.

In summer, on the headlands,
   The Baltic Sea along,
Sits Neckan with his harp of gold,
   And sings this plaintive song.   60

A DREAM

[First published 1853.   Reprinted 1854, '57.]

WAS it a dream ? We sail'd, I thought we sail'd,
Martin and I, down a green Alpine stream,
Under o'erhanging pines ; the morning sun,
On the wet umbrage of their glossy tops,

A Dream *Title*] Switzerland. III. A Dream *1853, 1854, 1857.*

On the red pinings of their forest floor,
Drew a warm scent abroad ; behind the pines
The mountain skirts, with all their sylvan change
Of bright-leaf'd chestnuts, and moss'd walnut-trees,
And the frail scarlet-berried ash, began.
Swiss chalets glitter'd on the dewy slopes,   10
And from some swarded shelf high up, there came
Notes of wild pastoral music : over all
Rang'd, diamond-bright, the eternal wall of snow.
Upon the mossy rocks at the stream's edge,
Back'd by the pines, a plank-built cottage stood,
Bright in the sun ; the climbing gourd-plant's leaves
Muffled its walls, and on the stone-strewn roof
Lay the warm golden gourds ; golden, within,
Under the eaves, peer'd rows of Indian corn.
We shot beneath the cottage with the stream.   20
On the brown rude-carv'd balcony two Forms
Came forth—Olivia's, Marguerite ! and thine.
Clad were they both in white, flowers in their breast ;
Straw hats bedeck'd their heads, with ribbons blue
Which wav'd, and on their shoulders fluttering play'd.
They saw us, they conferr'd ; their bosoms heav'd,
And more than mortal impulse fill'd their eyes.
Their lips mov'd ; their white arms, wav'd eagerly,
Flash'd once, like falling streams :—we rose, we gaz'd :
One moment, on the rapid's top, our boat   30
Hung pois'd—and then the darting River of Life,
Loud thundering, bore us by : swift, swift it foam'd ;
Black under cliffs it rac'd, round headlands shone.
Soon the plank'd cottage 'mid the sun-warm'd pines
Faded, the moss, the rocks ; us burning Plains
Bristled with cities, us the Sea receiv'd.

REQUIESCAT

[First published 1853.   Reprinted 1854, '57.]

STREW on her roses, roses,
    And never a spray of yew.
In quiet she reposes :
    Ah ! would that I did too.

23 breast] breasts *1853*.

Her mirth the world required :
   She bath'd it in smiles of glee.
But her heart was tired, tired,
   And now they let her be.

Her life was turning, turning,
   In mazes of heat and sound.   10
But for peace her soul was yearning,
   And now peace laps her round.

Her cabin'd, ample Spirit,
   It flutter'd and fail'd for breath.
To-night it doth inherit
   The vasty Hall of Death.

THE SCHOLAR GIPSY

[First published 1853.   Reprinted 1854, '57.]

Go, for they call you, Shepherd, from the hill ;
   Go, Shepherd, and untie the wattled cotes :
      No longer leave thy wistful flock unfed,
Nor let thy bawling fellows rack their throats,
      Nor the cropp'd grasses shoot another head.
         But when the fields are still,
   And the tired men and dogs all gone to rest,
   And only the white sheep are sometimes seen
      Cross and recross the strips of moon-blanch'd green ;
   Come, Shepherd, and again renew the quest.

Here, where the reaper was at work of late,   11
   In this high field's dark corner, where he leaves
      His coat, his basket, and his earthen cruise,
And in the sun all morning binds the sheaves,
      Then here, at noon, comes back his stores to use ;
         Here will I sit and wait,
While to my ear from uplands far away
   The bleating of the folded flocks is borne,
   With distant cries of reapers in the corn—
      All the live murmur of a summer's day.   20

Screen'd is this nook o'er the high, half-reap'd field,
   And here till sun-down, Shepherd, will I be.
     Through the thick corn the scarlet poppies peep,
   And round green roots and yellowing stalks I see
     Pale blue convolvulus in tendrils creep:
       And air-swept lindens yield
   Their scent, and rustle down their perfum'd showers
   Of bloom on the bent grass where I am laid,
     And bower me from the August sun with shade ;
     And the eye travels down to Oxford's towers:

And near me on the grass lies Glanvil's book—   31
   Come, let me read the oft-read tale again,
     The story of that Oxford scholar poor
   Of pregnant parts and quick inventive brain,
     Who, tir'd of knocking at Preferment's door,
       One summer morn forsook
   His friends, and went to learn the Gipsy lore,
     And roam'd the world with that wild brotherhood,
     And came, as most men deem'd, to little good,
       But came to Oxford and his friends no more.

But once, years after, in the country lanes,   41
   Two scholars whom at college erst he knew
     Met him, and of his way of life inquir'd.
   Whereat he answer'd, that the Gipsy crew,
     His mates, had arts to rule as they desir'd
       The workings of men's brains ;
   And they can bind them to what thoughts they will:
     'And I,' he said, ' the secret of their art,
     When fully learn'd, will to the world impart: 49
       But it needs heaven-sent moments for this skill.'

This said, he left them, and return'd no more,
   But rumours hung about the country side
     That the lost Scholar long was seen to stray,
   Seen by rare glimpses, pensive and tongue-tied,
     In hat of antique shape, and cloak of grey,
       The same the Gipsies wore.
   Shepherds had met him on the Hurst in spring ;
     At some lone alehouse in the Berkshire moors,
     On the warm ingle bench, the smock-frock'd boors
       Had found him seated at their entering,   60

But, mid their drink and clatter, he would fly :
  And I myself seem half to know thy looks,
    And put the shepherds, Wanderer, on thy trace ;
  And boys who in lone wheatfields scare the rooks
    I ask if thou hast pass'd their quiet place ;
      Or in my boat I lie
  Moor'd to the cool bank in the summer heats,
    Mid wide grass meadows which the sunshine fills,
    And watch the warm green-muffled Cumner hills,
      And wonder if thou haunt'st their shy retreats.

For most, I know, thou lov'st retired ground.   71
  Thee, at the ferry, Oxford riders blithe,
    Returning home on summer nights, have met
  Crossing the stripling Thames at Bab-lock-hithe,
    Trailing in the cool stream thy fingers wet,
      As the slow punt swings round :
  And leaning backwards in a pensive dream,
    And fostering in thy lap a heap of flowers
    Pluck'd in shy fields and distant Wychwood bowers,
      And thine eyes resting on the moonlit stream :

And then they land, and thou art seen no more.   81
  Maidens who from the distant hamlets come
    To dance around the Fyfield elm in May,
  Oft through the darkening fields have seen thee roam,
    Or cross a stile into the public way.
      Oft thou hast given them store
  Of flowers—the frail-leaf'd, white anemone—
    Dark bluebells drench'd with dews of summer
      eves—
    And purple orchises with spotted leaves—
      But none has words she can report of thee.   90

And, above Godstow Bridge, when hay-time's here
  In June, and many a scythe in sunshine flames,
    Men who through those wide fields of breezy grass
  Where black-wing'd swallows haunt the glittering
      Thames,
    To bathe in the abandon'd lasher pass,
      Have often pass'd thee near

79 Wychwood] woodland *1853, 1854.*

Sitting upon the river bank o'ergrown :
　Mark'd thy outlandish garb, thy figure spare,
　　Thy dark vague eyes, and soft abstracted air ;
　　　But, when they came from bathing, thou wert
　　　　gone.   100

At some lone homestead in the Cumner hills,
　Where at her open door the housewife darns,
　　Thou hast been seen, or hanging on a gate
　To watch the threshers in the mossy barns.
　　　Children, who early range these slopes and late
　　　　For cresses from the rills,
　Have known thee watching, all an April day,
　　The springing pastures and the feeding kine ;
　　And mark'd thee, when the stars come out and
　　　shine,   109
　　　Through the long dewy grass move slow away.

In Autumn, on the skirts of Bagley wood,
　Where most the Gipsies by the turf-edg'd way
　　Pitch their smok'd tents, and every bush you see
　With scarlet patches tagg'd and shreds of grey,
　　　Above the forest ground call'd Thessaly—
　　　　The blackbird picking food
Sees thee, nor stops his meal, nor fears at all ;
　So often has he known thee past him stray
　　Rapt, twirling in thy hand a wither'd spray,   119
　　　And waiting for the spark from Heaven to fall.

And once, in winter, on the causeway chill
　Where home through flooded fields foot-travellers go,
　　Have I not pass'd thee on the wooden bridge
　Wrapt in thy cloak and battling with the snow,
　　　Thy face towards Hinksey and its wintry ridge ?
　　　　And thou hast climb'd the hill
And gain'd the white brow of the Cumner range,
　Turn'd once to watch, while thick the snowflakes
　　fall,
　　The line of festal light in Christ-Church hall—
　　　Then sought thy straw in some sequester'd
　　　　grange.   130

But what—I dream ! Two hundred years are flown
  Since first thy story ran through Oxford halls,
    And the grave Glanvil did the tale inscribe
  That thou wert wander'd from the studious walls
    To learn strange arts, and join a Gipsy tribe:
      And thou from earth art gone
  Long since, and in some quiet churchyard laid;
    Some country nook, where o'er thy unknown grave
    Tall grasses and white flowering nettles wave—
      Under a dark red-fruited yew-tree's shade.   140

—No, no, thou hast not felt the lapse of hours.
  For what wears out the life of mortal men?
    'Tis that from change to change their being rolls:
  'Tis that repeated shocks, again, again,
    Exhaust the energy of strongest souls,
      And numb the elastic powers.
  Till having us'd our nerves with bliss and teen,
    And tir'd upon a thousand schemes our wit,
    To the just-pausing Genius we remit   149
      Our worn-out life, and are—what we have been.

Thou hast not liv'd, why should'st thou perish, so?
  Thou hadst *one* aim, *one* business, *one* desire:
    Else wert thou long since number'd with the
      dead—
  Else hadst thou spent, like other men, thy fire.
    The generations of thy peers are fled,
      And we ourselves shall go;
  But thou possessest an immortal lot,
    And we imagine thee exempt from age
    And living as thou liv'st on Glanvil's page,   159
      Because thou hadst—what we, alas, have not!

For early didst thou leave the world, with powers
  Fresh, undiverted to the world without,
    Firm to their mark, not spent on other things;
  Free from the sick fatigue, the languid doubt,
    Which much to have tried, in much been baffled,
      brings.
      O Life unlike to ours!

Who fluctuate idly without term or scope,
   Of whom each strives, nor knows for what he
      strives,   168
  And each half lives a hundred different lives ;
   Who wait like thee, but not, like thee, in hope.

Thou waitest for the spark from Heaven: and we,
  Vague half-believers of our casual creeds,
   Who never deeply felt, nor clearly will'd,
  Whose insight never has borne fruit in deeds,
   Whose weak resolves never have been fulfill'd ;
    For whom each year we see
  Breeds new beginnings, disappointments new ;
   Who hesitate and falter life away,
   And lose to-morrow the ground won to-day—
    Ah, do not we, Wanderer, await it too ?   180

Yes, we await it, but it still delays,
  And then we suffer ; and amongst us One,
   Who most has suffer'd, takes dejectedly
  His seat upon the intellectual throne ;
   And all his store of sad experience he
    Lays bare of wretched days ;
  Tells us his misery's birth and growth and signs,
   And how the dying spark of hope was fed,
   And how the breast was sooth'd, and how the
    head,
    And all his hourly varied anodynes.   190

This for our wisest : and we others pine,
  And wish the long unhappy dream would end,
   And waive all claim to bliss, and try to bear,
  With close-lipp'd Patience for our only friend,
   Sad Patience, too near neighbour to Despair :
    But none has hope like thine.
  Thou through the fields and through the woods dost
    stray,
   Roaming the country side, a truant boy,
   Nursing thy project in unclouded joy,   199
    And every doubt long blown by time away.

172 Vague] Light *1853, 1854.*   175 weak] vague *1853, 1854.*

O born in days when wits were fresh and clear,
  And life ran gaily as the sparkling Thames ;
    Before this strange disease of modern life,
  With its sick hurry, its divided aims,
    Its heads o'ertax'd, its palsied hearts, was rife—
      Fly hence, our contact fear !
  Still fly, plunge deeper in the bowering wood !
    Averse, as Dido did with gesture stern
    From her false friend's approach in Hades turn,
      Wave us away, and keep thy solitude.   210

Still nursing the unconquerable hope,
  Still clutching the inviolable shade,
    With a free onward impulse brushing through,
  By night, the silver'd branches of the glade—
    Far on the forest skirts, where none pursue,
      On some mild pastoral slope
  Emerge, and resting on the moonlit pales,
    Freshen thy flowers, as in former years,
    With dew, or listen with enchanted ears,
      From the dark dingles, to the nightingales.

But fly our paths, our feverish contact fly !   221
  For strong the infection of our mental strife,
    Which, though it gives no bliss, yet spoils for rest ;
  And we should win thee from thy own fair life,
    Like us distracted, and like us unblest.
      Soon, soon thy cheer would die,
  Thy hopes grow timorous, and unfix'd thy powers,
    And thy clear aims be cross and shifting made :
    And then thy glad perennial youth would fade,
      Fade, and grow old at last, and die like ours.

Then fly our greetings, fly our speech and smiles !
  —As some grave Tyrian trader, from the sea,   232
    Descried at sunrise an emerging prow
  Lifting the cool-hair'd creepers stealthily,
    The fringes of a southward-facing brow
      Among the Aegean isles ;
  And saw the merry Grecian coaster come,
    Freighted with amber grapes, and Chian wine,
    Green bursting figs, and tunnies steep'd in brine ;
      And knew the intruders on his ancient home,

The young light-hearted Masters of the waves ; 241
 And snatch'd his rudder, and shook out more sail,
  And day and night held on indignantly
O'er the blue Midland waters with the gale,
 Betwixt the Syrtes and soft Sicily,
  To where the Atlantic raves
Outside the Western Straits, and unbent sails
 There, where down cloudy cliffs, through sheets
   of foam,
 Shy traffickers, the dark Iberians come ;
  And on the beach undid his corded bales. 250

STANZAS

IN MEMORY OF THE LATE EDWARD QUILLINAN, ESQ.

[First published 1853. Reprinted 1854, '57.]

I saw him sensitive in frame,
 I knew his spirits low ;
And wish'd him health, success, and fame :
 I do not wish it now.

For these are all their own reward,
 And leave no good behind ;
They try us, oftenest make us hard,
 Less modest, pure, and kind.

Alas ! Yet to the suffering man,
 In this his mortal state,   10
Friends could not give what Fortune can—
 Health, ease, a heart elate.

But he is now by Fortune foil'd
 No more ; and we retain
The memory of a man unspoil'd,
 Sweet, generous, and humane ;

With all the fortunate have not—
 With gentle voice and brow.
Alive, we would have chang'd his lot :
 We would not change it now.   20

Ἡμεῖς δὲ κλέος οἶον ἀκούομεν, οὐδέ τι ἴδμεν.

BALDER DEAD

AN EPISODE

[First published 1855.]

I

SENDING

So on the floor lay Balder dead ; and round
Lay thickly strewn swords axes darts and spears
Which all the Gods in sport had idly thrown
At Balder, whom no weapon pierc'd or clove :
But in his breast stood fixt the fatal bough
Of mistletoe, which Lok the Accuser gave
To Hoder, and unwitting Hoder threw :
'Gainst that alone had Balder's life no charm.
And all the Gods and all the Heroes came
And stood round Balder on the bloody floor   10
Weeping and wailing ; and Valhalla rang
Up to its golden roof with sobs and cries :
And on the tables stood the untasted meats,
And in the horns and gold-rimm'd skulls the wine :
And now would Night have fall'n, and found them yet
Wailing ; but otherwise was Odin's will :
And thus the Father of the Ages spake :—

' Enough of tears, ye Gods, enough of wail !
Not to lament in was Valhalla made.
If any here might weep for Balder's death   20
I most might weep, his Father ; such a son
I lose to-day, so bright, so lov'd a God.
But he has met that doom which long ago
The Nornies, when his mother bare him, spun,
And Fate set seal, that so his end must be.
Balder has met his death, and ye survive :
Weep him an hour ; but what can grief avail ?
For you yourselves, ye Gods, shall meet your doom,
All ye who hear me, and inhabit Heaven,
And I too, Odin too, the Lord of all ;   30

But ours we shall not meet, when that day comes,
With woman's tears and weak complaining cries—
Why should we meet another's portion so ?
Rather it fits you, having wept your hour,
With cold dry eyes, and hearts compos'd and stern,
To live, as erst, your daily life in Heaven :
By me shall vengeance on the murderer Lok,
The Foe, the Accuser, whom, though Gods, we hate,
Be strictly car'd for, in the appointed day.   39
Meanwhile, to-morrow, when the morning dawns,
Bring wood to the seashore to Balder's ship,
And on the deck build high a funeral pile,
And on the top lay Balder's corpse, and put
Fire to the wood, and send him out to sea
To burn ; for that is what the dead desire.'

So having spoke, the King of Gods arose
And mounted his horse Sleipner, whom he rode,
And from the hall of Heaven he rode away
To Lidskialf, and sate upon his throne,   49
The Mount, from whence his eye surveys the world.
And far from Heaven he turn'd his shining orbs
To look on Midgard, and the earth, and men :
And on the conjuring Lapps he bent his gaze
Whom antler'd reindeer pull over the snow ;
And on the Finns, the gentlest of mankind,
Fair men, who live in holes under the ground :
Nor did he look once more to Ida's plain,
Nor towards Valhalla, and the sorrowing Gods ;
For well he knew the Gods would heed his word,
And cease to mourn, and think of Balder's pyre.   60

But in Valhalla all the Gods went back
From around Balder, all the Heroes went ;
And left his body stretch'd upon the floor.
And on their golden chairs they sate again,
Beside the tables, in the hall of Heaven ;
And before each the cooks who serv'd them plac'd
New messes of the boar Serimner's flesh,
And the Valkyries crown'd their horns with mead.
So they, with pent-up hearts and tearless eyes,
Wailing no more, in silence ate and drank,   70
While Twilight fell, and sacred Night came on.

But the blind Hoder left the feasting Gods
In Odin's hall, and went through Asgard streets,
And past the haven where the Gods have moor'd
Their ships, and through the gate, beyond the wall.
Though sightless, yet his own mind led the God.
Down to the margin of the roaring sea
He came, and sadly went along the sand
Between the waves and black o'erhanging cliffs
Where in and out the screaming seafowl fly ;   80
Until he came to where a gully breaks
Through the cliff wall, and a fresh stream runs down
From the high moors behind, and meets the sea.
There in the glen Fensaler stands, the house
Of Frea, honour'd Mother of the Gods,
And shows its lighted windows to the main.
There he went up, and pass'd the open doors :
And in the hall he found those women old,
The Prophetesses, who by rite eterne
On Frea's hearth feed high the sacred fire   90
Both night and day ; and by the inner wall
Upon her golden chair the Mother sate,
With folded hands, revolving things to come :
To her drew Hoder near, and spake, and said :—

'Mother, a child of bale thou bar'st in me.
For, first, thou barest me with blinded eyes,
Sightless and helpless, wandering weak in Heaven ;
And, after that, of ignorant witless mind
Thou barest me, and unforeseeing soul :
That I alone must take the branch from Lok,   100
The Foe, the Accuser, whom, though Gods, we hate,
And cast it at the dear-lov'd Balder's breast
At whom the Gods in sport their weapons threw—
'Gainst that alone had Balder's life no charm.
Now therefore what to attempt, or whither fly ?
For who will bear my hateful sight in Heaven ?—
Can I, O Mother, bring them Balder back ?
Or—for thou know'st the Fates, and things allow'd—
Can I with Hela's power a compact strike,
And make exchange, and give my life for his ?'   110

He spoke : the Mother of the Gods replied :—
'Hoder, ill-fated, child of bale, my son,

Sightless in soul and eye, what words are these?
That one, long portion'd with his doom of death,
Should change his lot, and fill another's life,
And Hela yield to this, and let him go!
On Balder Death hath laid her hand, not thee;
Nor doth she count this life a price for that.
For many Gods in Heaven, not thou alone,
Would freely die to purchase Balder back,   120
And wend themselves to Hela's gloomy realm.
For not so gladsome is that life in Heaven
Which Gods and Heroes lead, in feast and fray,
Waiting the darkness of the final times,
That one should grudge its loss for Balder's sake,
Balder their joy, so bright, so lov'd a God.
But Fate withstands, and laws forbid this way.
Yet in my secret mind one way I know,
Nor do I judge if it shall win or fail: 129
But much must still be tried, which shall but fail.'

    And the blind Hoder answer'd her, and said :—
'What way is this, O Mother, that thou show'st?
Is it a matter which a God might try?'

    And straight the Mother of the Gods replied :—
'There is a way which leads to Hela's realm,
Untrodden, lonely, far from light and Heaven.
Who goes that way must take no other horse
To ride, but Sleipner, Odin's horse, alone.
Nor must he choose that common path of Gods
Which every day they come and go in Heaven,   140
O'er the bridge Bifrost, where is Heimdall's watch,
Past Midgard Fortress, down to Earth and men ;
But he must tread a dark untravell'd road
Which branches from the north of Heaven, and ride
Nine days, nine nights, towards the northern ice,
Through valleys deep-engulph'd, with roaring streams.
And he will reach on the tenth morn a bridge
Which spans with golden arches Giall's stream,
Not Bifrost, but that bridge a Damsel keeps,
Who tells the passing troops of dead their way   150
To the low shore of ghosts, and Hela's realm.
And she will bid him northward steer his course:
Then he will journey through no lighted land,

Nor see the sun arise, nor see it set ;
But he must ever watch the northern Bear
Who from her frozen height with jealous eye
Confronts the Dog and Hunter in the south,
And is alone not dipt in Ocean's stream.
And straight he will come down to Ocean's strand ;
Ocean, whose watery ring enfolds the world,   160
And on whose marge the ancient Giants dwell.
But he will reach its unknown northern shore,
Far, far beyond the outmost Giant's home,
At the chink'd fields of ice, the waste of snow :
And he will fare across the dismal ice
Northward, until he meets a stretching wall
Barring his way, and in the wall a grate.
But then he must dismount, and on the ice
Tighten the girths of Sleipner, Odin's horse,
And make him leap the grate, and come within.   170
And he will see stretch round him Hela's realm,
The plains of Niflheim, where dwell the dead,
And hear the roaring of the streams of Hell.
And he will see the feeble shadowy tribes,
And Balder sitting crown'd, and Hela's throne.
Then he must not regard the wailful ghosts
Who all will flit, like eddying leaves, around ;
But he must straight accost their solemn Queen,
And pay her homage, and entreat with prayers,
Telling her all that grief they have in Heaven   180
For Balder, whom she holds by right below :
If haply he may melt her heart with words,
And make her yield, and give him Balder back.'

    She spoke : but Hoder answer'd her and said :—
' Mother, a dreadful way is this thou show'st.
No journey for a sightless God to go.'

    And straight the Mother of the Gods replied :—
' Therefore thyself thou shalt not go, my son.
But he whom first thou meetest when thou com'st
To Asgard, and declar'st this hidden way,   190
Shall go, and I will be his guide unseen.'

    She spoke, and on her face let fall her veil,
And bow'd her head, and sate with folded hands.

But at the central hearth those Women old,
Who while the Mother spake had ceased their toil,
Began again to heap the sacred fire:
And Hoder turn'd, and left his mother's house,
Fensaler, whose lit windows look to sea ;
And came again down to the roaring waves,
And back along the beach to Asgard went,   200
Pondering on that which Frea said should be.

　　But Night came down, and darken'd Asgard streets.
Then from their loathèd feast the Gods arose,
And lighted torches, and took up the corpse
Of Balder from the floor of Odin's hall,
And laid it on a bier, and bare him home
Through the fast-darkening streets to his own house
Breidablik, on whose columns Balder grav'd
The enchantments, that recall the dead to life :
For wise he was, and many curious arts,   210
Postures of runes, and healing herbs he knew ;
Unhappy : but that art he did not know
To keep his own life safe, and see the sun :—
There to his hall the Gods brought Balder home,
And each bespake him as he laid him down :—
　' Would that ourselves, O Balder, we were borne
Home to our halls, with torchlight, by our kin,
So thou might'st live, and still delight the Gods.'

　　They spake : and each went home to his own house.
But there was one, the first of all the Gods   220
For speed, and Hermod was his name in Heaven ;
Most fleet he was, but now he went the last,
Heavy in heart for Balder, to his house
Which he in Asgard built him, there to dwell,
Against the harbour, by the city wall :
Him the blind Hoder met, as he came up
From the sea cityward, and knew his step ;
Nor yet could Hermod see his brother's face,
For it grew dark ; but Hoder touch'd his arm :
And as a spray of honeysuckle flowers   230
Brushes across a tired traveller's face
Who shuffles through the deep dew-moisten'd dust,
On a May evening, in the darken'd lanes,
And starts him, that he thinks a ghost went by—

So Hoder brush'd by Hermod's side, and said : —

'Take Sleipner, Hermod, and set forth with dawn
To Hela's kingdom, to ask Balder back ;
And they shall be thy guides, who have the power.'

He spake, and brush'd soft by, and disappear'd.
And Hermod gaz'd into the night, and said:—   240

'Who is it utters through the dark his hest
So quickly, and will wait for no reply ?
The voice was like the unhappy Hoder's voice.
Howbeit I will see, and do his hest ;
For there rang note divine in that command.'

So speaking, the fleet-footed Hermod came
Home, and lay down to sleep in his own house,
And all the Gods lay down in their own homes.
And Hoder too came home, distraught with grief,
Loathing to meet, at dawn, the other Gods :   250
And he went in, and shut the door, and fixt
His sword upright, and fell on it, and died.

But from the hill of Lidskialf Odin rose,
The throne, from which his eye surveys the world ;
And mounted Sleipner, and in darkness rode
To Asgard.   And the stars came out in Heaven,
High over Asgard, to light home the King.
But fiercely Odin gallop'd, mov'd in heart ;
And swift to Asgard, to the gate, he came ·
And terribly the hoofs of Sleipner rang   260
Along the flinty floor of Asgard streets ;
And the Gods trembled on their golden beds
Hearing the wrathful Father coming home ;
For dread, for like a whirlwind, Odin came :
And to Valhalla's gate he rode, and left
Sleipner ; and Sleipner went to his own stall :
And in Valhalla Odin laid him down.

But in Breidablik Nanna, Balder's wife,
Came with the Goddesses who wrought her will,
And stood round Balder lying on his bier :   270
And at his head and feet she station'd Scalds
Who in their lives were famous for their song ;
These o'er the corpse inton'd a plaintive strain,

A dirge ; and Nanna and her train replied.
And far into the night they wail'd their dirge :
But when their souls were satisfied with wail,
They went, and laid them down, and Nanna went
Into an upper chamber, and lay down ;
And Frea seal'd her tired lids with sleep.

    And 'twas when Night is bordering hard on Dawn,
When air is chilliest, and the stars sunk low,   281
Then Balder's spirit through the gloom drew near,
In garb, in form, in feature as he was
Alive, and still the rays were round his head
Which were his glorious mark in Heaven ; he stood
Over against the curtain of the bed,
And gaz'd on Nanna as she slept, and spake :—

    ' Poor lamb, thou sleepest, and forgett'st thy woe.
Tears stand upon the lashes of thine eyes,
Tears wet the pillow by thy cheek ; but thou,   290
Like a young child, hast cried thyself to sleep.
Sleep on : I watch thee, and am here to aid.
Alive I kept not far from thee, dear soul,
Neither do I neglect thee now, though dead.
For with to-morrow's dawn the Gods prepare
To gather wood, and build a funeral pile
Upon my ship, and burn my corpse with fire,
That sad, sole honour of the dead ; and thee
They think to burn, and all my choicest wealth,
With me, for thus ordains the common rite :   300
But it shall not be so : but mild, but swift,
But painless shall a stroke from Frea come,
To cut thy thread of life, and free thy soul,
And they shall burn thy corpse with mine, not thee.
And well I know that by no stroke of death,
Tardy or swift, wouldst thou be loath to die,
So it restor'd thee, Nanna, to my side,
Whom thou so well hast lov'd ; but I can smooth
Thy way, and this at least my prayers avail.
Yes, and I fain would altogether ward   310
Death from thy head, and with the Gods in Heaven
Prolong thy life, though not by thee desir'd :
But Right bars this, not only thy desire.
Yet dreary, Nanna, is the life they lead

In that dim world, in Hela's mouldering realm ;
And doleful are the ghosts, the troops of dead,
Whom Hela with austere control presides ;
For of the race of Gods is no one there
Save me alone, and Hela, solemn Queen :
And all the nobler souls of mortal men   320
On battle-field have met their death, and now
Feast in Valhalla, in my Father's hall ;
Only the inglorious sort are there below,
The old, the cowards, and the weak are there,
Men spent by sickness, or obscure decay.
But even there, O Nanna, we might find
Some solace in each other's look and speech,
Wandering together through that gloomy world.
And talking of the life we led in Heaven,
While we yet liv'd, among the other Gods.'   330

   He spake, and straight his lineaments began
To fade : and Nanna in her sleep stretch'd out
Her arms towards him with a cry ; but he
Mournfully shook his head, and disappear'd.
And as the woodman sees a little smoke
Hang in the air, afield, and disappear—
So Balder faded in the night away.
And Nanna on her bed sunk back : but then
Frea, the Mother of the Gods, with stroke
Painless and swift, set free her airy soul,   340
Which took, on Balder's track, the way below :
And instantly the sacred Morn appear'd.

II

JOURNEY TO THE DEAD

   FORTH from the East, up the ascent of Heaven,
Day drove his courser with the Shining Mane ;
And in Valhalla, from his gable perch,
The golden-crested Cock began to crow :
Hereafter, in the blackest dead of night,
With shrill and dismal cries that Bird shall crow,
Warning the Gods that foes draw nigh to Heaven ;
But now he crew at dawn, a cheerful note,
To wake the Gods and Heroes to their tasks.
And all the Gods, and all the Heroes, woke.   10

And from their beds the Heroes rose, and donn'd
Their arms, and led their horses from the stall,
And mounted them, and in Valhalla's court
Were rang'd ; and then the daily fray began.
And all day long they there are hack'd and hewn
'Mid dust, and groans, and limbs lopp'd off, and blood;
But all at night return to Odin's hall
Woundless and fresh : such lot is theirs in Heaven.
And the Valkyries on their steeds went forth
Toward Earth and fights of men ; and at their side 20
Skulda, the youngest of the Nornies, rode :
And over Bifrost, where is Heimdall's watch,
Past Midgard Fortress, down to Earth they came :
There through some battle-field, where men fall fast,
Their horses fetlock-deep in blood, they ride,
And pick the bravest warriors out for death,
Whom they bring back with them at night to Heaven,
To glad the Gods, and feast in Odin's hall.

But the Gods went not now, as otherwhile,
Into the Tilt-Yard, where the Heroes fought, 30
To feast their eyes with looking on the fray :
Nor did they to their Judgement-Place repair
By the ash Igdrasil, in Ida's plain,
Where they hold council, and give laws for men :
But they went, Odin first, the rest behind,
To the hall Gladheim, which is built of gold ;
Where are in circle rang'd twelve golden chairs,
And in the midst one higher, Odin's throne :
There all the Gods in silence sate them down ;
And thus the Father of the Ages spake :— 40

Go quickly, Gods, bring wood to the seashore,
With all, which it beseems the dead to have
And make a funeral pile on Balder's ship.
On the twelfth day the Gods shall burn his corpse.
But Hermod, thou, take Sleipner, and ride down
To Hela's kingdom, to ask Balder back.'

So said he ; and the Gods arose, and took
Axes and ropes, and at their head came Thor,
Shouldering his Hammer, which the Giants know :
Forth wended they, and drove their steeds before : 50

And up the dewy mountain tracks they far'd
To the dark forests, in the early dawn ;
And up and down and side and slant they roam'd :
And from the glens all day an echo came
Of crashing falls ; for with his hammer Thor'
Smote 'mid the rocks the lichen-bearded pines
And burst their roots ; while to their tops the Gods
Made fast the woven ropes, and hal'd them down,
And lopp'd their boughs, and clove them on the sward,
And bound the logs behind their steeds to draw,　　60
And drove them homeward ; and the snorting steeds
Went straining through the crackling brushwood down,
And by the darkling forest paths the Gods
Follow'd, and on their shoulders carried boughs.
And they came out upon the plain, and pass'd
Asgard, and led their horses to the beach,
And loos'd them of their loads on the seashore,
And rang'd the wood in stacks by Balder's ship ;
And every God went home to his own house.

But when the Gods were to the forest gone　　70
Hermod led Sleipner from Valhalla forth
And saddled him ; before that, Sleipner brook'd
No meaner hand than Odin's on his mane,
On his broad back no lesser rider bore :
Yet docile now he stood at Hermod's side,
Arching his neck, and glad to be bestrode,
Knowing the God they went to seek, how dear.
But Hermod mounted him, and sadly far'd,
In silence, up the dark untravell'd road
Which branches from the north of Heaven, and went
All day ; and Daylight wan'd, and Night came on.　　81
And all that night he rode, and journey'd so,
Nine days, nine nights, towards the northern ice,
Through valleys deep-engulph'd, by roaring streams :
And on the tenth morn he beheld the bridge
Which spans with golden arches Giall's stream,
And on the bridge a Damsel watching arm'd,
In the strait passage, at the further end,
Where the road issues between walling rocks.
Scant space that Warder left for passers by ;　　90
But, as when cowherds in October drive

Their kine across a snowy mountain pass
To winter pasture on the southern side,
And on the ridge a wagon chokes the way,
Wedg'd in the snow ; then painfully the hinds
With goad and shouting urge their cattle past,
Plunging through deep untrodden banks of snow
To right and left, and warm steam fills the air—
So on the bridge that Damsel block'd the way,
And question'd Hermod as he came, and said :—   100

'Who art thou on thy black and fiery horse
Under whose hoofs the bridge o'er Giall's stream
Rumbles and shakes ?   Tell me thy race and home.
But yestermorn five troops of dead pass'd by
Bound on their way below to Hela's realm,
Nor shook the bridge so much as thou alone.
And thou hast flesh and colour on thy cheeks
Like men who live and draw the vital air ;
Nor look'st thou pale and wan, like men deceas'd,
Souls bound below, my daily passers here.'   110

And the fleet-footed Hermod answer'd her :—
'O Damsel, Hermod am I call'd, the son
Of Odin ; and my high-roof'd house is built
Far hence, in Asgard, in the City of Gods :
And Sleipner, Odin's horse, is this I ride.
And I come, sent this road on Balder's track :
Say then, if he hath cross'd thy bridge or no ?'

He spake ; the Warder of the bridge replied :—
'O Hermod, rarely do the feet of Gods
Or of the horses of the Gods resound   120
Upon my bridge ; and, when they cross, I know.
Balder hath gone this way, and ta'en the road
Below there, to the north, toward Hela's realm.
From here the cold white mist can be discern'd,
Not lit with sun, but through the darksome air
By the dim vapour-blotted light of stars,
Which hangs over the ice where lies the road.
For in that ice are lost those northern streams
Freezing and ridging in their onward flow,
Which from the fountain of Vergelmer run,   130
The spring that bubbles up by Hela's throne.

There are the joyless seats, the haunt of ghosts,
Hela's pale swarms ; and there was Balder bound.
Ride on ; pass free : but he by this is there.'

    She spake, and stepp'd aside, and left him room.
And Hermod greeted her, and gallop'd by
Across the bridge ; then she took post again.
But northward Hermod rode, the way below :
And o'er a darksome tract, which knows no sun,
But by the blotted light of stars, he far'd ;   140
And he came down to Ocean's northern strand
At the drear ice, beyond the Giants' home :
Thence on he journey'd o'er the fields of ice
Still north, until he met a stretching wall
Barring his way, and in the wall a grate.
Then he dismounted, and drew tight the girths,
On the smooth ice, of Sleipner, Odin's horse,
And made him leap the grate, and came within.
And he beheld spread round him Hela's realm,
The plains of Niflheim, where dwell the dead,   150
And heard the thunder of the streams of Hell.
For near the wall the river of Roaring flows,
Outmost : the others near the centre run—
The Storm, the Abyss, the Howling, and the Pain :
These flow by Hela's throne, and near their spring.
And from the dark flock'd up the shadowy tribes :
And as the swallows crowd the bulrush-beds
Of some clear river, issuing from a lake,
On autumn days, before they cross the sea ;
And to each bulrush-crest a swallow hangs   160
Swinging, and others skim the river streams,
And their quick twittering fills the banks and shores—
So around Hermod swarm'd the twittering ghosts.
Women, and infants, and young men who died
Too soon for fame, with white ungraven shields ;
And old men, known to Glory, but their star
Betray'd them, and of wasting age they died,
Not wounds : yet, dying, they their armour wore,
And now have chief regard in Hela's realm.
Behind flock'd wrangling up a piteous crew,   170
Greeted of none, disfeatur'd and forlorn—
Cowards, who were in sloughs interr'd alive :

And round them still the wattled hurdles hung
Wherewith they stamp'd them down, and trod them deep,
To hide their shameful memory from men.
But all he pass'd unhail'd, and reach'd the throne
Of Hela, and saw, near it, Balder crown'd,
And Hela sat thereon, with countenance stern ;
And thus bespake him first the solemn Queen :—

'Unhappy, how hast thou endur'd to leave   180
The light, and journey to the cheerless land
Where idly flit about the feeble shades ?
How didst thou cross the bridge o'er Giall's stream,
Being alive, and come to Ocean's shore ?
Or how o'erleap the grate that bars the wall ?'

She spake : but down off Sleipner Hermod sprang,
And fell before her feet, and clasp'd her knees ;
And spake, and mild entreated her, and said :—

'O Hela, wherefore should the Gods declare
Their errands to each other, or the ways   190
They go ? the errand and the way is known.
Thou know'st, thou know'st, what grief we have in
        Heaven
For Balder, whom thou hold'st by right below :
Restore him, for what part fulfils he here ?
Shall he shed cheer over the cheerless seats,
And touch the apathetic ghosts with joy ?
Not for such end, O Queen, thou hold'st thy realm.
For Heaven was Balder born, the City of Gods
And Heroes, where they live in light and joy :
Thither restore him, for his place is there.'   200

He spoke ; and grave replied the solemn Queen :—
'Hermod, for he thou art, thou Son of Heaven !
A strange unlikely errand, sure, is thine.
Do the Gods send to me to make them blest ?
Small bliss my race hath of the Gods obtain'd.
Three mighty children to my Father Lok
Did Angerbode, the Giantess, bring forth—
Fenris the Wolf, the Serpent huge, and Me :
Of these the Serpent in the sea ye cast,
Who since in your despite hath wax'd amain,   210

And now with gleaming ring enfolds the world:
Me on this cheerless nether world ye threw
And gave me nine unlighted realms to rule:
While on his island in the lake, afar,
Made fast to the bor'd crag, by wile not strength
Subdu'd, with limber chains lives Fenris bound.
Lok still subsists in Heaven, our Father wise,
Your mate, though loath'd, and feasts in Odin's hall;
But him too foes await, and netted snares,
And in a cave a bed of needle rocks,   220
And o'er his visage serpents dropping gall.
Yet he shall one day rise, and burst his bonds,
And with himself set us his offspring free,
When he guides Muspel's children to their bourne.
Till then in peril or in pain we live,
Wrought by the Gods: and ask the Gods our aid?
Howbeit we abide our day: till then,
We do not as some feebler haters do,
Seek to afflict our foes with petty pangs,
Helpless to better us, or ruin them.   230
Come then; if Balder was so dear belov'd,
And this is true, and such a loss is Heaven's—
Hear, how to Heaven may Balder be restor'd.
Show me through all the world the signs of grief:
Fails but one thing to grieve, here Balder stops:
Let all that lives and moves upon the earth
Weep him, and all that is without life weep:
Let Gods, men, brutes, beweep him; plants and stones.
So shall I know the lost was dear indeed,   239
And bend my heart, and give him back to Heaven.'

    She spake; and Hermod answer'd her, and said:—
'Hela, such as thou say'st, the terms shall be.
But come, declare me this, and truly tell:
May I, ere I depart, bid Balder hail?
Or is it here withheld to greet the dead?'

    He spake; and straightway Hela answer'd him:—
'Hermod, greet Balder if thou wilt, and hold
Converse: his speech remains, though he be dead.'

    And straight to Balder Hermod turn'd, and spake:—
'Even in the abode of Death, O Balder, hail!   250

Thou hear'st, if hearing, like as speech, is thine,
The terms of thy releasement hence to Heaven:
Fear nothing but that all shall be fulfill'd.
For not unmindful of thee are the Gods
Who see the light, and blest in Asgard dwell;
Even here they seek thee out, in Hela's realm.
And sure of all the happiest far art thou
Who ever have been known in Earth or Heaven:
Alive, thou wert of Gods the most belov'd:
And now thou sittest crown'd by Hela's side,   260
Here, and hast honour among all the dead.'

He spake; and Balder utter'd him reply,
But feebly, as a voice far off; he said :—

'Hermod the nimble, gild me not my death.
Better to live a slave, a captur'd man,
Who scatters rushes in a master's hall,
Than be a crown'd king here, and rule the dead.
And now I count not of these terms as safe
To be fulfill'd, nor my return as sure,
Though I be lov'd, and many mourn my death: 270
For double-minded ever was the seed
Of Lok, and double are the gifts they give.
Howbeit, report thy message; and therewith,
To Odin, to my Father, take this ring,
Memorial of me, whether sav'd or no:
And tell the Heaven-born Gods how thou hast seen
Me sitting here below by Hela's side,
Crown'd, having honour among all the dead.'

He spake, and rais'd his hand, and gave the ring.
And with inscrutable regard the Queen   280
Of Hell beheld them, and the ghosts stood dumb.
But Hermod took the ring, and yet once more
Kneel'd and did homage to the solemn Queen;
Then mounted Sleipner, and set forth to ride
Back, through the astonish'd tribes of dead, to Heaven.
And to the wall he came, and found the grate
Lifted, and issued on the fields of ice;
And o'er the ice he far'd to Ocean's strand,
And up from thence, a wet and misty road,
To the arm'd Damsel's bridge, and Giall's stream.   290

Worse was that way to go than to return,
For him: for others all return is barr'd.
Nine days he took to go, two to return;
And on the twelfth morn saw the light of Heaven.
And as a traveller in the early dawn
To the steep edge of some great valley comes
Through which a river flows, and sees beneath
Clouds of white rolling vapours fill the vale,
But o'er them, on the farther slope, descries   299
Vineyards, and crofts, and pastures, bright with sun—
So Hermod, o'er the fog between, saw Heaven.
And Sleipner snorted, for he smelt the air
Of Heaven: and mightily, as wing'd, he flew.
And Hermod saw the towers of Asgard rise:
And he drew near, and heard no living voice
In Asgard; and the golden halls were dumb.
Then Hermod knew what labour held the Gods:
And through the empty streets he rode, and pass'd
Under the gate-house to the sands, and found
The Gods on the seashore by Balder's ship.   310

III

FUNERAL

The Gods held talk together, group'd in knots,
Round Balder's corpse, which they had thither borne;
And Hermod came down towards them from the gate.
And Lok, the Father of the Serpent, first
Beheld him come, and to his neighbour spake:—

'See, here is Hermod, who comes single back
From Hell; and shall I tell thee how he seems?
Like as a farmer, who hath lost his dog,
Some morn, at market, in a crowded town—
Through many streets the poor beast runs in vain,   10
And follows this man after that, for hours;
And, late at evening, spent and panting, falls
Before a stranger's threshold, not his home,
With flanks a-tremble, and his slender tongue
Hangs quivering out between his dust-smear'd jaws,
And piteously he eyes the passers by:
But home his master comes to his own farm,
Far in the country, wondering where he is—
So Hermod comes to-day unfollow'd home.'

And straight his neighbour, mov'd with wrath,
    replied :—   20
'Deceiver, fair in form, but false in heart,
Enemy, Mocker, whom, though Gods, we hate—
Peace, lest our Father Odin hear thee gibe.
Would I might see him snatch thee in his hand,
And bind thy carcase, like a bale, with cords,
And hurl thee in a lake, to sink or swim.
If clear from plotting Balder's death, to swim ;
But deep, if thou devisedst it, to drown,
And perish, against fate, before thy day !'

So they two soft to one another spake.   30
But Odin look'd toward the land, and saw
His messenger ; and he stood forth, and cried :
And Hermod came, and leapt from Sleipner down,
And in his Father's hand put Sleipner's rein,
And greeted Odin and the Gods, and said :—

'Odin, my Father, and ye, Gods of Heaven !
Lo, home, having perform'd your will, I come.
Into the joyless kingdom have I been,
Below, and look'd upon the shadowy tribes
Of ghosts, and commun'd with their solemn Queen ; 40
And to your prayer she sends you this reply :
Show her through all the world the signs of grief :
Fails but one thing to grieve, there Balder stops.
Let Gods, men, brutes, beweep him, plants and stones.
So shall she know your loss was dear indeed,
And bend her heart, and give you Balder back.'

He spoke ; and all the Gods to Odin look'd :
And straight the Father of the Ages said :—

'Ye Gods, these terms may keep another day.
But now, put on your arms, and mount your steeds, 50
And in procession all come near, and weep
Balder ; for that is what the dead desire.
When ye enough have wept, then build a pile
Of the heap'd wood, and burn his corpse with fire
Out of our sight ; that we may turn from grief,
And lead, as erst, our daily life in Heaven.'

He spoke ; and the Gods arm'd : and Odin donn'd
His dazzling corslet and his helm of gold,
And led the way on Sleipner : and the rest
Follow'd, in tears, their Father and their King.   60
And thrice in arms around the dead they rode,
Weeping ; the sands were wetted, and their arms,
With their thick-falling tears : so good a friend
They mourn'd that day, so bright, so lov'd a God.
And Odin came, and laid his kingly hands
On Balder's breast, and thus began the wail :—

'Farewell, O Balder, bright and lov'd, my Son !
In that great day, the Twilight of the Gods,
When Muspel's children shall beleaguer Heaven,
Then we shall miss thy counsel and thy arm.'   70

Thou camest near the next, O Warrior Thor !
Shouldering thy Hammer, in thy chariot drawn,
Swaying the long-hair'd Goats with silver'd rein ;
And over Balder's corpse these words didst say :—

'Brother, thou dwellest in the darksome land,
And talkest with the feeble tribes of ghosts,
Now, and I know not how they prize thee there,
But here, I know, thou wilt be miss'd and mourn'd.
For haughty spirits and high wraths are rife
Among the Gods and Heroes here in Heaven,   80
As among those, whose joy and work is war :
And daily strifes arise, and angry words :
But from thy lips, O Balder, night or day,
Heard no one ever an injurious word
To God or Hero, but thou keptest back
The others, labouring to compose their brawls.
Be ye then kind, as Balder too was kind :
For we lose him, who smooth'd all strife in Heaven.'

He spake : and all the Gods assenting wail'd.
And Freya next came nigh, with golden tears :   90
The loveliest Goddess she in Heaven, by all
Most honour'd after Frea, Odin's wife :
Her long ago the wandering Oder took
To mate, but left her to roam distant lands ;
Since then she seeks him, and weeps tears of gold :
Names hath she many ; Vanadis on earth

They call her ; Freya is her name in Heaven :
She in her hands took Balder's head, and spake :—

  ' Balder, my brother, thou art gone a road
Unknown and long, and haply on that way   100
My long-lost wandering Oder thou hast met,
For in the paths of Heaven he is not found.
Oh, if it be so, tell him what thou wert
To his neglected wife, and what he is,
And wring his heart with shame, to hear thy word.
For he, my husband, left me here to pine,
Not long a wife, when his unquiet heart
First drove him from me into distant lands.
Since then I vainly seek him through the world,
And weep from shore to shore my golden tears,   110
But neither god nor mortal heeds my pain.
Thou only, Balder, wert for ever kind,
To take my hand, and wipe my tears, and say :—
Weep not, O Freya, weep no golden tears !
One day the wandering Oder will return,
Or thou wilt find him in thy faithful search
On some great road, or resting in an inn,
Or at a ford, or sleeping by a tree.—
So Balder said ; but Oder, well I know,
My truant Oder I shall see no more   120
To the world's end ; and Balder now is gone ;
And I am left uncomforted in Heaven.'

  She spake ; and all the Goddesses bewail'd.
Last, from among the Heroes one came near,
No God, but of the Hero-troop the chief—
Regner, who swept the northern sea with fleets,
And rul'd o'er Denmark and the heathy isles,
Living ; but Ella captur'd him and slew :
A king, whose fame then fill'd the vast of Heaven,
Now time obscures it, and men's later deeds :   130
He last approach'd the corpse, and spake, and said :—

  ' Balder, there yet are many Scalds in Heaven
Still left, and that chief Scald, thy brother Brage,
Whom we may bid to sing, though thou art gone :
And all these gladly, while we drink, we hear,
After the feast is done, in Odin's hall :

But they harp ever on one string, and wake
Remembrance in our soul of wars alone,
Such as on earth we valiantly have wag'd,
And blood, and ringing blows, and violent death :   140
But when thou sangest, Balder, thou didst strike
Another note, and, like a bird in spring,
Thy voice of joyance minded us, and youth,
And wife, and children, and our ancient home.
Yes, and I too remember'd then no more
My dungeon, where the serpents stung me dead,
Nor Ella's victory on the English coast ;
But I heard Thora laugh in Gothland Isle ;
And saw my shepherdess, Aslauga, tend
Her flock along the white Norwegian beach :   150
Tears started to mine eyes with yearning joy :
Therefore with grateful heart I mourn thee dead.'

So Regner spake, and all the Heroes groan'd.
But now the sun had pass'd the height of Heaven,
And soon had all that day been spent in wail ;
But then the Father of the Ages said :—

'Ye Gods, there well may be too much of wail.
Bring now the gather'd wood to Balder's ship ;
Heap on the deck the logs, and build the pyre.'   159

But when the Gods and Heroes heard, they brought
The wood to Balder's ship, and built a pile,
Full the deck's breadth, and lofty ; then the corpse
Of Balder on the highest top they laid,
With Nanna on his right, and on his left
Hoder, his brother, whom his own hand slew.
And they set jars of wine and oil to lean
Against the bodies, and stuck torches near,
Splinters of pine-wood, soak'd with turpentine ;
And brought his arms and gold, and all his stuff,
And slew the dogs which at his table fed,   170
And his horse, Balder's horse, whom most he lov'd,
And threw them on the pyre, and Odin threw
A last choice gift thereon, his golden ring.
They fixt the mast, and hoisted up the sails,
Then they put fire to the wood ; and Thor

Set his stout shoulder hard against the stern
To push the ship through the thick sand: sparks flew
From the deep trench she plough'd—so strong a God
Furrow'd it—and the water gurgled in.
And the Ship floated on the waves, and rock'd: 180
But in the hills a strong East-Wind arose,
And came down moaning to the sea; first squalls
Ran black o'er the sea's face, then steady rush'd
The breeze, and fill'd the sails, and blew the fire.
And, wreath'd in smoke, the Ship stood out to sea.
Soon with a roaring rose the mighty fire,
And the pile crackled; and between the logs
Sharp quivering tongues of flame shot out, and leapt,
Curling and darting, higher, until they lick'd
The summit of the pile, the dead, the mast,   190
And ate the shrivelling sails; but still the Ship
Drove on, ablaze, above her hull, with fire.
And the Gods stood upon the beach, and gaz'd:
And, while they gaz'd, the Sun went lurid down
Into the smoke-wrapt sea, and Night came on.
Then the wind fell, with night, and there was calm.
But through the dark they watch'd the burning Ship
Still carried o'er the distant waters on
Farther and farther, like an Eye of Fire.
And as in the dark night a travelling man   200
Who bivouacs in a forest 'mid the hills,
Sees suddenly a spire of flame shoot up
Out of the black waste forest, far below,
Which woodcutters have lighted near their lodge
Against the wolves; and all night long it flares:—
So flar'd, in the far darkness, Balder's pyre.
But fainter, as the stars rose high, it burn'd;
The bodies were consum'd, ash chok'd the pile:
And as in a decaying winter fire   209
A charr'd log, falling, makes a shower of sparks—
So, with a shower of sparks, the pile fell in,
Reddening the sea around; and all was dark.

But the Gods went by starlight up the shore
To Asgard, and sate down in Odin's hall
At table, and the funeral-feast began.
All night they ate the boar Serimner's flesh,

And from their horns, with silver rimm'd, drank mead,
Silent, and waited for the sacred Morn.

And Morning over all the world was spread.
Then from their loathèd feast the Gods arose,　　　220
And took their horses, and set forth to ride
O'er the bridge Bifrost, where is Heimdall's watch,
To the ash Igdrasil, and Ida's plain:
Thor came on foot; the rest on horseback rode.
And they found Mimir sitting by his Fount
Of Wisdom, which beneath the ashtree springs;
And saw the Nornies watering the roots
Of that world-shadowing tree with Honey-dew:
There came the Gods, and sate them down on stones:
And thus the Father of the Ages said:—　　　230

'Ye Gods, the terms ye know, which Hermod brought.
Accept them or reject them; both have grounds.
Accept them, and they bind us, unfulfill'd,
To leave for ever Balder in the grave,
An unrecover'd prisoner, shade with shades.
But how, ye say, should the fulfilment fail?
Smooth sound the terms, and light to be fulfill'd;
For dear-belov'd was Balder while he liv'd
In Heaven and Earth, and who would grudge him tears?
But from the traitorous seed of Lok they come,　　　240
These terms, and I suspect some hidden fraud.
Bethink ye, Gods, is there no other way?—
Speak, were not this a way, the way for Gods?
If I, if Odin, clad in radiant arms,
Mounted on Sleipner, with the Warrior Thor
Drawn in his car beside me, and my sons,
All the strong brood of Heaven, to swell my train,
Should make irruption into Hela's realm,
And set the fields of gloom ablaze with light,
And bring in triumph Balder back to Heaven?'　　　250

He spake; and his fierce sons applauded loud.
But Frea, Mother of the Gods, arose,
Daughter and wife of Odin; thus she said:—

'Odin, thou Whirlwind, what a threat is this!
Thou threatenest what transcends thy might, even thine.

For of all powers the mightiest far art thou,
Lord over men on Earth, and Gods in Heaven ;
Yet even from thee thyself hath been withheld
One thing ; to undo what thou thyself hast rul'd.
For all which hath been fixt, was fixt by thee :   260
In the beginning, ere the Gods were born,
Before the Heavens were builded, thou didst slay
The Giant Ymir, whom the Abyss brought forth,
Thou and thy brethren fierce, the Sons of Bor,
And threw his trunk to choke the abysmal void :
But of his flesh and members thou didst build
The Earth and Ocean, and above them Heaven :
And from the flaming world, where Muspel reigns,
Thou sent'st and fetched'st fire, and madest lights,
Sun Moon and Stars, which thou hast hung in Heaven,
Dividing clear the paths of night and day :   271
And Asgard thou didst build, and Midgard Fort :
Then me thou mad'st ; of us the Gods were born :
Then, walking by the sea, thou foundest spars
Of wood, and framed'st men, who till the earth,
Or on the sea, the field of pirates, sail :
And all the race of Ymir thou didst drown,
Save one, Bergelmer ; he on shipboard fled
Thy deluge, and from him the Giants sprang ;
But all that brood thou hast remov'd far off,   280
And set by Ocean's utmost marge to dwell :
But Hela into Niflheim thou threw'st,
And gav'st her nine unlighted worlds to rule,
A Queen, and empire over all the dead.
That empire wilt thou now invade, light up
Her darkness, from her grasp a subject tear ?—
Try it ; but I, for one, will not applaud.
Nor do I merit, Odin, thou should'st slight
Me and my words, though thou be first in Heaven :
For I too am a Goddess, born of thee,   290
Thine eldest, and of me the Gods are sprung ;
And all that is to come I know, but lock
In my own breast, and have to none reveal'd.
Come then ; since Hela holds by right her prey,
But offers terms for his release to Heaven,
Accept the chance ;—thou canst no more obtain.
Send through the world thy messengers : entreat

All living and unliving things to weep
For Balder ; if thou haply thus may'st melt
Hela, and win the lov'd one back to Heaven.'   300

She spake, and on her face let fall her veil,
And bow'd her head, and sate with folded hands.
Nor did the all-ruling Odin slight her word ;
Straightway he spake, and thus address'd the Gods :

'Go quickly forth through all the world, and pray
All living and unliving things to weep
Balder, if haply he may thus be won.'

When the Gods heard, they straight arose, and took
Their horses, and rode forth through all the world.
North south east west they struck, and roam'd the
          world,   310
Entreating all things to weep Balder's death :
And all that liv'd, and all without life, wept.
And as in winter, when the frost breaks up,
At winter's end, before the spring begins,
And a warm west wind blows, and thaw sets in—
After an hour a dripping sound is heard
In all the forests, and the soft-strewn snow
Under the trees is dibbled thick with holes,
And from the boughs the snowloads shuffle down ;
And in fields sloping to the south dark plots   320
Of grass peep out amid surrounding snow,
And widen, and the peasant's heart is glad—
So through the world was heard a dripping noise
Of all things weeping to bring Balder back :
And there fell joy upon the Gods to hear.

But Hermod rode with Niord, whom he took
To show him spits and beaches of the sea
Far off, where some unwarn'd might fail to weep—
Niord, the God of storms, whom fishers know :
Not born in Heaven ; he was in Vanheim rear'd,   330
With men, but lives a hostage with the Gods :
He knows each frith, and every rocky creek
Fring'd with dark pines, and sands where seafowl
          scream :—
They two scour'd every coast, and all things wept.
And they rode home together, through the wood

Of Jarnvid, which to east of Midgard lies
Bordering the Giants, where the trees are iron;
There in the wood before a cave they came
Where sate, in the cave's mouth, a skinny Hag,
Toothless and old; she gibes the passers by : 340
Thok is she call'd; but now Lok wore her shape :
She greeted them the first, and laugh'd, and said :—

'Ye Gods, good lack, is it so dull in Heaven,
That ye come pleasuring to Thok's Iron Wood?
Lovers of change ye are, fastidious sprites.
Look, as in some boor's yard a sweet-breath'd cow
Whose manger is stuff'd full of good fresh hay
Snuffs at it daintily, and stoops her head
To chew the straw, her litter, at her feet— 349
So ye grow squeamish, Gods, and sniff at Heaven.'

She spake; but Hermod answer'd her and said :—
'Thok, not for gibes we come, we come for tears.
Balder is dead, and Hela holds her prey,
But will restore, if all things give him tears.
Begrudge not thine; to all was Balder dear.'

But, with a louder laugh, the Hag replied :—
'Is Balder dead? and do ye come for tears?
Thok with dry eyes will weep o'er Balder's pyre.
Weep him all other things, if weep they will—
I weep him not : let Hela keep her prey!' 360

She spake; and to the cavern's depth she fled,
Mocking : and Hermod knew their toil was vain.
And as seafaring men, who long have wrought
In the great deep for gain, at last come home,
And towards evening see the headlands rise
Of their own country, and can clear descry
A fire of wither'd furze which boys have lit
Upon the cliffs, or smoke of burning weeds
Out of a till'd field inland;—then the wind
Catches them, and drives out again to sea : 370
And they go long days tossing up and down
Over the grey sea ridges; and the glimpse
Of port they had makes bitterer far their toil—
So the Gods' cross was bitterer for their joy.

Then, sad at heart, to Niord Hermod spake :—
'It is the Accuser Lok, who flouts us all.
Ride back, and tell in Heaven this heavy news.
I must again below, to Hela's realm.'

He spoke ; and Niord set forth back to Heaven.
But northward Hermod rode, the way below ;   380
The way he knew: and travers'd Giall's stream,
And down to Ocean grop'd, and cross'd the ice,
And came beneath the wall, and found the grate
Still lifted ; well was his return foreknown.
And once more Hermod saw around him spread
The joyless plains, and heard the streams of Hell.
But as he enter'd, on the extremest bound
Of Niflheim, he saw one Ghost come near,
Hovering, and stopping oft, as if afraid ;
Hoder, the unhappy, whom his own hand slew :   390
And Hermod look'd, and knew his brother's ghost,
And call'd him by his name, and sternly said :—

'Hoder, ill-fated, blind in heart and eyes !
Why tarriest thou to plunge thee in the gulph
Of the deep inner gloom, but flittest here,
In twilight, on the lonely verge of Hell,
Far from the other ghosts, and Hela's throne ?
Doubtless thou fearest to meet Balder's voice,
Thy brother, whom through folly thou didst slay.'

He spoke ; but Hoder answer'd him, and said :—
'Hermod the nimble, dost thou still pursue   401
The unhappy with reproach, even in the grave ?
For this I died, and fled beneath the gloom,
Not daily to endure abhorring Gods,
Nor with a hateful presence cumber Heaven—
And canst thou not, even here, pass pitying by ?
No less than Balder have I lost the light
Of Heaven, and communion with my kin :
I too had once a wife, and once a child,
And substance, and a golden house in Heaven :   410
But all I left of my own act, and fled
Below, and dost thou hate me even here ?
Balder upbraids me not, nor hates at all,
Though he has cause, have any cause ; but he,

When that with downcast looks I hither came,
Stretch'd forth his hand, and, with benignant voice,
Welcome, he said, *if there be welcome here,*
Brother and fellow-sport of Lok with me.
And not to offend thee, Hermod, nor to force
My hated converse on thee, came I up   420
From the deep gloom, where I will now return ;
But earnestly I long'd to hover near,
Not too far off, when that thou camest by,
To feel the presence of a brother God,
And hear the passage of a horse of Heaven,
For the last time : for here thou com'st no more.'

He spake, and turn'd to go to the inner gloom.
But Hermod stay'd him with mild words, and said :—

'Thou doest well to chide me, Hoder blind.
Truly thou say'st, the planning guilty mind   430
Was Lok's ; the unwitting hand alone was thine.
But Gods are like the sons of men in this—
When they have woe, they blame the nearest cause.
Howbeit stay, and be appeas'd ; and tell—
Sits Balder still in pomp by Hela's side,
Or is he mingled with the unnumber'd dead ?'

And the blind Hoder answer'd him and spake :—
'His place of state remains by Hela's side,
But empty : for his wife, for Nanna came
Lately below, and join'd him ; and the Pair   440
Frequent the still recesses of the realm
Of Hela, and hold converse undisturb'd.
But they too doubtless, will have breath'd the balm
Which floats before a visitant from Heaven,
And have drawn upwards to this verge of Hell.'

He spake ; and, as he ceas'd, a puff of wind
Roll'd heavily the leaden mist aside
Round where they stood, and they beheld Two Forms
Make towards them o'er the stretching cloudy plain.
And Hermod straight perceiv'd them, who they were,
Balder and Nanna ; and to Balder said :—   451

'Balder, too truly thou foresaw'st a snare.
Lok triumphs still, and Hela keeps her prey.

No more to Asgard shalt thou come, nor lodge
In thy own house, Breidablik, nor enjoy
The love all bear towards thee, nor train up
Forset, thy son, to be belov'd like thee.
Here must thou lie, and wait an endless age.
Therefore for the last time, O Balder, hail!'   459

He spake; and Balder answer'd him and said:—
'Hail and farewell, for here thou com'st no more.
Yet mourn not for me, Hermod, when thou sitt'st
In Heaven, nor let the other Gods lament,
As wholly to be pitied, quite forlorn:
For Nanna hath rejoin'd me, who, of old,
In Heaven, was seldom parted from my side;
And still the acceptance follows me, which crown'd
My former life, and cheers me even here.
The iron frown of Hela is relax'd
When I draw nigh, and the wan tribes of dead   470
Trust me, and gladly bring for my award
Their ineffectual feuds and feeble hates,
Shadows of hates, but they distress them still.'

And the fleet-footed Hermod made reply:—
'Thou hast then all the solace death allows,
Esteem and function: and so far is well.
Yet here thou liest, Balder, underground,
Rusting for ever: and the years roll on,
The generations pass, the ages grow,
And bring us nearer to the final day   480
When from the south shall march the Fiery Band
And cross the Bridge of Heaven, with Lok for guide,
And Fenris at his heel with broken chain:
While from the east the Giant Rymer steers
His ship, and the great Serpent makes to land;
And all are marshall'd in one flaming square
Against the Gods, upon the plains of Heaven.
I mourn thee, that thou canst not help us then.'   488

He spake; but Balder answer'd him and said:—
'Mourn not for me: Mourn, Hermod, for the Gods:
Mourn for the men on Earth, the Gods in Heaven,
Who live, and with their eyes shall see that day.
The day will come, when Asgard's towers shall fall,

And Odin, and his Sons, the seed of Heaven :
But what were I, to save them in that hour ?
If strength could save them, could not Odin save,
My Father, and his pride, the Warrior Thor,
Vidar the Silent, the Impetuous Tyr ?
I, what were I, when these can naught avail ?
Yet, doubtless, when the day of battle comes,   500
And the two Hosts are marshall'd, and in Heaven
The golden-crested Cock shall sound alarm,
And his black Brother-Bird from hence reply,
And bucklers clash, and spears begin to pour—
Longing will stir within my breast, though vain.
But not to me so grievous, as, I know,
To other Gods it were, is my enforc'd
Absence from fields where I could nothing aid :
For I am long since weary of your storm
Of carnage, and find, Hermod, in your life   510
Something too much of war and broils, which make
Life one perpetual fight, a bath of blood.
Mine eyes are dizzy with the arrowy hail ;
Mine ears are stunn'd with blows, and sick for calm.
Inactive therefore let me lie, in gloom,
Unarm'd, inglorious : I attend the course
Of ages, and my late return to light,
In times less alien to a spirit mild,
In new-recover'd seats, the happier day.'   519

He spake ; and the fleet Hermod thus replied : —
'Brother, what seats are these, what happier day ?
Tell me, that I may ponder it when gone.'

And the ray-crowned Balder answer'd him :—
'Far to the south, beyond The Blue, there spreads
Another Heaven, The Boundless : no one yet
Hath reach'd it : there hereafter shall arise
The second Asgard, with another name.
Thither, when o'er this present Earth and Heavens
The tempest of the latter days hath swept,   529
And they from sight have disappear'd, and sunk,
Shall a small remnant of the Gods repair :
Hoder and I shall join them from the grave.
There re-assembling we shall see emerge

From the bright Ocean at our feet an Earth
More fresh, more verdant than the last, with fruits
Self-springing, and a seed of man preserv'd,
Who then shall live in peace, as now in war.
But we in Heaven shall find again with joy
The ruin'd palaces of Odin, seats
Familiar, halls where we have supp'd of old ;   540
Re-enter them with wonder, never fill
Our eyes with gazing, and rebuild with tears.
And we shall tread once more the well-known plain
Of Ida, and among the grass shall find
The golden dice with which we play'd of yore ;
And that will bring to mind the former life
And pastime of the Gods, the wise discourse
Of Odin, the delights of other days.
O Hermod, pray that thou mayst join us then !
Such for the future is my hope : meanwhile,   550
I rest the thrall of Hela, and endure
Death, and the gloom which round me even now
Thickens, and to its inner gulph recalls.
Farewell, for longer speech is not allow'd.'

He spoke, and wav'd farewell, and gave his hand
To Nanna ; and she gave their brother blind
Her hand, in turn, for guidance ; and The Three
Departed o'er the cloudy plain, and soon
Faded from sight into the interior gloom.
But Hermod stood beside his drooping horse,   560
Mute, gazing after them in tears : and fain,
Fain had he follow'd their receding steps,
Though they to Death were bound, and he to Heaven,
Then ; but a Power he could not break withheld.
And as a stork which idle boys have trapp'd,
And tied him in a yard, at autumn sees
Flocks of his kind pass flying o'er his head
To warmer lands, and coasts that keep the sun ;
He strains to join their flight, and, from his shed,
Follows them with a long complaining cry—   570
So Hermod gaz'd, and yearn'd to join his kin.

At last he sigh'd, and set forth back to Heaven.

SEPARATION

[First published 1855.]

Stop—Not to me, at this bitter departing,
  Speak of the sure consolations of Time.
Fresh be the wound, still-renew'd be its smarting,
  So but thy image endure in its prime.

But, if the stedfast commandment of Nature
  Wills that remembrance should always decay;
If the lov'd form and the deep-cherish'd feature
  Must, when unseen, from the soul fade away—

Me let no half-effac'd memories cumber!
  Fled, fled at once, be all vestige of thee—   10
Deep be the darkness, and still be the slumber—
  Dead be the Past and its phantoms to me!

Then, when we meet, and thy look strays towards me,
  Scanning my face and the changes wrought there,—
Who, let me say, *is this Stranger regards me,*
  With the grey eyes, and the lovely brown hair?

Separation—*Title*] Faded Leaves. III. Separation *1855*.

TWO POEMS FROM MAGAZINES, 1855

STANZAS FROM THE GRANDE CHARTREUSE

[First published in *Fraser's Magazine*, April, 1855.
Reprinted 1867.]

THROUGH Alpine meadows soft-suffused
With rain, where thick the crocus blows,
Past the dark forges long disused,
The mule-track from Saint Laurent goes.
The bridge is cross'd, and slow we ride,
Through forest, up the mountain-side.

The autumnal evening darkens round,
The wind is up, and drives the rain ;
While hark ! far down, with strangled sound
Doth the Dead Guiers' stream complain,   10
Where that wet smoke among the woods
Over his boiling cauldron broods.

Swift rush the spectral vapours white
Past limestone scars with ragged pines,
Showing—then blotting from our sight.
Halt ! through the cloud-drift something shines !
High in the valley, wet and drear,
The huts of Courrerie appear.

Strike leftward ! cries our guide ; and higher
Mounts up the stony forest-way.   20
At last the encircling trees retire ;
Look ! through the showery twilight grey
What pointed roofs are these advance ?
A palace of the Kings of France ?

Approach, for what we seek is here.
Alight and sparely sup and wait
For rest in this outbuilding near ;
Then cross the sward and reach that gate ;

13 Swift] Fast *Fraser 1855.*

Knock; pass the wicket! Thou art come
To the Carthusians' world-famed home. 30

The silent courts, where night and day
Into their stone-carved basins cold
The splashing icy fountains play,
The humid corridors behold,
Where ghostlike in the deepening night
Cowl'd forms brush by in gleaming white.

The chapel, where no organ's peal
Invests the stern and naked prayer.
With penitential cries they kneel
And wrestle; rising then, with bare 40
And white uplifted faces stand,
Passing the Host from hand to hand;

Each takes; and then his visage wan
Is buried in his cowl once more.
The cells—the suffering Son of Man
Upon the wall! the knee-worn floor!
And, where they sleep, that wooden bed,
Which shall their coffin be, when dead.

The library, where tract and tome
Not to feed priestly pride are there, 50
To hymn the conquering march of Rome,
Nor yet to amuse, as ours are;
They paint of souls the inner strife,
Their drops of blood, their death in life.

The garden, overgrown—yet mild
Those fragrant herbs are flowering there!
Strong children of the Alpine wild
Whose culture is the brethren's care;
Of human tasks their only one,
And cheerful works beneath the sun. 60

Those halls too, destined to contain
Each its own pilgrim host of old,
From England, Germany, or Spain—
All are before me! I behold
The House, the Brotherhood austere!
And what am I, that I am here?

For rigorous teachers seized my youth,
And purged its faith, and trimm'd its fire,
Show'd me the high white star of Truth,
There bade me gaze, and there aspire ;   70
Even now their whispers pierce the gloom :
What dost thou in this living tomb ?

Forgive me, masters of the mind !
At whose behest I long ago
So much unlearnt, so much resign'd !
I come not here to be your foe.
I seek these anchorites, not in ruth,
To curse and to deny your truth ;

Not as their friend or child I speak !
But as on some far northern strand,   80
Thinking of his own Gods, a Greek
In pity and mournful awe might stand
Before some fallen Runic stone—
For both were faiths, and both are gone.

Wandering between two worlds, one dead,
The other powerless to be born,
With nowhere yet to rest my head,
Like these, on earth I wait forlorn.
Their faith, my tears, the world deride ;
I come to shed them at their side.   90

Oh, hide me in your gloom profound,
Ye solemn seats of holy pain !
Take me, cowl'd forms, and fence me round,
Till I possess my soul again !
Till free my thoughts before me roll,
Not chafed by hourly false control.

For the world cries your faith is now
But a dead time's exploded dream ;
My melancholy, sciolists say,
Is a pass'd mode, an outworn theme—   100
As if the world had ever had
A faith, or sciolists been sad.

68 purged . . . trimm'd] prun'd . . . quench'd *Fraser 1855.*
69 high white] pale cold *Fraser 1855.*
93 Invest me, steep me, fold me round, *Fraser 1855.*
101 ever] *ever Fraser 1855.*

Ah, if it *be* pass'd, take away,
At least, the restlessness—the pain !
Be man henceforth no more a prey
To these out-dated stings again !
The nobleness of grief is gone—
Ah, leave us not the fret alone !

But, if you cannot give us ease,
Last of the race of them who grieve   110
Here leave us to die out with these
Last of the people who believe !
Silent, while years engrave the brow ;
Silent—the best are silent now.

Achilles ponders in his tent,
The kings of modern thought are dumb ;
Silent they are, though not content,
And wait to see the future come.
They have the grief men had of yore,
But they contend and cry no more.   120

Our fathers water'd with their tears
This sea of time whereon we sail ;
Their voices were in all men's ears
Who pass'd within their puissant hail.
Still the same Ocean round us raves,
But we stand mute and watch the waves.

For what avail'd it, all the noise
And outcry of the former men ?
Say, have their sons obtain'd more joys ?
Say, is life lighter now than then ?   130
The sufferers died, they left their pain ;
The pangs which tortured them remain.

What helps it now, that Byron bore,
With haughty scorn which mock'd the smart,
Through Europe to the Aetolian shore
The pageant of his bleeding heart ?
That thousands counted every groan,
And Europe made his woe her own ?

108 fret] pang *Fraser 1855*.   121 Our] Their *Fraser 1855*.
126 we] they *Fraser 1855*.   129 obtain'd] achiev'd *Fraser 1855*.

ARNOLD   T

What boots it, Shelley! that the breeze
Carried thy lovely wail away, 140
Musical through Italian trees
That fringe thy soft blue Spezzian bay?
Inheritors of thy distress
Have restless hearts one throb the less?

Or are we easier, to have read,
O Obermann! the sad, stern page,
Which tells us how thou hidd'st thy head
From the fierce tempest of thine age
In the lone brakes of Fontainebleau,
Or chalets near the Alpine snow? 150

Ye slumber in your silent grave!
The world, which for an idle day
Grace to your mood of sadness gave,
Long since hath flung her weeds away.
The eternal trifler breaks your spell;
But we—we learnt your lore too well!

There may, perhaps, yet dawn an age,
More fortunate, alas! than we,
Which without hardness will be sage,
And gay without frivolity. 160
Sons of the world, oh, haste those years;
But, till they rise, allow our tears!

Allow them! We admire with awe
The exulting thunder of your race;
You give the universe your law,
You triumph over time and space.
Your pride of life, your tireless powers,
We mark them, but they are not ours.

We are like children rear'd in shade
Beneath some old-world abbey wall 170
Forgotten in a forest-glade
And secret from the eyes of all;
Deep, deep the greenwood round them waves,
Their abbey, and its close of graves.

142 soft] dark *Fraser 1855*.   151 Ye . . . your] They . . .
their *Fraser 1855*.   153, 155, 156 your] their *Fraser 1855*.   154
flung] thrown *Fraser 1855*.   168 We mark them] They awe
us *Fraser 1855*.

But where the road runs near the stream,
Oft through the trees they catch a glance
Of passing troops in the sun's beam—
Pennon, and plume, and flashing lance!
Forth to the world those soldiers fare,
To life, to cities, and to war.   180

And through the woods, another way,
Faint bugle-notes from far are borne,
Where hunters gather, staghounds bay,
Round some old forest-lodge at morn;
Gay dames are there in sylvan green,
Laughter and cries—those notes between!

The banners flashing through the trees
Make their blood dance and chain their eyes;
That bugle-music on the breeze
Arrests them with a charm'd surprise.   190
Banner by turns and bugle woo:
Ye shy recluses, follow too!

O children, what do ye reply?—
'Action and pleasure, will ye roam
Through these secluded dells to cry
And call us? but too late ye come!
Too late for us your call ye blow
Whose bent was taken long ago.

'Long since we pace this shadow'd nave;
We watch those yellow tapers shine,   200
Emblems of hope over the grave,
In the high altar's depth divine;
The organ carries to our ear
Its accents of another sphere.

'Fenced early in this cloistral round
Of reverie, of shade, of prayer,
How should we grow in other ground?
How should we flower in foreign air?
Pass, banners, pass, and bugles, cease!
And leave our desert to its peace!'   210

179 the world those soldiers] the mighty world they *Fraser
1855.*   201 hope over] light above *Fraser 1855.*   210 desert]
forest *Fraser 1855.*

HAWORTH CHURCHYARD

APRIL, 1855

[First published in *Fraser's Magazine*, May, 1855.]

WHERE, under Loughrigg, the stream
Of Rotha sparkles, the fields
Are green, in the house of one
Friendly and gentle, now dead,
Wordsworth's son-in-law, friend—
Four years since, on a mark'd
Evening, a meeting I saw.

Two friends met there, two fam'd
Gifted women.   The one,
Brilliant with recent renown,   10
Young, unpractis'd, had told
With a Master's accent her feign'd
Story of passionate life :
The other, maturer in fame,
Earning, she too, her praise
First in Fiction, had since
Widen'd her sweep, and survey'd
History, Politics, Mind.

They met, held converse : they wrote
In a book which of glorious souls   20
Held memorial : Bard,
Warrior, Statesman, had left
Their names :—chief treasure of all,
Scott had consign'd there his last
Breathings of song, with a pen
Tottering, a death-stricken hand.

I beheld ; the obscure
Saw the famous.   Alas !
Years in number, it seem'd,
Lay before both, and a fame   30
Heighten'd, and multiplied power.
Behold ! The elder, to-day,
Lies expecting from Death,
In mortal weakness, a last
Summons : the younger is dead.

First to the living we pay
Mournful homage : the Muse
Gains not an earth-deafen'd ear.

Hail to the steadfast soul,
Which, unflinching and keen,   40
Wrought to erase from its depth
Mist, and illusion, and fear !
Hail to the spirit which dar'd
Trust its own thoughts, before yet
Echoed her back by the crowd !
Hail to the courage which gave
Voice to its creed, ere the creed
Won consecration from Time !

Turn, O Death, on the vile,
Turn on the foolish the stroke   50
Hanging now o'er a head
Active, beneficent, pure !
But, if the prayer be in vain—
But, if the stroke *must* fall—
Her, whom we cannot save,
What might we say to console ?

She will not see her country lose
Its greatness, nor the reign of fools prolong'd.
She will behold no more
This ignominious spectacle,   60
Power dropping from the hand
Of paralytic factions, and no soul
To snatch and wield it : will not see
Her fellow people sit
Helplessly gazing on their own decline.

Myrtle and rose fit the young,
Laurel and oak the mature.
Private affections, for these,
Have run their circle, and left
Space for things far from themselves,   70
Thoughts of the general weal,
Country, and public cares :
Public cares, which move
Seldom and faintly the depth

Of younger passionate souls
Plung'd in themselves, who demand
Only to live by the heart,
Only to love and be lov'd.

How shall we honour the young,
The ardent, the gifted? how mourn?   80
Console we cannot; her ear
Is deaf.   Far northward from here,
In a churchyard high mid the moors
Of Yorkshire, a little earth
Stops it for ever to praise.

Where, behind Keighley, the road
Up to the heart of the moors
Between heath-clad showery hills
Runs, and colliers' carts
Poach the deep ways coming down,   90
And a rough, grim'd race have their homes—
There, on its slope, is built
The moorland town.   But the church
Stands on the crest of the hill,
Lonely and bleak; at its side
The parsonage-house and the graves.

See! in the desolate house
The childless father! Alas—
Age, whom the most of us chide,
Chide, and put back, and delay—   100
Come, unupbraided for once!
Lay thy benumbing hand,
Gratefully cold, on this brow!
Shut out the grief, the despair!
Weaken the sense of his loss!
Deaden the infinite pain!

Another grief I see,
Younger: but this the Muse,
In pity and silent awe
Revering what she cannot soothe,   110
With veil'd face and bow'd head,
Salutes, and passes by.

Strew with roses the grave
Of the early-dying.   Alas !
Early she goes on the path
To the Silent Country, and leaves
Half her laurels unwon,
Dying too soon : yet green
Laurels she had, and a course
Short, but redoubled by Fame.   120

For him who must live many years
That life is best which slips away
Out of the light, and mutely ; which avoids
Fame, and her less-fair followers, Envy, Strife,
Stupid Detraction, Jealousy, Cabal,
Insincere Praises :—which descends
The mossy quiet track to Age.

But, when immature Death
Beckons too early the guest
From the half-tried Banquet of Life,   130
Young, in the bloom of his days ;
Leaves no leisure to press,
Slow and surely, the sweet
Of a tranquil life in the shade—
Fuller for him be the hours !
Give him emotion, though pain !
Let him live, let him feel, *I have liv'd.*
Heap up his moments with life !
Quicken his pulses with Fame !

And not friendless, nor yet   140
Only with strangers to meet,
Faces ungreeting and cold,
Thou, O Mourn'd One, to-day
Enterest the House of the Grave.
Those of thy blood, whom thou lov'dst,
Have preceded thee ; young,
Loving, a sisterly band :
Some in gift, some in art
Inferior ; all in fame.
They, like friends, shall receive   150
This comer, greet her with joy ;
Welcome the Sister, the Friend ;
Hear with delight of thy fame.

Round thee they lie ; the grass
Blows from their graves toward thine.
She, whose genius, though not
Puissant like thine, was yet
Sweet and graceful : and She—
(How shall I sing her ?)—whose soul
Knew no fellow for might,   160
Passion, vehemence, grief,
Daring, since Byron died,
That world-fam'd Son of Fire ; She, who sank
Baffled, unknown, self-consum'd ;
Whose too bold dying song
Shook, like a clarion-blast, my soul.

Of one too I have heard,
A Brother—sleeps he here ?—
Of all his gifted race
Not the least gifted ; young,   170
Unhappy, beautiful ; the cause
Of many hopes, of many tears.
O Boy, if here thou sleep'st, sleep well !
On thee too did the Muse
Bright in thy cradle smile :
But some dark Shadow came
(I know not what) and interpos'd.

Sleep, O cluster of friends,
Sleep ! or only, when May,
Brought by the West Wind, returns   180
Back to your native heaths,
And the plover is heard on the moors,
Yearly awake, to behold
The opening summer, the sky,
The shining moorland ; to hear
The drowsy bee, as of old,
Hum o'er the thyme, the grouse
Call from the heather in bloom :

Sleep : or only for this
Break your united repose.   190

TO MARGUERITE

[First published 1857.]

WE were apart : yet, day by day,
I bade my heart more constant be ;
I bade it keep the world away,
And grow a home for only thee :
Nor fear'd but thy love likewise grew,
Like mine, each day more tried, more true.

The fault was grave : I might have known,
What far too soon, alas, I learn'd—
The heart can bind itself alone,
And faith is often unreturn'd.—   10
   Self-sway'd our feelings ebb and swell :
Thou lov'st no more : Farewell ! Farewell !

Farewell ! and thou, thou lonely heart,
Which never yet without remorse
Even for a moment did'st depart
From thy remote and spherèd course
To haunt the place where passions reign,
Back to thy solitude again !

Back, with the conscious thrill of shame
Which Luna felt, that summer night,   20
Flash through her pure immortal frame,
When she forsook the starry height
To hang over Endymion's sleep
Upon the pine-grown Latmian steep ;—

Yet she, chaste Queen, had never prov'd
How vain a thing is mortal love,
Wandering in Heaven, far remov'd.
But thou hast long had place to prove
This truth—to prove, and make thine own :
   Thou hast been, shalt be, art, alone.   30

To Marguerite *Title*] Switzerland. VI. To Marguerite *1857*.

Or, if not quite alone, yet they
Which touch thee are unmating things—
Ocean, and Clouds, and Night, and Day ;
Lorn Autumns and triumphant Springs ;
And life, and others' joy and pain,
And love, if love, of happier men.

Of happier men—for they, at least,
Have *dream'd* two human hearts might blend
In one, and were through faith releas'd
From isolation without end   40
Prolong'd, nor knew, although not less
Alone than thou, their loneliness.

MEROPE.   A TRAGEDY.   1858

Φιλοκαλοῦμεν μετ᾽ εὐτελείας

[First published 1858.]

PREFACE

I AM not about to defend myself for having taken the
story of the following tragedy from classical antiquity.
On this subject I have already said all which appears
to me to be necessary.   For those readers to whom my
tragedy will give pleasure, no argument on such a
matter is required : one critic, whose fine intelligence
it would have been an honour to convince, lives, alas !
no longer : there are others, upon whom no arguments
which I could possibly use would produce any impression.   The Athenians fined Phrynichus for repre- 10
senting to them their own sufferings : there are critics
who would fine us for representing to them anything else.

But, as often as it has happened to me to be blamed
or praised for my supposed addiction to the classical
school in poetry, I have thought, with real humilia-
tion, how little any works of mine were entitled to
rank among the genuine works of that school ; how
little they were calculated to give, to readers unac-
quainted with the great creations of classical antiquity, 20
any adequate impression of their form or of their spirit.
And yet, whatever the critics may say, there exists,
I am convinced, even in England, even in this strong-
hold of the romantic school, a wide though an ill-
informed curiosity on the subject of the so-called classical
school, meriting a more complete satisfaction than it
has hitherto obtained.   Greek art—the antique—classical beauty—a nameless hope and interest attaches,
I can often see, to these words, even in the minds of
those who have been brought up among the productions 30
of the romantic school ; of those who have been taught

to consider classicalism as inseparable from coldness, and the antique as another phrase for the unreal. So immortal, so indestructible is the power of true beauty, of consummate form : it may be submerged, but the tradition of it survives : nations arise which know it not, which hardly believe in the report of it ; but they, too, are haunted with an indefinable interest in its name, with an inexplicable curiosity as to its nature.

But however the case may be with regard to the
10 curiosity of the public, I have long had the strongest desire to attempt, for my own satisfaction, to come to closer quarters with the form which produces such grand effects in the hands of the Greek masters ; to try to obtain, through the medium of a living, familiar language, a fuller and more intense feeling of that beauty, which, even when apprehended through the medium of a dead language, so powerfully affected me. In his delightful *Life of Goethe*, Mr. Lewes has most truly observed that Goethe's *Iphigeneia* enjoys an ines-
20 timable advantage in being written in a language which, being a modern language, is in some sort our own. Not only is it vain to expect that the vast majority of mankind will ever undertake the toil of mastering a dead language, above all, a dead language so difficult as the Greek ; but it may be doubted whether even those, whose enthusiasm shrinks from no toil, can ever so thoroughly press into the intimate feeling of works composed in a dead language as their enthusiasm would desire.

I desired to try, therefore, how much of the effec-
30 tiveness of the Greek poetical forms I could retain in an English poem constructed under the conditions of those forms ; of those forms, too, in their severest and most definite expression, in their application to dramatic poetry.

I thought at first that I might accomplish my object by a translation of one of the great works of Aeschylus or Sophocles. But a translation is a work not only inferior to the original by the whole difference of talent between the first composer and his
40 translator : it is even inferior to the best which the translator could do under more inspiring circum-

stances. No man can do his best with a subject which
does not penetrate him : no man can be penetrated by a
subject which he does not conceive independently.

Should I take some subject on which we have an
extant work by one of the great Greek poets, and treat
it independently ? Something was to be said for such
a course : in antiquity, the same tragic stories were
handled by all the tragic poets : Voltaire says truly
that to see the same materials differently treated by
different poets is most interesting ; accordingly, we 10
have an *Oedipus* of Corneille, an *Oedipus* of Voltaire :
innumerable are the *Agamemnons*, the *Electras*, the
Antigones, of the French and Italian poets from the
sixteenth to the nineteenth century. But the same
disadvantage which we have in translating clings to us
in our attempt to treat these subjects independently :
their treatment by the ancient masters is so over-
whelmingly great and powerful that we can henceforth conceive them only as they are there treated : an
independent conception of them has become impossible 20
for us : in working upon them we are still, therefore,
subject to conditions under which no man can do his
best.

It remained to select a subject from among those
which had been considered to possess the true requi-
sites of good tragic subjects ; on which great works
had been composed, but had not survived to chill
emulation by their grandeur. Of such subjects there
is, fortunately, no lack. In the writings of Hyginus,
a Latin mythographer of uncertain date, we possess a 30
large stock of them. The heroic stories in Hyginus,
Maffei, the reformer of the Italian theatre, imagined
rightly or wrongly to be the actual summaries of lost
Greek dramas : they are, at any rate, subjects on
which lost dramas were founded. Maffei counsels
the poets of his nation to turn from the inferior subjects on which they were employing themselves, to
this ' *miniera di tragici argomenti*,' this rich mine of
subjects for tragedy. Lessing, the great German critic,
echoes Maffei's counsel, but adds a warning. ' Yes,' he 40
cries, ' the great subjects are there, but they await an
intelligent eye to regard them : they can be handled,

not by the great majority of poets, but only by the
small minority.'

Among these subjects presented in the collection
of Hyginus, there is one which has long attracted my
interest, from the testimony of the ancients to its
excellence, and from the results which that testimony
has called forth from the emulation of the moderns.
That subject is the story of Merope. To the effectiveness of the situations which this story offered,
10 Aristotle and Plutarch have borne witness: a celebrated tragedy upon it, probably by Euripides, existed
in antiquity. 'The *Cresphontes* of Euripides is lost,'
exclaims the reviewer of Voltaire's *Mérope*, a Jesuit,
and not unwilling to conciliate the terrible pupil of
his order; 'the *Cresphontes* of Euripides is lost:
M. de Voltaire has restored it to us.' 'Aristotle,' says
Voltaire, 'Aristotle, in his immortal work on Poetry,
does not hesitate to affirm that the recognition between
Merope and her son was the most interesting moment
20 of the Greek stage.' Aristotle affirms no such thing;
but he *does* say that the story of Merope, like the
stories of Iphigeneia and Antiope, supplies an example
of a recognition of the most affecting kind. And
Plutarch says; 'Look at Merope in the tragedy, lifting
up the axe against her own son as being the murderer
of her own son, and crying—

$$\dot{o}\sigma\iota\omega\tau\dot{\epsilon}\rho\alpha\nu\ \delta\dot{\eta}\ \tau\dot{\eta}\nu\delta'\ \dot{\epsilon}\gamma\omega\ \delta\dot{\iota}\delta\omega\mu\dot{\iota}\ \sigma\omega$$
$$\pi\lambda\eta\gamma\dot{\eta}\nu\text{———}$$

A more just stroke than that thou gav'st my son,
30   Take ———

What an agitation she makes in the theatre ! how she
fills the spectators with terror lest she should be too
quick for the old man who is trying to stop her, and
should strike the lad !'

It is singular that neither Aristotle nor Plutarch
names the author of the tragedy : scholiasts and other
late writers quote from it as from a work of Euripides ;
but the only writer of authority who names him as
its author is Cicero. About fifty lines of it have come
40 down to us: the most important of these remains are
the passage just quoted, and a choral address to Peace ;

of these I have made use in my tragedy, translating the
former, and of the latter adopting the general thought,
that of rejoicing at the return of peace : the other
fragments consist chiefly of detached moral sentences,
of which I have not made any use.

It may be interesting to give some account of the
more celebrated of those modern works which have
been founded upon this subject. But before I proceed
to do this, I will state what accounts we have of the
story itself. 10

These proceed from three sources—Apollodorus,
Pausanias, and Hyginus. Of their accounts that of
Apollodorus is the most ancient, that of Pausanias the
most historically valuable, and that of Hyginus the
fullest. I will begin with the last-named writer.

Hyginus says :—

'Merope sent away and concealed her infant son.
Polyphontes sought for him everywhere, and promised
gold to whoever should slay him. He, when he grew
up, laid a plan to avenge the murder of his father and 20
brothers. In pursuance of this plan he came to king
Polyphontes and asked for the promised gold, saying
that he had slain the son of Cresphontes and Merope.
The king ordered him to be hospitably entertained,
intending to inquire further of him. He, being very
tired, went to sleep, and an old man, who was the
channel through whom the mother and son used to
communicate, arrives at this moment in tears, bringing
word to Merope that her son had disappeared from his
protector's house. Merope, believing that the sleeping 30
stranger is the murderer of her son, comes into the
guest-chamber with an axe, not knowing that he
whom she would slay was her son : the old man
recognized him, and withheld Merope from slaying
him. After the recognition had taken place, Merope,
to prepare the way for her vengeance, affected to be
reconciled with Polyphontes. The king, overjoyed,
celebrated a sacrifice : his guest, pretending to strike
the sacrificial victim, slew the king, and so got back
his father's kingdom.' 40

Apollodorus says :—

'Cresphontes had not reigned long in Messenia when

he was murdered together with two of his sons. And
Polyphontes reigned in his stead, he, too, being of the
family of Hercules ; and he had for his wife, against
her will, Merope, the widow of the murdered king.
But Merope had borne to Cresphontes a third son,
called Aepytus: him she gave to her own father to
bring up. He, when he came to man's estate, returned
secretly to Messenia, and slew Polyphontes and the
other murderers of his father.'

10 Pausanias adds nothing to the facts told by Apollodorus, except that he records the proceedings of
Cresphontes which had provoked the resentment of
his Dorian nobles, and led to his murder. His state-
ments on this point will be found in the Historical
Introduction which follows this Preface.

The account of the modern fortunes of the story of
Merope is a curious chapter in literary history. In the
early age of the French theatre this subject attracted
the notice of a great man, if not a great poet, the
20 cardinal Richelieu. At his theatre, in the Palais
Royal, was brought out, in 1641, a tragedy under the
title of *Téléphonte*, the name given by Hyginus to the
surviving son of Merope. This piece is said by
Voltaire to have contained about a hundred lines by
the great cardinal, who had, as is well known, more
bent than genius for dramatic composition. There his
vein appears to have dried up, and the rest is by an
undistinguished hand. This tragedy was followed
by another on the same subject from the resident
30 minister, at Paris, of the celebrated Christina of
Sweden. Two pieces with the title of *Mérope*, besides
others on the same story, but with different names,
were brought out at Paris before the *Mérope* of Voltaire
appeared. It seems that none of them created any
memorable impression.

The first eminent success was in Italy. There too,
as in France, more than one *Merope* was early produced : one of them in the sixteenth century, by a
Count Torelli, composed with choruses : but the first
40 success was achieved by Maffei. Scipio Maffei, called
by Voltaire the Sophocles and Varro of Verona, was
a noble and cultivated person. He became in middle

life the historian of his native place, Verona; and may claim the honour of having partly anticipated Niebuhr in his famous discovery, in the Capitular library of that city, of the lost works of Gaius, the Roman lawyer. He visited France and England, and received an honorary degree at Oxford. But in earlier life he signalized himself as the reviver of the study of Greek literature in Italy; and with the aim to promote that study, and to rescue the Italian theatre from the debasement into which it had fallen, 10 he brought out at Modena, in 1713, his tragedy of *Merope*.

The effect was immense. 'Let the Greek and Roman writers give place: here is a greater production than the *Oedipus!*' wrote, in Latin verse, an enthusiastic admirer. In the winter following its appearance, the tragedy kept constant possession of the stage in Italy; and its reputation travelled into France and England. In England a play was produced in 1731, by a writer called Jeffreys, professedly taken 20 from the *Merope* of Maffei. But at this period a love-intrigue was considered indispensable in a tragedy: Voltaire was even compelled by the actors to introduce one in his *Oedipus*: and although in Maffei's work there is no love-intrigue, the English adapter felt himself bound to supply the deficiency. Accordingly he makes, if we may trust Voltaire, the unknown son of Merope in love with one of her maids of honour: he is brought before his mother as his own supposed murderer: she gives him the choice of death by the 30 dagger or by poison: he chooses the latter, drinks off the poison and falls insensible: but reappears at the end of the tragedy safe and sound, a friend of the maid of honour having substituted a sleeping-draught for the poison. Such is Voltaire's account of this English *Merope*, of which I have not been able to obtain sight. Voltaire is apt to exaggerate; but the work was, without doubt, sufficiently absurd. A better English translation, by Ayre, appeared in 1740. I have taken from Maffei a line in my tragedy— 40

Tyrants think, him they murder not, they spare.

Maffei has—

> Ecco il don dei tiranni: a lor rassembra,
> Morte non dando altrui, di dar la vita.

Maffei makes some important changes in the story as told by its ancient relaters. In his tragedy the unknown prince, Merope's son, is called Egisto: Merope herself is not, as the ancients represented her, at the time of her son's return the wife of Polyphontes, but is repelling the importunate offer of his hand by her
10 husband's murderer: Egisto does not, like Orestes, know his own parentage, and return secretly to his own home in order to wreak vengeance, in concert with his mother, upon his father's murderer: he imagines himself the son of Messenian parents, but of a rank not royal, entrusted to an old man, Polidoro, to be brought up; and is driven by curiosity to quit his protector and visit his native land. He enters Messenia, and is attacked by a robber, whom he kills. The blood upon his dress attracts the notice of some
20 soldiers of Polyphontes whom he falls in with; he is seized and brought to the royal palace. On hearing his story, a suspicion seizes Merope, who has heard from Polidoro that her son has quitted him, that the slain person must have been her own son. The suspicion is confirmed by the sight of a ring on the finger of Egisto, which had belonged to Cresphontes, and which Merope supposes the unknown stranger to have taken from her murdered son: she twice attempts his life: the arrival of Polidoro at last clears up the
30 mystery for her; but at the very moment when she recognizes Egisto, they are separated, and no interview of recognition takes place between the mother and son. Finally, the prince is made acquainted with his origin, and kills Polyphontes in the manner described by Hyginus.

This is an outline of the story as arranged by Maffei. This arrangement has been followed, in the main, by all his successors. His treatment of the subject has, I think, some grave defects, which I shall presently
40 notice: but his work has much nobleness and feeling; it seems to me to possess, on the whole, more merit

of a strictly poetical kind than any of the subsequent
works upon the same subject.

Voltaire's curiosity, which never slumbered, was
attracted by the success of Maffei. It was not until
1736, however, when his interest in Maffei's tragedy
had been increased by a personal acquaintance with
its author, that his own *Mérope* was composed. It
was not brought out upon the stage until 1743. It
was received, like its Italian predecessor, with an
enthusiasm which, assuredly, the English *Merope* will 10
not excite. From its exhibition dates the practice of
calling for a successful author to appear at the close
of his piece : the audience were so much enchanted
with Voltaire's tragedy, that they insisted on seeing
the man who had given them such delight. To Corneille had been paid the honour of reserving for him
the same seat in the theatre at all representations ; but
neither he nor Racine were ever 'called for.'

Voltaire, in a long complimentary letter, dedicated
his tragedy to Maffei. He had at first intended, he 20
says, merely to translate the *Merope* of his predecessor,
which he so greatly admired : he still admired it ;
above all, he admired it because it possessed *simplicity* ;
that simplicity which is, he says, his own idol. But
he has to deal with a Parisian audience, with an
audience who have been glutted with masterpieces until
their delicacy has become excessive ; until they can
no longer support the simple and rustic air, the details
of country life, which Maffei had imitated from the
Greek theatre. The audience of Paris, of that city in 30
which some thirty thousand spectators daily witnessed
theatrical performances, and thus acquired, by constant practice, a severity of taste, to which the ten
thousand Athenians who saw tragedies but four times
a year could not pretend—of that terrible city, in
which

> Et pueri nasum rhinocerotis habent :

this audience loved simplicity, indeed, but not the
same simplicity which was loved at Athens and imitated by Maffei. 'I regret this,' says Voltaire, 'for 40
how fond I am of simple nature ! but, *il faut se plier au*

goût d'une nation, one must accommodate oneself to the
taste of one's countrymen.'

He does himself less than justice. When he objects,
indeed, to that in Maffei's work which is truly 'naïf et
rustique,' to that which is truly in a Greek spirit, he
is wrong. His objection, for instance, to the passage
in which the old retainer of Cresphontes describes, in
the language of a man of his class, the rejoicings which
celebrated his master's accession, is, in my opinion,
10 perfectly groundless. But the wonderful penetration
and clear sense of Voltaire seizes, in general, upon
really weak points in Maffei's work : upon points
which, to an Athenian, would have seemed as weak
as they seemed to Voltaire. A French audience, he
says, would not have borne to witness Polyphontes
making love to Merope, whose husband he had
murdered : neither would an Athenian audience have
borne it. To hear Polyphontes say to Merope '*Io
t'amo,*' even though he is but feigning, for state pur-
20 poses, a love which he has not really, shocks the
natural feeling of mankind. Our usages, says
Voltaire, would not permit that Merope should twice
rush upon her son to slay him, once with a javelin,
the next time with an axe. The French dramatic
usages, then, would on this point have perfectly agreed
with the laws of reason and good taste : this repetition
of the same incident is tasteless and unmeaning. It
is a grave fault of art, says Voltaire, that, at the critical
moment of recognition, not a word passes between
30 Merope and her son. He is right ; a noble opportunity
is thus thrown away. He objects to Maffei's excessive
introduction of conversations between subaltern personages : these conversations are, no doubt, tiresome.
Other points there are, with respect to which we may
say that Voltaire's objections would have been perfectly
sound had Maffei really done what is imputed to him :
but he has not. Voltaire has a talent for misrepresen-
tation, and he often uses it unscrupulously.

He never used it more unscrupulously than on this
40 occasion. The French public, it appears, took Voltaire's expressions of obligation to Maffei somewhat
more literally than Voltaire liked : they imagined

that the French *Mérope* was rather a successful adaptation of the Italian *Merope* than an original work. It
was necessary to undeceive them. A letter appeared,
addressed by a M. de La Lindelle to Voltaire, in which
Voltaire is reproached for his excessive praises of
Maffei's tragedy, in which that work is rigorously
analysed, its faults remorselessly displayed. No merit
is allowed to it: it is a thoroughly bad piece on
a thoroughly good subject. Lessing, who, in 1768, in
his *Hamburgische Dramaturgie*, reviewed Voltaire's 10
Mérope at great length, evidently has divined, what is
the truth, that M. de La Lindelle and Voltaire are one
and the same person. It required indeed but little of
the great Lessing's sagacity to divine that. An unknown
M. de La Lindelle does not write one letter in that
style of unmatched incisiveness and animation, that
style compared to which the style of Lord Macaulay is
tame, and the style of Isocrates is obscure, and then
pass for ever from the human stage. M. de La Lindelle
is Voltaire ; but that does not hinder Voltaire from 20
replying to him with perfect gravity. 'You terrify
me!' he exclaims to his correspondent—that is, to
himself : 'you terrify me! you are as hypercritical as
Scaliger. Why not fix your attention rather on the
beauties of M. Maffei's work, than on its undoubted
defects ? It is my sincere opinion that, in some points,
M. Maffei's *Merope* is superior to my own.' The transaction is one of the most signal instances of literary
sharp practice on record. To this day, in the ordinary
editions of Voltaire, M. de La Lindelle's letter figures, 30
in the correspondence prefixed to the tragedy of *Mérope*,
as the letter of an authentic person ; although the true
history of the proceeding has long been well known,
and Voltaire's conduct in it was severely blamed by
La Harpe.

Voltaire had said that his *Mérope* was occasioned by
that of Maffei. '*Occasioned*,' says Lessing, 'is too
weak a word : M. de Voltaire's tragedy owes *everything*
to that of M. Maffei.' This is not just. We have seen
the faults in Maffei's work pointed out by Voltaire. 40
Some of these faults he avoids : at the same time he
discerns, with masterly clearness, the true difficulties

of the subject. 'Comment se prendre,' he says, 'pour
faire penser à Mérope que son fils est l'assassin de son
fils même?' That is one problem; here is another:
'Comment trouver des motifs nécessaires pour que
Polyphonte veuille épouser Mérope?' Let us see
which of Maffei's faults Voltaire avoids: let us see
how far he solves the problems which he himself has
enunciated.

The story, in its main outline, is the same with
10 Voltaire as with Maffei; but in some particulars it is
altered, so as to have more probability. Like Maffei's
Egisto, Voltaire's Égisthe does not know his own
origin: like him, youthful curiosity drives him to
quit his aged protector, and to re-enter Messenia.
Like him he has an encounter with a stranger, whom
he slays, and whose blood, staining his clothes, leads
to his apprehension. But this stranger is an emissary
of Polyphontes, sent to effect the young prince's
murder. This is an improvement upon the robber of
20 Maffei, who has no connexion whatever with the
action of the piece. Suspicion falls upon Égisthe on
the same grounds as those on which it fell upon
Egisto. The suspicion is confirmed in Égisthe's case
by the appearance of a coat of armour, as, in Egisto's
case, it was confirmed by the appearance of a ring.
In neither case does Merope seem to have sufficient
cause to believe the unknown youth to be her son's
murderer. In Voltaire's tragedy, Merope is ignorant
until the end of the third act that Polyphontes is her
30 husband's murderer; nay, she believes that Cresphontes,
murdered by the brigands of Pylos, has been avenged
by Polyphontes, who claims her gratitude on that
ground. He desires to marry her in order to strengthen
his position. 'Of interests in the state,' he says,

'Il ne reste aujourd'hui que le vôtre et le mien :
Nous devons l'un à l'autre un mutuel soutien.'

Voltaire thus departs widely from the tradition ; but
he can represent Merope as entertaining and discuss-
ing the tyrant's offer of marriage without shocking
40 our feelings. The style, however, in which Voltaire
makes Polyphontes urge his addresses, would some-

times, I think, have wounded a Greek's taste as much
as Maffei's *Io t'amo*—

Je sais que vos appas, encor dans le printemps,
Pourraient s'effaroucher de l'hiver de mes ans.

What an address from a stern, care-haunted ruler to
a widowed queen, the mother of a grown-up son!
The tragedy proceeds; and Merope is about to slay
her son, when his aged guardian arrives and makes
known to her who the youth is. This is as in Maffei's
piece; but Voltaire avoids the absurdity of the double 10
attempt by Merope on her son's life. Yet he, too,
permits Égisthe to leave the stage without exchanging
a word with his mother: the very fault which he
justly censures in Maffei. Égisthe, indeed, does not
even learn, on this occasion, that Merope is his mother: the recognition is thus cut in half. The second
half of it comes afterwards, in the presence of Polyphontes; and his presence imposes, of course, a re-
straint upon the mother and son. Merope is driven,
by fear for her son's safety, to consent to marry 20
Polyphontes, although his full guilt is now revealed
to her; but she is saved by her son, who slays
the tyrant in the manner told in the tradition and
followed by Maffei.

What is the real merit of Voltaire's tragedy? We
must forget the rhymed Alexandrines; that metre,
faulty not so much because it is disagreeable in itself,
as because it has in it something which is essentially
unsuited to perfect tragedy; that metre which is so
indefensible, and which Voltaire has so ingeniously 30
laboured to defend. He takes a noble passage from
Racine's *Phèdre*, alters words so as to remove the
rhyme, and asks if the passage now produces as good
an effect as before. But a fine passage which we are
used to we like in the form in which we are used to it,
with all its faults. Prose is, undoubtedly, a less
noble vehicle for tragedy than verse; yet we should
not like the fine passages in Goethe's prose tragedy of
Egmont the better for having them turned into verse.
Besides, it is not clear that the unrhymed Alexandrine 40
is a better tragic metre than the rhymed. Voltaire

says that usage has now established the metre in
France, and that the dramatic poet has no escape from
it. For him and his contemporaries this is a valid
plea ; but how much one regrets that the poetical
feeling of the French nation did not, at a period when
such an alteration was still possible, change for a better
this unsuitable tragic metre, as the Greeks, in the
early period of their tragic art, changed for the more
fitting iambus their trochaic tetrameter.

10   To return to Voltaire's *Mérope*. It is admirably
constructed, and must have been most effective on the
stage. One feels, as one reads it, that a poet gains
something by living amongst a population who have
the nose of the rhinoceros : his ingenuity becomes
sharpened. This work has, besides, that stamp of
a prodigious talent which none of Voltaire's works
are without ; it has vigour, clearness, rapid movement ;
it has lines which are models of terse observation—

> Le premier qui fut roi fut un soldat heureux :
20 > Qui sert bien son pays n'a pas besoin d'aïeux.

It has lines which are models of powerful, animated
rhetoric—

MÉROPE

Courons à Polyphonte—implorons son appui.

NARBAS

N'implorez que les dieux, et ne craignez que lui.

What it wants is a charm of poetical feeling, which
Racine's tragedies possess, and which has given to
them the decisive superiority over those of Voltaire.
30 He has managed his story with great adroitness ; but
he has departed from the original tradition yet further
than Maffei. He has avoided several of Maffei's
faults : why has he not avoided his fault of omitting
to introduce, at the moment of recognition, a scene
between the mother and son ? Lessing thinks that
he wanted the double recognition in order to enable
him to fill his prescribed space, that terrible 'carrière
de cinq actes' of which he so grievously complains.
I believe, rather, that he cut the recognition in two, in
40 order to produce for his audience two distinct shocks
of surprise : for to inspire *surprise*, Voltaire considered

the dramatic poet's true aim ; an opinion which, as we shall hereafter see, sometimes led him astray.

Voltaire's *Mérope* was adapted for the English stage by Aaron Hill, a singular man ; by turns, poet, soldier, theatrical manager, and Lord Peterborough's private secretary ; but always, and above all, an indefatigable projector. He originated a beech-oil company, a Scotch timber company, and a plan to colonize Florida. He published Essays on Reducing the Price of Coals, on Repairing Dagenham Breach, and on English Grape 10 Wines ; an epic poem on Gideon, a tragedy called *The Fatal Vision, or Fall of Siam*, and a translation of Voltaire's *Zaïre*. His *Merope* was his last work. It appeared in 1749 with a dedication to Lord Bolingbroke ; it was brought on the stage with great success, Garrick acting in it ; and Hill, who was at this time in poverty, and who died soon after, received a considerable sum from his benefit nights. I have not seen this work, which is not included in the Inchbald collection of acted plays. Warton calls Aaron Hill an affected and 20 fustian writer, and this seems to have been his reputation among his contemporaries. His *Zara*, which I have seen, has the fault of so much of English literature of the second class—an incurable defect of *style*.

One other *Merope* remains to be noticed—the *Merope* of Alfieri. In this tragedy, which appeared in 1783, Alfieri has entirely followed Maffei and Voltaire. He seems to have followed Maffei in the first half of it ; Voltaire in the second. His Polyphontes, however, does not make love to Merope : desiring to obtain her 30 hand, in order by this marriage to make the Messenians forget their attachment to Cresphontes, he appeals to her self-interest. 'You are miserable,' he says ; 'but a throne is a great consolation. A throne is—

> la sola
> Non vile ammenda, che al fallir mio resti.'

Egisto, in Alfieri's piece, falls under suspicion from the blood left on his clothes in a struggle with a stranger, whom he kills and throws into the river Pamisus. The suspicion is confirmed by the appearance of a 40 girdle recognized by Merope as having belonged to her son ; as it was confirmed in Maffei's piece by the appearance of a ring, in Voltaire's, by that of a coat of armour. The rest is, in the main, as with Voltaire, except that Alfieri makes Polyphontes perish upon the stage, under circumstances of considerable improbability.

This work of Alfieri has the characteristic merit, and the characteristic fault, of Alfieri's tragedies : it has the merit of elevation, and the fault of narrowness. *Narrow elevation ;* that seems to me exactly to express
10 the quality of Alfieri's poetry : he is a noble-minded, deeply interesting man, but a monotonous poet.

A mistake, a grave mistake it seems to me, in the treatment of their subject, is common to Maffei, Voltaire, and Alfieri. They have abandoned the tradition where they had better have followed it ; they have followed it, where they had better have abandoned it.

The tradition is a great matter to a poet ; it is an unspeakable support ; it gives him the feeling that he
20 is treading on solid ground. Aristotle tells the tragic poet that he must not destroy the received stories. A noble and accomplished living poet, M. Manzoni, has, in an admirable dissertation, developed this thesis of the importance to the poet of a basis of tradition. Its importance I feel so strongly, that, where driven to invent in the false story told by Merope's son, as by Orestes in the *Electra*, of his own death, I could not satisfy myself until I discovered in Pausanias a tradition, which I took for my basis, of an Arcadian
30 hunter drowned in the lake Stymphalus, down one of those singular Katabothra, or chasms in the limestone rock, so well known in Greece, in a manner similar to that in which Aepytus is represented to have perished.

Maffei did right, I think, in altering the ancient tradition where it represents Merope as actually the wife of Polyphontes. It revolts our feeling to consider her as married to her husband's murderer ; and it is no great departure from the tradition to represent her as sought in marriage by him, but not yet obtained.
40 But why did Maffei (for he, it will be remembered, gave the story its modern arrangement, which Voltaire and Alfieri have, in all its leading points, followed),

why did Maffei abandon that part of the tradition
which represents Aepytus, the Messenian prince, as
acquainted with his own origin ? Why did he and his
followers prefer to attribute to curiosity a return
which the tradition attributed to a far more tragic
motive ? Why did they compel themselves to invent a
machinery of robbers, assassins, guards, rings, girdles,
and I know not what, to effect that which the tradition
effects in a far simpler manner, to place Aepytus before
his mother as his own murderer ? Lessing imagines 10
that Maffei, who wished to depict, above all, the
maternal anxiety of Merope, conceived that this anxiety
would be more naturally and powerfully awakened by
the thought of her child reared in hardship and
obscurity as a poor man's son, than by the thought of
him reared in splendour as a prince in the palace of her
own father. But what a conception of the sorrow of a
queen, whose husband has been murdered, and whose
son is an exile from his inheritance, to suppose that such
a sorrow is enhanced by the thought that her child is 20
rudely housed and plainly fed ; to assume that it
would take a less tragic complexion if she knew that
he lived in luxury ! No ; the true tragic motive of
Merope's sorrow is elsewhere : the tradition amply
supplied it.

Here, then, the moderns have invented amiss, because they have invented needlessly ; because, on this
point, the tradition, as it stood, afforded perfect materials to the tragic poet : and, by Maffei's change, not
a higher tragic complication, but merely a greater 30
puzzle and intricacy is produced. I come now to a
point on which the tradition might with advantage, as
I think, have been set aside ; and that is, the character
of Polyphontes.

Yet, on this point, to speak of *setting aside the tradition*
is to speak too strongly ; for the tradition is here not
complete. Neither Pausanias nor Apollodorus mention
circumstances which definitely fix the character of
Polyphontes ; Hyginus, no doubt, represents him as a
villain, and, if Hyginus follows Euripides, Euripides 40
also thus represented him. Euripides may possibly
have done so ; yet a purer tragic feeling, it seems to me,

is produced, if Polyphontes is represented as not wholly black and inexcusable, than if he is represented as a mere monster of cruelty and hypocrisy. Aristotle's profound remark is well known, that the tragic personage whose ruin is represented, should be a personage neither eminently good, nor yet one brought to ruin by sheer iniquity ; nay, that his character should incline rather to good than to bad, but that he should have some fault which impels him to his fall. For, as
10 he explains, the two grand tragic feelings, pity and terror, which it is the business of tragedy to excite, will not be excited by the spectacle of the ruin of a mere villain ; since pity is for those who suffer undeservedly, and such a man suffers deservedly : terror is excited by the fall of one of like nature with ourselves, and we feel that the mere villain is not as ourselves. Aristotle, no doubt, is here speaking, above all, of the Protagonist, or principal personage of the drama ; but the noblest tragic poets of Greece rightly extended their
20 application of the truth on which his remark is based to all the personages of the drama : neither the Creon of Sophocles, nor the Clytemnestra of Aeschylus, are wholly inexcusable ; in none of the extant dramas of Aeschylus or Sophocles is there a character which is entirely bad. For such a character we must go to Euripides ; we must go to an art—wonderful indeed, for I entirely dissent from the unreserved disparagers of this great poet—but an art of less moral significance than the art of Sophocles and Aeschylus ; we must go to
30 tragedies like the *Hecuba*, for villains like Polymestor.

What is the main dramatic difficulty of the story of Merope, as usually treated ? It is, as Alfieri rightly saw, that the interest naturally declines from the moment of Merope's recognition of her son ; that the destruction of the tyrant is not, after this, matter of interest enough to affect us deeply. This is true, if Polyphontes is a mere villain. It is not true, if he is one for the ruin of whom we may, in spite of his crime, feel a profound compassion. Then our interest
40 in the story lasts to the end : for to the very end we are inspired with the powerful tragic emotions of commiseration and awe. Pausanias states circumstances

which suggest the possibility of representing Polyphontes, not as a mere cruel and selfish tyrant, but as
a man whose crime was a truly tragic fault, the error
of a noble nature. Assume such a nature in him, and
the turn of circumstances in the drama takes a new
aspect : Merope and her son triumph, but the fall of
their foe leaves us awestruck and compassionate : the
story issues *tragically*, as Aristotle has truly said that
the best tragic stories ought to issue.

Neither Maffei, nor Voltaire, nor Alfieri have drawn
Polyphontes with a character to inspire any feeling
but aversion, with any traits of nobleness to mitigate
our satisfaction at his death. His character being
such, it is difficult to render his anxiety to obtain
Merope's hand intelligible, for Merope's situation is
not such as to make her enmity really dangerous to
Polyphontes ; he has, therefore, no sufficient motive of
self-interest, and the nobler motives of reparation and
pacification could have exercised, on such a character,
no force. Voltaire accordingly, whose keen eye no
weak place of this kind escaped, felt his difficulty.
' Neither M. Maffei nor I,' he confesses, ' have assigned
any sufficient motives for the desire of Polyphontes to
marry Merope.'

To criticize is easier than to create ; and if I have
been led, in this review of the fortunes of my story, to
find fault with the works of others, I do not on that
account assume that I have myself produced a work
which is not a thousand times more faulty.

It remains to say something, for those who are not
familiar with the Greek dramatic forms, of the form
in which this tragedy is cast. Greek tragedy, as is
well known, took its origin from the songs of a chorus,
and the stamp of its origin remained for ever impressed
upon it. A chorus, or band of dancers, moving around
the altar of Bacchus, sang the adventures of the god.
To this band Thespis joined an actor, who held
dialogue with the chorus, and who was called ὑποκριτὴς,
the answerer, because he answered the songs of the
chorus. The drama thus commenced ; for the dialogue of this actor with the chorus brought before
the audience some action of Bacchus, or of one of the

heroes ; this action, narrated by the actor, was com-
mented on in song, at certain intervals, by the chorus
alone.   Aeschylus added a second actor, thus making
the character of the representation more *dramatic,* for
the chorus was never itself so much an actor as a hearer
and observer of the actor : Sophocles added a third.
These three actors might successively personate several
characters in the same piece ; but to three actors and
a chorus the dramatic poet limited himself : only in
10 a single piece of Sophocles, not brought out until after
his death, was the employment of a fourth actor, it
appears, necessary.

The chorus consisted, in the time of Sophocles, of
fifteen persons.   After their first entrance they remained before the spectators, without withdrawing,
until the end of the piece.   Their place was in the
orchestra ; that of the actors was upon the stage.   The
orchestra was a circular space, like the pit of our
theatres : the chorus arrived in it by side-entrances,
20 and not by the stage.   In the centre of the orchestra
was the altar of Bacchus, around which the chorus
originally danced ; but in dramatic representations
their place was between this altar and the stage : here
they stood, a little lower than the persons on the stage,
but looking towards them, and holding, through their
leaders, conversation with them : then, at pauses in
the action, the united chorus sang songs expressing
their feelings at what was happening upon the stage,
making, as they sang, certain measured stately move-
30 ments between the stage and the altar, and occasionally
standing still.   Steps led from the orchestra to the
stage, and the chorus, or some members of it, might
thus, if necessary, join the actors on the stage ; but
this seldom happened, the proper place for the chorus
was the orchestra.   The dialogue of the chorus with
the actors on the stage passed generally in the ordinary
form of dramatic dialogue ; but, on occasions where
strong feeling was excited, the dialogue took a lyrical
form.   Long dialogues of this kind sometimes took
40 place between the leaders of the chorus and one of the
actors upon the stage, their burden being a lamentation
for the dead.

The Greek theatres were vast, and open to the sky ; the actors, masked, and in a somewhat stiff tragic costume, were to be regarded from a considerable distance : a solemn, clearly marked style of gesture, a sustained tone of declamation, were thus rendered necessary. Under these conditions, intricate by-play, rapid variations in the action, requiring great mobility, ever-changing shades of tone and gesture in the actor, were impossible. Broad and simple effects were, under these conditions, above all to be aimed at ; a profound 10 and clear impression was to be effected. Unity of plan in the action, and symmetry in the treatment of it, were indispensable. The action represented, therefore, was to be a single, rigorously developed action ; the masses of the composition were to be balanced, each bringing out the other into stronger and distincter relief. In the best tragedies, not only do the divisions of the full choral songs accurately correspond to one another, but the divisions of the lyrical dialogue, nay, even the divisions of the regular dramatic dialogue, 20 form corresponding members, of which one member is the answer, the counter-stroke to the other ; and an indescribable sense of distinctness and depth of impression is thus produced.

From what has been said, the reader will see that the Greek tragic forms were not chosen as being, in the nature of things, the best tragic forms ; such would be a wholly false conception of them. They are an adaptation to dramatic purposes, under certain theatrical conditions, of forms previously existing for 30 other purposes ; that adaptation at which the Greeks, after several stages of improvement, finally rested. The laws of Greek tragic art, therefore, are not exclusive ; they are for Greek dramatic art itself, but they do not pronounce other modes of dramatic art unlawful ; they are, at most, *prophecies of the improbability of dramatic success under other conditions.* 'Tragedy,' says Aristotle, in a remarkable passage, 'after going through many changes, got the nature which suited it, and there it stopped. Whether or no the kinds of tragedy are 40 yet exhausted,' he presently adds, 'tragedy being considered either in itself, or in respect to the stage,

I shall not now inquire.' Travelling in a certain path, the spirit of man arrived at Greek tragedy; travelling in other paths, it may arrive at other kinds of tragedy.

But it cannot be denied that the Greek tragic forms, although not the only possible tragic forms, satisfy, in the most perfect manner, some of the most urgent demands of the human spirit. If, on the one hand, the human spirit demands variety and the widest possible range, it equally demands, on the other hand,
10 depth and concentration in its impressions. Powerful thought and emotion, flowing in strongly marked channels, make a stronger impression: this is the main reason why a metrical form is a more effective vehicle for them than prose: in prose there is more freedom, but, in the metrical form, the very limit gives a sense of precision and emphasis. This sense of emphatic distinctness in our impressions rises, as the thought and emotion swell higher and higher without overflowing their boundaries, to a lofty sense of the
20 mastery of the human spirit over its own stormiest agitations; and this, again, conducts us to a state of feeling which it is the highest aim of tragedy to produce, to *a sentiment of sublime acquiescence in the course of fate, and in the dispensations of human life.*

What has been said explains, I think, the reason of the effectiveness of the severe forms of Greek tragedy, with its strongly marked boundaries, with its recurrence, even in the most agitating situations, of mutually replying masses of metrical arrangement. Sometimes
30 the agitation becomes overwhelming, and the correspondence is for a time lost, the torrent of feeling flows for a space without check: this disorder amid the general order produces a powerful effect; but the balance is restored before the tragedy closes: the final sentiment in the mind must be one not of trouble, but of acquiescence.

This sentiment of acquiescence is, no doubt, a sentiment of *repose;* and, therefore, I cannot agree with Mr. Lewes when he says, in his remarks on Goethe's
40 *Iphigeneia,* that 'the Greek Drama is distinguished by its absence of repose; by the currents of passion being for ever kept in agitation.' I entirely agree, however,

in his criticism of Goethe's tragedy; of that noble
poem which Schiller so exactly characterized when he
said that it was 'full of soul': I entirely agree with
him when he says that 'the tragic situation in the
story of Iphigeneia is not touched by Goethe; that his
tragedy addresses the conscience rather than the
emotions.' But Goethe does not err from Greek
ideas when he thinks that there is repose in tragedy:
he errs from Greek practice in the mode in which he
strives to produce that repose. Sophocles does not 10
produce the sentiment of repose, of acquiescence, by
inculcating it, by avoiding agitating circumstances: he
produces it by exhibiting to us the most agitating
matter under the conditions of the severest form.
Goethe has truly recognized that this sentiment is the
grand final effect of Greek tragedy: but he produces
it, not in the manner of Sophocles, but, as Mr. Lewes
has most ably pointed out, in a manner of his own;
he produces it by inculcating it; by avoiding agitating
matter; by keeping himself in the domain of the soul 20
and conscience, not in that of the passions.

I have now to speak of the chorus; for of this, as of
the other forms of Greek tragedy, it is not enough,
considering how Greek tragedy arose, to show that the
Greeks used it; it is necessary to show that it is
effective. Johnson says, that 'it could only be by
long prejudice and the bigotry of learning that Milton
could prefer the ancient tragedies, with their encumbrance of a chorus, to the exhibitions of the French
and English stages:' and his tragedy of *Irene* suffi- 30
ciently proves that he himself, in his practice, adopted
Greek art as arranged at Paris, by those

> Juges plus éclairés que ceux qui dans Athène
> Firent naître et fleurir les lois de Melpomène;

as Voltaire calls them in the prologue to his *Éryphile*.
Johnson merely calls the chorus an encumbrance.
Voltaire, who, in his *Oedipus*, had made use of the
chorus in a singular manner, argued, at a later period,
against its introduction. Voltaire is always worth
listening to, because his keenness of remark is always 40
suggestive. 'In an interesting piece the intrigue

generally requires,' says Voltaire, 'that the principal
actors should have secrets to tell one another—*Eh! le
moyen de dire son secret à tout un peuple.* And, if the
songs of the chorus allude to what has already happened, they must,' he says, 'be tiresome ; if they
allude to what is about to happen, their effect will
be to *dérober le plaisir de la surprise.*' How ingenious,
and how entirely in Voltaire's manner ! The sense to
be appealed to in tragedy is *curiosity* ; the impression
10 to be awakened in us is *surprise.* But the Greeks
thought differently. For them, the aim of tragedy
was *profound moral impression :* and the ideal spectator,
as Schlegel and Müller have called the chorus, was
designed to enable the actual spectator to feel his own
impressions more distinctly and more deeply. The
chorus was, at each stage in the action, to collect and
weigh the impressions which the action would at that
stage naturally make on a pious and thoughtful mind ;
and was at last, at the end of the tragedy, when the
20 issue of the action appeared, to strike the final balance.
If the feeling with which the actual spectator regarded
the course of the tragedy could be deepened by remind-
ing him of what was past, or by indicating to him
what was to come, it was the province of the ideal
spectator so to deepen it. To combine, to harmonize,
to deepen for the spectator the feelings naturally
excited in him by the sight of what was passing upon
the stage—this is one grand effect produced by the
chorus in Greek tragedy.
30 There is another. Coleridge observes that Shakespeare, after one of his grandest scenes, often plunges,
as if to relax and relieve himself, into a scene of
buffoonery. After tragic situations of the greatest
intensity, a desire for relief and relaxation is no
doubt natural, both to the poet and to the spectator ;
but the finer feeling of the Greeks found this relief,
not in buffoonery, but in lyrical song. The noble and
natural relief from the emotion produced by tragic
events is in the transition to the emotion produced by
40 lyric poetry, not in the contrast and shock of a totally
opposite order of feelings. The relief afforded to excited feeling by lyrical song every one has experienced

at the opera: the delight and facility of this relief renders so universal the popularity of the opera, of this '*beau monstre*,' which still, as in Voltaire's time, '*étouffe Melpomène*.' But in the opera, the lyrical element, the element of feeling and relaxation, is in excess: the dramatic element, the element of intellect and labour, is in defect. In the best Greek tragedy, the lyrical element occupies its true place; it is the relief and solace in the stress and conflict of the action; it is not the substantive business.   10

Few can have read the *Samson Agonistes* of Milton without feeling that the chorus imparts a peculiar and noble effect to that poem; but I regret that Milton determined, induced probably by his preference for Euripides, to adopt, in the songs of the chorus, 'the measure,' as he himself says, 'called by the Greeks Monostrophic, or rather Apolelymenon, without regard had to Strophe, Antistrophe, or Epode.' In this relaxed form of the later Greek tragedy, the means are sacrificed by which the chorus could produce, 20 within the limits of a single choric song, the same effect which it was their business, as we have seen, to produce in the tragedy as a whole. The regular correspondence of part with part, the antithesis, in answering stanzas, of thought to thought, feeling to feeling, with the balance of the whole struck in one independent final stanza or epode, is lost; something of the peculiar distinctness and symmetry, which constitute the vital force of the Greek tragic forms, is thus forfeited. The story of Samson, although it has no 30 mystery or complication, to inspire, like tragic stories of the most perfect kind, a foreboding and anxious gloom in the mind of him who hears it, is yet a truly dramatic and noble one; but the forms of Greek tragedy, which are founded on Greek manners, on the practice of chorus-dancing, and on the ancient habitual transaction of affairs in the open air in front of the dwellings of kings, are better adapted to Greek stories than to Hebrew or any other. These reserves being made, it is impossible to praise the *Samson Agonistes* 40 too highly: it is great with all the greatness of Milton. Goethe might well say to Eckermann, after re-reading it, that hardly any work had been composed so entirely in the spirit of the ancients.

Milton's drama has the true oratorical flow of ancient tragedy, produced mainly, I think, by his making it, as the Greeks made it, the rule, not the exception, to put the pause at the end of the line, not in the middle. Shakespeare has some noble passages, particularly in his *Richard the Third*, constructed with this, the true oratorical rhythm; indeed, that wonderful poet, who
10 has so much besides rhetoric, is also the greatest poetical rhetorician since Euripides : still, it is to the Elizabethan poets that we owe the bad habit, in dramatic poetry, of perpetually dividing the line in the middle. Italian tragedy has the same habit : in Alfieri's plays it is intolerable. The constant occurrence of such lines produces, not a sense of variety, but a sense of perpetual interruption.

Some of the measures used in the choric songs of my tragedy are ordinary measures of English verse :
20 others are not so ; but it must not be supposed that these last are the reproduction of any Greek choric measures. So to adapt Greek measures to English verse is impossible : what I have done is to try to follow rhythms which produced on my own feeling a similar impression to that produced on it by the rhythms of Greek choric poetry. In such an endeavour, when the ear is guided solely by its own feeling, there is, I know, a continual risk of failure and of offence. I believe, however, that there are no existing English
30 measures which produce the same effect on the ear, and therefore on the mind, as that produced by many measures indispensable to the nature of Greek lyric poetry. He, therefore, who would obtain certain effects obtained by that poetry, is driven to invent new measures, whether he will or no.

Pope and Dryden felt this. Pope composed two choruses for the Duke of Buckingham's *Brutus*, a tragedy altered from Shakespeare, and performed at Buckingham House. A short specimen will show what
40 these choruses were—

Love's purer flames the Gods approve :
The Gods and Brutus bend to love :

> Brutus for absent Portia sighs,
> And sterner Cassius melts at Junia's eyes.

In this style he proceeds for eight lines more, and then the antistrophe duly follows. Pope felt that the peculiar effects of Greek lyric poetry were here missed; the measure in itself makes them impossible : in his ode on St. Cecilia's day, accordingly, he tries to come nearer to the Greeks. Here is a portion of his fourth stanza ; of one of those stanzas in which Johnson thinks that 'we have all that can be performed by 10 sweetness of diction, or elegance of versification : '—

> Dreadful gleams,
> Dismal screams,
> Fires that glow,
> Shrieks of woe,
> Sullen moans,
> Hollow groans,
> And cries of tortured ghosts.

Horrible ! yet how dire must have been the necessity, how strong the feeling of the inadequacy of existing 20 metres to produce effects demanded, which could drive a man of Pope's taste to such prodigies of invention ! Dryden in his *Alexander's Feast* deviates less from ordinary English measures ; but to deviate from them in some degree he was compelled. My admiration for Dryden's genius is warm : my delight in this incomparable ode, the mighty son of his old age, is unbounded : but it seems to me that in only one stanza and chorus of the *Alexander's Feast*, the fourth, does the rhythm from first to last completely satisfy 30 the ear.

I must have wearied my reader's patience : but I was desirous, in laying before him my tragedy, that it should not lose what benefit it can derive from the foregoing explanations. To his favourable reception of it there will still be obstacles enough, in its unfamiliar form, and in the incapacity of its author.

How much do I regret that the many poets of the present day who possess that capacity which I have not, should not have forestalled me in an endeavour 40 far beyond my powers ! How gladly should I have applauded their better success in the attempt to enrich

with what, in the forms of the most perfectly-formed
literature in the world, is most perfect, our noble
English literature; to extend its boundaries in the
one direction, in which, with all its force and variety,
it has not yet advanced! They would have lost
nothing by such an attempt, and English literature
would have gained much.

Only their silence could have emboldened to undertake it one with inadequate time, inadequate know-
10 ledge, and a talent, alas! still more inadequate: one
who brings to the task none of the requisite qualifica-
tions of genius or learning: nothing but a passion
for the great Masters, and an effort to study them
without fancifulness.

LONDON: December, 1857.

HISTORICAL INTRODUCTION

IN the foregoing Preface the story of Merope is detailed: what
is here added may serve to explain allusions which occur in the
course of the tragedy, and to illustrate the situation of its chief
20 personages at the moment when it commences.

The events on which the action turns belong to the period
of transition from the heroic and fabulous to the human and
historic age of Greece. The hero Hercules, the ancestor of the
Messenian Aepytus, belongs to fable: but the invasion of Peloponnesus by the Dorians under chiefs claiming to be descended
from Hercules, and their settlement in Argos, Lacedaemon, and
Messenia, belong to history. Aepytus is descended on the
father's side from Hercules, Perseus, and the kings of Argos:
on the mother's side from Pelasgus, and the aboriginal kings
30 of Arcadia. Callisto, the daughter of the wicked Lycaon, and
the mother, by Zeus, of Arcas, from whom the Arcadians took
their name, was the grand-daughter of Pelasgus. The birth
of Arcas brought upon Callisto the anger of the virgin-Goddess
Artemis, whose service she followed: she was changed into
a she-bear, and in this form was chased by her own son, grown
to manhood. At the critical moment Zeus interposed, and the
mother and son were removed from the earth, and placed
among the stars: Callisto became the famous constellation of
the Great Bear; her son became Arcturus, Arctophylax, or

Boötes. From him, Cypselus, the maternal grandfather of Aepytus, and the children of Cypselus, Laias and Merope, were lineally descended.

The events of the life of Hercules, the paternal ancestor of Aepytus, are so well known that it is hardly necessary to record them. It is sufficient to remind the reader, that, although entitled to the throne of Argos by right of descent from Perseus and Danaus, and to the thrones of Sparta and Messenia by right of conquest, he yet passed his life in labours and wanderings, subjected by the decree of fate to the commands of his 10 far inferior kinsman, the feeble and malignant Eurystheus. Hercules, who is represented with the violence as well as the virtues of an adventurous ever-warring hero, attacked and slew Eurytus, an Euboean king, with whom he had a quarrel, and carried off the daughter of Eurytus, the beautiful Iole. The wife of Hercules, Deianeira, seized with jealous anxiety, remembered that long ago the centaur Nessus, dying by the poisoned arrows of Hercules, had assured her that the blood flowing from his mortal wound would prove an infallible lovecharm to win back the affections of her husband, if she should 20 ever lose them. With this philtre Deianeira now anointed a robe of triumph, which she sent to her victorious husband : he received it when about to offer public sacrifice, and immediately put it on : but the sun's rays called into activity the poisoned blood with which the robe was smeared : it clung to the flesh of the hero and consumed it. In dreadful agonies Hercules caused himself to be transported from Euboea to Mount Oeta : there, under the crags of Trachis, an immense funeral pile was constructed. Recognizing the divine will in the fate which had overtaken him, the hero ascended the pile, 30 and called on his children and followers to set it on fire. They refused ; but the office was performed by Poeas, the father of Philoctetes, who, passing near, was attracted by the concourse round the pile, and who received the bow and arrows of Hercules for his reward. The flames arose, and the apotheosis of Hercules was consummated.

He bequeathed to his offspring, the Heracleidae, his own claims to the kingdoms of Peloponnesus, and to the persecution of Eurystheus. They at first sought shelter with Ceyx, king of Trachis : he was too weak to protect them ; and they then 40 took refuge at Athens. The Athenians refused to deliver them up at the demand of Eurystheus : he invaded Attica, and a battle was fought near Marathon, in which, after Macaria, a daughter of Hercules, had devoted herself for the preservation of her house, Eurystheus fell, and the Heracleidae and their Athenian protectors were victorious. The memory of Macaria's self-sacrifice was perpetuated by the name of a spring of water on the plain of Marathon, the spring Macaria. The Heracleidae then endeavoured to effect their return to Peloponnesus. Hyllus, the eldest of them, inquired of the oracle at 50 Delphi respecting their return ; he was told to return by the *narrow passage*, and in the *third harvest*. Accordingly, in the

third year from that time, Hyllus led an army to the Isthmus
of Corinth; but there he was encountered by an army of
Achaians and Arcadians, and fell in single combat with
Echemus, king of Tegea. Upon this defeat the Heracleidae
retired to Northern Greece : there, after much wandering,
they finally took refuge with Aegimius, king of the Dorians,
who appears to have been the fastest friend of their house, and
whose Dorian warriors formed the army which at last achieved
their return. But, for a hundred years from the date of their
10 first attempt, the Heracleidae were defeated in their successive
invasions of Peloponnesus. Cleolaus and Aristomachus, the
son and grandson of Hyllus, fell in unsuccessful expeditions.
At length the sons of Aristomachus, Temenus, Cresphontes,
and Aristodemus, when grown up, repaired to Delphi and
taxed the oracle with the non-fulfilment of the promise made
to their ancestor Hyllus. But Apollo replied that his oracle
had been misunderstood ; for that by the *third harvest* he had
meant the third generation, and by the *narrow passage* he had
meant the straits of the Corinthian Gulf. After this explana-
20 tion the sons of Aristomachus built a fleet at Naupactus; and
finally, in the hundredth year from the death of Hyllus, and
the eightieth from the fall of Troy, the invasion was again
attempted, and was this time successful. The son of Orestes,
Tisamenus, who ruled both Argos and Lacedaemon, fell in
battle ; many of his vanquished subjects left their homes and
retired to Achaia.

The spoil was now to be divided among the conquerors.
Aristodemus, the youngest of the sons of Aristomachus, did
not survive to enjoy his share. He was slain at Delphi by
30 the sons of Pylades and Electra, the kinsmen of the house of
Agamemnon, that house which the Heracleidae with their
Dorian army dispossessed. The claims of Aristodemus descended to his two sons, Procles and Eurysthenes, children
under the guardianship of their maternal uncle, Theras.
Temenus, the eldest of the sons of Aristomachus, took the
kingdom of Argos ; for the two remaining kingdoms, that of
Sparta and that of Messenia, his two nephews, who were to
rule jointly, and their uncle Cresphontes, were to cast lots.
Cresphontes wished to have the fertile Messenia, and induced
40 his brother to acquiesce in a trick which secured it to him.
The lot of Cresphontes and that of his two nephews were to
be placed in a water-jar, and thrown out. Messenia was to
belong to him whose lot came out first. With the connivance
of Temenus, Cresphontes marked as his own lot a pellet composed of baked clay ; as the lot of his nephews, a pellet of
unbaked clay : the unbaked pellet was of course dissolved in
the water, while the brick pellet fell out alone. Messenia,
therefore, was assigned to Cresphontes.

Messenia was at this time ruled by Melanthus, a descendant
50 of Neleus. This ancestor, a prince of the great house of Aeolus,
had come from Thessaly, and succeeded to the Messenian
throne on the failure of the previous dynasty. Melanthus and

his race were thus foreigners in Messenia, and were unpopular. His subjects offered little or no opposition to the invading Dorians : Melanthus abandoned his kingdom to Cresphontes, and retired to Athens.

Cresphontes married Merope, whose native country, Arcadia, was not affected by the Dorian invasion. This marriage, the issue of which was three sons, connected him with the native population of Peloponnesus. He built a new capital of Messenia, Stenyclaros, and transferred thither, from Pylos, the seat of government : he at first proposed, it is said by Pausanias, to 10 divide Messenia into five states, and to confer on the native Messenians equal privileges with their Dorian conquerors. The Dorians complained that his administration unduly favoured the vanquished people : his chief magnates, headed by Polyphontes, himself a descendant of Hercules, formed a cabal against him, in which he was slain with his two eldest sons. The youngest son of Cresphontes, Aepytus, then an infant, was saved by his mother, who sent him to her father, Cypselus, the king of Arcadia, under whose protection he was brought up.   20

The drama begins at the moment when Aepytus, grown to manhood, returns secretly to Messenia to take vengeance on his father's murderers. At this period Temenus was no longer reigning at Argos : he had been murdered by his sons, jealous of their brother-in-law, Deiphontes : the sons of Aristodemus, Procles and Eurysthenes, at variance with their guardian, were reigning at Sparta.

PERSONS OF THE DRAMA

LAIAS, *uncle of* AEPYTUS, *brother of* MEROPE.
AEPYTUS, *son of* MEROPE *and* CRESPHONTES.
POLYPHONTES, *king of* MESSENIA.
MEROPE, *widow of* CRESPHONTES, *the murdered king of* MESSENIA.
THE CHORUS, *of* MESSENIAN *maidens.*
ARCAS, *an old man of* MEROPE'S *household.*
MESSENGER.
GUARDS, ATTENDANTS, &c.

The Scene is before the royal palace in STENYCLAROS, *the capital of*
   MESSENIA. *In the foreground is the tomb of* CRESPHONTES. *The*
   action commences at day-break.

MEROPE

LAIAS. AEPYTUS

LAIAS

Son of Cresphontes, we have reach'd the goal
Of our night-journey, and thou see'st thy home.
Behold thy heritage, thy father's realm !
This is that fruitful, fam'd Messenian land,
Wealthy in corn and flocks, which, when at last
The late-relenting Gods with victory brought
The Heracleidae back to Pelops' isle,
Fell to thy father's lot, the second prize.
Before thy feet this recent city spreads
Of Stenyclaros, which he built, and made   10
Of his fresh-conquer'd realm the royal seat,
Degrading Pylos from its ancient rule.
There stands the temple of thine ancestor,
Great Hercules ; and, in that public place,
Zeus hath his altar, where thy father fell.
Thence to the south, behold those snowy peaks,
Taygetus, Laconia's border-wall :
And, on this side, those confluent streams which make
Pamisus watering the Messenian plain :
Then to the north, Lycaeus and the hills   20
Of pastoral Arcadia, where, a babe
Snatch'd from the slaughter of thy father's house,
Thy mother's kin receiv'd thee, and rear'd up.—
Our journey is well made, the work remains
Which to perform we made it ; means for that
Let us consult, before this palace sends
Its inmates on their daily tasks abroad.
Haste and advise, for day comes on apace.

AEPYTUS

O brother of my mother, guardian true,
And second father from that hour when first   30
My mother's faithful servant laid me down,
An infant, at the hearth of Cypselus,
My grandfather, the good Arcadian king— .

Thy part it were to advise, and mine to obey.
But let us keep that purpose, which, at home,
We judg'd the best ; chance finds no better way.
Go thou into the city, and seek out
Whate'er in the Messenian city stirs
Of faithful fondness towards their former king
Or hatred to their present ; in this last   40
Will lie, my grandsire said, our fairest chance.
For tyrants make man good beyond himself ;
Hate to their rule, which else would die away,
Their daily-practis'd chafings keep alive.
Seek this ; revive, unite it, give it hope ;
Bid it rise boldly at the signal given.
Meanwhile within my father's palace I,
An unknown guest, will enter, bringing word
Of my own death ; but, Laias, well I hope
Through that pretended death to live and reign.   50
                              [The Chorus *comes forth.*

Softly, stand back !—see, tow'rd the palace gates
What black procession slowly makes approach ?—
Sad-chanting maidens clad in mourning robes,
With pitchers in their hands, and fresh-pull'd flowers:
Doubtless, they bear them to my father's tomb.—
                              [Merope *comes forth.*

And see, to meet them, that one, grief-plung'd Form,
Severer, paler, statelier than they all,
A golden circlet on her queenly brow.—
O Laias, Laias, let the heart speak here !
Shall I not greet her ? shall I not leap forth ?   60
                [Polyphontes *comes forth, following* Merope.

Laias

Not so : thy heart would pay its moment's speech
By silence ever after ; for, behold !
The King (I know him, even through many years)
Follows the issuing Queen, who stops, as call'd.
No lingering now ! straight to the city I :
Do thou, till for thine entrance to this house
The happy moment comes, lurk here unseen
Behind the shelter of thy father's tomb :
Remove yet further off, if aught comes near.

But, here while harbouring, on its margin lay, 70
Sole offering that thou hast, locks from thy head :
And fill thy leisure with an earnest prayer
To his avenging Shade, and to the Gods
Who under earth watch guilty deeds of men,
To guide our effort to a prosperous close.

[LAIAS *goes out.* POLYPHONTES, MEROPE, *and* THE
CHORUS *come forward. As they advance,* AEPYTUS,
*who at first conceals himself behind the tomb, moves
off the stage.*

POLYPHONTES (*To* THE CHORUS)

Set down your pitchers, maidens ! and fall back ;
Suspend your melancholy rites awhile :
Shortly ye shall resume them with your Queen.—

(*To* MEROPE)

I sought thee, Merope ; I find thee thus,
As I have ever found thee ; bent to keep, 80
By sad observances and public grief,
A mournful feud alive, which else would die.
I blame thee not, I do thy heart no wrong :
Thy deep seclusion, thine unyielding gloom,
Thine attitude of cold, estrang'd reproach,
These punctual funeral honours, year by year
Repeated, are in thee, I well believe,
Courageous, faithful actions, nobly dar'd.
But, Merope, the eyes of other men
Read in these actions, innocent in thee, 90
Perpetual promptings to rebellious hope,
War-cries to faction, year by year renew'd,
Beacons of vengeance, not to be let die.
And me, believe it, wise men gravely blame,
And ignorant men despise me, that I stand
Passive, permitting thee what course thou wilt.
Yes, the crowd mutters that remorseful fear
And paralysing conscience stop my arm,
When it should pluck thee from thy hostile way.
All this I bear, for, what I seek, I know ; 100
Peace, peace is what I seek, and public calm :
Endless extinction of unhappy hates :
Union cemented for this nation's weal.

And even now, if to behold me here,
This day, amid these rites, this black-rob'd train,
Wakens, O Queen! remembrance in thy heart
Too wide at variance with the peace I seek—
I will not violate thy noble grief,
The prayer I came to urge I will defer.

MEROPE

This day, to-morrow, yesterday, alike   110
I am, I shall be, have been, in my mind
Tow'rds thee ; towards thy silence as thy speech.
Speak, therefore, or keep silence, which thou wilt.

POLYPHONTES

Hear me, then, speak ; and let this mournful day,
The twentieth anniversary of strife,
Henceforth be honour'd as the date of peace.
Yes, twenty years ago this day beheld
The king Cresphontes, thy great husband, fall:
It needs no yearly offerings at his tomb
To keep alive that memory in my heart ;   120
It lives, and, while I see the light, will live.
For we were kinsmen—more than kinsmen—friends :
Together we had sprung, together liv'd ;
Together to this isle of Pelops came
To take the inheritance of Hercules ;
Together won this fair Messenian land—
Alas, that, how to rule it, was our broil !
He had his counsel, party, friends—I mine ;
He stood by what he wish'd for—I the same ;
I smote him, when our wishes clash'd in arms ;   130
He had smit me, had he been swift as I.
But while I smote him, Queen, I honour'd him ;
Me, too, had he prevail'd, he had not scorn'd.
Enough of this !—since then, I have maintain'd
The sceptre—not remissly let it fall—
And I am seated on a prosperous throne:
Yet still, for I conceal it not, ferments
In the Messenian people what remains
Of thy dead husband's faction ; vigorous once,
Now crush'd but not quite lifeless by his fall.   140
And these men look to thee, and from thy grief—

Something too studiously, forgive me, shown—
Infer thee their accomplice; and they say
That thou in secret nurturest up thy son,
Him whom thou hiddest when thy husband fell,
To avenge that fall, and bring them back to power.
Such are their hopes—I ask not if by thee
Willingly fed or no—their most vain hopes;
For I have kept conspiracy fast-chain'd
Till now, and I have strength to chain it still.   150
But, Merope, the years advance;—I stand
Upon the threshold of old age, alone,
Always in arms, always in face of foes.
The long repressive attitude of rule
Leaves me austerer, sterner, than I would;
Old age is more suspicious than the free
And valiant heart of youth, or manhood's firm,
Unclouded reason; I would not decline
Into a jealous tyrant, scourg'd with fears,
Closing, in blood and gloom, his sullen reign.   160
The cares which might in me with time, I feel,
Beget a cruel temper, help me quell;
The breach between our parties help me close;
Assist me to rule mildly: let us join
Our hands in solemn union, making friends
Our factions with the friendship of their chiefs.
Let us in marriage, King and Queen, unite
Claims ever hostile else; and set thy son—
No more an exile fed on empty hopes,
And to an unsubstantial title heir,   170
But prince adopted by the will of power,
And future king—before this people's eyes.
Consider him; consider not old hates:
Consider, too, this people, who were dear
To their dead king, thy husband—yea, too dear,
For that destroy'd him. Give them peace; thou
    can'st.
O Merope, how many noble thoughts,
How many precious feelings of man's heart,
How many loves, how many gratitudes,
Do twenty years wear out, and see expire!   180
Shall they not wear one hatred out as well?

MEROPE

Thou hast forgot, then, who I am who hear,
And who thou art who speakest to me ?   I
Am Merope, thy murder'd master's wife . . .
And thou art Polyphontes, first his friend,
And then . . . his murderer.   These offending tears
That murder draws . . . this breach that thou would'st
   close
Was by that murder open'd . . . that one child
(If still, indeed, he lives) whom thou would'st seat
Upon a throne not thine to give, is heir   190
Because thou slew'st his brothers with their father. . .
Who can patch union here ? . . . What can there be
But everlasting horror 'twixt us two,
Gulfs of estranging blood ? . . . Across that chasm
Who can extend their hands ? . . . Maidens, take back
These offerings home ! our rites are spoil'd to-day.

POLYPHONTES

Not so : let these Messenian maidens mark
The fear'd and blacken'd ruler of their race,
Albeit with lips unapt to self-excuse,
Blow off the spot of murder from his name.— 200
Murder !—but what *is* murder ? When a wretch
For private gain or hatred takes a life,
We call it murder, crush him, brand his name :
But when, for some great public cause, an arm
Is, without love or hate, austerely rais'd
Against a Power exempt from common checks,
Dangerous to all, to be but thus annull'd—
Ranks any man with murder such an act ?
With grievous deeds, perhaps ; with murder—no !
Find then such cause, the charge of murder falls :
Be judge thyself if it abound not here.— 211
All know how weak the Eagle, Hercules,
Soaring from his death-pile on Oeta, left
His puny, callow Eaglets ; and what trials—
Infirm protectors, dubious oracles
Construed awry, misplann'd invasions—us'd
Two generations of his offspring up ;
Hardly the third, with grievous loss, regain'd
Their fathers' realm, this isle, from Pelops nam'd.—

Who made that triumph, though deferr'd, secure?
Who, but the kinsmen of the royal brood   221
Of Hercules, scarce Heracleidae less
Than they? these, and the Dorian lords, whose king
Aegimius gave our outcast house a home
When Thebes, when Athens dar'd not; who in arms
Thrice issued with us from their pastoral vales,
And shed their blood like water in our cause?—
Such were the dispossessors: of what stamp
Were they we dispossessed?—of us I speak,
Who to Messenia with thy husband came—   230
I speak not now of Argos, where his brother,
Not now of Sparta, where his nephews reign'd:—
What we found here were tribes of fame obscure,
Much turbulence, and little constancy,
Precariously rul'd by foreign lords
From the Aeolian stock of Neleus sprung,
A house once great, now dwindling in its sons.
Such were the conquer'd, such the conquerors: who
Had most thy husband's confidence? Consult
His acts; the wife he chose was—full of virtues—
But an Arcadian princess, more akin   241
To his new subjects than to us; his friends
Were the Messenian chiefs; the laws he fram'd
Were aim'd at their promotion, our decline;
And, finally, this land, then half-subdued,
Which from one central city's guarded seat
As from a fastness in the rocks our scant
Handful of Dorian conquerors might have curb'd,
He parcell'd out in five confederate states,
Sowing his victors thinly through them all,   250
Mere prisoners, meant or not, among our foes.
If this was fear of them, it sham'd the king:
If jealousy of us, it sham'd the man.—
Long we refrain'd ourselves, submitted long,
Construed his acts indulgently, rever'd,
Though found perverse, the blood of Hercules:
Reluctantly the rest; but, against all,
One voice preach'd patience, and that voice was mine.
At last it reach'd us, that he, still mistrustful,
Deeming, as tyrants deem, our silence hate,   260
Unadulating grief conspiracy,

Had to this city, Stenyclaros, call'd
A general assemblage of the realm,
With compact in that concourse to deliver,
For death, his ancient to his new-made friends.
Patience was thenceforth self-destruction.   I,
I his chief kinsman, I his pioneer
And champion to the throne, I honouring most
Of men the line of Hercules, preferr'd
The many of that lineage to the one :   270
What his foes dar'd not, I, his lover, dar'd :
I, at that altar, where mid shouting crowds
He sacrific'd, our ruin in his heart,
To Zeus, before he struck his blow, struck mine :
Struck once, and aw'd his mob, and sav'd this realm.
Murder let others call this, if they will ;
I, self-defence and righteous execution.

MEROPE

Alas, how fair a colour can his tongue,
Who self-exculpates, lend to foulest deeds.
Thy trusting lord didst thou, his servant, slay ;   280
Kinsman, thou slew'st thy kinsman; friend, thy friend:
This were enough ; but let me tell thee, too,
Thou hadst no cause, as feign'd, in his misrule.
For ask at Argos, ask in Lacedaemon,
Whose people, when the Heracleidae came,
Were hunted out, and to Achaia fled,
Whether is better, to abide alone,
A wolfish band, in a dispeopled realm,
Or conquerors with conquer'd to unite
Into one puissant folk, as he design'd ?   290
These sturdy and unworn Messenian tribes,
Who shook the fierce Neleidae on their throne,
Who to the invading Dorians stretch'd a hand,
And half bestow'd, half yielded up their soil—
He would not let his savage chiefs alight,
A cloud of vultures, on this vigorous race ;
Ravin a little while in spoil and blood,
Then, gorg'd and helpless, be assail'd and slain.
He would have sav'd you from your furious selves,
Not in abhorr'd estrangement let you stand ;   300
He would have mix'd you with your friendly foes,

Foes dazzled with your prowess, well inclin'd
To reverence your lineage, more, to obey:
So would have built you, in a few short years,
A just, therefore a safe, supremacy.
For well he knew, what you, his chiefs, did not—
How of all human rules the over-tense
Are apt to snap; the easy-stretch'd endure.—
O gentle wisdom, little understood!
O arts, above the vulgar tyrant's reach!   310
O policy too subtle far for sense
Of heady, masterful, injurious men!
This good he meant you, and for this he died.
Yet not for this—else might thy crime in part
Be error deem'd—but that pretence is vain.
For, if ye slew him for suppos'd misrule,
Injustice to his kin and Dorian friends,
Why with the offending father did ye slay
Two unoffending babes, his innocent sons?
Why not on them have plac'd the forfeit crown,   320
Rul'd in their name, and train'd them to your will?
Had *they* misrul'd? had *they* forgot their friends?
Forsworn their blood? ungratefully had *they*
Preferr'd Messenian serfs to Dorian lords?
No: but to thy ambition their poor lives
Were bar; and this, too, was their father's crime.
That thou might'st reign he died, not for his fault
Even fancied; and his death thou wroughtest chief.
For, if the other lords desir'd his fall
Hotlier than thou, and were by thee kept back,   330
Why dost thou only profit by his death?
Thy crown condemns thee, while thy tongue absolves.
And now to me thou tenderest friendly league,
And to my son reversion to thy throne:
Short answer is sufficient; league with thee,
For me I deem such impious; and for him,
Exile abroad more safe than heirship here.

POLYPHONTES

I ask thee not to approve thy husband's death,
No, nor expect thee to admit the grounds,
In reason good, which justified my deed: 340
With women the heart argues, not the mind.

But, for thy children's death, I stand assoil'd :
I sav'd them, meant them honour : but thy friends
Rose, and with fire and sword assailed my house
By night ; in that blind tumult they were slain.
To chance impute their deaths, then, not to me.

MEROPE

Such chance as kill'd the father, kill'd the sons.

POLYPHONTES

One son at least I spar'd, for still he lives.

MEROPE

Tyrants think him they murder not they spare.

POLYPHONTES

Not much a tyrant thy free speech displays me.   350

MEROPE

Thy shame secures my freedom, not thy will.

POLYPHONTES

Shame rarely checks the genuine tyrant's will.

MEROPE

One merit, then, thou hast : exult in that.

POLYPHONTES

Thou standest out, I see, repellest peace.

MEROPE

Thy sword repell'd it long ago, not I.

POLYPHONTES

Doubtless thou reckonest on the hope of friends.

MEROPE

Not help of men, although, perhaps, of Gods.

POLYPHONTES

What Gods ? the Gods of concord, civil weal ?

MEROPE

No : the avenging Gods, who punish crime.

Polyphontes

Beware! from thee upbraidings I receive   360
With pity, nay, with reverence; yet, beware!
I know, I know how hard it is to think
That right, that conscience pointed to a deed,
Where interest seems to have enjoin'd it too.
Most men are led by interest; and the few
Who are not, expiate the general sin,
Involv'd in one suspicion with the base.
Dizzy the path and perilous the way
Which in a deed like mine a just man treads,
But it is sometimes trodden, oh! believe it.   370
Yet how *canst* thou believe it? therefore thou
Hast all impunity. Yet, lest thy friends,
Embolden'd by my lenience, think it fear,
And count on like impunity, and rise,
And have to thank thee for a fall, beware!
To rule this kingdom I intend: with sway
Clement, if may be, but to rule it: there
Expect no wavering, no retreat, no change.—
And now I leave thee to these rites, esteem'd
Pious, but impious, surely, if their scope   380
Be to foment old memories of wrath.
Pray, as thou pour'st libations on this tomb,
To be delivered from thy foster'd hate,
Unjust suspicion, and erroneous fear.

[Polyphontes *goes into the palace.* The Chorus *and*
Merope *approach the tomb with their offerings.*

The Chorus

Draw, draw near to the tomb.   *strophe.*
Lay honey-cakes on its marge,
Pour the libation of milk,
Deck it with garlands of flowers.
Tears fall thickly the while!
Behold, O King, from the dark   390
House of the grave, what we do.

O Arcadian hills,   *antistrophe.*
Send us the Youth whom ye hide,
Girt with his coat for the chase,
With the low broad hat of the tann'd

Hunter o'ershadowing his brow:
Grasping firm, in his hand
Advanc'd, two javelins, not now
Dangerous alone to the deer.

MEROPE

What shall I bear, O lost   *str.* 1.   400
Husband and King, to thy grave?—
Pure libations, and fresh
Flowers? But thou, in the gloom,
Discontented, perhaps,
Demandest vengeance, not grief?
Sternly requirest a man,
Light to spring up to thy race?

THE CHORUS

Vengeance, O Queen, is his due,   *str.* 2.
His most just prayer: yet his race—
If that might soothe him below—   410
Prosperous, mighty, came back
In the third generation, the way
Order'd by Fate, to their home.
And now, glorious, secure,
Fill the wealth-giving thrones
Of their heritage, Pelops' isle.

MEROPE

Suffering sent them, Death   *ant.* 1.
March'd with them, Hatred and Strife
Met them entering their halls.
For from the day when the first   420
Heracleidae receiv'd
That Delphic hest to return,
What hath involv'd them but blind
Error on error, and blood?

THE CHORUS

Truly I hear of a Maid   *ant.* 2.
Of that stock born, who bestow'd
Her blood that so she might make
Victory sure to her race,
When the fight hung in doubt: but she now,

Honour'd and sung of by all, 430
Far on Marathon plain
Gives her name to the spring
Macaria, blessed Child.

Merope

She led the way of death. *str.* 3.
And the plain of Tegea,
And the grave of Orestes—
Where, in secret seclusion
Of his unreveal'd tomb,
Sleeps Agamemnon's unhappy,
Matricidal, world-fam'd, 440
Seven-cubit-statur'd son—
Sent forth Echemus, the victor, the king,
By whose hand, at the Isthmus,
At the Fate-denied Straits,
Fell the eldest of the sons of Hercules,
Hyllus, the chief of his house.—
Brother follow'd sister
The all-wept way.

The Chorus

Yes; but his son's seed, wiser-counsell'd, 449
Sail'd by the Fate-meant Gulf to their conquest;
Slew their enemies' king, Tisamenus.
Wherefore accept that happier omen!
Yet shall restorers appear to the race.

Merope

Three brothers won the field, *ant.* 3.
And to two did Destiny
Give the thrones that they conquer'd.
But the third, what delays him
From his unattain'd crown? . . .
Ah Pylades and Electra,
Ever faithful, untir'd, 460
Jealous, blood-exacting friends!
Ye lie watching for the foe of your kin,
In the passes of Delphi,
In the temple-built gorge.—

There the youngest of the band of conquerors
Perish'd, in sight of the goal.
Grandson follow'd sire
The all-wept way.

The Chorus

Thou tellest the fate of the last   *str.* 4.
Of the three Heracleidae.   470
Not of him, of Cresphontes thou shared'st the lot.
A king, a king was he while he liv'd,
Swaying the sceptre with predestin'd hand.
And now, minister lov'd,
Holds rule——

Merope

Ah me . . . Ah . . .

The Chorus

For the awful Monarchs below.

Merope

Thou touchest the worst of my ills.   *str.* 5.
Oh had he fallen of old
At the Isthmus, in fight with his foes,
By Achaian, Arcadian spear !   480
Then had his sepulchre risen
On the high sea-bank, in the sight
Of either Gulf, and remain'd
All-regarded afar,
Noble memorial of worth
Of a valiant Chief, to his own.

The Chorus

There rose up a cry in the streets   *ant.* 4.
From the terrified people.
From the altar of Zeus, from the crowd, came a wail.
A blow, a blow was struck, and he fell,   490
Sullying his garment with dark-streaming blood :
While stood o'er him a Form—
Some Form——

Merope

Ah me . . . Ah . .

The Chorus

Of a dreadful Presence of fear.

Merope

More piercing the second cry rang, *ant.* 5.
Wail'd from the palace within,
From the Children. . . . The Fury to them,
Fresh from their father, draws near.
Ah bloody axe! dizzy blows!
In these ears, they thunder, they ring, 500
These poor ears, still :—and these eyes
Night and day see them fall,
Fiery phantoms of death,
On the fair, curl'd heads of my sons.

The Chorus

Not to thee only hath come *str.* 6.
Sorrow, O Queen, of mankind.
Had not Electra to haunt
A palace defil'd by a death unaveng'd,
For years, in silence, devouring her heart?
But her nursling, her hope, came at last. 510
Thou, too, rearest in joy,
Far 'mid Arcadian hills,
Somewhere, in safety, a nursling, a light.
Yet, yet shall Zeus bring him home!
Yet shall he dawn on this land!

Merope

Him in secret, in tears, *str.* 7.
Month after month, through the slow-dragging year,
Longing, listening, I wait, I implore.
But he comes not. What dell,
O Erymanthus! from sight 520
Of his mother, which of thy glades,
O Lycaeus! conceals
The happy hunter? He basks
In youth's pure morning, nor thinks
On the blood-stain'd home of his birth.

The Chorus

Give not thy heart to despair. *ant.* 6.
No lamentation can loose

Prisoners of death from the grave:
But Zeus, who accounteth thy quarrel his own,
Still rules, still watches, and numbers the hours   530
Till the sinner, the vengeance, be ripe.
Still, by Acheron stream,
Terrible Deities thron'd
Sit, and make ready the serpent, the scourge.
Still, still the Dorian boy,
Exil'd, remembers his home.

MEROPE

Him if high-ruling Zeus   *ant.* 7.
Bring to his mother, the rest I commit,
Willing, patient, to Zeus, to his care.
Blood I ask not.   Enough   540
Sated, and more than enough,
Are mine eyes with blood.   But if this,
O my comforters! strays
Amiss from Justice, the Gods
Forgive my folly, and work
What they will!—but to me give my son!

THE CHORUS

Hear us and help us, Shade of our King!   *str.* 8.

MEROPE

A return, O Father! give to thy boy!   *str.* 9.

THE CHORUS

Send an avenger, Gods of the dead!   *ant.* 8.

MEROPE

An avenger I ask not: send me my son!   *ant.* 9.   550

THE CHORUS

O Queen, for an avenger to appear,
Thinking that so I pray'd aright, I pray'd:
If I pray'd wrongly, I revoke the prayer.

MEROPE

Forgive me, maidens, if I seem too slack
In calling vengeance on a murderer's head.

Impious I deem the alliance which he asks ;
Requite him words severe, for seeming kind ;
And righteous, if he falls, I count his fall.
With this, to those unbrib'd inquisitors,
Who in man's inmost bosom sit and judge,   560
The true avengers these, I leave his deed,
By him shown fair, but, I believe, most foul.
If these condemn him, let them pass his doom!
That doom obtain effect, from Gods or men!
So be it! yet will that more solace bring
To the chaf'd heart of Justice than to mine.—
To hear another tumult in these streets,
To have another murder in these halls,
To see another mighty victim bleed—
There is small comfort for a woman here.   570
A woman, O my friends, has one desire—
To see secure, to live with, those she loves.
Can Vengeance give me back the murdered? no!
Can it bring home my child? Ah, if it can,
I pray the Furies' ever-restless band,
And pray the Gods, and pray the all-seeing Sun—
'Sun, who careerest through the height of Heaven,
When o'er the Arcadian forests thou art come,
And seest my stripling hunter there afield,
Put tightness in thy gold-embossèd rein,   580
And check thy fiery steeds, and, leaning back,
Throw him a pealing word of summons down,
To come, a late avenger, to the aid
Of this poor soul who bore him, and his sire.'
If this will bring him back, be this my prayer!—
But Vengeance travels in a dangerous way,
Double of issue, full of pits and snares
For all who pass, pursuers and pursued—
That way is dubious for a mother's prayer.
Rather on thee I call, Husband belov'd!—   590
May Hermes, herald of the dead, convey
My words below to thee, and make thee hear.—
Bring back our son! if may be, without blood!
Install him in thy throne, still without blood!
Grant him to reign there wise and just like thee,
More fortunate than thee, more fairly judg'd!
This for our son : and for myself I pray,

Soon, having once beheld him, to descend
Into the quiet gloom, where thou art now.
These words to thine indulgent ear, thy wife,   600
I send, and these libations pour the while.
  [*They make their offerings at the tomb.* MEROPE
                then goes towards the palace.

THE CHORUS

The dead hath now his offerings duly paid.
But whither go'st thou hence, O Queen, away?

MEROPE

To receive Arcas, who to-day should come,
Bringing me of my boy the annual news.

THE CHORUS

No certain news if like the rest it run.

MEROPE

Certain in this, that 'tis uncertain still.

THE CHORUS

What keeps him in Arcadia from return?

MEROPE

His grandsire and his uncles fear the risk.

THE CHORUS

Of what? it lies with them to make risk none.   610

MEROPE

Discovery of a visit made by stealth.

THE CHORUS

With arms then they should send him, not by stealth.

MEROPE

With arms they dare not, and by stealth they fear.

THE CHORUS

I doubt their caution little suits their ward.

MEROPE

The heart of youth I know; that most I fear.

THE CHORUS

I augur thou wilt hear some bold resolve.

MEROPE

I dare not wish it; but, at least, to hear
That my son still survives, in health, in bloom;
To hear that still he loves, still longs for, me;
Yet, with a light uncareworn spirit, turns   620
Quick from distressful thought, and floats in joy—
Thus much from Arcas, my old servant true,
Who sav'd him from these murderous halls a babe,
And since has fondly watch'd him night and day
Save for this annual charge, I hope to hear.
If this be all, I know not; but I know,
These many years I live for this alone.

[MEROPE *goes in.*

THE CHORUS

Much is there which the Sea   *str.* 1.
Conceals from man, who cannot plumb its depths.
Air to his unwing'd form denies a way,   630
And keeps its liquid solitudes unscal'd.
Even Earth, whereon he treads,
So feeble is his march, so slow,
Holds countless tracts untrod.

But, more than all unplumb'd,   *ant.* 1.
Unscal'd, untrodden, is the heart of Man.
More than all secrets hid, the way it keeps.
Nor any of our organs so obtuse,
Inaccurate, and frail,
As those with which we try to test   640
Feelings and motives there.

Yea, and not only have we not explor'd   *str.* 2.
That wide and various world, the heart of others,
But even our own heart, that narrow world
Bounded in our own breast, we hardly know,
Of our own actions dimly trace the causes.
Whether a natural obscureness, hiding
That region in perpetual cloud,
Or our own want of effort, be the bar.

Therefore—while acts are from their motives judg'd,
ant. 2. 650
And to one act many most unlike motives,
This pure, that guilty, may have each impell'd—
Power fails us to try clearly if that cause
Assign'd us by the actor be the true one:
Power fails the man himself to fix distinctly
The cause which drew him to his deed,
And stamp himself, thereafter, bad or good.

The most are bad, wise men have said. *str.* 3.
Let the best rule, they say again.
The best, then, to dominion have the right. 660
Rights unconceded and denied,
Surely, if rights, may be by force asserted—
May be, nay should, if for the general weal.
The best, then, to the throne may carve his way,
And hew opposers down,
Free from all guilt of lawlessness,
Or selfish lust of personal power:
Bent only to serve Virtue,
Bent to diminish wrong.

And truly, in this ill-rul'd world, *ant.* 3. 670
Well sometimes may the good desire
To give to Virtue her dominion due.
Well may they long to interrupt
The reign of Folly, usurpation ever,
Though fenc'd by sanction of a thousand years.
Well thirst to drag the wrongful ruler down.
Well purpose to pen back
Into the narrow path of right,
The ignorant, headlong multitude,
Who blindly follow ever 680
Blind leaders, to their bane.

But who can say, without a fear, *str.* 4.
That best, who ought to rule, am I;
The mob, who ought to obey, are these;
I the one righteous, they the many bad?—
Who, without check of conscience, can aver
That he to power makes way by arms,

Sheds blood, imprisons, banishes, attaints,
Commits all deeds the guilty oftenest do,
Without a single guilty thought, 690
Arm'd for right only, and the general good?

Therefore, with censure unallay'd, *ant.* 4.
Therefore, with unexcepting ban,
Zeus and pure-thoughted Justice brand
Imperious self-asserting Violence.
Sternly condemn the too bold man, who dares
Elect himself Heaven's destin'd arm.
And, knowing well man's inmost heart infirm,
However noble the committer be,
His grounds however specious shown, 700
Turn with averted eyes from deeds of blood.

Thus, though a woman, I was school'd *epode.*
By those whom I revere.
Whether I learnt their lessons well,
Or, having learnt them, well apply
To what hath in this house befall'n,
If in the event be any proof,
The event will quickly show.

[AEPYTUS *comes in.*

AEPYTUS

Maidens, assure me if they told me true
Who told me that the royal house was here. 710

THE CHORUS

Rightly they told thee, and thou art arriv'd.

AEPYTUS

Here, then, it is, where Polyphontes dwells?

THE CHORUS

He doth: thou hast both house and master right.

AEPYTUS

Might some one straight inform him he is sought?

THE CHORUS

Inform him that thyself, for here he comes.

[POLYPHONTES *comes forth, with* ATTENDANTS
and GUARDS.

AEPYTUS

O King, all hail ! I come with weighty news:
Most likely, grateful ; but, in all case, sure.

POLYPHONTES

Speak them, that I may judge their kind myself.

AEPYTUS

Accept them in one word, for good or bad :
Aepytus, the Messenian prince, is dead !   720

POLYPHONTES

Dead !—and when died he ? where ? and by what
        hand ?
And who art thou, who bringest me such news ?

AEPYTUS

He perish'd in Arcadia, where he liv'd
With Cypselus ; and two days since he died.
One of the train of Cypselus am I.

POLYPHONTES

Instruct me of the manner of his death.

AEPYTUS

That will I do, and to this end I came.
For, being of like age, of birth not mean,
The son of an Arcadian noble, I
Was chosen his companion from a boy ;   730
And on the hunting-rambles which his heart,
Unquiet, drove him ever to pursue,
Through all the lordships of the Arcadian dales,
From chief to chief, I wander'd at his side,
The captain of his squires, and his guard.
On such a hunting-journey, three morns since,
With beaters, hounds, and huntsmen, he and I
Set forth from Tegea, the royal town.
The prince at start seem'd sad, but his regard
Clear'd with blithe travel and the morning air.   740
We rode from Tegea, through the woods of oaks,

Past Arnê spring, where Rhea gave the babe
Poseidon to the shepherd-boys to hide
From Saturn's search among the new-yean'd lambs,
To Mantinea, with its unbak'd walls ;
Thence, by the Sea-God's Sanctuary, and the tomb
Whither from wintry Maenalus were brought
The bones of Arcas, whence our race is nam'd,
On, to the marshy Orchomenian plain,
And the Stone Coffins ;—then, by Caphyae Cliffs,   750
To Pheneos with its craggy citadel.
There, with the chief of that hill-town, we lodg'd
One night ; and the next day, at dawn, far'd on
By the Three Fountains and the Adder's Hill
To the Stymphalian Lake, our journey's end,
To draw the coverts on Cyllene's side.
There, on a grassy spur which bathes its root
Far in the liquid lake, we sate, and drew
Cates from our hunters' pouch, Arcadian fare,
Sweet chestnuts, barley-cakes, and boar's-flesh dried :
And as we ate, and rested there, we talk'd   761
Of places we had pass'd, sport we had had,
Of beasts of chase that haunt the Arcadian hills,
Wild hog, and bear, and mountain-deer, and roe :
Last, of our quarters with the Arcadian chiefs.
For courteous entertainment, welcome warm,
Sad, reverential homage, had our prince
From all, for his great lineage and his woes :
All which he own'd, and prais'd with grateful mind.
But still over his speech a gloom there hung,   770
As of one shadow'd by impending death ;
And strangely, as we talk'd, he would apply
The story of spots mention'd to his own :
Telling us, Arnê minded him, he too
Was sav'd a babe, but to a life obscure,
Which he, the seed of Hercules, dragg'd on
Inglorious, and should drop at last unknown,
Even as those dead unepitaph'd, who lie
In the stone coffins at Orchomenus.
And, then, he bade remember how we pass'd   780
The Mantinean Sanctuary, forbid
To foot of mortal, where his ancestor,
Nam'd Aepytus like him, having gone in,

Was blinded by the outgushing springs of brine.
Then, turning westward to the Adder's Hill—
Another ancestor, nam'd, too, like me,
Died of a snake-bite, said he, *on that brow :*
Still at his mountain tomb men marvel, built
Where, as life ebb'd, his bearers laid him down.
So he play'd on ; then ended, with a smile—   790
This region is not happy for my race.
We cheer'd him ; but, that moment, from the copse
By the lake-edge, broke the sharp cry of hounds ;
The prickers shouted that the stag was gone :
We sprang upon our feet, we snatch'd our spears,
We bounded down the swarded slope, we plung'd
Through the dense ilex-thickets to the dogs.
Far in the woods ahead their music rang ;
And many times that morn we cours'd in ring
The forests round which belt Cyllene's side ;   800
Till I, thrown out and tired, came to halt
On the same spur where we had sate at morn.
And resting there to breathe, I saw below
Rare, straggling hunters, foil'd by brake and crag,
And the prince, single, pressing on the rear
Of that unflagging quarry and the hounds.
Now, in the woods far down, I saw them cross
An open glade ; now he was high aloft
On some tall scar fring'd with dark feathery pines,
Peering to spy a goat-track down the cliff,   810
Cheering with hand, and voice, and horn his dogs.
At last the cry drew to the water's edge—
And through the brushwood, to the pebbly strand,
Broke, black with sweat, the antler'd mountain stag,
And took the lake : two hounds alone pursued ;
Then came the prince—he shouted and plung'd in.—
There is a chasm rifted in the base
Of that unfooted precipice, whose rock
Walls on one side the deep Stymphalian Lake :
There the lake-waters, which in ages gone   820
Wash'd, as the marks upon the hills still show,
All the Stymphalian plain, are now suck'd down.
A headland, with one agèd plane-tree crown'd,
Parts from the cave-pierc'd cliff the shelving bay
Where first the chase plung'd in : the bay is smooth,

But round the headland's point a current sets,
Strong, black, tempestuous, to the cavern-mouth.
Stoutly, under the headland's lee, they swam :
But when they came abreast the point, the race
Caught them, as wind takes feathers, whirl'd them
    round   830
Struggling in vain to cross it, swept them on,
Stag, dogs, and hunter, to the yawning gulph.
All this, O King, not piecemeal, as to thee
Now told, but in one flashing instant pass'd :
While from the turf whereon I lay I sprang,
And took three strides, quarry and dogs were gone ;
A moment more—I saw the prince turn round
Once in the black and arrowy race, and cast
One arm aloft for help ; then sweep beneath
The low-brow'd cavern-arch, and disappear.   840
And what I could, I did—to call by cries
Some straggling hunters to my aid, to rouse
Fishers who live on the lake-side, to launch
Boats, and approach, near as we dar'd, the chasm.
But of the prince nothing remain'd, save this,
His boar-spear's broken shaft, back on the lake
Cast by the rumbling subterranean stream ;
And this, at landing spied by us and sav'd,
His broad-brimm'd hunter's hat, which, in the bay,
Where first the stag took water, floated still.   850
And I across the mountains brought with haste
To Cypselus, at Basilis, this news :
Basilis, his new city, which he now
Near Lycosura builds, Lycaon's town,
First city founded on the earth by men.
He to thee sends me on, in one thing glad
While all else grieves him, that his grandchild's death
Extinguishes distrust 'twixt him and thee.
But I from our deplor'd mischance learn this—
The man who to untimely death is doom'd,   860
Vainly you hedge him from the assault of harm ;
He bears the seed of ruin in himself.

The Chorus

So dies the last shoot of our royal tree !
Who shall tell Merope this heavy news ?

POLYPHONTES

Stranger, the news thou bringest is too great
For instant comment, having many sides
Of import, and in silence best receiv'd,
Whether it turn at last to joy or woe.
But thou, the zealous bearer, hast no part
In what it has of painful, whether now,   870
First heard, or in its future issue shown.
Thou for thy labour hast deserv'd our best
Refreshment, needed by thee, as I judge,
With mountain-travel and night-watching spent.—
To the guest-chamber lead him, some one! give
All entertainment which a traveller needs,
And such as fits a royal house to show:
To friends, still more, and labourers in our cause.

     [ATTENDANTS *conduct* AEPYTUS *within the palace.*

THE CHORUS

The youth is gone within; alas! he bears
A presence sad for some one through those doors.   880

POLYPHONTES

Admire then, maidens, how in one short hour
The schemes, pursued in vain for twenty years,
Are by a stroke, though undesir'd, complete,
Crown'd with success, not in my way, but Heaven's!
This at a moment, too, when I had urg'd
A last, long-cherish'd project, in my aim
Of concord, and been baffled with disdain.
Fair terms of reconcilement, equal rule,
I offer'd to my foes, and they refus'd:
Worse terms than mine they have obtain'd from
    Heaven.   890
Dire is this blow for Merope; and I
Wish'd, truly wish'd, solution to our broil
Other than by this death: but it hath come!
I speak no word of boast, but this I say,
A private loss here founds a nation's peace.

     [POLYPHONTES *goes out.*

THE CHORUS

Peace, who tarriest too long;   *strophe.*
Peace, with Delight in thy train;

Come, come back to our prayer!
Then shall the revel again
Visit our streets, and the sound   900
Of the harp be heard with the pipe,
When the flashing torches appear
In the marriage-train coming on,
With dancing maidens and boys:
While the matrons come to the doors,
And the old men rise from their bench,
When the youths bring home the bride.

Not decried by my voice   *antistrophe.*
He who restores thee shall be,
Not unfavour'd by Heaven.   910
Surely no sinner the man,
Dread though his acts, to whose hand
Such a boon to bring hath been given.
Let her come, fair Peace! let her come!
But the demons long nourish'd here,
Murder, Discord, and Hate,
In the stormy desolate waves
Of the Thracian Sea let her leave,
Or the howling outermost Main.

[MEROPE *comes forth.*

MEROPE

A whisper through the palace flies of one   920
Arriv'd from Tegea with weighty news;
And I came, thinking to find Arcas here.
Ye have not left this gate, which he must pass:
Tell me—hath one not come? or, worse mischance,
Come, but been intercepted by the King?

THE CHORUS

A messenger, sent from Arcadia here,
Arriv'd, and of the King had speech but now.

MEROPE

Ah me! the wrong expectant got his news.

THE CHORUS

The message brought was for the King design'd.

MEROPE

How so? was Arcas not the messenger?   930

The Chorus

A younger man, and of a different name.

Merope

And what Arcadian news had he to tell?

The Chorus

Learn that from other lips, O Queen, than mine.

Merope

He kept his tale, then, for the King alone?

The Chorus

His tale was meeter for that ear than thine.

Merope

Why dost thou falter, and make half reply?

The Chorus

O thrice unhappy, how I groan thy fate!

Merope

Thou frightenest and confound'st me by thy words.
O were but Arcas come, all would be well!

The Chorus

If so, all 's well: for look, the old man speeds   940
Up from the city tow'rds this gated hill.

> [Arcas *comes in.*

Merope

Not with the failing breath and foot of age
My faithful follower comes.   Welcome, old friend!

Arcas

Faithful, not welcome, when my tale is told.
O that my over-speed and bursting grief
Had on the journey chok'd my labouring breath,
And lock'd my speech for ever in my breast!
Yet then another man would bring this news.—
O honour'd Queen, thy son, my charge, is gone.

The Chorus

Too suddenly thou tellest such a loss.   950
Look up, O Queen! look up, O mistress dear!
Look up, and see thy friends who comfort thee.

MEROPE

Ah . . . Ah . . . Ah me!

THE CHORUS

And I, too, say, ah me!

ARCAS

Forgive, forgive the bringer of such news!

MEROPE

Better from thine than from an enemy's tongue.

THE CHORUS

And yet no enemy did this, O Queen:
But the wit-baffling will and hand of Heaven.

ARCAS

No enemy! and what hast thou, then, heard?
Swift as I came, hath Falsehood been before?

THE CHORUS

A youth arriv'd but now, the son, he said,   960
Of an Arcadian lord, our prince's friend,
Jaded with travel, clad in hunter's garb.
He brought report that his own eyes had seen
The prince, in chase after a swimming stag,
Swept down a chasm broken in the cliff
Which hangs o'er the Stymphalian Lake, and drown'd.

ARCAS

Ah me! with what a foot doth Treason post,
While Loyalty, with all her speed, is slow!
Another tale, I trow, thy messenger
For the King's private ear reserves, like this   970
In one thing only, that the prince is dead.

THE CHORUS

And how then runs this true and private tale?

ARCAS

As much to the King's wish, more to his shame.
This young Arcadian noble, guard and mate

To Aepytus, the king seduc'd with gold,
And had him at the prince's side in leash,
Ready to slip on his unconscious prey.
He on a hunting party three days since,
Among the forests on Cyllene's side,
Perform'd good service for his bloody wage ;   980
The prince, his uncle Laias, whom his ward
Had in a father's place, he basely murder'd.
Take this for true, the other tale for feign'd.

THE CHORUS

And this perfidious murder who reveal'd ?

ARCAS

The faithless murderer's own, no other tongue.

THE CHORUS

Did conscience goad him to denounce himself ?

ARCAS

To Cypselus at Basilis he brought
This strange unlikely tale, the prince was drown'd.

THE CHORUS

But not a word appears of murder here.

ARCAS

Examin'd close, he own'd this story false.   990
Then evidence came—his comrades of the hunt,
Who saw the prince and Laias last with him,
Never again in life—next, agents, fee'd
To ply 'twixt the Messenian king and him,
Spoke, and reveal'd that traffic, and the traitor.
So charg'd, he stood dumb-founder'd : Cypselus,
On this suspicion, cast him into chains.
Thence he escap'd—and next I find him here.

THE CHORUS

His presence with the King, thou mean'st, implies——

ARCAS

He comes to tell his prompter he hath sped.   1000

The Chorus

Still he repeats the drowning story here.

Arcas

To thee—that needs no Oedipus to explain.

The Chorus

Interpret, then ; for we, it seems, are dull.

Arcas

Your King desir'd the profit of his death,
Not the black credit of his murderer.
That stern word '*murder*' had too dread a sound
For the Messenian hearts, who lov'd the prince.

The Chorus

Suspicion grave I see, but no clear proof.   1008

Merope

Peace ! peace ! all 's clear.—The wicked watch and work
While the good sleep : the workers have the day.
He who was sent hath sped, and now comes back,
To chuckle with his sender o'er the game
Which foolish innocence plays with subtle guilt.
Ah ! now I comprehend the liberal grace
Of this far-scheming tyrant, and his boon
Of heirship to his kingdom for my son :
He had his murderer ready, and the sword
Lifted, and that unwish'd-for heirship void—
A tale, meanwhile, forg'd for his subjects' ears :
And me, henceforth sole rival with himself   1020
In their allegiance, me, in my son's death-hour,
When all turn'd tow'rds me, me he would have shown
To my Messenians, dup'd, disarm'd, despis'd,
The willing sharer of his guilty rule,
All claim to succour forfeit, to myself
Hateful, by each Messenian heart abhorr'd.—
His offers I repelled—but what of that ?
If with no rage, no fire of righteous hate,
Such as ere now hath spurr'd to fearful deeds
Weak women with a thousandth part my wrongs,
But calm, but unresentful, I endur'd   1031
His offers, coldly heard them, cold repell'd ?

While all this time I bear to linger on
In this blood-delug'd palace, in whose halls
Either a vengeful Fury I should stalk,
Or else not live at all—but here I haunt,
A pale, unmeaning ghost, powerless to fright
Or harm, and nurse my longing for my son,
A helpless one, I know it :—but the Gods
Have temper'd me e'en thus ; and, in some souls,
Misery, which rouses others, breaks the spring.   1041
And even now, my son, ah me ! my son,
Fain would I fade away, as I have liv'd,
Without a cry, a struggle, or a blow,
All vengeance unattempted, and descend
To the invisible plains, to roam with thee,
Fit denizen, the lampless under-world——
But with what eyes should I encounter there
My husband, wandering with his stern compeers,
Amphiaraos, or Mycenae's king,   1050
Who led the Greeks to Ilium, Agamemnon,
Betray'd like him, but, not like him, aveng'd?
Or with what voice shall I the questions meet
Of my two elder sons, slain long ago,
Who sadly ask me, what, if not revenge,
Kept me, their mother, from their side so long?
Or how reply to thee, my child, last-born,
Last-murder'd, who reproachfully wilt say—
Mother, I well believ'd thou lived'st on
In the detested palace of thy foe,   1060
With patience on thy face, death in thy heart,
Counting, till I grew up, the laggard years,
That our joint hands might then together pay
To one unhappy house the debt we owe.
My death makes my debt void, and doubles thine—
But down thou fleest here, and leav'st our scourge
Triumphant, and condemnest all our race
To lie in gloom for ever unappeas'd.
What shall I have to answer to such words?—
No, something must be dar'd ; and, great as erst
Our dastard patience, be our daring now !   1071
Come, ye swift Furies, who to him ye haunt
Permit no peace till your behests are done ;
Come Hermes, who dost watch the unjustly kill'd,

And can'st teach simple ones to plot and feign ;
Come, lightning Passion, that with foot of fire
Advancest to the middle of a deed
Almost before 'tis plann'd ; come, glowing Hate ;
Come, baneful Mischief, from thy murky den
Under the dripping black Tartarean cliff   1080
Which Styx's awful waters trickle down—
Inspire this coward heart, this flagging arm !
How say ye, maidens, do ye know these prayers ?
Are these words Merope's—is this voice mine ?
Old man, old man, thou had'st my boy in charge,
And he is lost, and thou hast that to atone.
Fly, find me on the instant where confer
The murderer and his impious setter-on :
And ye, keep faithful silence, friends, and mark
What one weak woman can achieve alone.   1090

ARCAS

O mistress, by the Gods, do nothing rash !

MEROPE

Unfaithful servant, dost thou, too, desert me ?

ARCAS

I go ! I go !—yet, Queen, take this one word :
Attempting deeds beyond thy power to do,
Thou nothing profitest thy friends, but mak'st
Our misery more, and thine own ruin sure.

[ARCAS *goes out.*

THE CHORUS

I have heard, O Queen, how a prince,   *str.* 1.
Agamemnon's son, in Mycenae,
Orestes, died but in name,
Liv'd for the death of his foes.   1100

MEROPE

Peace !

THE CHORUS
What is it ?

MEROPE

Alas,

Thou destroyest me !

The Chorus
How?

Merope

Whispering hope of a life
Which no stranger unknown,
But the faithful servant and guard,
Whose tears warrant his truth,
Bears sad witness is lost.

The Chorus

Wheresoe'er men are, there is grief.   *ant.* 1.
In a thousand countries, a thousand
Homes, e'en now is there wail;   1110
Mothers lamenting their sons.

Merope

Yes——

The Chorus
Thou knowest it?

Merope

This,
Who lives, witnesses.

The Chorus
True.

Merope
But, is it only a fate
Sure, all-common, to lose
In a land of friends, by a friend.
One last, murder-sav'd child?

The Chorus
Ah me!   *str.* 2.

Merope

Thou confessest the prize
In the rushing, thundering, mad,   1120
Cloud-envelop'd, obscure,
Unapplauded, unsung
Race of calamity, mine?

The Chorus

None can truly claim that
Mournful pre-eminence, not
Thou.

Merope

Fate *gives* it, ah me!

The Chorus

Not, above all, in the doubts,
Double and clashing, that hang——

Merope

What then?   *ant. 2.*
Seems it lighter, my loss,   1130
If, perhaps, unpierc'd by the sword,
My child lies in a jagg'd
Sunless prison of rocks,
On the black wave borne to and fro?

The Chorus

Worse, far worse, if his friend,
If the Arcadian within,
If——

Merope (*with a start*)

How say'st thou? within? . . .

The Chorus

He in the guest-chamber now,
Faithlessly murder'd his friend.

Merope

Ye, too, ye, too, join to betray, then,   1140
Your Queen!

The Chorus
What is this?

Merope

Ye knew,

O false friends! into what
Haven the murderer had dropp'd?
Ye kept silence?

The Chorus
In fear,
O lov'd mistress! in fear,
Dreading thine over-wrought mood,
What I knew, I conceal'd.

Merope
Swear by the Gods henceforth to obey me!

The Chorus
Unhappy one, what deed
Purposes thy despair?　　　　　　　　　　1150
I promise; but I fear.

Merope
From the altar, the unaveng'd tomb,
Fetch me the sacrifice-axe!——
　　　[The Chorus *goes towards the tomb of* Cres-
　　　　　phontes, *and their leader brings back the axe.*

O Husband, O cloth'd
With the grave's everlasting,
All-covering darkness! O King,
Well mourn'd, but ill-aveng'd!
Approv'st thou thy wife now?——
The axe!—who brings it?

The Chorus
　　　　　　　'Tis here!
But thy gesture, thy look,　　　　　　　　1160
Appals me, shakes me with awe.

Merope
Thrust back now the bolt of that door!

The Chorus
Alas! alas!—
Behold the fastenings withdrawn
Of the guest-chamber door!—
Ah! I beseech thee—with tears——

Merope
Throw the door open!

The Chorus
　　　　　　　'Tis done! . . .

*[The door of the house is thrown open : the interior
    of the guest-chamber is discovered, with
    AEPYTUS asleep on a couch.*

MEROPE

He sleeps—sleeps calm.   O ye all-seeing Gods !
Thus peacefully do ye let sinners sleep,
While troubled innocents toss, and lie awake ?   1170
What sweeter sleep than this could I desire
For thee, my child, if thou wert yet alive ?
How often have I dream'd of thee like this,
With thy soil'd hunting-coat, and sandals torn,
Asleep in the Arcadian glens at noon,
Thy head droop'd softly, and the golden curls
Clustering o'er thy white forehead, like a girl's ;
The short proud lip showing thy race, thy cheeks
Brown'd with thine open-air, free, hunter's life.
Ah me ! . . .   1180
And where dost thou sleep now, my innocent boy ?—
In some dark fir-tree's shadow, amid rocks
Untrodden, on Cyllene's desolate side ;
Where travellers never pass, where only come
Wild beasts, and vultures sailing overhead.
There, there thou liest now, my hapless child !
Stretch'd among briers and stones, the slow, black gore
Oozing through thy soak'd hunting-shirt, with limbs
Yet stark from the death-struggle, tight-clench'd hands,
And eyeballs staring for revenge in vain.   1190
Ah miserable ! . . .
And thou, thou fair-skinn'd Serpent ! thou art laid
In a rich chamber, on a happy bed,
In a king's house, thy victim's heritage ;
And drink'st untroubled slumber, to sleep off
The toils of thy foul service, till thou wake
Refresh'd, and claim thy master's thanks and gold.—
Wake up in hell from thine unhallow'd sleep,
Thou smiling Fiend, and claim thy guerdon there !
Wake amid gloom, and howling, and the noise   1200
Of sinners pinion'd on the torturing wheel,
And the stanch Furies' never-silent scourge.
And bid the chief-tormentors there provide
For a grand culprit shortly coming down.

Go thou the first, and usher in thy lord!
A more just stroke than that thou gav'st my son,
Take——

> [MEROPE *advances towards the sleeping* AEPYTUS,
> *with the axe uplifted. At the same moment*
> ARCAS *returns.*

ARCAS (*to the Chorus*)

  Not with him to council did the King
Carry his messenger, but left him here.
>   [*Sees* MEROPE *and* AEPYTUS.
O Gods!...

MEROPE

  Foolish old man, thou spoil'st my blow!

ARCAS

What do I see?...

MEROPE

    A murderer at death's door. 1210
Therefore no words!

ARCAS

    A murderer?...

MEROPE

      And a captive
To the dear next-of-kin of him he murder'd.
Stand, and let vengeance pass!

ARCAS

     Hold, O Queen, hold!
Thou know'st not whom thou strik'st....

MEROPE

     I know his crime.

ARCAS

Unhappy one! thou strik'st——

MEROPE

     A most just blow.

ARCAS

No, by the Gods, thou slay'st——

MEROPE

Stand off!

ARCAS

Thy son!

MEROPE

Ah!...   [*She lets the axe drop, and falls insensible.*

AEPYTUS (*awaking*)

Who are these?   What shrill, ear-piercing scream
Wakes me thus kindly from the perilous sleep
Wherewith fatigue and youth had bound mine eyes,
Even in the deadly palace of my foe?—   1220
Arcas!   Thou here?

ARCAS (*embracing him*)

O my dear master!   O
My child, my charge belov'd, welcome to life!
As dead we held thee, mourn'd for thee as dead.

AEPYTUS

In word I died, that I in deed might live.
But who are these?

ARCAS

Messenian maidens, friends.

AEPYTUS

And, Arcas!—but I tremble!

ARCAS

Boldly ask.

AEPYTUS

That black-rob'd, swooning figure?...

ARCAS

Merope.

AEPYTUS

O mother! mother!

MEROPE

Who upbraids me?   Ah!...
                    [*seeing the axe.*

ARNOLD   A a

AEPYTUS

Upbraids thee? no one.

MEROPE

Thou dost well: but take . . .

AEPYTUS

What wav'st thou off?

MEROPE

That murderous axe away!

AEPYTUS

Thy son is here.

MEROPE

One said so, sure, but now.　1231

AEPYTUS

Here, here thou hast him!

MEROPE

Slaughter'd by this hand! . . .

AEPYTUS

No, by the Gods, alive and like to live!

MEROPE

What, thou?—I dream——

AEPYTUS

May'st thou dream ever so!

MEROPE (*advancing towards him*)

My child? unhurt? . . .

AEPYTUS

Only by over joy.

MEROPE

Art thou, then, come? . . .

AEPYTUS

Never to part again.

[*They fall into one another's arms. Then* MEROPE,
holding AEPYTUS *by the hand, turns to* THE
CHORUS.

Merope

O kind Messenian maidens, O my friends,
Bear witness, see, mark well, on what a head
My first stroke of revenge had nearly fallen!

The Chorus

We see, dear mistress: and we say, the Gods,   1240
As hitherto they kept him, keep him now.

Merope

O my son!   *strophe.*
I have, I have thee . . . . the years
Fly back, my child! and thou seem'st
Ne'er to have gone from these eyes,
Never been torn from this breast.

Aepytus

Mother, my heart runs over: but the time
Presses me, chides me, will not let me weep.

Merope

Fearest thou now?

Aepytus

I fear not, but I think on my design.   1250

Merope

At the undried fount of this breast,
A babe, thou smilest again.
Thy brothers play at my feet,
Early-slain innocents! near,
Thy kind-speaking father stands.

Aepytus

Remember, to revenge his death I come!

Merope

Ah . . . revenge!   *antistrophe.*
That word! it kills me! I see
Once more roll back on my house,
Never to ebb, the accurs'd   1260
All-flooding ocean of blood.

Aepytus

Mother, sometimes the justice of the Gods
Appoints the way to peace through shedding blood.

Mérope

Sorrowful peace !

Aepytus

And yet the only peace to us allow'd.

Merope

From the first-wrought vengeance is born
A long succession of crimes.
Fresh blood flows, calling for blood:
Fathers, sons, grandsons, are all
One death-dealing vengeful train.   1270

Aepytus

Mother, thy fears are idle: for I come
To close an old wound, not to open new.
In all else willing to be taught, in this
Instruct me not ; I have my lesson clear.—
Arcas, seek out my uncle Laias, now
Concerting in the city with our friends ;
Here bring him, ere the king come back from council:
That, how to accomplish what the Gods enjoin,
And the slow-ripening time at last prepares,
We two with thee, my mother, may consult: 1280
For whose help dare I count on if not thine ?

Merope

Approves my brother Laias this design ?

Aepytus

Yes, and alone is with me here to share.

Merope

And what of thine Arcadian mate, who bears
Suspicion from thy grandsire of thy death,
For whom, as I suppose, thou passest here ?

Aepytus

Sworn to our plot he is : but, that surmise
Fix'd him the author of my death, I knew not.

Merope

Proof, not surmise, shows him in commerce close——

AEPYTUS

With this Messenian tyrant—that I know.   1290

MEROPE

And entertain'st thou, child, such dangerous friends?

AEPYTUS

This commerce for my best behoof he plies.

MEROPE

That thou may'st read thine enemy's counsel plain?

AEPYTUS

Too dear his secret wiles have cost our house.

MEROPE

And of his unsure agent what demands he?

AEPYTUS

News of my business, pastime, temper, friends.

MEROPE

His messages, then, point not to thy murder?

AEPYTUS

Not yet; though such, no doubt, his final aim.

MEROPE

And what Arcadian helpers bring'st thou here?

AEPYTUS

Laias alone; no errand mine for crowds.   1300

MEROPE

On what relying, to crush such a foe?

AEPYTUS

One sudden stroke, and the Messenians' love.

MEROPE

O thou long-lost, long seen in dreams alone,
But now seen face to face, my only child!
Why wilt thou fly to lose as soon as found
My new-won treasure, thy belovèd life?
Or how expectest not to lose, who com'st

With such slight means to cope with such a foe?
Thine enemy thou know'st not, nor his strength.
The stroke thou purposest is desperate, rash—   1310
Yet grant that it succeeds ;—thou hast behind
The stricken king a second enemy
Scarce dangerous less than him, the Dorian lords.
These are not now the savage band who erst
Follow'd thy father from their northern hills,
Mere ruthless and uncounsell'd tools of war,
Good to obey, without a leader naught.
Their chief hath train'd them, made them like himself,
Sagacious, men of iron, watchful, firm,
Against surprise and sudden panic proof: 1320
Their master fall'n, these will not flinch, but band
To keep their master's power : thou wilt find
Behind his corpse their hedge of serried spears.
But, to match these, thou hast the people's love?
On what a reed, my child, thou leanest there !
Knowest thou not how timorous, how unsure,
How useless an ally a people is
Against the one and certain arm of power?
Thy father perish'd in this people's cause,
Perish'd before their eyes, yet no man stirr'd :   1330
For years, his widow, in their sight I stand,
A never-changing index to revenge—
What help, what vengeance, at their hands have I ?—
At least, if thou wilt trust them, try them first:
Against the King himself array the host
Thou countest on to back thee 'gainst his lords :
First rally the Messenians to thy cause,
Give them cohesion, purpose, and resolve,
Marshal them to an army—then advance,
Then try the issue ; and not, rushing on   1340
Single and friendless, throw to certain death
That dear-belov'd, that young, that gracious head.
Be guided, O my son ! spurn counsel not:
For know thou this, a violent heart hath been
Fatal to all the race of Hercules.

The Chorus

With sage experience she speaks ; and thou,
O Aepytus, weigh well her counsel given.

Aepytus

Ill counsel, in my judgement, gives she here,
Maidens, and reads experience much amiss ;
Discrediting the succour which our cause   1350
Might from the people draw, if rightly us'd :
Advising us a course which would, indeed,
If followed, make their succour slack and null.
A people is no army, train'd to fight,
A passive engine, at their general's will ;
And, if so us'd, proves, as thou say'st, unsure.
A people, like a common man, is dull,
Is lifeless, while its heart remains untouch'd ;
A fool can drive it, and a fly may scare :
When it admires and loves, its heart awakes ;   1360
Then irresistibly it lives, it works :
A people, then, is an ally indeed ;
It is ten thousand fiery wills in one.
Now I, if I invite them to run risk
Of life for my advantage, and myself,
Who chiefly profit, run no more than they—
How shall I rouse their love, their ardour so ?
But, if some signal, unassisted stroke,
Dealt at my own sole risk, before their eyes,
Announces me their rightful prince return'd—
The undegenerate blood of Hercules—   1371
The daring claimant of a perilous throne—
How might not such a sight as this revive
Their loyal passion tow'rd my father's house ?
Electrify their hearts ? make them no more
A craven mob, but a devouring fire ?
Then might I use them, then, for one who thus
Spares not himself, themselves they will not spare.
Haply, had but one daring soul stood forth
To rally them and lead them to revenge,   1380
When my great father fell, they had replied :—
Alas ! our foe alone stood forward then.
And·thou, my mother, hadst thou made a sign—
Hadst thou, from thy forlorn and captive state
Of widowhood in these polluted halls,
Thy prison-house, rais'd one imploring cry—
Who knows but that avengers thou hadst found ?

But mute thou sat'st, and each Messenian heart
In thy despondency desponded too.
Enough of this!—though not a finger stir   1390
To succour me in my extremest need ;
Though all free spirits in this land be dead,
And only slaves and tyrants left alive—
Yet for me, mother, I had liefer die
On native ground, than drag the tedious hours
Of a protected exile any more.
Hate, duty, interest, passion call one way:
Here stand I now, and the attempt shall be.

The Chorus

Prudence is on the other side ; but deeds
Condemn'd by prudence have sometimes gone well.

Merope

Not till the ways of prudence all are tried,   1401
And tried in vain, the turn of rashness comes.
Thou leapest to thy deed, and hast not ask'd
Thy kinsfolk and thy father's friends for aid.

Aepytus

And to what friends should I for aid apply ?

Merope

The royal race of Temenus, in Argos——

Aepytus

That house, like ours, intestine murder maims.

Merope

Thy Spartan cousins, Procles and his brother——

Aepytus

Love a won cause, but not a cause to win.

Merope

My father, then, and his Arcadian chiefs——   1410

Aepytus

Mean still to keep aloof from Dorian broil.

MEROPE

Wait, then, until sufficient help appears.

AEPYTUS

Orestes in Mycenae had no more.

MEROPE

He to fulfil an order rais'd his hand.

AEPYTUS

What order more precise had he than I ?

MEROPE

Apollo peal'd it from his Delphian cave.

AEPYTUS

A mother's murder needed hest divine.

MEROPE

He had a hest, at least, and thou hast none.

AEPYTUS

The Gods command not where the heart speaks clear.

MEROPE

Thou wilt destroy, I see, thyself and us.   1420

AEPYTUS

O suffering ! O calamity ! how ten,
How twentyfold worse are ye, when your blows
Not only wound the sense, but kill the soul,
The noble thought, which is alone the man !
That I, to-day returning, find myself
Orphan'd of both my parents—by his foes
My father, by your strokes my mother slain !—
For this is not my mother, who dissuades,
At the dread altar of her husband's tomb,
His son from vengeance on his murderer ;   1430
And not alone dissuades him, but compares
His just revenge to an unnatural deed,
A deed so awful, that the general tongue
Fluent of horrors, falters to relate it—
Of darkness so tremendous, that its author,

Though to his act empower'd, nay, impell'd,
By the oracular sentence of the Gods,
Fled, for years after, o'er the face of earth,
A frenzied wanderer, a God-driven man,   1439
And hardly yet, some say, hath found a grave—
With such a deed as *this* thou matchest mine,
Which Nature sanctions, which the innocent blood
Clamours to find fulfill'd, which good men praise,
And only bad men joy to see undone?
O honour'd father! hide thee in thy grave
Deep as thou canst, for hence no succour comes;
Since from thy faithful subjects what revenge
Canst thou expect, when thus thy widow fails?
Alas! an adamantine strength indeed,
Past expectation, hath thy murderer built: 1450
For this is the true strength of guilty kings,
When they corrupt the souls of those they rule.

The Chorus

Zeal makes him most unjust: but, in good time,
Here, as I guess, the noble Laias comes.

Laias

Break off, break off your talking, and depart
Each to his post, where the occasion calls;
Lest from the council-chamber presently
The King return, and find you prating here.
A time will come for greetings; but to-day
The hour for words is gone, is come for deeds.   1460

Aepytus

O princely Laias! to what purpose calls
The occasion, if our chief confederate fails?
My mother stands aloof, and blames our deed.

Laias

My royal sister? . . . but, without some cause,
I know, she honours not the dead so ill.

Merope

Brother, it seems thy sister must present,
At this first meeting after absence long,
Not welcome, exculpation to her kin:

Yet exculpation needs it, if I seek,
A woman and a mother, to avert   1470
Risk from my new-restor'd, my only son ?—
Sometimes, when he was gone, I wish'd him back,
Risk what he might ; now that I have him here,
Now that I feed mine eyes on that young face,
Hear that fresh voice, and clasp that gold-lock'd head,
I shudder, Laias, to commit my child
To Murder's dread arena, where I saw
His father and his ill-starr'd brethren fall :
I loathe for him the slippery way of blood ;
I ask if bloodless means may gain his end.   1480
In me the fever of revengeful hate,
Passion's first furious longing to imbrue
Our own right hand in the detested blood
Of enemies, and count their dying groans—
If in this feeble bosom such a fire
Did ever burn—is long by time allay'd,
And I would now have Justice strike, not me.
Besides—for from my brother and my son
I hide not even this—the reverence deep,
Remorseful, tow'rd my hostile solitude,   1490
By Polyphontes never fail'd-in once
Through twenty years ; his mournful anxious zeal
To efface in me the memory of his crime—
Though it efface not that, yet makes me wish
His death a public, not a personal act,
Treacherously plotted 'twixt my son and me ;
To whom this day he came to proffer peace,
Treaty, and to this kingdom for my son
Heirship, with fair intent, as I believe :—
For that he plots thy death, account it false ;   1500

　　　　　　　　　　　　　　　　[*to* AEPYTUS.

Number it with the thousand rumours vain,
Figments of plots, wherewith intriguers fill
The enforcèd leisure of an exile's ear :—
Immers'd in serious state-craft is the King,
Bent above all to pacify, to rule,
Rigidly, yet in settled calm, this realm ;
Not prone, all say, to useless bloodshed now.—
So much is due to truth, even tow'rds our foe.

　　　　　　　　　　　　　　　　[*to* LAIAS.

Do I, then, give to usurpation grace,
And from his natural rights my son debar?   1510
Not so : let him—and none shall be more prompt
Than I to help—raise his Messenian friends ;
Let him fetch succours from Arcadia, gain
His Argive or his Spartan cousins' aid ;
Let him do this, do aught but recommence
Murder's uncertain, secret, perilous game—
And I, when to his righteous standard down
Flies Victory wing'd, and Justice raises *then*
Her sword, will be the first to bid it fall.
If, haply, at this moment, such attempt   1520
Promise not fair, let him a little while
Have faith, and trust the future and the Gods.
He may—for never did the Gods allow
Fast permanence to an ill-gotten throne.—
These are but woman's words ;—yet, Laias, thou
Despise them not ! for, brother, thou, like me,
Wert not among the feuds of warrior-chiefs,
Each sovereign for his dear-bought hour, born ;
But in the pastoral Arcadia rear'd,
With Cypselus our father, where we saw   1530
The simple patriarchal state of kings,
Where sire to son transmits the unquestion'd crown,
Unhack'd, unsmirch'd, unbloodied, and hast learnt
That spotless hands unshaken sceptres hold.
Having learnt this, then, use thy knowledge now.

The Chorus

Which way to lean I know not : bloody strokes
Are never free from doubt, though sometimes due.

Laias

O Merope, the common heart of man
Agrees to deem some deeds so horrible,
That neither gratitude, nor tie of race,   1540
Womanly pity, nor maternal fear,
Nor any pleader else, shall be indulg'd
To breathe a syllable to bar revenge.
All this, no doubt, thou to thyself hast urg'd—
Time presses, so that theme forbear I now :
Direct to thy dissuasions I reply.

Blood-founded thrones, thou say'st, are insecure ;
Our father's kingdom, because pure, is safe.
True ; but what cause to our Arcadia gives
Its privileg'd immunity from blood,   1550
But that, since first the black and fruitful Earth
In the primeval mountain-forests bore
Pelasgus, our forefather and mankind's,
Legitimately sire to son, with us,
Bequeaths the allegiance of our shepherd-tribes,
More loyal, as our line continues more ?—
How can your Heracleidan chiefs inspire
This awe which guards our earth-sprung, lineal kings ?
What permanence, what stability like ours,
Whether blood flows or no, can yet invest   1560
The broken order of your Dorian thrones,
Fix'd yesterday, and ten times chang'd since then ?—
Two brothers, and their orphan nephews, strove
For the three conquer'd kingdoms of this isle :
The eldest, mightiest brother, Temenus, took
Argos : a juggle to Cresphontes gave
Messenia : to those helpless Boys, the lot
Worst of the three, the stony Sparta, fell.
August, indeed, was the foundation here !
What followed ?—His most trusted kinsman slew
Cresphontes in Messenia ; Temenus   1571
Perish'd in Argos by his jealous sons ;
The Spartan Brothers with their guardian strive :—
Can houses thus ill-seated—thus embroil'd—
Thus little founded in their subjects' love,
Practise the indulgent, bloodless policy
Of dynasties long-fix'd, and honour'd long ?
No ! Vigour and severity must chain
Popular reverence to these recent lines ;
If their first-founded order be maintain'd—   1580
Their murder'd rulers terribly aveng'd—
Ruthlessly their rebellious subjects crush'd.—
Since policy bids thus, what fouler death
Than thine illustrious husband's to avenge
Shall we select ?—than Polyphontes, what
More daring and more grand offender find ?
Justice, my sister, long demands this blow,
And Wisdom, now thou see'st, demands it too :

To strike it, then, dissuade thy son no more ;
For to live disobedient to these two,   1590
Justice and Wisdom, is no life at all.

The Chorus

The Gods, O mistress dear ! the hard-soul'd man,
Who spar'd not others, bid not us to spare.

Merope

Alas ! against my brother, son, and friends,
One, and a woman, how can I prevail ?—
O brother ! thou hast conquer'd ; yet, I fear. . . .
Son ! with a doubting heart thy mother yields . . .
May it turn happier than my doubts portend !

Laias

Meantime on thee the task of silence only
Shall be impos'd ; to us shall be the deed.   1600
Now, not another word, but to our act !
Nephew ! thy friends are sounded, and prove true :
Thy father's murderer, in the public place,
Performs, this noon, a solemn sacrifice :
Go with him—choose the moment—strike thy blow !
If prudence counsels thee to go unarm'd,
The sacrificer's axe will serve thy turn.
To me and the Messenians leave the rest,
With the Gods' aid—and, if they give but aid
As our just cause deserves, I do not fear.   1610

[Aepytus, Laias, *and* Arcas *go out.*

The Chorus

O Son and Mother,   *str.* 1.
Whom the Gods o'ershadow,
In dangerous trial,
With certainty of favour !
As erst they shadow'd
Your race's founders
From irretrievable woe :
When the seed of Lycaon
Lay forlorn, lay outcast,
Callisto and her Boy.   1620

What deep-grass'd meadow   *ant.* 1.
At the meeting valleys—

Where clear-flowing Ladon,
Most beautiful of waters,
Receives the river
Whose trout are vocal,
The Aroanian stream—
Without home, without mother,
Hid the babe, hid Arcas,
The nursling of the dells? 1630

But the sweet-smelling myrtle, *str.* 2.
And the pink-flower'd oleander,
And the green agnus-castus,
To the West-Wind's murmur,
Rustled round his cradle ;
And Maia rear'd him.
Then, a boy, he startled
In the snow-fill'd hollows
Of high Cyllene
The white mountain-birds ; 1640
Or surpris'd, in the glens,
The basking tortoises,
Whose strip'd shell founded
In the hand of Hermes
The glory of the lyre.

But his mother, Callisto, *ant.* 2.
In her hiding-place of the thickets
Of the lentisk and ilex,
In her rough form, fearing
The hunter on the outlook, 1650
Poor changeling ! trembled.
Or the children, plucking
In the thorn-chok'd gullies
Wild gooseberries, scar'd her,
The shy mountain-bear.
Or the shepherds, on slopes
With pale-spik'd lavender
And crisp thyme tufted,
Came upon her, stealing
At day-break through the dew. 1660

Once, 'mid the gorges, *str.* 3.
Spray-drizzled, lonely,
Unclimb'd by man—

O'er whose cliffs the townsmen
Of crag-perch'd Nonacris
Behold in summer
The slender torrent
Of Styx come dancing,
A wind-blown thread—
By the precipices of Khelmos,　　　　　1670
The fleet, desperate hunter,
The youthful Arcas, born of Zeus,
His fleeing mother,
Transform'd Callisto,
Unwitting follow'd—
And rais'd his spear.

Turning, with piteous　　　　　　*unt. 3.*
Distressful longing,
Sad, eager eyes,
Mutely she regarded　　　　　　　1680
Her well-known enemy.
Low moans half utter'd
What speech refus'd her ;
Tears cours'd, tears human,
Down those disfigur'd
Once human cheeks.
With unutterable foreboding
Her son, heart-stricken, ey'd her.
The Gods had pity, made them Stars.
Stars now they sparkle　　　　　　1690
In the northern Heaven ;
The guard Arcturus,
The guard-watch'd Bear.

So, o'er thee and thy child,　　　　*epode.*
Some God, Merope, now,
In dangerous hour, stretches his hand.
So, like a star, dawns thy son,
Radiant with fortune and joy.

　　　　　　　[POLYPHONTES *comes in.*

POLYPHONTES

O Merope, the trouble on thy face
Tells me enough thou know'st the news which all
Messenia speaks: the prince, thy son, is dead.　　　1701

Not from my lips should consolation fall:
To offer that, I came not; but to urge,
Even after news of this sad death, our league.
Yes, once again I come; I will not take
This morning's angry answer for thy last:
To the Messenian kingdom thou and I
Are the sole claimants left; what cause of strife
Lay in thy son is buried in his grave.
Most honourably I meant, I call the Gods   1710
To witness, offering him return and power:
Yet, had he liv'd, suspicion, jealousy,
Inevitably had surg'd up, perhaps,
'Twixt thee and me; suspicion, that I nurs'd
Some ill design against him; jealousy,
That he enjoy'd but part, being heir to all.
And he himself, with the impetuous heart
Of youth, 'tis like, had never quite forgone
The thought of vengeance on me, never quite
Unclos'd his itching fingers from his sword.   1720
But thou, O Merope, though deeply wrong'd,
Though injur'd past forgiveness, as men deem,
Yet hast been long at school with thoughtful Time,
And from that teacher may'st have learn'd, like me,
That all may be endur'd, and all forgiv'n;
Have learn'd that we must sacrifice the thirst
Of personal vengeance to the public weal;
Have learn'd, that there are guilty deeds, which leave
The hand that does them guiltless; in a word,
That kings live for their peoples, not themselves.
This having learn'd, let us a union found   1731
(For the last time I ask, ask earnestly)
Bas'd on pure public welfare; let us be—
Not Merope and Polyphontes, foes
Blood-sever'd—but Messenia's King and Queen:
Let us forget ourselves for those we rule.
Speak: I go hence to offer sacrifice
To the Preserver Zeus; let me return
Thanks to him for our amity as well.

MEROPE

Oh had'st thou, Polyphontes, still but kept   1740
The silence thou hast kept for twenty years!

Polyphontes

Henceforth, if what I urge displease, I may:
But fair proposal merits fair reply.

Merope

And thou shalt have it ! Yes, because thou *hast*
For twenty years forborne to interrupt
The solitude of her whom thou hast wrong'd—
That scanty grace shall earn thee this reply.—
First, for our union. Trust me, 'twixt us two
The brazen-footed Fury ever stalks,
Waving her hundred hands, a torch in each,   1750
Aglow with angry fire, to keep us twain.
Now, for thyself. Thou com'st with well-cloak'd joy,
To announce the ruin of my husband's house,
To sound thy triumph in his widow's ears,
To bid her share thine unendanger'd throne:—
To this thou would'st have answer.—Take it: Fly !
Cut short thy triumph, seeming at its height ;
Fling off thy crown, suppos'd at last secure ;
Forsake this ample, proud Messenian realm :
To some small, humble, and unnoted strand,   1760
Some rock more lonely than that Lemnian isle
Where Philoctetes pin'd, take ship and flee :
Some solitude more inaccessible
Than the ice-bastion'd Caucasean Mount,
Chosen a prison for Prometheus, climb :
There in unvoic'd oblivion hide thy name,
And bid the sun, thine only visitant,
Divulge not to the far-off world of men
What once-fam'd wretch he hath seen lurking there.
There nurse a late remorse, and thank the Gods,   1770
And thank thy bitterest foe, that, having lost
All things but life, thou lose not life as well.

Polyphontes

What mad bewilderment of grief is this ?

Merope

Thou art bewilder'd : the sane head is mine.

Polyphontes

I pity thee, and wish thee calmer mind.

MEROPE
Pity thyself; none needs compassion more.

POLYPHONTES
Yet, oh! could'st thou but act as reason bids!

MEROPE
And in my turn I wish the same for thee.

POLYPHONTES
All I could do to soothe thee has been tried.

MEROPE
For that, in this my warning, thou art paid.   1780

POLYPHONTES
Know'st thou then aught, that thus thou sound'st the
    alarm?

MEROPE
Thy crime: that were enough to make one fear.

POLYPHONTES
My deed is of old date, and long aton'd.

MEROPE
Aton'd this very day, perhaps, it is.

POLYPHONTES
My final victory proves the Gods appeas'd.

MEROPE
O victor, victor, trip not at the goal!

POLYPHONTES
Hatred and passionate Envy blind thine eyes.

MEROPE
O Heaven-abandon'd wretch, that envies thee!

POLYPHONTES
Thou hold'st so cheap, then, the Messenian crown?

MEROPE

I think on what the future hath in store. 1790

POLYPHONTES

To-day I reign: the rest I leave to Fate.

MEROPE

For Fate thou wait'st not long; since, in this hour——

POLYPHONTES

What? for so far she hath not prov'd my foe—

MEROPE

Fate seals my lips, and drags to ruin thee.

POLYPHONTES

Enough! enough! I will no longer hear
The ill-boding note which frantic Envy sounds
To affright a fortune which the Gods secure.
Once more my friendship thou rejectest: well!
More for this land's sake grieve I, than mine own.
I chafe not with thee, that thy hate endures, 1800
Nor bend myself too low, to make it yield.
What I have done is done; by my own deed,
Neither exulting nor asham'd, I stand.
Why should this heart of mine set mighty store
By the construction and report of men?
Not men's good-word hath made me what I am.
Alone I master'd power; and alone,
Since so thou wilt, I will maintain it still.

[POLYPHONTES *goes out.*

THE CHORUS

Did I then waver *str.* 1.
(O woman's judgement!) 1810
Misled by seeming
Success of crime?
And ask, if sometimes
The Gods, perhaps, allow'd you,
O lawless daring of the strong,
O self-will recklessly indulg'd?

Not time, not lightning, *ant.* 1.
Not rain, not thunder,
Efface the endless
Decrees of Heaven— 1820
Make Justice alter,
Revoke, assuage her sentence,
Which dooms dread ends to dreadful deeds,
And violent deaths to violent men.

But the signal example *str.* 2.
Of invariableness of justice
Our glorious founder
Hercules gave us,
Son lov'd of Zeus his father: for he err'd,

And the strand of Euboea, *ant.* 2. 1830
And the promontory of Cenaeum,
His painful, solemn
Punishment witness'd,
Beheld his expiation: for he died.

O villages of Oeta *str.* 3.
With hedges of the wild rose!
O pastures of the mountain,
Of short grass, beaded with dew,
Between the pine-woods and the cliffs!
O cliffs, left by the eagles, 1840
On that morn, when the smoke-cloud
From the oak-built, fiercely-burning pyre,
Up the precipices of Trachis,
Drove them screaming from their eyries!
A willing, a willing sacrifice on that day
Ye witness'd, ye mountain lawns,
When the shirt-wrapt, poison-blister'd Hero
Ascended, with undaunted heart,
Living, his own funeral-pile,
And stood, shouting for a fiery torch; 1850
And the kind, chance-arriv'd Wanderer,
The inheritor of the bow,
Coming swiftly through the sad Trachinians,
Put the torch to the pile:
That the flame tower'd on high to the Heaven
Bearing with it, to Olympus,

To the side of Hebe,
To immortal delight,
The labour-releas'd Hero.

O heritage of Neleus,   *ant.* 3.   1860
Ill-kept by his infirm heirs !
O kingdom of Messenê,
Of rich soil, chosen by craft,
Possess'd in hatred, lost in blood !
O town, high Stenyclaros,
With new walls, which the victors
From the four-town'd, mountain-shadow'd Doris,
For their Hercules-issu'd princes
Built in strength against the vanquish'd !
Another, another sacrifice on this day   1870
Ye witness, ye new-built towers !
When the white-rob'd, garland-crowned Monarch
Approaches, with undoubting heart,
Living, his own sacrifice-block,
And stands, shouting for a slaughterous axe ;
And the stern, Destiny-brought Stranger,
The inheritor of the realm,
Coming swiftly through the jocund Dorians,
Drives the axe to its goal :
That the blood rushes in streams to the dust ;   1880
Bearing with it, to Erinnys,
To the Gods of Hades,
To the dead unaveng'd,
The fiercely-requir'd Victim.

Knowing he did it, unknowing pays for it.   [*epode.*
Unknowing, unknowing,
Thinking aton'd-for
Deeds unatonable,
Thinking appeas'd
Gods unappeasable,   1890
Lo, the Ill-fated One,
Standing for harbour,
Right at the harbour-mouth,
Strikes, with all sail set,
Full on the sharp-pointed
Needle of ruin !

                       [*A* MESSENGER *comes in.*

Messenger

O honour'd Queen, O faithful followers
Of your dead master's line, I bring you news
To make the gates of this long-mournful house
Leap, and fly open of themselves for joy !   1900
[noise and shouting heard.
Hark how the shouting crowds tramp hitherward
With glad acclaim !   Ere they forestall my news,
Accept it :—Polyphontes is no more.

Merope

Is my son safe ? that question bounds my care.

Messenger

He is, and by the people hail'd for king.

Merope

The rest to me is little : yet, since that
Must from some mouth be heard, relate it thou.

Messenger

Not little, if thou saw'st what love, what zeal,
At thy dead husband's name the people show.
For when this morning in the public square   1910
I took my stand, and saw the unarm'd crowds
Of citizens in holiday attire,
Women and children intermix'd ; and then,
Group'd around Zeus's altar, all in arms,
Serried and grim, the ring of Dorian lords—
I trembled for our prince and his attempt.
Silence and expectation held us all :
Till presently the King came forth, in robe
Of sacrifice, his guards clearing the way
Before him—at his side, the prince, thy son,   1920
Unarm'd and travel-soil'd, just as he was :
With him conferring the King slowly reach'd
The altar in the middle of the square,
Where, by the sacrificing minister,
The flower-dress'd victim stood, a milk-white bull,
Swaying from side to side his massy head
With short impatient lowings : there he stopp'd,
And seem'd to muse awhile, then rais'd his eyes

To Heaven, and laid his hand upon the steer,
And cried—*O Zeus, let what blood-guiltiness*   1930
Yet stains our land be by this blood wash'd out,
And grant henceforth to the Messenians peace!
That moment, while with upturn'd eyes he pray'd,
The prince snatch'd from the sacrificer's hand
The axe, and on the forehead of the King,
Where twines the chaplet, dealt a mighty blow
Which fell'd him to the earth, and o'er him stood,
And shouted—*Since by thee defilement came,*
What blood so meet as thine to wash it out?
What hand to strike thee meet as mine, the hand   1940
Of Aepytus, thy murder'd master's son?—
But, gazing at him from the ground, the King . . .
Is it, then, thou? he murmur'd; and with that,
He bow'd his head, and deeply groan'd, and died.
Till then we all seem'd stone: but then a cry
Broke from the Dorian lords: forward they rush'd
To circle the prince round: when suddenly
Laias in arms sprang to his nephew's side,
Crying—*O ye Messenians, will ye leave*
The son to perish as ye left the sire?   1950
And from that moment I saw nothing clear:
For from all sides a deluge, as it seem'd,
Burst o'er the altar and the Dorian lords,
Of holiday-clad citizens transform'd
To armèd warriors: I heard vengeful cries;
I heard the clash of weapons; then I saw
The Dorians lying dead, thy son hail'd king.
And, truly, one who sees, what seem'd so strong,
The power of this tyrant and his lords,
Melt like a passing smoke, a nightly dream,   1960
At one bold word, one enterprising blow—
Might ask, why we endur'd their yoke so long:
But that we know how every perilous feat
Of daring, easy as it seems when done,
Is easy at no moment but the right.

The Chorus

Thou speakest well; but here, to give our eyes
Authentic proof of what thou tell'st our ears,
The conquerors, with the King's dead body, come.

*[*Aepytus, Laias, *and* Arcas *come in with the dead body of* Polyphontes, *followed by a crowd of the* Messenians.*]*

Laias

Sister, from this day forth thou art no more
The widow of a husband unaveng'd,   1970
The anxious mother of an exil'd son.
Thine enemy is slain, thy son is king!
Rejoice with us! and trust me, he who wish'd
Welfare to the Messenian state, and calm,
Could find no way to found them sure as this.

Aepytus

Mother, all these approve me: but if thou
Approve not too, I have but half my joy.

Merope

O Aepytus, my son, behold, behold
This iron man, my enemy and thine,
This politic sovereign, lying at our feet,   1980
With blood-bespatter'd robes, and chaplet shorn!
Inscrutable as ever, see, it keeps
Its sombre aspect of majestic care,
Of solitary thought, unshar'd resolve,
Even in death, that countenance austere.
So look'd he, when to Stenyclaros first,
A new-made wife, I from Arcadia came,
And found him at my husband's side, his friend,
His kinsman, his right hand in peace and war;
Unsparing in his service of his toil,   1990
His blood; to me, for I confess it, kind:
So look'd he in that dreadful day of death:
So, when he pleaded for our league but now.
What meantest thou, O Polyphontes, what
Desired'st thou, what truly spurr'd thee on?
Was policy of state, the ascendancy
Of the Heracleidan conquerors, as thou said'st,
Indeed thy lifelong passion and sole aim?
Or did'st thou but, as cautious schemers use,
Cloak thine ambition with these specious words?
I know not; just, in either case, the stroke   2001

Which laid thee low, for blood requires blood:
But yet, not knowing this, I triumph not
Over thy corpse, triumph not, neither mourn;
For I find worth in thee, and badness too.
What mood of spirit, therefore, shall we call
The true one of a man—what way of life
His fix'd condition and perpetual walk?
None, since a twofold colour reigns in all.
But thou, my son, study to make prevail   2010
One colour in thy life, the hue of truth:
That Justice, that sage Order, not alone
Natural Vengeance, may maintain thine act,
And make it stand indeed the will of Heaven.
Thy father's passion was this people's ease,
This people's anarchy, thy foe's pretence;
As the chiefs rule, indeed, the people are:
Unhappy people, where the chiefs themselves
Are, like the mob, vicious and ignorant!
So rule, that even thine enemies may fail   2020
To find in thee a fault whereon to found,
Of tyrannous harshness, or remissness weak:
So rule, that as thy father thou be lov'd;
So rule, that as thy foe thou be obey'd.
Take these, my son, over thine enemy's corpse
Thy mother's prayers: and this prayer last of all,
That even in thy victory thou show,
Mortal, the moderation of a man.

Aepytus

O mother, my best diligence shall be
In all by thy experience to be rul'd   2030
Where my own youth falls short.   But, Laias, now,
First work after such victory, let us go
To render to my true Messenians thanks,
To the Gods grateful sacrifice; and then,
Assume the ensigns of my father's power.

The Chorus

Son of Cresphontes, past what perils
Com'st thou, guided safe, to thy home!
What things daring! what enduring!
And all this by the will of the Gods.

POEMS FROM MAGAZINES, 1860–1866

MEN OF GENIUS

[First published in the *Cornhill Magazine*, July, 1860.]

SILENT, the Lord of the world
  Eyes from the heavenly height,
    Girt by his far-shining train,
Us, who with banners unfurl'd
  Fight life's many-chanc'd fight
    Madly below, in the plain.

Then saith the Lord to his own :—
  ' See ye the battle below ?
    Turmoil of death and of birth !
Too long let we them groan.   10
  Haste, arise ye, and go ;
    Carry my peace upon earth.'

Gladly they rise at his call ;
  Gladly they take his command ;
    Gladly descend to the plain.
Alas ! How few of them all—
  Those willing servants—shall stand
    In their Master's presence again !

Some in the tumult are lost :
  Baffled, bewilder'd, they stray.   20
    Some as prisoners draw breath.
Others—the bravest—are cross'd,
  On the height of their bold-follow'd way,
    By the swift-rushing missile of Death.

Hardly, hardly shall one
  Come, with countenance bright,
    O'er the cloud-wrapt, perilous plain :
His Master's errand well done,
  Safe through the smoke of the fight,
    Back to his Master again.   30

SAINT BRANDAN

[First published in *Fraser's Magazine*, July, 1860.   Reprinted
separately 1867, also in *New Poems*, 1867.]

SAINT BRANDAN sails the northern main ;
The brotherhoods of saints are glad.
He greets them once, he sails again.
So late !—such storms !—The Saint is mad !

He heard across the howling seas
Chime convent bells on wintry nights,
He saw on spray-swept Hebrides
Twinkle the monastery lights ;

But north, still north, Saint Brandan steer'd ;
And now no bells, no convents more !   10
The hurtling Polar lights are near'd,
The sea without a human shore.

At last—(it was the Christmas night,
Stars shone after a day of storm)—
He sees float past an iceberg white,
And on it—Christ !—a living form !

That furtive mien, that scowling eye,
Of hair that red and tufted fell——
It is—Oh, where shall Brandan fly ?—
The traitor Judas, out of hell !   20

Palsied with terror, Brandan sate ;
The moon was bright, the iceberg near.
He hears a voice sigh humbly : ' Wait !
By high permission I am here.

' One moment wait, thou holy man !
On earth my crime, my death, they knew ;
My name is under all men's ban ;
Ah, tell them of my respite too !

' Tell them, one blessed Christmas night—
(It was the first after I came,   30
Breathing self-murder, frenzy, spite,
To rue my guilt in endless flame)—

15 past] near *1860*.   18 red] black *1860*.

'I felt, as I in torment lay
'Mid the souls plagued by heavenly power,
An angel touch mine arm, and say :
Go hence, and cool thyself an hour !

' " Ah, whence this mercy, Lord ? " I said.
The Leper recollect, said he,
*Who ask'd the passers-by for aid,
In Joppa, and thy charity.*   40

' Then I remember'd how I went,
In Joppa, through the public street,
One morn, when the sirocco spent
Its storms of dust, with burning heat ;

' And in the street a Leper sate,
Shivering with fever, naked, old ;
Sand raked his sores from heel to pate,
The hot wind fever'd him five-fold.

' He gazed upon me as I pass'd,
And murmur'd : *Help me, or I die !*—   50
To the poor wretch my cloak I cast,
Saw him look eased, and hurried by.

' Oh, Brandan, think what grace divine,
What blessing must true goodness shower,
If semblance of it faint, like mine,
Hath such inestimable power !

' Well-fed, well-clothed, well-friended, I
Did that chance act of good, that one !
Then went my way to kill and lie—
Forgot my good as soon as done.   60

' That germ of kindness, in the womb
Of mercy caught, did not expire ;
Outlives my guilt, outlives my doom,
And friends me in the pit of fire.

' Once every year, when carols wake,
On earth, the Christmas night's repose,
Arising from the sinners' lake,
I journey to these healing snows.

55 If] When *1860*.   56 inestimable] inalienable *1860*.
60 good] deed *1860*.

'I stanch with ice my burning breast,
With silence balm my whirling brain.   70
O Brandan ! to this hour of rest,
That Joppan leper's ease was pain !'——

Tears started to Saint Brandan's eyes ;
He bow'd his head ; he breathed a prayer.
When he look'd up—tenantless lies
The iceberg in the frosty air !

A SOUTHERN NIGHT

[First published in *The Victoria Regia*, 1861.   Reprinted 1867.]

THE sandy spits, the shore-lock'd lakes,
    Melt into open, moonlit sea;
The soft Mediterranean breaks
        At my feet, free.

Dotting the fields of corn and vine
    Like ghosts, the huge, gnarl'd olives stand ;
Behind, that lovely mountain-line !
        While by the strand

Cette, with its glistening houses white,
    Curves with the curving beach away   10
To where the lighthouse beacons bright
        Far in the bay.

Ah, such a night, so soft, so lone,
    So moonlit, saw me once of yore
Wander unquiet, and my own
        Vext heart deplore !

But now that trouble is forgot ;
    Thy memory, thy pain, to-night,
My brother ! and thine early lot,
        Possess me quite.   20

The murmur of this Midland deep
    Is heard to-night around thy grave
There where Gibraltar's cannon'd steep
        O'erfrowns the wave.

For there, with bodily anguish keen,
  With Indian heats at last fordone,
With public toil and private teen,
    Thou sank'st, alone.

Slow to a stop, at morning grey,
  I see the smoke-crown'd vessel come ;   30
Slow round her paddles dies away
    The seething foam.

A boat is lower'd from her side ;
  Ah, gently place him on the bench !
That spirit—if all have not yet died—
    A breath might quench.

Is this the eye, the footstep fast,
  The mien of youth we used to see,
Poor, gallant boy !—for such thou wast,
    Still art, to me.   40

The limbs their wonted tasks refuse,
  The eyes are glazed, thou canst not speak ;
And whiter than thy white burnous
    That wasted cheek !

Enough ! The boat, with quiet shock,
  Unto its haven coming nigh,
Touches, and on Gibraltar's rock
    Lands thee, to die.

Ah me ! Gibraltar's strand is far,
  But farther yet across the brine   50
Thy dear wife's ashes buried are,
    Remote from thine.

For there where Morning's sacred fount
  Its golden rain on earth confers,
The snowy Himalayan Mount
    O'ershadows hers.

Strange irony of Fate, alas,
  Which for two jaded English saves,
When from their dusty life they pass,
    Such peaceful graves !   60

26 heats] suns *1861*.   37 footstep fast] form alert *1861*.
39 wast] wert *1861*.

In cities should we English lie,
  Where cries are rising ever new,
And men's incessant stream goes by ;
    We who pursue

Our business with unslackening stride,
  Traverse in troops, with care-fill'd breast,
The soft Mediterranean side,
    The Nile, the East,

And see all sights from pole to pole,
  And glance, and nod, and bustle by ;   70
And never once possess our soul
    Before we die.

Not by those hoary Indian hills,
  Not by this gracious Midland sea
Whose floor to-night sweet moonshine fills,
    Should our graves be !

Some sage, to whom the world was dead,
  And men were specks, and life a play ;
Who made the roots of trees his bed,
    And once a day   80

With staff and gourd his way did bend
  To villages and homes of man,
For food to keep him till he end
    His mortal span,

And the pure goal of Being reach ;
  Grey-headed, wrinkled, clad in white,
Without companion, without speech,
    By day and night

Pondering God's mysteries untold,
  And tranquil as the glacier snows—   90
He by those Indian mountains old
    Might well repose !

Some grey crusading knight austere
  Who bore Saint Louis company
And came home hurt to death and here
    Landed to die ;

Some youthful troubadour whose tongue
 Fill'd Europe once with his love-pain,
Who here outwearied sunk, and sung
  His dying strain ;   100

Some girl who here from castle-bower,
 With furtive step and cheek of flame,
'Twixt myrtle-hedges all in flower
  By moonlight came

To meet her pirate-lover's ship,
 And from the wave-kiss'd marble stair
Beckon'd him on, with quivering lip
  And unbound hair,

And lived some moons in happy trance,
 Then learnt his death, and pined away— 110
Such by these waters of romance
  'Twas meet to lay !

But you—a grave for knight or sage,
 Romantic, solitary, still,
O spent ones of a work-day age !
  Befits you ill.

So sang I ; but the midnight breeze
 Down to the brimm'd moon-charmèd main
Comes softly through the olive-trees,
  And checks my strain.   120

I think of her, whose gentle tongue
 All plaint in her own cause controll'd ;
Of thee I think, my brother ! young
  In heart, high-soul'd ;

That comely face, that cluster'd brow,
 That cordial hand, that bearing free,
I see them still, I see them now,
  Shall always see !

And what but gentleness untired,
 And what but noble feeling warm, 130
Wherever shown, howe'er attired,
  Is grace, is charm ?

100 His] A *1861*. 101 castle-bower] palace-bower *1861*.
108 unbound] floating *1861*. 113 knight] Girl *1861*.

What else is all these waters are,
  What else is steep'd in lucid sheen,
What else is bright, what else is fair,
  What else serene?

Mild o'er her grave, ye mountains, shine!
  Gently by his, ye waters, glide!
To that in you which is divine
  They were allied.   140

THYRSIS

A MONODY, *to commemorate the author's friend*, ARTHUR
  HUGH CLOUGH, *who died at Florence*, 1861

[First published in *Macmillan's Magazine*, April, 1866.
Reprinted 1867.]

> Thus yesterday, to-day, to-morrow come,
> They hustle one another and they pass;
> But all our hustling morrows only make
> The smooth to-day of God.
>   *From* LUCRETIUS, *an unpublished Tragedy.*

How changed is here each spot man makes or fills!
  In the two Hinkseys nothing keeps the same;
    The village-street its haunted mansion lacks,
And from the sign is gone Sibylla's name,
    And from the roofs the twisted chimney-stacks;
      Are ye too changed, ye hills?
See, 'tis no foot of unfamiliar men
  To-night from Oxford up your pathway strays
Here came I often, often, in old days;
Thyrsis and I; we still had Thyrsis then.

Runs it not here, the track by Childsworth Farm,
  Up past the wood, to where the elm-tree crowns
    The hill behind whose ridge the sunset flames?
The signal-elm, that looks on Ilsley Downs,
    The Vale, the three lone weirs, the youthful
        Thames?—
      This winter-eve is warm,

135 bright] good *1861.*
Thyrsis] *Motto first inserted in 1867.*

Humid the air; leafless, yet soft as spring,
　　The tender purple spray on copse and briers;
　　And that sweet City with her dreaming spires,
She needs not June for beauty's heightening,　　20

Lovely all times she lies, lovely to-night!
　Only, methinks, some loss of habit's power
　　Befalls me wandering through this upland dim;
　Once pass'd I blindfold here, at any hour,
　　　Now seldom come I, since I came with him.
　　　That single elm-tree bright
　Against the west—I miss it! is it gone?
　　We prized it dearly; while it stood, we said,
　　Our friend, the Scholar-Gipsy, was not dead;
While the tree lived, he in these fields lived on.　30

Too rare, too rare, grow now my visits here!
　But once I knew each field, each flower, each stick;
　　And with the country-folk acquaintance made
　By barn in threshing-time, by new-built rick.
　　　Here, too, our shepherd-pipes we first assay'd.
　　　Ah me! this many a year
　My pipe is lost, my shepherd's-holiday!
　　Needs must I lose them, needs with heavy heart
　　Into the world and wave of men depart;
But Thyrsis of his own will went away.　　40

It irk'd him to be here, he could not rest.
　He loved each simple joy the country yields,
　　He loved his mates; but yet he could not keep,
　For that a shadow lower'd on the fields,
　　　Here with the shepherds and the silly sheep.
　　　Some life of men unblest
　He knew, which made him droop, and fill'd his head.
　　He went; his piping took a troubled sound
　　Of storms that rage outside our happy ground;
He could not wait their passing, he is dead!　　50

So, some tempestuous morn in early June,
　When the year's primal burst of bloom is o'er,
　　Before the roses and the longest day—
　When garden-walks, and all the grassy floor,
　　　With blossoms, red and white, of fallen May,
　　　And chestnut-flowers are strewn—

So have I heard the cuckoo's parting cry,
  From the wet field, through the vext garden-trees,
    Come with the volleying rain and tossing breeze:
The bloom is gone, and with the bloom go I.   60

Too quick despairer, wherefore wilt thou go?
  Soon will the high Midsummer pomps come on,
    Soon will the musk carnations break and swell,
  Soon shall we have gold-dusted snapdragon,
    Sweet-William with its homely cottage-smell.
      And stocks in fragrant blow;
  Roses that down the alleys shine afar,
    And open, jasmine-muffled lattices,
    And groups under the dreaming garden-trees,
And the full moon, and the white evening-star.   70

He hearkens not! light comer, he is flown!
  What matters it? next year he will return,
    And we shall have him in the sweet spring-days,
  With whitening hedges, and uncrumpling fern,
    And blue-bells trembling by the forest-ways,
      And scent of hay new-mown.
  But Thyrsis never more we swains shall see!
    See him come back, and cut a smoother reed,
    And blow a strain the world at last shall heed—
For Time, not Corydon, hath conquer'd thee.   80

Alack, for Corydon no rival now!—
  But when Sicilian shepherds lost a mate,
    Some good survivor with his flute would go,
  Piping a ditty sad for Bion's fate,
    And cross the unpermitted ferry's flow,
      And relax Pluto's brow,
  And make leap up with joy the beauteous head
    Of Proserpine, among whose crownèd hair
    Are flowers, first open'd on Sicilian air,
And flute his friend, like Orpheus, from the dead.

O easy access to the hearer's grace   91
  When Dorian shepherds sang to Proserpine!
    For she herself had trod Sicilian fields,
  She knew the Dorian water's gush divine,

71 flown] gone *1866*.   86 relax] unbend *1866*.

She knew each lily white which Enna yields,
 Each rose with blushing face ;
She loved the Dorian pipe, the Dorian strain.
 But ah, of our poor Thames she never heard !
 Her foot the Cumner cowslips never stirr'd ! 99
And we should tease her with our plaint in vain.

Well ! wind-dispers'd and vain the words will be,
 Yet, Thyrsis, let me give my grief its hour
  In the old haunt, and find our tree-topp'd hill !
 Who, if not I, for questing here hath power ?
  I know the wood which hides the daffodil,
   I know the Fyfield tree,
 I know what white, what purple fritillaries
  The grassy harvest of the river-fields, 108
  Above by Ensham, down by Sandford, yields,
And what sedg'd brooks are Thames's tributaries ;

I know these slopes ; who knows them if not I ?—
 But many a dingle on the loved hill-side,
  With thorns once studded, old, white-blossom'd
   trees,
 Where thick the cowslips grew, and, far descried,
  High tower'd the spikes of purple orchises,
   Hath since our day put by
 The coronals of that forgotten time.
  Down each green bank hath gone the ploughboy's
   team,
  And only in the hidden brookside gleam
Primroses, orphans of the flowery prime. 120

Where is the girl, who, by the boatman's door,
 Above the locks, above the boating throng,
  Unmoor'd our skiff, when, through the Wytham
   flats,
 Red loosestrife and blond meadow-sweet among,
  And darting swallows, and light water-gnats,
   We track'd the shy Thames shore ?
 Where are the mowers, who, as the tiny swell
  Of our boat passing heav'd the river-grass,
  Stood with suspended scythe to see us pass ?—
They all are gone, and thou art gone as well. 130

Yes, thou art gone! and round me too the night
  In ever-nearing circle weaves her shade.
    I see her veil draw soft across the day,
  I feel her slowly chilling breath invade
    The cheek grown thin, the brown hair sprent with
        grey;
       I feel her finger light
Laid pausefully upon life's headlong train;
  The foot less prompt to meet the morning dew,
  The heart less bounding at emotion new,   139
And hope, once crush'd, less quick to spring again.

And long the way appears, which seem'd so short
  To the unpractis'd eye of sanguine youth;
    And high the mountain-tops, in cloudy air,
The mountain-tops where is the throne of Truth,
    Tops in life's morning-sun so bright and bare!
      Unbreachable the fort
Of the long-batter'd world uplifts its wall.
  And strange and vain the earthly turmoil grows,
  And near and real the charm of thy repose,
And night as welcome as a friend would fall.   150

But hush! the upland hath a sudden loss
  Of quiet;—Look! adown the dusk hill-side,
    A troop of Oxford hunters going home,
  As in old days, jovial and talking, ride!
    From hunting with the Berkshire hounds they
      come—
      Quick, let me fly, and cross
Into yon further field!—'Tis done; and see,
  Back'd by the sunset, which doth glorify
  The orange and pale violet evening-sky,
Bare on its lonely ridge, the Tree! the Tree!   160

I take the omen!   Eve lets down her veil,
  The white fog creeps from bush to bush about,
    The west unflushes, the high stars grow bright,
  And in the scatter'd farms the lights come out.
    I cannot reach the Signal-Tree to-night,
      Yet, happy omen, hail!

Hear it from thy broad lucent Arno vale
(For there thine earth-forgetting eyelids keep
The morningless and unawakening sleep
Under the flowery oleanders pale),   170

Hear it, O Thyrsis, still our Tree is there !—
Ah, vain ! These English fields, this upland dim,
These brambles pale with mist engarlanded,
That lone, sky-pointing tree, are not for him.
To a boon southern country he is fled,
And now in happier air,
Wandering with the great Mother's train divine
(And purer or more subtle soul than thee,
I trow, the mighty Mother doth not see !)
Within a folding of the Apennine,   180

Thou hearest the immortal strains of old.
Putting his sickle to the perilous grain
In the hot cornfield of the Phrygian king,
For thee the Lityerses song again
Young Daphnis with his silver voice doth sing ;
Sings his Sicilian fold,
His sheep, his hapless love, his blinded eyes ;
And how a call celestial round him rang
And heavenward from the fountain-brink he sprang,
And all the marvel of the golden skies.   190

There thou art gone, and me thou leavest here
Sole in these fields ; yet will I not despair ;
Despair I will not, while I yet descry
'Neath the soft canopy of English air
That lonely Tree against the western sky.
Still, still these slopes, 'tis clear,
Our Gipsy-Scholar haunts, outliving thee !
Fields where soft sheep from cages pull the hay,
Woods with anemonies in flower till May,
Know him a wanderer still ; then why not me ?

A fugitive and gracious light he seeks,   201
Shy to illumine ; and I seek it too.
This does not come with houses or with gold,
With place, with honour, and a flattering crew ;

198 soft] the *1866*.

'Tis not in the world's market bought and sold.
　　But the smooth-slipping weeks
Drop by, and leave its seeker still untired ;
　　Out of the heed of mortals he is gone,
　　He wends unfollow'd, he must house alone ;
Yet on he fares, by his own heart inspired.　　210

Thou too, O Thyrsis, on like quest wert bound,
　　Thou wanderedst with me for a little hour ;
　　Men gave thee nothing, but this happy quest,
If men esteem'd thee feeble, gave thee power,
　　If men procured thee trouble, gave thee rest.
　　And this rude Cumner ground,
Its fir-topped Hurst, its farms, its quiet fields,
　　Here cam'st thou in thy jocund youthful time,
　　Here was thine height of strength, thy golden prime ;
And still the haunt beloved a virtue yields.　　220

What though the music of thy rustic flute
　　Kept not for long its happy, country tone,
　　Lost it too soon, and learnt a stormy note
Of men contention-tost, of men who groan,
　　　Which task'd thy pipe too sore, and tired thy
　　　　　throat—
　　　It fail'd, and thou wast mute ;
Yet hadst thou alway visions of our light,
　　And long with men of care thou couldst not stay,
　　And soon thy foot resumed its wandering way,
Left human haunt, and on alone till night.　　230

Too rare, too rare, grow now my visits here !
　　'Mid city-noise, not, as with thee of yore,
　　Thyrsis, in reach of sheep-bells is my home !
Then through the great town's harsh, heart-wearying
　　　　　roar,
　　　Let in thy voice a whisper often come,
　　　To chase fatigue and fear :
Why faintest thou ?　I wander'd till I died.
　　Roam on ! the light we sought is shining still.
　　Dost thou ask proof ?　Our Tree yet crowns the hill,
Our Scholar travels yet the loved hillside.　　240

　　　208 he is] is he 1866.　　226 wast] wert 1866.

NEW POEMS

1867

Though the Muse be gone away,
Though she move not earth to-day,
Souls, erewhile who caught her word,
Ah! still harp on what they heard.

A PICTURE AT NEWSTEAD

[First published 1867.]

WHAT made my heart, at Newstead, fullest swell?—
'Twas not the thought of Byron, of his cry
Stormily sweet, his Titan agony;
It was the sight of that Lord Arundel

Who struck, in heat, the child he loved so well,
And the child's reason flickered, and did die.
Painted (he will'd it) in the gallery
They hang; the picture doth the story tell.

Behold the stern, mail'd father, staff in hand!
The little fair-hair'd son, with vacant gaze,   10
Where no more lights of sense or knowledge are!

Methinks the woe which made that father stand
Baring his dumb remorse to future days,
Was woe than Byron's woe more tragic far.

RACHEL

[First published 1867.]

I

In Paris all look'd hot and like to fade.
Brown in the garden of the Tuileries,
Brown with September, droop'd the chestnut-trees.
'Twas dawn ; a brougham roll'd through the streets,
  and made

Halt at the white and silent colonnade
Of the French Theatre.   Worn with disease,
Rachel, with eyes no gazing can appease,
Sate in the brougham, and those blank walls survey'd.

She follows the gay world, whose swarms have fled
To Switzerland, to Baden, to the Rhine ;   10
Why stops she by this empty play-house drear ?

Ah, where the spirit its highest life hath led,
All spots, match'd with that spot, are less divine ;
And Rachel's Switzerland, her Rhine, is here !

II

Unto a lonely villa in a dell
Above the fragrant warm Provençal shore
The dying Rachel in a chair they bore
Up the steep pine-plumed paths of the Estrelle,

And laid her in a stately room, where fell
The shadow of a marble Muse of yore—
The rose-crown'd queen of legendary lore,
Polymnia—full on her death-bed.   'Twas well !

The fret and misery of our northern towns,
In this her life's last day, our poor, our pain,   10
Our jangle of false wits, our climate's frowns,

Do for this radiant Greek-soul'd artist cease ;
Sole object of her dying eyes remain
The beauty and the glorious art of Greece.

III

Sprung from the blood of Israel's scatter'd race,
At a mean inn in German Aarau born,
To forms from antique Greece and Rome uptorn,
Trick'd out with a Parisian speech and face,

Imparting life renew'd, old classic grace ;
Then soothing with thy Christian strain forlorn,
A-Kempis ! her departing soul outworn,
While by her bedside Hebrew rites have place—

Ah, not the radiant spirit of Greece alone   9
She had—one power, which made her breast its home !
In her, like us, there clash'd, contending powers,

Germany, France, Christ, Moses, Athens, Rome.
The strife, the mixture in her soul, are ours ;
Her genius and her glory are her own.

EAST LONDON

[First published 1867.]

'Twas August, and the fierce sun overhead
Smote on the squalid streets of Bethnal Green,
And the pale weaver, through his windows seen
In Spitalfields, look'd thrice dispirited ;

I met a preacher there I knew, and said :
'Ill and o'erwork'd, how fare you in this scene ?'
'Bravely !' said he ; 'for I of late have been
Much cheer'd with thoughts of Christ, *the living bread.*'

O human soul ! as long as thou canst so
Set up a mark of everlasting light,   10
Above the howling senses' ebb and flow,

To cheer thee, and to right thee if thou roam,
Not with lost toil thou labourest through the night !
Thou mak'st the heaven thou hop'st indeed thy home.

WEST LONDON

[First published 1867.]

CROUCH'D on the pavement close by Belgrave Square
A tramp I saw, ill, moody, and tongue-tied ;
A babe was in her arms, and at her side
A girl ; their clothes were rags, their feet were bare.

Some labouring men, whose work lay somewhere there,
Pass'd opposite ; she touch'd her girl, who hied
Across, and begg'd, and came back satisfied.
The rich she had let pass with frozen stare.

Thought I : Above her state this spirit towers ;
She will not ask of aliens, but of friends,   10
Of sharers in a common human fate.

She turns from that cold succour, which attends
The unknown little from the unknowing great,
And points us to a better time than ours.

ANTI-DESPERATION

[First published 1867.]

LONG fed on boundless hopes, O race of man,
How angrily thou spurn'st all simpler fare !
Christ, some one says, was human as we are ;
No judge eyes us from heaven, our sin to scan ;

We live no more, when we have done our span.
' Well, then, for Christ,' thou answerest, ' who can
          care ?
' From sin, which heaven records not, why forbear ?
' Live we like brutes our life without a plan ! '

So answerest thou ; but why not rather say :
' Hath man no second life ?—Pitch this one high !   10
' Sits there no judge in heaven, our sin to see ?—

' More strictly, then, the inward judge obey !
' Was Christ a man like us ?—Ah ! let us try
' If we then, too, can be such men as he ! '

IMMORTALITY

[First published 1867.]

FOIL'D by our fellow men, depress'd, outworn,
We leave the brutal world to take its way,
And, *Patience! in another life,* we say,
The world shall be thrust down, and we up-borne!

And will not, then, the immortal armies scorn
The world's poor, routed leavings ; or will they,
Who fail'd under the heat of this life's day,
Support the fervours of the heavenly morn ?

No, no ! the energy of life may be
Kept on after the grave, but not begun ;   10
And he who flagg'd not in the earthly strife,

From strength to strength advancing—only he,
His soul well-knit, and all his battles won,
Mounts, and that hardly, to eternal life.

WORLDLY PLACE

[First published 1867.]

Even in a palace, life may be led well!
So spoke the imperial sage, purest of men,
Marcus Aurelius.—But the stifling den
Of common life, where, crowded up pell-mell.

Our freedom for a little bread we sell,
And drudge under some foolish master's ken,
Who rates us, if we peer outside our pen—
Match'd with a palace, is not this a hell?

Even in a palace!   On his truth sincere,
Who spoke these words, no shadow ever came ;   10
And when my ill-school'd spirit is aflame

Some nobler, ampler stage of life to win,
I'll stop, and say : 'There were no succour here !
'The aids to noble life are all within.'

THE DIVINITY

[First published 1867.]

'YES, write it in the rock!' Saint Bernard said,
'Grave it on brass with adamantine pen!
''Tis God himself becomes apparent, when
'God's wisdom and God's goodness are display'd,

'For God of these his attributes is made.'—
Well spake the impetuous Saint, and bore of men
The suffrage captive; now, not one in ten
Recalls the obscure opposer he outweigh'd.

God's wisdom and *God's goodness!*—Ay, but fools
Mis-define these till God knows them no more.   10
Wisdom and goodness, they are God!—what schools

Have yet so much as heard this simpler lore?
This no Saint preaches, and this no Church rules;
'Tis in the desert, now and heretofore.

THE GOOD SHEPHERD WITH THE KID

[First published 1867.]

HE saves the sheep, the goats he doth not save!
So rang Tertullian's sentence, on the side
Of that unpitying Phrygian sect which cried:
'Him can no fount of fresh forgiveness lave,

'Who sins, once wash'd by the baptismal wave!'
So spake the fierce Tertullian.   But she sigh'd,
The infant Church; of love she felt the tide
Stream on her from her Lord's yet recent grave.

And then she smiled, and in the Catacombs,
With eye suffused but heart inspired true,   10
On those walls subterranean, where she hid

Her head in ignominy, death, and tombs,
She her Good Shepherd's hasty image drew;
And on his shoulders, not a lamb, a kid.

AUSTERITY OF POETRY

[First published 1867.]

THAT son of Italy who tried to blow,
Ere Dante came, the trump of sacred song,
In his light youth amid a festal throng
Sate with his bride to see a public show.

Fair was the bride, and on her front did glow
Youth like a star ; and what to youth belong,
Gay raiment, sparkling gauds, elation strong.
A prop gave way ! crash fell a platform ! lo,

Mid struggling sufferers, hurt to death, she lay !
Shuddering they drew her garments off—and found
A robe of sackcloth next the smooth, white skin.   11

Such, poets, is your bride, the Muse ! young, gay,
Radiant, adorn'd outside ; a hidden ground
Of thought and of austerity within.

EAST AND WEST

[First published 1867.]

IN the bare midst of Anglesey they show
Two springs which close by one another play,
And, 'Thirteen hundred years agone,' they say,
'Two saints met often where those waters flow.

'One came from Penmon, westward, and a glow
'Whiten'd his face from the sun's fronting ray.
'Eastward the other, from the dying day ;
'And he with unsunn'd face did always go.'

Seiriol the Bright, Kybi the Dark, men said.
The Seër from the East was then in light,   10
The Seër from the West was then in shade.

Ah ! now 'tis changed.   In conquering sunshine bright
The man of the bold West now comes array'd ;
He of the mystic East is touch'd with night.

MONICA'S LAST PRAYER

[First published 1867.]

'OH could thy grave at home, at Carthage, be! '—
Care not for that, and lay me where I fall.
Everywhere heard will be the judgment-call.
But at God's altar, oh! remember me.

Thus Monica, and died in Italy.
Yet fervent had her longing been, through all
Her course, for home at last, and burial
With her own husband, by the Libyan sea.

Had been; but at the end, to her pure soul
All tie with all beside seem'd vain and cheap,　　10
And union before God the only care.

Creeds pass, rites change, no altar standeth whole;
Yet we her memory, as she pray'd, will keep,
Keep by this: *Life in God, and union there!*

CALAIS SANDS

[First published 1867.]

A THOUSAND knights have rein'd their steeds
To watch this line of sand-hills run,
Along the never silent Strait,
To Calais glittering in the sun:

To look toward Ardres' Golden Field
Across this wide aërial plain,
Which glows as if the Middle Age
Were gorgeous upon earth again.

Oh, that to share this famous scene
I saw, upon the open sand,　　10
Thy lovely presence at my side,
Thy shawl, thy look, thy smile, thy hand!

How exquisite thy voice would come,
My darling, on this lonely air !
How sweetly would the fresh sea-breeze
Shake loose some lock of soft brown hair !

But now my glance but once hath roved
O'er Calais and its famous plain ;
To England's cliffs my gaze is turn'd,
O'er the blue Strait mine eyes I strain.   20

Thou comest !   Yes, the vessel's cloud
Hangs dark upon the rolling sea !—
Oh that yon seabird's wings were mine
To win one instant's glimpse of thee !

I must not spring to grasp thy hand,
To woo thy smile, to seek thine eye ;
But I may stand far off, and gaze,
And watch thee pass unconscious by,

And spell thy looks, and guess thy thoughts,
Mixt with the idlers on the pier.—   30
Ah, might I always rest unseen,
So I might have thee always near !

To-morrow hurry through the fields
Of Flanders to the storied Rhine !
To-night those soft-fringed eyes shall close
Beneath one roof, my queen ! with mine.

DOVER BEACH

[First published 1867.]

THE sea is calm to-night,
The tide is full, the moon lies fair
Upon the Straits ;—on the French coast, the light
Gleams, and is gone ; the cliffs of England stand,
Glimmering and vast, out in the tranquil bay.
Come to the window, sweet is the night air !
Only, from the long line of spray
Where the ebb meets the moon-blanch'd sand,
Listen ! you hear the grating roar

ARNOLD   D d

Of pebbles which the waves suck back, and fling,　　10
At their return, up the high strand,
Begin, and cease, and then again begin,
With tremulous cadence slow, and bring
The eternal note of sadness in.

　Sophocles long ago
Heard it on the Aegaean, and it brought
Into his mind the turbid ebb and flow
Of human misery ; we
Find also in the sound a thought,
Hearing it by this distant northern sea.　　20

The sea of faith
Was once, too, at the full, and round earth's shore
Lay like the folds of a bright girdle furl'd ;
But now I only hear
Its melancholy, long, withdrawing roar,
Retreating to the breath
Of the night-wind down the vast edges drear
And naked shingles of the world.

Ah, love, let us be true
To one another ! for the world, which seems　　30
To lie before us like a land of dreams,
So various, so beautiful, so new,
Hath really neither joy, nor love, nor light,
Nor certitude, nor peace, nor help for pain ;
And we are here as on a darkling plain
Swept with confused alarms of struggle and flight,
Where ignorant armies clash by night.

THE TERRACE AT BERNE

[First published 1867.]

TEN years !—and to my waking eye
Once more the roofs of Berne appear ;
The rocky banks, the terrace high,
The stream—and do I linger here ?

The clouds are on the Oberland,
The Jungfrau snows look faint and far ;
But bright are those green fields at hand,
And through those fields comes down the Aar,

And from the blue twin lakes it comes,
Flows by the town, the church-yard fair,   10
And 'neath the garden-walk it hums,
The house—and is my Marguerite there?

Ah, shall I see thee, while a flush
Of startled pleasure floods thy brow,
Quick through the oleanders brush,
And clap thy hands, and cry: *'Tis thou!*

Or hast thou long since wander'd back,
Daughter of France! to France, thy home;
And flitted down the flowery track
Where feet like thine too lightly come?   20

Doth riotous laughter now replace
Thy smile, and rouge, with stony glare,
Thy cheek's soft hue, and fluttering lace
The kerchief that enwound thy hair?

Or is it over?—art thou dead?—
Dead?—and no warning shiver ran
Across my heart, to say thy thread
Of life was cut, and closed thy span!

Could from earth's ways that figure slight
Be lost, and I not feel 'twas so?   30
Of that fresh voice the gay delight
Fail from earth's air, and I not know?

Or shall I find thee still, but changed,
But not the Marguerite of thy prime?
With all thy being re-arranged,
Pass'd through the crucible of time;

With spirit vanish'd, beauty waned,
And hardly yet a glance, a tone,
A gesture—anything—retain'd
Of all that was my Marguerite's own?   40

I will not know!—for wherefore try
To things by mortal course that live
A shadowy durability
For which they were not meant, to give?

Like driftwood spars which meet and pass
Upon the boundless ocean-plain,
So on the sea of life, alas !
Man nears man, meets, and leaves again.

I knew it when my life was young,
I feel it still, now youth is o'er !   50
The mists are on the mountains hung,
And Marguerite I shall see no more.

STANZAS COMPOSED AT CARNAC

MAY 6, 1859

[First published 1867.]

FAR on its rocky knoll descried
Saint Michael's chapel cuts the sky.
I climb'd ;—beneath me, bright and wide,
Lay the lone coast of Brittany.

Bright in the sunset, weird and still,
It lay beside the Atlantic wave,
As if the wizard Merlin's will
Yet charm'd it from his forest grave.

Behind me on their grassy sweep,
Bearded with lichen, scrawl'd and grey,   10
The giant stones of Carnac sleep,
In the mild evening of the May.

No priestly stern procession now
Streams through their rows of pillars old ;
No victims bleed, no Druids bow ;
Sheep make the furze-grown aisles their fold.

From bush to bush the cuckoo flies,
The orchis red gleams everywhere ;
Gold broom with furze in blossom vies,
The blue-bells perfume all the air.   20

And o'er the glistening, lonely land,
Rise up, all round, the Christian spires.
The church of Carnac, by the strand,
Catches the westering sun's last fires.

And there across the watery way,
See, low above the tide at flood,
The sickle-sweep of Quiberon bay
Whose beach once ran with loyal blood !

And beyond that, the Atlantic wide !—
All round, no soul, no boat, no hail !   30
But, on the horizon's verge descried,
Hangs, touch'd with light, one snowy sail !

Ah, where is he, who should have come
Where that far sail is passing now,
Past the Loire's mouth, and by the foam
Of Finistère's unquiet brow,

Home, round into the English wave ?—
He tarries where the Rock of Spain
Mediterranean waters lave ;
He enters not the Atlantic main.   40

Oh, could he once have reach'd this air
Freshen'd by plunging tides, by showers !
Have felt this breath he loved, of fair
Cool northern fields, and grass, and flowers !

He long'd for it—press'd on !—In vain.
At the Straits fail'd that spirit brave.
The South was parent of his pain,
The South is mistress of his grave.

FRAGMENT OF CHORUS OF A *DEJANEIRA*

[First published 1867.]

O FRIVOLOUS mind of man,
Light ignorance, and hurrying, unsure thoughts,
Though man bewails you not,
How I bewail you !

Little in your prosperity
Do you seek counsel of the Gods.
Proud, ignorant, self-adored, you live alone.
In profound silence stern
Among their savage gorges and cold springs
Unvisited remain   10
The great oracular shrines.

Thither in your adversity
Do you betake yourselves for light,
But strangely misinterpret all you hear.
For you will not put on
New hearts with the inquirer's holy robe,
And purged, considerate minds.

And him on whom, at the end
Of toil and dolour untold,
The Gods have said that repose   20
At last shall descend undisturb'd,
Him you expect to behold
In an easy old age, in a happy home ;
No end but this you praise.

But him, on whom, in the prime
Of life, with vigour undimm'd,
With unspent mind, and a soul
Unworn, undebased, undecay'd,
Mournfully grating, the gates
Of the city of death have for ever closed—   30
Him, I count *him*, well-starr'd.

PALLADIUM

[First published 1867.]

SET where the upper streams of Simois flow
Was the Palladium, high 'mid rock and wood ;
And Hector was in Ilium, far below,
And fought, and saw it not, but there it stood.

It stood ; and sun and moonshine rain'd their light
On the pure columns of its glen-built hall.
Backward and forward roll'd the waves of fight
Round Troy ; but while this stood, Troy could not
          fall.

So, in its lovely moonlight, lives the soul.
Mountains surround it, and sweet virgin air ;   10
Cold plashing, past it, crystal waters roll ;
We visit it by moments, ah ! too rare.

Men will renew the battle in the plain
To-morrow ; red with blood will Xanthus be ;
Hector and Ajax will be there again ;
Helen will come upon the wall to see.

Then we shall rust in shade, or shine in strife,
And fluctuate 'twixt blind hopes and blind despairs,
And fancy that we put forth all our life,
And never know how with the soul it fares.   20

Still doth the soul, from its lone fastness high,
Upon our life a ruling effluence send ;
And when it fails, fight as we will, we die,
And while it lasts, we cannot wholly end.

EARLY DEATH AND FAME

[First published 1867.]

FOR him who must see many years,
I praise the life which slips away
Out of the light and mutely ; which avoids
Fame, and her less fair followers, envy, strife,
Stupid detraction, jealousy, cabal,
Insincere praises ; which descends
The quiet mossy track to age.

But, when immature death
Beckons too early the guest
From the half-tried banquet of life,   10
Young, in the bloom of his days ;
Leaves no leisure to press,
Slow and surely, the sweets
Of a tranquil life in the shade ;
Fuller for him be the hours !
Give him emotion, though pain !
Let him live, let him feel : *I have lived !*
Heap up his moments with life,
Triple his pulses with fame !

YOUTH AND CALM

[First published in this form 1867.]

'TIS death! and peace, indeed, is here,
And ease from shame, and rest from fear.
There's nothing can dismarble now
The smoothness of that limpid brow.
But is a calm like this, in truth,
The crowning end of life and youth,
And when this boon rewards the dead,
Are all debts paid, has all been said?
And is the heart of youth so light,
Its step so firm, its eye so bright,   10
Because on its hot brow there blows
A wind of promise and repose
From the far grave, to which it goes;
Because it has the hope to come,
One day, to harbour in the tomb?
Ah no, the bliss youth dreams is one
For daylight, for the cheerful sun,
For feeling nerves and living breath—
Youth dreams a bliss on this side death!
It dreams a rest, if not more deep,   20
More grateful than this marble sleep.
It hears a voice within it tell:
Calm's not life's crown, though calm is well.
'Tis all perhaps which man acquires,
But 'tis not what our youth desires.

GROWING OLD

[First published 1867.]

WHAT is it to grow old?
Is it to lose the glory of the form,
The lustre of the eye?
Is it for beauty to forgo her wreath?
Yes, but not this alone.

Youth and Calm = *ll*. 17–41 *of* Lines written by a Death-bed,
1852. [*See pp. 138, 139.*]
 1 'Tis death! and] But ah, though *1852.*   3 There's]
Though *1852.*   5 But] Yet *1852.*

Is it to feel our strength—
Not our bloom only, but our strength—decay ?
Is it to feel each limb
Grow stiffer, every function less exact,
Each nerve more weakly strung ?   10

Yes, this, and more ! but not,
Ah, 'tis not what in youth we dream'd 'twould be !
'Tis not to have our life
Mellow'd and soften'd as with sunset glow,
A golden day's decline !

'Tis not to see the world
As from a height, with rapt prophetic eyes,
And heart profoundly stirr'd ;
And weep, and feel the fullness of the past,
The years that are no more !   20

It is to spend long days
And not once feel that we were ever young.
It is to add, immured
In the hot prison of the present, month
To month with weary pain.

It is to suffer this,
And feel but half, and feebly, what we feel.
Deep in our hidden heart
Festers the dull remembrance of a change,
But no emotion—none.   30

It is—last stage of all—
When we are frozen up within, and quite
The phantom of ourselves,
To hear the world applaud the hollow ghost
Which blamed the living man.

THE PROGRESS OF POESY

A Variation

[First published 1867.]

YOUTH rambles on life's arid mount,
And strikes the rock, and finds the vein,
And brings the water from the fount,
The fount which shall not flow again.

The man mature with labour chops
For the bright stream a channel grand,
And sees not that the sacred drops
Ran off and vanish'd out of hand.

And then the old man totters nigh
And feebly rakes among the stones.   10
The mount is mute, the channel dry ;
And down he lays his weary bones.

A NAMELESS EPITAPH

[First published 1867.]

THIS sentence have I left behind :
An aching body, and a mind
Not wholly clear, nor wholly blind,
Too keen to rest, too weak to find,
That travails sore, and brings forth wind,
Are God's worst portion to mankind.

Another

Ask not my name, O friend !
That Being only, which hath known each man
From the beginning, can
Remember each unto the end.

THE LAST WORD

[First published 1867.]

CREEP into thy narrow bed,
Creep, and let no more be said !
Vain thy onset ! all stands fast ;
Thou thyself must break at last.

Let the long contention cease !
Geese are swans, and swans are geese.
Let them have it how they will !
Thou art tired ; best be still !

They out-talk'd thee, hiss'd thee, tore thee.
Better men fared thus before thee ;   10
Fired their ringing shot and pass'd,
Hotly charged—and broke at last.

Charge once more, then, and be dumb !
Let the victors, when they come,
When the forts of folly fall,
Find thy body by the wall.

A WISH

[First published 1867.]

I ASK not that my bed of death
From bands of greedy heirs be free ;
For these besiege the latest breath
Of fortune's favour'd sons, not me.

I ask not each kind soul to keep
Tearless, when of my death he hears ;
Let those who will, if any, weep !
There are worse plagues on earth than tears.

I ask but that my death may find
The freedom to my life denied ;   10
Ask but the folly of mankind,
Then, then at last, to quit my side.

Spare me the whispering, crowded room,
The friends who come, and gape, and go ;
The ceremonious air of gloom—
All, that makes death a hideous show !

Nor bring, to see me cease to live,
Some doctor full of phrase and fame,
To shake his sapient head and give
The ill he cannot cure a name.   20

Nor fetch, to take the accustom'd toll
Of the poor sinner bound for death,
His brother doctor of the soul,
To canvass with official breath

The future and its viewless things—
That undiscover'd mystery
Which one who feels death's winnowing wings
Must needs read clearer, sure, than he!

Bring none of these! but let me be,
While all around in silence lies, 30
Moved to the window near, and see
Once more before my dying eyes

Bathed in the sacred dews of morn
The wide aërial landscape spread—
The world which was ere I was born,
The world which lasts when I am dead.

Which never was the friend of *one*,
Nor promised love it could not give,
But lit for all its generous sun,
And lived itself, and made us live. 40

There let me gaze, till I become
In soul with what I gaze on wed!
To feel the universe my home;
To have before my mind—instead

Of the sick-room, the mortal strife,
The turmoil for a little breath—
The pure eternal course of life,
Not human combatings with death.

Thus feeling, gazing, let me grow
Compos'd, refresh'd, ennobled, clear; 50
Then willing let my spirit go
To work or wait elsewhere or here!

A CAUTION TO POETS

[First published 1867.]

WHAT poets feel not, when they make,
    A pleasure in creating,
The world, in *its* turn, will not take
    Pleasure in contemplating.

PIS-ALLER

[First published 1867.]

'Man is blind because of sin ;
' Revelation makes him sure.
' Without that, who looks within,
' Looks in vain, for all 's obscure.'

Nay, look closer into man !
Tell me, can you find indeed
Nothing sure, no moral plan
Clear prescribed, without your creed ?

' No, I nothing can perceive ;
' Without that, all 's dark for men.   10
' That, or nothing, I believe.'—
For God's sake, believe it then !

EPILOGUE TO LESSING'S LAOCOÖN

[First published 1867.]

One morn as through Hyde Park we walk'd
My friend and I, by chance we talk'd
Of Lessing's famed Laocoön ;
And after we awhile had gone
In Lessing's track, and tried to see
What painting is, what poetry—
Diverging to another thought,
' Ah,' cries my friend, ' but who hath taught
Why music and the other arts
Oftener perform aright their parts   10
Than poetry ? why she, than they,
Fewer real successes can display ?

' For 'tis so, surely ! Even in Greece
Where best the poet framed his piece,
Even in that Phoebus-guarded ground
Pausanias on his travels found
Good poems, if he look'd, more rare
(Though many) than good statues were—
For these, in truth, were everywhere !

Of bards full many a stroke divine   20
In Dante's, Petrarch's, Tasso's line,
The land of Ariosto show'd ;
And yet, e'en there, the canvas glow'd
With triumphs, a yet ampler brood,
Of Raphael and his brotherhood.
And nobly perfect, in our day
Of haste, half-work, and disarray,
Profound yet touching, sweet yet strong,
Hath risen Goethe's, Wordsworth's song ;
Yet even I (and none will bow   30
Deeper to these !) must needs allow,
They yield us not, to soothe our pains,
Such multitude of heavenly strains
As from the kings of sound are blown,
Mozart, Beethoven, Mendelssohn.'

While thus my friend discoursed, we pass
Out of the path, and take the grass.
The grass had still the green of May,
And still the unblacken'd elms were gay ;
The kine were resting in the shade,   40
The flies a summer murmur made ;
Bright was the morn and south the air,
The soft-couch'd cattle were as fair
As those that pastured by the sea,
That old-world morn, in Sicily,
When on the beach the Cyclops lay,
And Galatea from the bay
Mock'd her poor lovelorn giant's lay.
'Behold,' I said, ' the painter's sphere !
The limits of his art appear !   50
The passing group, the summer morn,
The grass, the elms, that blossom'd thorn ;
Those cattle couch'd, or, as they rise,
Their shining flanks, their liquid eyes ;
These, or much greater things, but caught
Like these, and in one aspect brought.
In outward semblance he must give
A moment's life of things that live ;
Then let him choose his moment well,
With power divine its story tell !'   60

Still we walk'd on, in thoughtful mood,
And now upon the Bridge we stood.
Full of sweet breathings was the air,
Of sudden stirs and pauses fair ;
Down o'er the stately Bridge the breeze
Came rustling from the garden trees
And on the sparkling waters play'd.
Light-plashing waves an answer made,
And mimic boats their haven near'd.
Beyond, the Abbey towers appear'd,   70
By mist and chimneys unconfined,
Free to the sweep of light and wind ;
While, through the earth-moor'd nave below,
Another breath of wind doth blow,
Sound as of wandering breeze—but sound
In laws by human artists bound.
' The world of music ! ' I exclaim'd,
' This breeze that rustles by, that famed
Abbey recall it ! what a sphere,
Large and profound, hath genius here !   80
Th' inspired musician what a range,
What power of passion, wealth of change !
Some pulse of feeling he must choose
And its lock'd fount of beauty use,
And through the stream of music tell
Its else unutterable spell ;
To choose it rightly is his part,
And press into its inmost heart.

' *Miserere, Domine !*
The words are utter'd, and they flee.   90
Deep is their penitential moan,
Mighty their pathos, but 'tis gone !
They have declared the spirit's sore
Sore load, and words can do no more.
Beethoven takes them then—those two
Poor, bounded words—and makes them new ;
Infinite makes them, makes them young,
Transplants them to another tongue
Where they can now, without constraint,
Pour all the soul of their complaint,   100

And roll adown a channel large
The wealth divine they have in charge.
Page after page of music turn,
And still they live and still they burn,
Eternal, passion-fraught and free—
Miserere, Domine ! '

Onward we moved, and reach'd the Ride
Where gaily flows the human tide.
Afar, in rest the cattle lay,
We heard, afar, faint music play ;   110
But agitated, brisk, and near,
Men, with their stream of life, were here.
Some hang upon the rails, and some,
On foot, behind them, go and come.
This through the Ride upon his steed
Goes slowly by, and this at speed ;
The young, the happy, and the fair,
The old, the sad, the worn were there ;
Some vacant, and some musing went,
And some in talk and merriment.   120
Nods, smiles, and greetings, and farewells !
And now and then, perhaps, there swells
A sigh, a tear—but in the throng
All changes fast, and hies along ;
Hies, ah, from whence, what native ground ?
And to what goal, what ending, bound ?
' Behold at last the poet's sphere !
But who,' I said, ' suffices here ?

' For, ah ! so much he has to do !
Be painter and musician too !   130
The aspect of the moment show,
The feeling of the moment know !
The aspect not, I grant, express
Clear as the painter's art can dress,
The feeling not, I grant, explore
So deep as the musician's lore—
But clear as words can make revealing,
And deep as words can follow feeling.
But, ah, then comes his sorest spell
Of toil ! he must life's *movement* tell !   140

The thread which binds it all in one,
And not its separate parts alone !
The movement he must tell of life,
Its pain and pleasure, rest and strife ;
His eye must travel down, at full,
The long, unpausing spectacle ;
With faithful unrelaxing force
Attend it from its primal source,
From change to change and year to year
Attend it of its mid career,   150
Attend it to the last repose
And solemn silence of its close.

' The cattle rising from the grass
His thought must follow where they pass ;
The penitent with anguish bow'd
His thought must follow through the crowd.
Yes, all this eddying, motley throng
That sparkles in the sun along,
Girl, statesman, merchant, soldier bold,
Master and servant, young and old,   160
Grave, gay, child, parent, husband, wife,
He follows home, and lives their life !

' And many, many are the souls
Life's movement fascinates, controls.
It draws them on, they cannot save
Their feet from its alluring wave ;
They cannot leave it, they must go
With its unconquerable flow.
But, ah, how few of all that try
This mighty march, do aught but die !   170
For ill prepared for such a way,
Ill found in strength, in wits, are they !
They faint, they stagger to and fro,
And wandering from the stream they go ;
In pain, in terror, in distress,
They see, all round, a wilderness.
Sometimes a momentary gleam
They catch of the mysterious stream ;
Sometimes, a second's space, their ear
The murmur of its waves doth hear.   180

That transient glimpse in song they say,
But not as painter can pourtray !
That transient sound in song they tell,
But not, as the musician, well !
And when at last these snatches cease,
And they are silent and at peace,
The stream of life's majestic whole
Hath ne'er been mirror'd on their soul.

'Only a few the life-stream's shore
With safe unwandering feet explore,   190
Untired its movement bright attend,
Follow its windings to the end.
Then from its brimming waves their eye
Drinks up delighted ecstasy,
And its deep-toned, melodious voice,
For ever makes their ear rejoice.
They speak ! the happiness divine
They feel, runs o'er in every line.
Its spell is round them like a shower ;
It gives them pathos, gives them power.   200
No painter yet hath such a way
Nor no musician made, as they ;
And gather'd on immortal knolls
Such lovely flowers for cheering souls !
Beethoven, Raphael, cannot reach
The charm which Homer, Shakespeare, teach.
To these, to these, their thankful race
Gives, then, the first, the fairest place !
And brightest is their glory's sheen
For greatest has their labour been.'   210

BACCHANALIA ; OR, THE NEW AGE

[First published 1867.]

I

THE evening comes, the field is still.
The tinkle of the thirsty rill,
Unheard all day, ascends again ;
Deserted is the new-reap'd grain.

Silent the sheaves! the ringing wain,
The reaper's cry, the dogs' alarms,
All housed within the sleeping farms!
The business of the day is done,
The last belated gleaner gone.
And from the thyme upon the height,   10
And from the elder-blossom white
And pale dog-roses in the hedge,
And from the mint-plant in the sedge,
In puffs of balm the night-air blows
The perfume which the day forgoes.
And on the pure horizon far,
See, pulsing with the first-born star,
The liquid sky above the hill!
The evening comes, the field is still.

Loitering and leaping,   20
With saunter, with bounds—
Flickering and circling
In files and in rounds—
Gaily their pine-staff green
Tossing in air,
Loose o'er their shoulders white
Showering their hair—
See! the wild Maenads
Break from the wood,
Youth and Iacchus   30
Maddening their blood!
See! through the quiet corn
Rioting they pass—
Fling the piled sheaves about,
Trample the grass!
Tear from the rifled hedge
Garlands, their prize;
Fill with their sports the field,
Fill with their cries!

Shepherd, what ails thee, then?   40
Shepherd, why mute?
Forth with thy joyous song!
Forth with thy flute!
Tempts not the revel blithe?

Lure not their cries?
Glow not their shoulders smooth?
Melt not their eyes?
Is not, on cheeks like those,
Lovely the flush?—
 Ah, so the quiet was!   50
So was the hush!

II

The epoch ends, the world is still.
The age has talk'd and work'd its fill—
The famous orators have done,
The famous poets sung and gone,
The famous men of war have fought,
The famous speculators thought,
The famous players, sculptors, wrought,
The famous painters fill'd their wall,
The famous critics judged it all.
The combatants are parted now,   10
Uphung the spear, unbent the bow,
The puissant crown'd, the weak laid low!
And in the after-silence sweet,
Now strife is hush'd, our ears doth meet,
Ascending pure, the bell-like fame
Of this or that down-trodden name,
Delicate spirits, push'd away
In the hot press of the noon-day.
And o'er the plain, where the dead age
Did its now silent warfare wage—   20
O'er that wide plain, now wrapt in gloom,
Where many a splendour finds its tomb,
Many spent fames and fallen mights—
The one or two immortal lights
Rise slowly up into the sky
To shine there everlastingly,
Like stars over the bounding hill.
The epoch ends, the world is still.

Thundering and bursting
In torrents, in waves—   30
Carolling and shouting
Over tombs, amid graves—

See! on the cumber'd plain
Clearing a stage,
Scattering the past about,
Comes the new age!
Bards make new poems,
Thinkers new schools,
Statesmen new systems,
Critics new rules!   40
All things begin again;
Life is their prize;
Earth with their deeds they fill,
Fill with their cries!

Poet, what ails thee, then?
Say, why so mute?
Forth with thy praising voice!
Forth with thy flute!
Loiterer! why sittest thou
Sunk in thy dream?   50
Tempts not the bright new age?
Shines not its stream?
Look, ah, what genius,
Art, science, wit!
Soldiers like Caesar,
Statesmen like Pitt!
Sculptors like Phidias,
Raphaels in shoals,
Poets like Shakespeare—
Beautiful souls!   60
See, on their glowing cheeks
Heavenly the flush!
  Ah, so the silence was!
So was the hush!

The world but feels the present's spell,
The poet feels the past as well;
Whatever men have done, might do,
Whatever thought, might think it too.

RUGBY CHAPEL

November, 1857

[First published 1867.]

Coldly, sadly descends
The autumn evening.   The Field
Strewn with its dank yellow drifts
Of wither'd leaves, and the elms,
Fade into dimness apace,
Silent ;—hardly a shout
From a few boys late at their play !
The lights come out in the street,
In the school-room windows ; but cold,
Solemn, unlighted, austere,   10
Through the gathering darkness, arise
The Chapel walls, in whose bound
Thou, my father ! art laid.

There thou dost lie, in the gloom
Of the autumn evening.   But ah !
That word, *gloom*, to my mind
Brings thee back in the light
Of thy radiant vigour again !
In the gloom of November we pass'd
Days not of gloom at thy side ;   20
Seasons impair'd not the ray
Of thine even cheerfulness clear.
Such thou wast ; and I stand
In the autumn evening, and think
Of bygone autumns with thee.

Fifteen years have gone round
Since thou arosest to tread,
In the summer morning, the road
Of death, at a call unforeseen,
Sudden.   For fifteen years,   30
We who till then in thy shade
Rested as under the boughs
Of a mighty oak, have endured
Sunshine and rain as we might,
Bare, unshaded, alone,
Lacking the shelter of thee.

O strong soul, by what shore
Tarriest thou now ?   For that force,
Surely, has not been left vain !
Somewhere, surely, afar,   40
In the sounding labour-house vast
Of being, is practised that strength,
Zealous, beneficent, firm !

Yes, in some far-shining sphere,
Conscious or not of the past,
Still thou performest the word
Of the Spirit in whom thou dost live,
Prompt, unwearied, as here !
Still thou upraisest with zeal
The humble good from the ground,   50
Sternly repressest the bad.
Still, like a trumpet, dost rouse
Those who with half-open eyes
Tread the border-land dim
'Twixt vice and virtue ; reviv'st,
Succourest ;—this was thy work,
This was thy life upon earth.

What is the course of the life
Of mortal men on the earth ?—
Most men eddy about   60
Here and there—eat and drink,
Chatter and love and hate,
Gather and squander, are raised
Aloft, are hurl'd in the dust,
Striving blindly, achieving
Nothing ; and, then they die—
Perish ; and no one asks
Who or what they have been,
More than he asks what waves
In the moonlit solitudes mild   70
Of the midmost Ocean, have swell'd,
Foam'd for a moment, and gone.

And there are some, whom a thirst
Ardent, unquenchable, fires,

Not with the crowd to be spent,
Not without aim to go round
In an eddy of purposeless dust,
Effort unmeaning and vain.
Ah yes, some of us strive
Not without action to die   80
Fruitless, but something to snatch
From dull oblivion, nor all
Glut the devouring grave!
We, we have chosen our path—
Path to a clear-purposed goal,
Path of advance! but it leads
A long, steep journey, through sunk
Gorges, o'er mountains in snow!
Cheerful, with friends, we set forth;
Then, on the height, comes the storm!   90
Thunder crashes from rock
To rock, the cataracts reply;
Lightnings dazzle our eyes;
Roaring torrents have breach'd
The track, the stream-bed descends.
In the place where the wayfarer once
Planted his footstep—the spray
Boils o'er its borders; aloft,
The unseen snow-beds dislodge
Their hanging ruin;—alas,   100
Havoc is made in our train!
Friends who set forth at our side
Falter, are lost in the storm!
We, we only, are left!
With frowning foreheads, with lips
Sternly compress'd, we strain on,
On—and at nightfall, at last,
Come to the end of our way,
To the lonely inn 'mid the rocks;
Where the gaunt and taciturn Host   110
Stands on the threshold, the wind
Shaking his thin white hairs—
Holds his lantern to scan
Our storm-beat figures, and asks:
Whom in our party we bring?
Whom we have left in the snow?

Sadly we answer: We bring
Only ourselves; we lost
Sight of the rest in the storm.
Hardly ourselves we fought through,   120
Stripp'd, without friends, as we are.
Friends, companions, and train
The avalanche swept from our side.

But thou would'st not *alone*
Be saved, my father! *alone*
Conquer and come to thy goal,
Leaving the rest in the wild.
We were weary, and we
Fearful, and we, in our march,
Fain to drop down and to die.   130
Still thou turnedst, and still
Beckonedst the trembler, and still
Gavest the weary thy hand!
If, in the paths of the world,
Stones might have wounded thy feet,
Toil or dejection have tried
Thy spirit, of that we saw
Nothing! to us thou wert still
Cheerful, and helpful, and firm.
Therefore to thee it was given   140
Many to save with thyself;
And, at the end of thy day,
O faithful shepherd! to come,
Bringing thy sheep in thy hand.

And through thee I believe
In the noble and great who are gone;
Pure souls honour'd and blest
By former ages, who else—
Such, so soulless, so poor,
Is the race of men whom I see—   150
Seem'd but a dream of the heart,
Seem'd but a cry of desire.
Yes! I believe that there lived
Others like thee in the past,
Not like the men of the crowd
Who all round me to-day
Bluster or cringe, and make life

Hideous, and arid, and vile ;
But souls temper'd with fire,
Fervent, heroic, and good,   160
Helpers and friends of mankind.

Servants of God !—or sons
Shall I not call you ? because
Not as servants ye knew
Your Father's innermost mind,
His, who unwillingly sees
One of his little ones lost—
Yours is the praise, if mankind
Hath not as yet in its march
Fainted, and fallen, and died !   170

See ! in the rocks of the world
Marches the host of mankind,
A feeble, wavering line.
Where are they tending ?—A God
Marshall'd them, gave them their goal.—
Ah, but the way is so long !
Years they have been in the wild !
Sore thirst plagues them ; the rocks,
Rising all round, overawe.
Factions divide them ; their host   180
Threatens to break, to dissolve.
Ah, keep, keep them combined !
Else, of the myriads who fill
That army, not one shall arrive !
Sole they shall stray ; in the rocks
Labour for ever in vain,
Die one by one in the waste.

Then, in such hour of need
Of your fainting, dispirited race,
Ye, like angels, appear,   190
Radiant with ardour divine.
Beacons of hope, ye appear !
Languor is not in your heart,
Weakness is not in your word,
Weariness not on your brow.

Ye alight in our van ; at your voice,
Panic, despair, flee away.
Ye move through the ranks, recall
The stragglers, refresh the outworn,
Praise, re-inspire the brave.   200
Order, courage, return.
Eyes rekindling, and prayers,
Follow your steps as ye go.
Ye fill up the gaps in our files,
Strengthen the wavering line,
Stablish, continue our march,
On, to the bound of the waste,
On, to the City of God.

HEINE'S GRAVE

[First published 1867.]

'*HENRI HEINE*'——'tis here !
The black tombstone, the name
Carved there—no more ! and the smooth,
Swarded alleys, the limes
Touch'd with yellow by hot
Summer, but under them still
In September's bright afternoon
Shadow, and verdure, and cool !
Trim Montmartre ! the faint
Murmur of Paris outside ;   10
Crisp everlasting-flowers,
Yellow and black, on the graves.

Half blind, palsied, in pain,
Hither to come, from the streets'
Uproar, surely not loath
Wast thou, Heine !—to lie
Quiet ! to ask for closed
Shutters, and darken'd room,
And cool drinks, and an eased
Posture, and opium, no more !   20
Hither to come, and to sleep
Under the wings of Renown.

Ah ! not little, when pain
Is most quelling, and man
Easily quell'd, and the fine
Temper of genius alive
Quickest to ill, is the praise
Not to have yielded to pain !
No small boast, for a weak
Son of mankind, to the earth   30
Pinn'd by the thunder, to rear
His bolt-scathed front to the stars ;
And, undaunted, retort
'Gainst thick-crashing, insane,
Tyrannous tempests of bale,
Arrowy lightnings of soul !

Hark ! through the alley resounds
Mocking laughter ! A film
Creeps o'er the sunshine ; a breeze
Ruffles the warm afternoon,   40
Saddens my soul with its chill.
Gibing of spirits in scorn
Shakes every leaf of the grove,
Mars the benignant repose
Of this amiable home of the dead.

Bitter spirits ! ye claim
Heine ?—Alas, he is yours !
Only a moment I long'd
Here in the quiet to snatch
From such mates the outworn   50
Poet, and steep him in calm.
Only a moment ! I knew
Whose he was who is here
Buried, I knew he was yours !
Ah, I knew that I saw
Here no sepulchre built
In the laurell'd rock, o'er the blue
Naples bay, for a sweet
Tender Virgil ! no tomb
On Ravenna sands, in the shade   60
Of Ravenna pines, for a high
Austere Dante ! no grave

By the Avon side, in the bright
Stratford meadows, for thee,
Shakespeare! loveliest of souls,
Peerless in radiance, in joy.

What so harsh and malign,
Heine! distils from thy life,
Poisons the peace of thy grave?

I chide with thee not, that thy sharp   70
Upbraidings often assail'd
England, my country; for we,
Fearful and sad, for her sons,
Long since, deep in our hearts,
Echo the blame of her foes.
We, too, sigh that she flags;
We, too, say that she now,
Scarce comprehending the voice
Of her greatest, golden-mouth'd sons
Of a former age any more,   80
Stupidly travels her round
Of mechanic business, and lets
Slow die out of her life
Glory, and genius, and joy.

So thou arraign'st her, her foe;
So we arraign her, her sons.

Yes, we arraign her! but she,
The weary Titan! with deaf
Ears, and labour-dimm'd eyes,
Regarding neither to right   90
Nor left, goes passively by,
Staggering on to her goal;
Bearing on shoulders immense,
Atlanteän, the load,
Wellnigh not to be borne,
Of the too vast orb of her fate.

But was it thou—I think
Surely it was—that bard
Unnamed, who, Goethe said,
Had every other gift, but wanted love;   100
Love, without which the tongue
Even of angels sounds amiss?

Charm is the glory which makes
Song of the poet divine ;
Love is the fountain of charm.
How without charm wilt thou draw,
Poet ! the world to thy way ?
Not by the lightnings of wit !
Not by the thunder of scorn !
These to the world, too, are given ;   110
Wit it possesses, and scorn—
Charm is the poet's alone.
Hollow and dull are the great,
And artists envious, and the mob profane.
We know all this, we know !
Cam'st thou from heaven, O child
Of light ! but this to declare ?
Alas ! to help us forget
Such barren knowledge awhile,
God gave the poet his song.   120

Therefore a secret unrest
Tortured thee, brilliant and bold !
Therefore triumph itself
Tasted amiss to thy soul.
Therefore, with blood of thy foes,
Trickled in silence thine own.
Therefore the victor's heart
Broke on the field of his fame.

Ah ! as of old, from the pomp
Of Italian Milan, the fair   130
Flower of marble of white
Southern palaces—steps
Border'd by statues, and walks
Terraced, and orange bowers
Heavy with fragrance—the blond
German Kaiser full oft
Long'd himself back to the fields,
Rivers, and high-roof'd towns
Of his native Germany ; so,
So, how often ! from hot   140
Paris drawing-rooms, and lamps
Blazing, and brilliant crowds,

Starr'd and jewell'd, of men
Famous, of women the queens
Of dazzling converse, and fumes
Of praise—hot, heady fumes, to the poor brain
That mount, that madden!—how oft
Heine's spirit outworn
Long'd itself out of the din
Back to the tranquil, the cool   150
Far German home of his youth!

See! in the May afternoon,
O'er the fresh short turf of the Hartz,
A youth, with the foot of youth,
Heine! thou climbest again.
Up, through the tall dark firs
Warming their heads in the sun,
Chequering the grass with their shade—
Up, by the stream with its huge
Moss-hung boulders and thin   160
Musical water half-hid—
Up, o'er the rock-strewn slope,
With the sinking sun, and the air
Chill, and the shadows now
Long on the grey hill-side—
To the stone-roof'd hut at the top.

Or, yet later, in watch
On the roof of the Brocken tower
Thou standest, gazing! to see
The broad red sun, over field   170
Forest and city and spire
And mist-track'd stream of the wide
Wide German land, going down
In a bank of vapours——again
Standest! at nightfall, alone.

Or, next morning, with limbs
Rested by slumber, and heart
Freshen'd and light with the May,
O'er the gracious spurs coming down
Of the Lower Hartz, among oaks,   180
And beechen coverts, and copse
Of hazels green in whose depth

Ilse, the fairy transform'd,
In a thousand water-breaks light
Pours her petulant youth—
Climbing the rock which juts
O'er the valley, the dizzily perch'd
Rock! to its Iron Cross
Once more thou cling'st ; to the Cross
Clingest! with smiles, with a sigh.   190

Goethe, too, had been there.
In the long-past winter he came
To the frozen Hartz, with his soul
Passionate, eager, his youth
All in ferment ;—but he
Destined to work and to live
Left it, and thou, alas!
Only to laugh and to die.

But something prompts me : Not thus
Take leave of Heine, not thus   200
Speak the last word at his grave!
Not in pity and not
With half censure—with awe
Hail, as it passes from earth
Scattering lightnings, that soul!

The spirit of the world
Beholding the absurdity of men—
Their vaunts, their feats—let a sardonic smile
For one short moment wander o'er his lips.
That smile was Heine! for its earthly hour   210
The strange guest sparkled ; now 'tis pass'd away.

That was Heine! and we,
Myriads who live, who have lived,
What are we all, but a mood,
A single mood, of the life
Of the Being in whom we exist,
Who alone is all things in one.

    Spirit, who fillest us all!
Spirit who utterest in each
New-coming son of mankind   220
Such of thy thoughts as thou wilt!

O thou, one of whose moods,
Bitter and strange, was the life
Of Heine—his strange, alas!
His bitter life—may a life
Other and milder be mine!
May'st thou a mood more serene,
Happier, have utter'd in mine!
May'st thou the rapture of peace
Deep have embreathed at its core!   230
Made it a ray of thy thought!
Made it a beat of thy joy!

OBERMANN ONCE MORE

[First published 1867.]

Savez-vous quelque bien qui console du regret d'un monde?
OBERMANN.

GLION?——Ah, twenty years, it cuts
All meaning from a name!
White houses prank where once were huts!
Glion! but not the same,

And yet I know not. All unchanged
The turf, the pines, the sky!
The hills in their old order ranged!
The lake, with Chillon by!

And 'neath those chestnut-trees, where stiff
And stony mounts the way,   10
Their crackling husk-heaps burn, as if
I left them yesterday.

Across the valley, on that slope.
The huts of Avant shine—
Its pines under their branches ope
Ways for the tinkling kine.

Full-foaming milk-pails, Alpine fare,
Sweet heaps of fresh-cut grass,
Invite to rest the traveller there
Before he climb the pass—   20

ARNOLD   F f

The gentian-flower'd pass, its crown
With yellow spires aflame,
Whence drops the path to Allière down
And walls where Byron came,

By their green river who doth change
His birth-name just below—
Orchard, and croft, and full-stored grange
Nursed by his pastoral flow.

But stop !—to fetch back thoughts that stray
Beyond this gracious bound,   30
The cone of Jaman, pale and grey,
See, in the blue profound !

Ah, Jaman ! delicately tall
Above his sun-warm'd firs—
What thoughts to me his rocks recall !
What memories he stirs !

And who but thou must be, in truth,
Obermann ! with me here ?
Thou master of my wandering youth,
But left this many a year !   40

Yes, I forget the world's work wrought,
Its warfare waged with pain !
An eremite with thee, in thought
Once more I slip my chain

And to thy mountain-chalet come
And lie beside its door
And hear the wild bee's Alpine hum
And thy sad, tranquil lore.

Again I feel its words inspire
Their mournful calm—serene,   50
Yet tinged with infinite desire
For all that *might* have been,

The harmony from which man swerved
Made his life's rule once more !
The universal order served !
Earth happier than before !

While thus I mused, night gently ran
Down over hill and wood.
Then, still and sudden, Obermann
On the grass near me stood.   60

Those pensive features well I knew,
On my mind, years before,
Imaged so oft, imaged so true !
A shepherd's garb he wore,

A mountain-flower was in his hand,
A book was in his breast ;
Bent on my face, with gaze that scann'd
My soul, his eyes did rest.

'And is it thou,' he cried, 'so long
Held by the world which we   70
Loved not, who turnest from the throng
Back to thy youth and me ?

'And from thy world, with heart opprest,
Choosest thou *now* to turn ?—
Ah me, we anchorites knew it best !
Best can its course discern !

'Thou fledd'st me when the ungenial earth,
Thou soughtest, lay in gloom.
Return'st thou in her hour of birth,
Of hopes and hearts in bloom ?   80

'Wellnigh two thousand years have brought
Their load, and gone away,
Since last on earth there lived and wrought
A world like ours to-day.

'Like ours it look'd in outward air !
Its head was clear and true,
Sumptuous its clothing, rich its fare,
No pause its action knew ;

'Stout was its arm, each pulse and bone
Seem'd puissant and alive—   90
But, ah, its heart, its heart was stone,
And so it could not thrive !

' On that hard Pagan world disgust
And secret loathing fell.
Deep weariness and sated lust
Made human life a hell.

' In his cool hall, with haggard eyes,
The Roman noble lay ;
He drove abroad, in furious guise,
Along the Appian way ;   100

' He made a feast, drank fierce and fast,
And crown'd his hair with flowers—
No easier nor no quicker pass'd
The impracticable hours.

' The brooding East with awe beheld
Her impious younger world ;
The Roman tempest swell'd and swell'd,
And on her head was hurl'd.

' The East bow'd low before the blast,
In patient, deep disdain.   110
She let the legions thunder past,
And plunged in thought again.

' So well she mused, a morning broke
Across her spirit grey.
A conquering, new-born joy awoke,
And fill'd her life with day.

' " Poor world," she cried, " so deep accurst !
That runn'st from pole to pole
To seek a draught to slake thy thirst—
Go, seek it in thy soul ! "   120

' She heard it, the victorious West !
In crown and sword array'd.
She felt the void which mined her breast,
She shiver'd and obey'd.

' She veil'd her eagles, snapp'd her sword,
And laid her sceptre down ;
Her stately purple she abhorr'd,
And her imperial crown ;

'She broke her flutes, she stopp'd her sports,
Her artists could not please ;   130
She tore her books, she shut her courts,
She fled her palaces ;

'Lust of the eye and pride of life
She left it all behind,
And hurried, torn with inward strife,
The wilderness to find.

'Tears wash'd the trouble from her face !
She changed into a child.
'Mid weeds and wrecks she stood—a place
Of ruin—but she smiled !   140

'Oh, had I lived in that great day,
How had its glory new
Fill'd earth and heaven, and caught away
My ravish'd spirit too !

'No cloister-floor of humid stone
Had been too cold for me ;
For me no Eastern desert lone
Had been too far to flee.

'No thoughts that to the world belong
Had stood against the wave   150
Of love which set so deep and strong
From Christ's then open grave.

'No lonely life had pass'd too slow
When I could hourly see
That wan, nail'd Form, with head droop'd low,
Upon the bitter tree ;

'Could see the Mother with the Child
Whose tender winning arts
Have to his little arms beguiled
So many wounded hearts !   160

'And centuries came, and ran their course,
And unspent all that time
Still, still went forth that Child's dear force,
And still was at its prime.

'Ay, ages long endured his span
Of life, 'tis true received,
That gracious Child, that thorn-crown'd Man!
He lived while we believed.

'While we believed, on earth he went,
And open stood his grave.   170
Men call'd from chamber, church, and tent,
And Christ was by to save.

'Now he is dead.   Far hence he lies
In the lorn Syrian town,
And on his grave, with shining eyes,
The Syrian stars look down.

'In vain men still, with hoping new,
Regard his death-place dumb,
And say the stone is not yet to,
And wait for words to come.   180

'Ah, from that silent sacred land,
Of sun, and arid stone,
And crumbling wall, and sultry sand,
Comes now one word alone!

'From David's lips this word did roll,
'Tis true and living yet:
No man can save his brother's soul,
Nor pay his brother's debt.

'Alone, self-poised, henceforward man
Must labour; must resign   190
His all too human creeds, and scan
Simply the way divine.

'But slow that tide of common thought,
Which bathed our life, retired.
Slow, slow the old world wore to naught,
And pulse by pulse expired.

'Its frame yet stood without a breach
When blood and warmth were fled;
And still it spake its wonted speech—
But every word was dead.   200

'And oh, we cried, that on this corse
Might fall a freshening storm!
Rive its dry bones, and with new force
A new-sprung world inform!

'Down came the storm! In ruin fell
The outworn world we knew.
It pass'd, that elemental swell!
Again appear'd the blue.

'The sun shone in the new-wash'd sky—
And what from heaven saw he?   210
Blocks of the past, like icebergs high,
Float in a rolling sea.

'Upon them ply the race of man
All they before endeavour'd ;
They come and go, they work and plan,
And know not they are sever'd.

'Poor fragments of a broken world
Whereon we pitch our tent !
Why were ye too to death not hurl'd
When your world's day was spent?   220

'The glow of central fire is done
Which with its fusing flame
Knit all your parts, and kept you one ;—
But ye, ye are the same !

'The past, its mask of union on,
Had ceased to live and thrive.
The past, its mask of union gone,
Say, is it more alive?

'Your creeds are dead, your rites are dead,
Your social order too.   230
Where tarries he, the power who said :
See, I make all things new?

'The millions suffer still, and grieve ;
And what can helpers heal
With old-world cures men half believe
For woes they wholly feel?

'And yet they have such need of joy!
And joy whose grounds are true!
And joy that should all hearts employ
As when the past was new !   240

'Ah, not the emotion of that past,
Its common hope, were vain !
A new such hope must dawn at last,
Or man must toss in pain.

'But now the past is out of date,
The future not yet born—
And who can be *alone* elate,
While the world lies forlorn ?

'Then to the wilderness I fled.
There among Alpine snows   250
And pastoral huts I hid my head,
And sought and found repose.

'It was not yet the appointed hour.
Sad, patient, and resign'd,
I watch'd the crocus fade and flower,
I felt the sun and wind.

'The day I lived in was not mine—
Man gets no second day.
In dreams I saw the future shine,
But ah, I could not stay !   260

'Action I had not, followers, fame.
I pass'd obscure, alone.
The after-world forgets my name,
Nor do I wish it known.

'Gloom-wrapt within, I lived and died,
And knew my life was vain.
With fate I murmur not, nor chide ;
At Sèvres by the Seine

'(If Paris that brief flight allow)
My humble tomb explore ;   270
It bears : *Eternity, be thou
My refuge !* and no more.

'But thou, whom fellowship of mood
Did make from haunts of strife
Come to my mountain solitude
And learn my frustrate life ;

'O thou, who, ere thy flying span
Was past of cheerful youth,
Didst seek the solitary man
And love his cheerless truth—   280

'Despair not thou as I despair'd,
Nor be cold gloom thy prison !
Forward the gracious hours have fared,
And see ! the sun is risen.

'He melts the icebergs of the past,
A green, new earth appears.
Millions, whose life in ice lay fast,
Have thoughts, and smiles, and tears.

'The world's great order dawns in sheen
After long darkness rude,   290
Divinelier imaged, clearer seen,
With happier zeal pursued.

'With hope extinct and brow composed
I mark'd the present die ;
Its term of life was nearly closed,
Yet it had more than I.

'But thou, though to the world's new hour
Thou come with aspect marr'd,
Shorn of the joy, the bloom, the power,
Which best beseem its bard ;   300

'Though more than half thy years be past,
And spent thy youthful prime ;
Though, round thy firmer manhood cast,
Hang weeds of our sad time,

'Whereof thy youth felt all the spell,
And traversed all the shade—
Though late, though dimm'd, though weak, yet tell
Hope to a world new-made !

' Help it to reach our deep desire,
The dream which fill'd our brain,   310
Fix'd in our soul a thirst like fire
Immedicable pain !

'Which to the wilderness drove out
Our life, to Alpine snow ;
And palsied all our deed with doubt
And all our word with woe—

'What still of strength is left, employ,
That end to help men gain :
One mighty wave of thought and joy
Lifting mankind amain !'   320

The vision ended ; I awoke
As out of sleep, and no
Voice moved—only the torrent broke
The silence, far below.

Soft darkness on the turf did lie ;
Solemn, o'er hut and wood,
In the yet star-sown nightly sky,
The peak of Jaman stood.

Still in my soul the voice I heard
Of Obermann—away   330
I turn'd ; by some vague impulse stirr'd,
Along the rocks of Naye

And Sonchaud's piny flanks I gaze
And the blanch'd summit bare
Of Malatrait, to where in haze
The Valais opens fair,

And the domed Velan with his snows
Behind the upcrowding hills
Doth all the heavenly opening close
Which the Rhone's murmur fills—   340

And glorious there, without a sound,
Across the glimmering lake,
High in the Valais depth profound,
I saw the morning break.

NOTES

[Arnold's own notes are signed [A] ; unsigned notes are by the present editor.]

PREFACE. Page 5, ll. 1, 2. Poems by Goethe, Byron, Lamartine, and Wordsworth respectively.

l. 42. *the grand style*: cp. Arnold's *On Translating Homer* (first published in 1861), *passim*, for a full discussion of the grand style.

7, l. 15. *pragmatic poetry*: pragmatic in this sense means treating the facts of history systematically, in their connexion with each other as cause and effect, and omitting the merely accidental and circumstantial.

10, l. 21. *a modern French poet* : Théophile Gautier.

15, l. 24. *Non me . . . hostis* : see Virgil, *Aeneid*, xii, ll. 894–5.

36. MYCERINUS.

'After Chephren, Mycerinus, son of Cheops, reigned over Egypt. He abhorred his father's courses, and judged his subjects more justly than any of their kings had done.— To him there came an oracle from the city of Buto, to the effect, that he was to live but six years longer, and to die in the seventh year from that time.'—HERODOTUS. [A.]

[Note first inserted in 1853. The 1849 edition gives only the reference 'Herodotus, ii. 133 ' in a footnote.]

40. TO A FRIEND. The three referred to are Homer, Epictetus, and Sophocles. *Vespasian's brutal son* (l. 7) is Domitian.

47, l. 231. *Alcmena's dreadful son* : Hercules.

50, 51. *the Dawn-Goddess* (l. 55) is Aurora, the *fair youth* (l. 56), Orion ; the *Argive Seer* (l. 82) is Tiresias, Zeus's *tired son* (l. 90), Hercules, and the *feebler wight* (l. 96), Eurystheus.

61. TO A REPUBLICAN FRIEND : i. e. A. H. Clough.

66. THE NEW SIRENS. In 1869 Arnold writes : 'Swinburne writes to urge me to reprint the " New Sirens ", but I think that had better wait for a posthumous collection.' He relented, however, and reprinted the poem in *Macmillan's Magazine* for Dec. 1876 with a note giving Swinburne's repeated requests as the main reason for republication 'after a disappearance of more than twenty-five years '.

75. DESIRE (STAGYRUS *1849*). Stagirius was a monk to whom St. Chrysostom addressed three books.

77. TO A GIPSY CHILD, l. 4 : Arnold in later editions reverted to the 1849 form of this line. In a letter dated June 26, 1869, he writes : 'I suppose I must change back the "Gipsy Child" to its old form, as no one seems to like the new one.'

87, l. 41. *That wayside inn* : at Wythburn in the Lake District.

94. EMPEDOCLES ON ETNA. I cannot deny myself the pleasure of saying that I reprint (I cannot say *republish*, for it was withdrawn from circulation before fifty copies were sold) this poem at the request of a man of genius, whom it had the honour and the good fortune to interest,—Mr. Robert Browning. [A. 1867.]

115, l. 41. *Typho* : a giant whom Zeus slew with a thunderbolt and buried beneath Etna. *The Mount of Gore* (l. 54) is Mt. Haemus.

117, l. 128. The Faun *Marsyas* at Pan's instigation challenged Apollo to a contest in music ; Apollo, having been adjudged victor by the Muses, had Marsyas seized and flayed alive.

119, l. 205. *Pytho* : the great serpent produced from the mud left on the earth after Deucalion's flood.

120, l. 239. *Ye Sun-born Virgins! on the road of truth.*
See the Fragments of Parmenides :

> . . . . κοῦραι δ' ὁδὸν ἡγεμόνευον,
> ἡλιάδες κοῦραι, προλιποῦσαι δώματα νυκτός,
> εἰς φάος . . . .   [A.]

126. THE RIVER. In this edition the poems are printed in the order of their first publication. (See *Note*, p. xvii.) In reprinting them in later editions of his poems Arnold rearranged several in two groups under the headings 'Switzerland' and 'Faded Leaves', varying the number of poems thus grouped and the constitution of the groups from time to time. The critical notes below each poem give full information about these changes of title, and the contents of the different editions, given on pp. xix to xxvii, show the changing constitution of the groups ; for convenient reference the final arrangement is given here :—

SWITZERLAND (1885) :

I. Meeting (*The Lake*), p. 131.
II. Parting, p. 131.
III. A Farewell, p. 171.
IV. Isolation. To Marguerite (*To Marguerite*), p. 281.
V. To Marguerite—Continued (*To Marguerite, in returning a volume of the Letters of Ortis*), p. 135.
VI. Absence, p. 134.
VII. The Terrace at Berne, p. 402.

FADED LEAVES (1855) :

I. The River, p. 126.
II. Too Late, p. 129.
III. Separation, p. 269.
IV. On the Rhine, p. 129.
V. Longing, p. 130.

To my Friends who ridiculed a tender leave-taking (p. 63) and *A Dream* (p. 228) are in the final arrangement not included among the 'Switzerland' poems, though they appear in this group in the 1854 and 1857 editions.

127. Excuse. The title was altered to *Urania* in 1869.

128. Indifference. The title was altered to *Euphrosyne* in 1869.

139. Tristram and Iseult. In 1857 Arnold called his hero Tristan ; but as in 1869 and all later editions he reverted to the spelling Tristram, which he had used in the first three editions of the poem, that spelling has been followed here, although the text printed is otherwise that of 1857.

'In the court of his uncle King Marc, the king of Cornwall, who at this time resided at the castle of Tyntagel, Tristram became expert in all knightly exercises.—The king of Ireland, at Tristram's solicitations, promised to bestow his daughter Iseult in marriage on King Marc. The mother of Iseult gave to her daughter's confidante a philtre, or love-potion, to be administered on the night of her nuptials. Of this beverage Tristram and Iseult, on their voyage to Cornwall, unfortunately partook. Its influence, during the remainder of their lives, regulated the affections and destiny of the lovers.—

'After the arrival of Tristram and Iseult in Cornwall, and the nuptials of the latter with King Marc, a great part of the romance is occupied with their contrivances to procure secret interviews.—Tristram, being forced to leave Cornwall on account of the displeasure of his uncle, repaired to Brittany, where lived Iseult with the White Hands.—He married her—more out of gratitude than love.—Afterwards he proceeded to the dominions of Arthur, which became the theatre of unnumbered exploits.

'Tristram, subsequent to these events, returned to Brittany, and to his long-neglected wife. There, being wounded and sick, he was soon reduced to the lowest ebb. In this situation, he dispatched a confidant to the queen of Cornwall, to try if he could induce her to accompany him to Brittany,' &c.—Dunlop's *History of Fiction* [A.]. Vol. I. pp. 260 et seqq. (ed. 1816).

[Note first inserted in *1853*. 'Tyntagel' (*1857*) is 'Tyntagil' in *1852, 1853, 1854*.]

162. Memorial Verses. Goethe died in 1832, Byron at Missolonghi in 1824.

163, ll. 29-33 : almost a translation of Virgil, *Georgics*, ii. 490-2.

164, l. 13. *Cato* : who committed suicide at Utica rather than yield to Julius Caesar.

174. Obermann : Senancour (1770-1846) was the author of *Obermann*, 'a collection of letters from Switzerland treating almost entirely of nature and of the human soul' [A.]. He also wrote *Rêveries sur la Nature primitive de l'Homme* and *Libres Méditations d'un Solitaire Inconnu*.

176, ll. 89-91. *Son of Thetis* : Achilles. The reference is to Achilles' words to Lycaon in *Iliad*, xxi. 106 et seqq.

186, ll. 18-24. The references are to two poems by Wordsworth, *Michael* and *Ruth*. *The Evening Star* was the name given
to Michael's solitary house from the 'constant light' of his lamp,
'so regular and so far seen.'

188, l. 77. *the Mighty Mother* : Rhea, the mother of the gods.

198. SOHRAB AND RUSTUM.

The story of *Sohrab and Rustum* is told in Sir John Malcolm's
History of Persia, as follows :—

'The young Sohrab was the fruit of one of Rustum's early
amours. He had left his mother, and sought fame under the
banners of Afrasiab, whose armies he commanded, and soon
obtained a renown beyond that of all contemporary heroes but
his father. He had carried death and dismay into the ranks
of the Persians, and had terrified the boldest warriors of that
country, before Rustum encountered him, which at last that
hero resolved to do, under a feigned name. They met three
times. The first time they parted by mutual consent, though
Sohrab had the advantage. The second, the youth obtained
a victory, but granted life to his unknown father. The third
was fatal to Sohrab, who, when writhing in the pangs of death,
warned his conqueror to shun the vengeance that is inspired by
parental woes, and bade him dread the rage of the mighty
Rustum, who must soon learn that he had slain his son Sohrab.
These words, we are told, were as death to the aged hero ; and
when he recovered from a trance, he called in despair for
proofs of what Sohrab had said. The afflicted and dying youth
tore open his mail, and showed his father a seal which his
mother had placed on his arm when she discovered to him the
secret of his birth, and bade him seek his father. The sight of
his own signet rendered Rustum quite frantic : he cursed himself, attempted to put an end to his existence, and was only
prevented by the efforts of his expiring son. After Sohrab's
death, he burnt his tents, and all his goods, and carried the
corpse to Seistan, where it was interred. The army of Turan
was, agreeably to the last request of Sohrab, permitted to cross
the Oxus unmolested. It was commanded by Haman : and
Zoarrah attended, on the part of Rustum, to see that this
engagement was respected by the Persians. To reconcile us to
the improbability of this tale we are informed that Rustum
could have no idea his son was in existence. The mother of
Sohrab had written to him her child was a daughter, fearing to
lose her darling infant if she revealed the truth ; and Rustum,
as before stated, fought under a feigned name, an usage not
uncommon in the chivalrous combats of those days.'

M. Sainte-Beuve, also, that most delightful of critics, in a
notice of an edition of Ferdousi's great poem by M. Mohl now
in course of publication at Paris, containing the original text
and a prose translation, gives an analysis of this episode, with
extracts from M. Mohl's translation, which I will quote at
length : commencing from the point where Rustum leaves
Tehmimeh, the future mother of Sohrab, before the birth of her

child ; having given her an onyx with instructions to let the child wear it in her hair, if a girl, and on his arm, if a boy. Of M. Mohl's book itself I have not been able to obtain sight.

' Là-dessus Roustem part au matin, monté sur son cheval Raksch ; il s'en retourne vers l'Iran, et, durant des années, il n'a plus que, de vagues nouvelles de la belle Tehmimeh et du fils qui lui est né ; car c'est un fils et non une fille. Ce fils est beau et au visage brillant ; on l'appelle Sohrab. "Quand il eut un mois, il était comme un enfant d'un an ; quand il eut trois ans, il s'exerçait au jeu des armes, et à cinq ans il avait le cœur d'un lion. Quand il eut atteint l'âge de dix ans, personne dans son pays n'osait lutter contre lui." Il se distinguait, à première vue, de tous les Turcs d'alentour ; il devenait manifeste qu'il était issu d'une autre race. L'enfant, sentant sa force, alla fièrement demander à sa mère le nom de son père, et, quand il le sut, il n'eut plus de cesse qu'il n'eût assemblé une armée pour aller combattre les Iraniens et se faire reconnaître du glorieux Roustem à ses exploits et à sa bravoure.

' Sohrab choisit un cheval assez fort pour le porter, un cheval fort comme un éléphant ; il assemble une armée et se met en marche, non pour combattre son père, mais pour combattre et détrôner le souverain dont Roustem est le feudataire, et afin de mettre la race vaillante de Roustem à la place de ce roi déjà fainéant. C'est ici que l'action commence à se nouer avec un art et une habileté qui appartiennent au poëte. La solution fatale est à la fois entrevue et retardée moyennant des gradations qui vont la rendre plus dramatique. Roustem, mandé en toute hâte par le roi effrayé, ne s'empresse point d'accourir. A cette nouvelle d'une armée de Turcs commandée par un jeune homme si vaillant et si héroïque, il a l'idée d'abord que ce pourrait bien être son fils ; mais non : ce rejeton de sa race est trop enfant, se dit-il, "et ses lèvres sentent encore le lait." Roustem arrive pourtant ; mais, mal accueilli par le roi, il entre dans une colère d'Achille, et il est tout prêt à s'en retourner dans sa tente. On ne le fléchit qu'en lui représentant que s'abstenir en une telle rencontre, ce serait paraître reculer devant le jeune héros. Cependant les armées sont en présence. Roustem, déguisé en Turc, s'introduit dans un château qu'occupe l'ennemi, pour juger de tout par lui-même. Il voit son fils assis à un festin : il l'admire, il le compare, pour la force et la beauté, à sa propre race ; on dirait, à un moment, que le sang au-dedans va parler et lui crier : *C'est lui !* Le jeune Sohrab, de son côté, quand vient le matin, en présence de cette armée dont le camp se déploie devant lui, est avide de savoir si son noble père n'en est pas. Monté sur un lieu élevé, il se fait nommer par un prisonnier tous les chefs illustres dont il voit se dérouler les étendards. Le prisonnier les énumère avec complaisance et les lui nomme tous, tous excepté un seul, excepté celui, précisément, qui l'intéresse. Le prisonnier fait semblant de croire que Roustem n'est pas venu, car il craint que ce jeune orgueilleux, dans sa force indomptable, ne veuille se signaler en s'attaquant de préférence à ce chef illustre, et qu'il ne cause un grand malheur.

Sohrab insiste et trouve étonnant qu'entre tant de chefs, le vaillant Roustem, le premier de tous, ait manqué cette fois à l'appel; il presse de questions le prisonnier, qui lutte de ruse, et qui s'obstine, sur ce point, à lui cacher la vérité; "Sans doute, réplique celui-ci, le héros sera allé dans le Zaboulistan, car c'est le temps des fêtes dans les jardins de roses." A quoi Sohrab, sentant bouillonner son sang, répond : "Ne parle pas ainsi, car le front de Roustem se tourne toujours vers le combat." Mais Sohrab a beau vouloir forcer le secret, la fatalité l'emporte : "Comment veux-tu gouverner ce monde que gouverne Dieu?" s'écrie le poëte. "C'est le Créateur qui a déterminé d'avance toutes choses. Le sort a écrit autrement que tu n'aurais voulu, et, comme il te mène, il faut que tu suives."

'Sohrab engage le combat; tout plie devant lui. Jamais nos vieux romans de chevalerie n'ont retenti de pareils coups d'épée. Les plus vaillants chefs reculent. Roustem est appelé; il arrive, il se trouve seul en présence de son fils, et le duel va s'entamer. La pitié, tout à coup, saisit le vieux chef, en voyant ce jeune guerrier si fier et si beau :

'"O jeune homme si tendre !" lui dit-il, "la terre est sèche et froide, l'air est doux et chaud. Je suis vieux ; j'ai vu maint champ de bataille, j'ai détruit mainte armée, et je n'ai jamais été battu ... Mais j'ai pitié de toi et ne voudrais pas t'arracher la vie. Ne reste pas avec les Turcs ; je ne connais personne dans l'Iran qui ait des épaules et des bras comme toi."

'En entendant ces paroles qui semblent sortir d'une âme amie, le cœur de Sohrab s'élance, il a un pressentiment soudain ; il demande ingénument au guerrier s'il n'est pas celui qu'il cherche, s'il n'est pas l'illustre Roustem. Mais le vieux chef, qui ne veut pas donner à ce jouvenceau trop d'orgueil, répond avec ruse qu'il n'est pas Roustem, et le cœur de Sohrab se resserre aussitôt; le nuage qui venait de s'entr'ouvrir se referme, et la destinée se poursuit.

'Le duel commence : il n'est pas sans vicissitudes et sans péripéties singulières; il dure deux jours. Dès le premier choc, les épées des combattants se brisent en éclats sous leurs coups : "Quels coups ! on eût dit qu'ils amenaient la Résurrection !" Le combat continue à coups de massue ; nous sommes en plein âge héroïque. Le premier jour, le duel n'a pas de résultat. Après une lutte acharnée, les deux chefs s'éloignent, se donnant rendez-vous pour le lendemain. Roustem s'étonne d'avoir rencontré pour la première fois son égal, presque son maître, et de sentir son cœur défaillir sans savoir pourquoi. Le second jour, au moment de reprendre la lutte, Sohrab a un mouvement de tendresse, et la nature, près de succomber, fait en lui comme un suprême effort. En abordant le vieux chef, il s'adresse à lui le sourire sur les lèvres et comme s'ils avaient passé la nuit amicalement ensemble :

'"Comment as-tu dormi ?" lui demande-t-il, "comment t'es-tu levé ce matin ? Pourquoi as-tu préparé ton cœur pour la lutte ? Jette cette massue et cette épée de la vengeance, jette tout cet appareil d'un combat impie. Asseyons-nous tous deux

à terre, et adoucissons avec au vin nos regards courroucés.
Faisons un traité en invoquant Dieu, et repentons-nous dans
notre cœur de cette inimitié. Attends qu'un autre se présente
pour le combat, et apprête avec moi une fête. Mon cœur te
communiquera son amour, et je ferai couler de tes yeux des
larmes de honte. Puisque tu es né d'une noble race, fais-moi
connaître ton origine ; ne me cache pas ton nom, puisque tu
vas me combattre : ne serais-tu pas Roustem ? "

'Roustem, par sentiment d'orgueil, et soupçonnant toujours
une feinte de la part d'un jeune homme avide de gloire,
dissimule une dernière fois, et, dès ce moment, le sort n'a
plus de trêve. Toutes les ruses de Roustem (et j'en supprime
encore) tournent contre lui ; il finit par plonger un poignard
dans la poitrine de son fils, et ne le reconnaît que dans l'instant
suprême. Le jeune homme meurt avec résignation, avec dou-
ceur, en pensant à sa mère, à ses amis, en recommandant
qu'on épargne après lui cette armée qu'il a engagée dans une
entreprise téméraire :

' " Pendant bien des jours, je leur ai donné de belles paroles,
je leur ai donné l'espoir de tout obtenir ; car comment pouvais-
je savoir, ô héros illustre, que je périrais de la main de mon
père ? . . . Je voyais les signes que ma mère m'avait indiqués,
mais je n'en croyais pas mes yeux. Mon sort était écrit au-
dessus de ma tête, et je devais mourir de la main de mon père.
Je suis venu comme la foudre, je m'en vais comme le vent ;
peut-être que je te retrouverai heureux dans le ciel ! "

'Ainsi parle en expirant cet autre Hippolyte, immolé ici de
la main de Thésée.'

A writer in the *Christian Remembrancer* (of the general tenour
of whose remarks I have, assuredly, no right to complain) having
made the discovery of this notice by M. Sainte-Beuve, has
pointed out the passages in which I have made use of the extracts from M. Mohl's translation which it contains; has observed,
apparently with blame, that I 'have not thought fit to offer a
single syllable of acknowledgment to an author to whom I have
been manifestly very largely indebted ;' has complained of being
'under some embarrassment from not being sure how much of
the treatment is Mr. Arnold's own ;' and, finally, has suggested
that 'the whole work of M. Mohl may have been used throughout, and the study of antiquity carried so far as simply to
reproduce an ancient poem as well as an ancient subject.'

It would have been more charitable, perhaps, had the reviewer, before making this goodnatured suggestion, ascertained,
by reference to M. Mohl's work, how far it was confirmed by
the fact.

The reader, however, is now in possession of the whole of the
sources from which I have drawn the story of *Sohrab and
Rustum*, and can determine, if he pleases, the exact amount of
my obligation to M. Mohl. But I hope that it will not in future
be supposed, if I am silent as to the sources from which a
poem has been derived, that I am trying to conceal obligations,
or to claim an absolute originality for all parts of it. When

any man endeavours to '*remanier et réinventer à sa manière*' a great story, which, as M. Sainte-Beuve says of that of *Sohrab and Rustum*, has '*couru le monde*', it may be considered quite certain that he has not drawn all the details of his work out of his own head. The reader is not, I think, concerned to ask, from what sources these have been drawn ; but only how the whole work, as it stands, affects him. Real plagiarism, such as the borrowing without acknowledgment of passages from other English poets— real dishonesty, such as the endeavouring to pass off the mere translation of a poem as an original work—are always certain enough to be discovered.

I must not be led on, from defending the morality of my imitation, to defend at length its aesthetics ; but I cannot forbear adding, that it would be a most unfortunate scruple which should restrain an author, treating matter of history or tradition, from placing, where he can, in the mouths of his personages the very words of the old chronicle, or romance, or poem (when the poem embodies, as that of Ferdousi, the tradition of a people) ; and which should lead him to substitute for these any '*eigens grosse[n] Erfindungen*'. For my part, I only regret that I could not meet with a translation from Ferdousi's poem of the whole of the episode of *Sohrab and Rustum* : with a prose translation, that is : for in a verse translation no original work is any longer recognizable. I should certainly have made all the use I could of it. The use of the tradition, above everything else, gives to a work that *naïveté*, that flavour of reality and truth, which is the very life of poetry.   [A.]

[Note first inserted in *1854*, omitted in *1857*.]

202, l. 166. *sugar'd mulberries*: Arnold says in a letter that his authority for this statement was Burnes (James Burnes, 1801–62, author of *Narrative of a Visit to Scinde*, 1830).

219. PHILOMELA : one of the two daughters of Pandion, king of Attica ; Tereus seduced her, feigning that her sister Procne, whom he had married, was dead. The dumb sister (l. 21) is Procne, whose tongue Tereus had cut out. The two sisters revenged themselves by killing Tereus's son Itys ; they then fled and, being overtaken, were changed by the gods into birds, Procne becoming a swallow, Philomela a nightingale. (This is the form of the story chosen by Arnold ; another version changes the parts assigned to the two sisters.)

230. THE SCHOLAR GIPSY.

'There was very lately a lad in the University of Oxford, who was by his poverty forced to leave his studies there ; and at last to join himself to a company of vagabond gipsies. Among these extravagant people, by the insinuating subtilty of his carriage, he quickly got so much of their love and esteem as that they discovered to him their mystery. After he had been a pretty while well exercised in the trade, there chanced to ride by a couple of scholars, who had formerly been of his acquaintance. They quickly spied out their old friend among the gipsies ; and he gave them an account of the necessity which drove him to that kind of life, and told them that the people he went with were not such impostors as they were taken for, but that they had a traditional kind of learning among them, and could do wonders by the power of imagination, their fancy binding that of others: that himself had learned much of their art, and when he had compassed the whole secret, he intended, he said, to leave their company, and give the world an account of what he had learned.'—GLANVIL's *Vanity of Dogmatizing*, 1661. [A.]

235, ll. 182–190. These lines perhaps refer to Carlyle.

237. STANZAS. Edward Quillinan married Wordsworth's daughter Dora. He died in 1851 (see p. 276, ll. 4, 5).

238. BALDER DEAD.

'Balder the Good having been tormented with terrible dreams, indicating that his life was in great peril, communicated them to the assembled Aesir, who resolved to conjure all things to avert from him the threatened danger. Then Frigga exacted an oath from fire and water, from iron and all other metals, as well as from stones, earths, diseases, beasts, birds, poisons, and creeping things, that none of them would do any harm to Baldur. When this was done, it became a favourite pastime of the Aesir, at their meetings, to get Baldur to stand up and serve them as a mark, some hurling darts at him, some stones, while others hewed at him with their swords and battle-axes, for do what they would, none of them could harm him, and this was regarded by all as a great honour shown to Baldur. But when Loki, the son of Laufey, beheld the scene, he was sorely vexed that Baldur was not hurt. Assuming, therefore, the shape of a woman, he went to Fensalir, the mansion of Frigga. That goddess, when she saw the pretended woman, inquired of her if she knew what the Aesir were doing at their meetings. She replied, that they were throwing darts and stones at Baldur without being able to hurt him.

'"Ay," said Frigga, "neither metal nor wood can hurt Baldur, for I have exacted an oath from all of them."

'"What!" exclaimed the woman, "have all things sworn to spare Baldur?"

'"All things," replied Frigga, "except one little shrub that grows on the eastern side of Valhalla, and is called Mistletoe, and which I thought too young and feeble to crave an oath from."

'As soon as Loki heard this he went away, and, resuming his natural shape, cut off the Mistletoe, and repaired to the place where the gods were assembled. There he found Hödur standing apart, without partaking of the sports, on account of his blindness, and, going up to him, said, "Why dost thou not also throw something at Baldur?"

'"Because I am blind," answered Hödur, "and see not where Baldur is, and have, moreover, nothing to throw with."

'"Come then," said Loki, "do like the rest, and show honour to Baldur by throwing this twig at him, and I will direct thy arm toward the place where he stands."

"Hödur then took the mistletoe, and, under the guidance of Loki, darted it at Baldur, who, pierced through and through, fell down lifeless. . . . When Baldur fell the Aesir were struck speechless with horror, and then they looked at each other, and all were of one mind to lay hands on him who had done the deed, but they were obliged to delay their vengeance out of respect for the sacred place (Peace-stead) where they were assembled. They at length gave vent to their grief by loud lamentations, though not one of them could find words to express the poignancy of his feelings. Odin, especially, was more sensible than the others of the loss they had suffered, for he foresaw what a detriment Baldur's death would be to the Aesir. When the gods came to themselves, Frigga asked who among them wished to gain all her love and good will ; "For this," said she, "shall he have who will ride to Hel and try to find Baldur, and offer Hela a ransom if she will let him return to Asgard"; whereupon Hermod, surnamed the Nimble, the son of Odin, offered to undertake the journey. Odin's horse Sleipner was then led forth, on which Hermod mounted, and galloped away on his mission.

'The Aesir then took the dead body and bore it to the sea-shore, where stood Baldur's ship Hringhorn, which passed for the largest in the world. But when they wanted to launch it in order to make Baldur's funeral pile on it, they were unable to make it stir. In this conjuncture they sent to Jötunheim for a certain giantess named Hyrrokin, who came mounted on a wolf, having twisted serpents for a bridle. . . . Hyrrokin then went to the ship, and with a single push set it afloat, but the motion was so violent that fire sparkled from the rollers, and the earth shook all round. Thor, enraged at the sight, grasped his mallet, and but for the interference of the Aesir would have broken the woman's skull. Baldur's body was then borne to the funeral pile on board the ship, and this ceremony had such an effect on Nanna, the daughter of Nep, that her heart broke with grief, and her body was burnt on the same pile with her husband's . . . There was a vast concourse of various kinds of people at Baldur's obsequies. First came Odin, accompanied by Frigga, the Valkyrjor and his ravens ; then Frey in his car drawn by the boar named Gullinbursti or Slidrugtanni ; Heimdall rode his horse called Gulltop, and Freyja drove in her chariot drawn by cats. There were also a great many Frost-giants and giants of the mountains present. Odin laid on the pile the gold ring called Draupnir, which afterwards acquired the property of producing every ninth night eight rings of equal weight. Baldur's horse was led to the pile fully caparisoned, and consumed in the same flames on the body of his master.

'Meanwhile, Hermod was proceeding on his mission. For the space of nine days, and as many nights, he rode through deep glens so dark that he could not discern anything until he arrived at the river Gjöll, which he passed over on a bridge covered with glittering gold. Modgudur, the maiden who kept the bridge, asked him his name and lineage, telling him that the day before five bands of dead persons had ridden over the bridge, and did not shake it so much as he alone. "But," she added, "thou hast not death's hue on thee, why then ridest thou here on the way to Hel?"

' "I ride to Hel," answered Hermod, "to seek Baldur. Hast thou perchance seen him pass this way?"

' "Baldur," she replied, "hath ridden over Gjöll's bridge, but there below, towards the north, lies the way to the abodes of death."

' Hermod then pursued his journey until he came to the barred gates of Hel. Here he alighted, girthed his saddle tighter, and remounting, clapped both spurs to his horse, who cleared the gate by a tremendous leap without touching it. Hermod then rode on to the palace, where he found his brother Baldur occupying the most distinguished seat in the hall, and passed the night in his company. The next morning he besought Hela (Death) to let Baldur ride home with him, assuring her that nothing but lamentations were to be heard among the gods. Hela answered that it should now be tried whether Baldur was so beloved as he was said to be.

' "If therefore," she added, "all things in the world, both living and lifeless, weep for him, then shall he return to the Aesir, but if any one thing speak against him or refuse to weep, he shall be kept in Hel."

' Hermod then rose, and Baldur led him out of the hall and gave him the ring Draupnir, to present as a keepsake to Odin. Nanna also sent Frigga a linen cassock and other gifts, and to Fulla a gold finger-ring. Hermod then rode back to Asgard, and gave an account of all he had heard and witnessed.

' The gods upon this dispatched messengers throughout the world, to beg everything to weep, in order that Baldur might be delivered from Hel. All things very willingly complied with this request, both men and every other living being, as well as earths and stones, and trees and metals, just as thou must have seen these things weep when they are brought from a cold place into a hot one. As the messengers were returning with the conviction that their mission had been quite successful, they found an old hag named Thaukt sitting in a cavern, and begged her to weep Baldur out of Hel. But she answered,

> ' "Thaukt will wail
> With arid tears
> Baldur's bale fire.
> Naught, quick or dead,
> By man's son gain I,
> Let Hela hold what's hers."

It was strongly suspected that this hag was no other than Loki himself, who never ceased to work evil among the Aesir.'—The Prose or Younger Edda, commonly ascribed to Snorri Sturleson, translated by J. A. Blackwell. Contained in P. H. Mallet's *Northern Antiquities.* Bohn's edition, 1847.

276, ll. 8, 9. *Two friends met there, two fam'd Gifted women.* Charlotte Brontë and Harriet Martineau. [A.]

454

NOTES

280, ll. 156, 158. Anne and Emily Brontë.

l. 168. Branwell Brontë.

283. MEROPE. In a letter dated Feb. 3, 1858, Arnold explains that everybody seems to think that *Merope* betrays a design to substitute tragedies *à la grecque* for all other kinds of poetry, and he continues : 'What I meant them to see in it was a specimen of the work created by the Greek imagination.'

In a later letter (May 17, 1865) he writes to Professor Conington : 'The chorus-rhythms are unsatisfactory, I admit, but I cannot yet feel that rhyme would do.'

291, l. 37. *Et pueri*, &c. : Martial, I. iii. 6.

373, l. 1351. *the kind, chance-arriv'd Wanderer* : Poias, father of Philoctetes.

382, l. 19. *My brother! and thine early lot.* The Author's brother, William Delafield Arnold, Director of Public Instruction in the Punjab, and author of *Oakfield, or Fellowship in the East*, died at Gibraltar, on his way home from India, April the 9th, 1859. [A.]

386. THYRSIS. Throughout this Poem there is reference to another piece, *The Scholar Gipsy*, printed in the first volume of the Author's Poems [*Poems, a new edition*, 1853]. [A.]

388, l. 80. Corydon and Thyrsis contend against one another in song in Virgil's sixth Eclogue ; Thyrsis is defeated.

391, ll. 181–91. Daphnis, a Greek shepherd, was blinded by a nymph whose love he would not return ; he afterwards had his sight restored and was carried up to heaven by Hermes. Another Daphnis was rescued by Hercules from Lityerses, a Phrygian king, who made all travellers enter into a reaping-match with him and killed those whom he vanquished. The 'Lityerses song' was a dirge sung over the dead bodies of the unfortunate travellers. Arnold has apparently blended these two stories.

398. THE DIVINITY, l. 8. *Recalls the obscure opposer he outweigh'd.* Gilbert de la Porrée, at the Council of Rheims, in 1148. [A.]

THE GOOD SHEPHERD, l. 4. The *Phrygian sect* : the Montanists.

399. AUSTERITY OF POETRY, l. 1. *That son of Italy who tried to blow.* Giacopone di Todi. [A.]

400. MONICA'S LAST PRAYER ; Monica was the mother of Augustine.

405, l. 38. *He tarries where the Rock of Spain.* See note to p. 382 above. [A.]

432, l. 191. *Goethe, too, had been there.* See *Harzreise im Winter*, in Goethe's *Gedichte*. [A.]

434, l. 21. *The gentian-flower'd pass, its crown.* The *Gentiana lutea* of the Alps. [A.]

l. 24. *And walls where Byron came.* Montbovon. See Byron's Journal, in his *Works*, vol. iii, p. 258. The river Saane becomes the Sarine below Montbovon. [A.]

INDEX OF TITLES

INDEX OF FIRST LINES